THE TRUTH ABOUT A PUBLISHER

By the same Author

THE TRUTH ABOUT PUBLISHING

'*The Truth About Publishing* is much more than a guide-book for young authors or an eye-opener for would-be publishers. It is the fascinating inside story of a little understood profession told by an acknowledged expert.'—*John o' London's Weekly*.

'All that could be said in praise of the original edition can be said with even greater truth of this edition, and in reading this new edition its lucidity, readability, clarity, fullness, and accuracy are impressed upon one.'—*Bookseller*.

'To authors, young and old, it is simply indispensable. It answers all those perplexing questions which arise in the course of a writer's career, and does it in the simple terms of a man who knows from experience the value of clarity, especially in a work such as this.'—*Western Mail and South Wales News*.

'This publisher-author belongs to the small category of writers who know how to say a lot in a little. . . . Sir Stanley Unwin's monograph tells all the ascertainable and communicable truth about publishing, as it has been and is practised by the best British publishers. Within these limits—and they are right and proper limits—it comes as near perfection as such a book can.'—GEOFFREY FABER in *The British Weekly*.

'As a guide to, and interpreter of, every publishing operation which can be codified, Sir Stanley is impeccable.'—MICHAEL SADLEIR in *The Sunday Times*.

'Candid, illuminating and frequently provocative about the economics of book publishing. . . . Every aspiring writer will find it useful to have the work beside him, not least those who have been brought up in the tradition of seeing each and every publisher as their natural enemy.'—*The Listener*.

'The large number of foreign languages into which this book has been translated proves the high value in which it is held throughout the literary world. There is no higher authority on, nor more widely experienced practitioner of, the craft and art of publishing than Sir Stanley Unwin, and the new edition of his book is most timely and welcome.'—*Quarterly Review*.

'The most readable and reliably instructive text-book of the whole business of book-publishing.'—*The Author*.

'I place it among the two or three text-books I know which are as fascinating to read as novels.'—*A Music Publisher*.

STANLEY UNWIN

THE TRUTH
ABOUT A PUBLISHER

AN AUTOBIOGRAPHICAL RECORD

by

SIR STANLEY UNWIN

Fellow of the Royal Society of Literature
Hon. LL.D. (Aberdeen)

'Sooner or later, near or far,
The strong have need of the weak.'

An Unwin family motto

LONDON
GEORGE ALLEN & UNWIN LTD

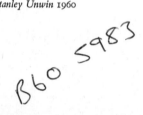

PRINTED IN GREAT BRITAIN
in 12 on 13 pt. Bembo type
BY UNWIN BROTHERS LIMITED
WOKING AND LONDON

When in my youth I read Arnold Bennett's *Truth About an Author*, I felt very strongly that someone ought to write *The Truth About a Publisher*; but the more I thought about it the clearer it became that what was even more needed was *The Truth About Publishing*. That I accordingly wrote for authors to remove the 'mystery' from publishing and with no thought that it would become a text-book.

Now that I have attempted to write *The Truth About a Publisher*, it has developed into something different from what I contemplated. The creation of George Allen & Unwin being my life work, my autobiography has inevitably become interwoven with it. Moreover, any account of my life would be incomplete were there no reference to my work for the Publishers Association, the International Publishers Association, and the British Council. But these I have confined to appendices. Some of my letters to *The Times*, through which I have probably become most widely known outside literary circles, are included in the chapter 'How to make a Nuisance of Oneself' in Part II.

I have written this story of my career primarily for my own amusement and as a record for my family. Some, however, whose opinions I respect, have urged me—rightly or wrongly—to publish it. I can only hope that it may not prove as damaging to my reputation as the publication of Trollope's autobiography, in which he revealed his method of work, at first did to his.

As I have explained on other occasions, publishing, not authorship, is my calling. I make no claims as a writer, except perhaps to lucidity.

There are several people whom I particularly wish to thank in connection with the preparation of this book. First and foremost, my good friend W. G. Taylor, who, over the course of years, patiently and critically read each chapter as it was written, and encouraged me to continue; then our excellent editor, Malcolm

Barnes, who, at my request, used his blue pencil to good effect on my first draft; my sons David and Rayner, who were wisely unsparing in their criticism; my two colleagues, Philip Unwin and C. A. Furth, who read the typescript at one stage or another and made helpful comments; and lastly my long-suffering secretary, Miss D. G. Davis, who has worked for me for over thirty-five years, and in odd moments typed the whole of the book, and retyped portions of it until she must have been weary of the sight of it. Finally, I should like to express my appreciation of the care devoted to its production by my family firm of printers, Unwin Brothers Limited.

CONTENTS

Part I

Part II

Appendices

LIST OF ILLUSTRATIONS

LIST OF ILLUSTRATIONS

Part I

CHAPTER I

CHILDHOOD

The arrival of a ninth child, particularly if he be a seventh son, may be a cause of rejoicing to his parents; but others may take a less favourable view. 'Fancy having to go away for *that thing*!' commented one of my elder brothers, who on my account had temporarily to leave the little suburban villa in Handen Road, Lee, SE, where Dr Hahnemann (grandson of the founder of homœopathy) assisted me into the world. 'If you can't do better than that, you had better stop', was the kindly advice given to my father by an all-too-candid friend. But this inauspicious start was considered to have been compensated for in some way by two privileges which the elder members of my family did not enjoy. I was christened by the son of Robert Moffat the missionary (the Rev. J. S. Moffat who married an Unwin), and I was sent to what was then an innovation, a Froebel kindergarten.

I am told that I showed no appreciation of the honour paid me by Mr Moffat, but I still recollect my affection for 'Miss Ethel', who induced an early interest in geography by encouraging me to produce peninsulas, islands, bays and mountains in a large and suitably low trough of damp sand. If the Jesuits are right, as I believe they are, that it is the first seven years that are decisive for a child's future, I was indeed blessed.

But those happy kindergarten days were soon followed by less placid times as a 'day bug' (as day boys were called at the School for Sons of Missionaries at Blackheath—now at Eltham—in which my father took a lifelong interest). To a small boy Blackheath seemed a long, long way away because we had by that time moved to the top of Burnt Ash Hill, whence a twopenny two-horse bus to Lee Green and a threepenny three-horse bus from Lee Green to Blackheath were needed if one was not prepared to walk. I was allowed fivepence for fares to cover one bus each way, and used proudly to clamber up to a seat next to the driver on the twopenny bus. I regarded the threepenny bus, which my sister used, as poor value, even on its uphill run, and felt that I could use the odd penny to much better purpose. Were there not four sweet shops on the way, each more difficult to pass than the other, and each with its speciality? And in those days what delights were to be had for a farthing! A whole ladder made of liquorice from one shop, two large aniseed balls at another, and at a third enough sherbet to make one froth at the mouth for the rest of the walk to school. There was a wide range of sweets at two ounces a penny, but as not all the shops were willing to sell less than an ounce excitement was intense when a new one opened with many excellent varieties at four ounces a penny! There was one tragic occasion, however, which made a lasting impression. I had a farthing left to spend, and entered with confidence the sweet shop next the Congregational Church in Burnt Ash Road where my father was a deacon, and of which I shall have more to say later. But once in the shop and my purchase made, that elusive farthing was not to be found. I was so careful of money that how I lost it puzzles me to this day. The good lady in the shop, evidently feeling that as a regular customer I was entitled to credit, pressed a further two aniseed balls into my hand and said that I could pay the halfpenny the next time. I knew that my parents would disapprove and I had a miserable time with my conscience. When at family prayers next morning my father substituted 'forgive us our debts' for 'trespasses' in the Lord's Prayer my agony of mind was intense. That incident possibly accounts for my lifelong horror of debts, and a disinclination to incur even a fully justified and well-secured bank overdraft.

My passion for sweets was indulged in another and curious way. For my own satisfaction I used regularly to see for how long I could keep up with the threepenny bus from Lee Green, possibly just to demonstrate how unnecessary it was for me to take it. This delighted an old gentleman who occupied the corner seat near the conductor, who for some mysterious reason called

The four
youngest
at the seaside
S. U. on left

1888

13 Handen Rd.
W. H. U.

S. U. at gate

The Go-cart
S. U. on left

The garden door at Handen Road, 1888
S. U. on his mother's lap

In the porch at 'The Mount', 1902
S. U. seated in centre

me Bosun, and rewarded my efforts with enormous white peppermints, of which he seemed to have an unlimited supply. We became firm friends!

But my journeys to and from school ceased to be either peaceful or pleasant when I had the company of two other boys who temporarily went also as day boys to Blackheath. To walk with the elder was like going with a dog which dislikes the smell of every other dog it meets. He positively loved fighting. No boy or boys could pass him without his trying to pick a quarrel. He would jeer at them, snatch their satchels, or try to trip them up without the slightest provocation. At that point, being temperamentally pacific and cowardly, I did my best (not always with success) to disown his company. The younger, though pacific, felt in loyalty bound to participate when his elder brother had taken on more than he could manage and was getting the worst of it. On one occasion when he had drawn a blank on his way to school, the elder brother decided to let loose his fighting instinct on me. I closed in upon him, and to his surprise and mine laid him flat upon his back, after which he ceased to trouble me. Curiously enough precisely the same thing occurred later at boarding school with another boy, but my successful defence did nothing to remove my detestation of fighting.

Life at SSM was far from uninteresting. The boys being the sons of missionaries were mostly impecunious, but they were rich in curios and foreign postage stamps. Stamp collecting was a passion with most of them and bartering was a highly skilled accomplishment. I may, and probably have, inherited business acumen from my maternal grandfather, James Spicer of the paper firm that bears his name, but it was SSM which gave it full play. I entered into the barter with avidity and enjoyment, and learnt a great deal.

Few of the younger generation have any conception of the extent to which religion and religious instruction occupied the lives and thoughts of a Nonconformist household in the 'seventies and 'eighties. Family prayers, at which the Bible was read morning and evening, were a matter of course. We acquired thereby a knowledge of the Bible—that most wonderful piece of English literature—which few, if any, of the younger generation possess today. There were week-day services, prayer meetings, church meetings, but it is the ritual of our Sundays that remains for ever in my mind. No Sunday papers crossed our threshold, for Sunday papers were wicked. We breakfasted late, and there were always hot pork sausages when there was an 'r' in the month— better ones than we ever seem to get today. Following breakfast the gong was rung for family prayers (as the youngest that was my job) and we all adjourned to the drawing-room. What memories those Victorian drawing-rooms evoke! I can see the alabaster clock and the small alabaster statues, all with glass covers, on the marble mantelpiece, above an old-fashioned fireplace with brass tongs, shovels and poker, endless small cupboards with glass doors, crammed with shells, curios and odd bits of china, and else-where more furniture of all kinds and descriptions than today we should think any room could hold, and the walls smothered with pictures of little merit. There were heavy curtains on heavy brass rods, as well, of course, as muslin curtains underneath. Everything that could be was under dust sheets during the week which were removed on Saturday evening.

In response to the gong all three maids[1] solemnly trooped into the drawing-room, where we sang a hymn for which as I grew older it was my privilege to play the tune on an old Erard piano. After the Bible reading we all knelt down and my father prayed. His capacity for extempore prayer was unrivalled. There seemed to be no reason why he should ever stop, and there were times when I irreligiously wondered whether he ever would. Prayers over, there was a bustle and a scurry to prepare for Chapel, particularly if Father had to attend a Deacons' Meeting or Prayer Meeting beforehand. We were all dressed in our Sunday best, my father in a frock coat and silk hat, and marched sedately and solemnly downhill to Burnt Ash Road Congregational Church,

[1] Two or three living-in maids were a normal feature of a suburban household of those days. Their wages were about £16 p.a. with cap and aprons provided by the employer. They had little time off, few expenses, and many saved money, incredible as that now sounds.

where the Rev. George Critchley officiated. He was an eloquent preacher, and my father absorbed his sermons with rapt attention. To us children they seemed, I fear, interminable and boring. But we were not neglected, because Mr Critchley had a reputation for his children's sermons, which I listened to with interest and respect. I still possess, or did until recently, a volume of them entitled *The Legend of the Silver Cup*. During the main sermon I found my mother's sealskin coat most comfortable to nestle against and provocative of pleasant daydreams.

After the service, while the deacons returned to the vestry, their respective families indulged in gossip. On the way home we would listen with awe to weighty discussions between our elders on the merits and demerits of the sermon. A visiting minister, or two sons of missionaries from the school at Blackheath, accompanied us.

And then Sunday lunch—always a sirloin of beef, with a large and delicious undercut. I watched my father's exquisite carving in anxiety to observe whether at long last when my turn came there would be any left. There usually was, because, greatly to my eldest brother's annoyance, my father believed in giving us all a small helping first, and then a second helping if we wanted it, whereas my eldest brother pressed in vain for one large helping. Although my father knew my mother would never eat it, he religiously carved off a little piece of fat for her (as well as for the rest of us) and continued to do so, despite her protests, for the whole of her life. There was a look of severe disapproval if any of us failed to consume our portions. When suitable fruit was available there was always 'camananda' pudding, followed by dessert. But there was little leisure to deal with the last because my father was Sunday School Superintendent, and I had to attend a Sunday School class, so down we trotted once again to the Chapel. I still think with sorrow of the unfortunate lady who took that class, and I still possess in my Bible some of the little texts she used to present for good behaviour. Poor soul, she had no idea of maintaining order, and I am afraid that we learnt little.

Grace was said before and after all meals, but at Sunday teatime it was sung. Usually my mother pitched the opening note, but as we grew older we developed the facetious habit of intervening and pitching the start a tone or two too high in order to watch with perverse enjoyment the struggle of the sopranos to reach the top note.

Tea over, there was once again a bustle to get ready for evening service. My father liked us all to attend, but with one accord we tried to make excuse. His sorrow at our unwillingness to go was so real that most of us succumbed. Occasionally I succeeded in persuading my mother that it was desirable that I should go to bed early, but that meant going without supper—a great deprivation. On the other hand, it meant an hour's hymn-singing with my mother which I enjoyed, and on my way to bed the maid who was in could usually be persuaded to give me a custard. In my elder brothers' time they had the option of supper if they went to church, no supper if they didn't, and they used to inspect the larder before deciding. But in my time the late Sunday evening supper never varied; it always consisted of soup and bread-and-butter pudding, with probably some other sweets. My mother disapproved of the absence of a meat course and insisted upon the cold beef being put on the sideboard. She partook of a small portion, and with equal regularity the rest of us, including my father, refrained.

It was part of the Sunday ritual to wait on ourselves at supper, to clear away and wash up, to give the maids a Sunday evening's rest. As we grew older, Sunday supper became more and more hilarious—a reaction no doubt from the solemnity of the day.

As soon as we had washed up the gong was rung for prayers. Once again the maids trooped into the drawing-room; a hymn was sung and the twenty-third psalm read, followed by a long extempore prayer. Then at last we were free, but it was usually time to go to bed.

My two greatest treats of those days were a visit to the Rectory Field to watch Blackheath (or Kent) play Rugby Football, and the acquisition of a $2\frac{1}{2}$d tin of sweetened condensed milk, which I would suck dry in an afternoon. They are both things I could still enjoy if given the opportunity.

Not all of us remember the part played by fear in our childhood. It loomed so large in mine that I can never forget. My fear of the dark, so common in children, was acute. I shared a room on the top floor with an elder brother studying medicine, who for his own excellent purposes possessed a skeleton. But what I think intimidated me even more was the collection of lion and tiger heads and skins stored there for members of the Moffat family, who made our home their headquarters when in London. My reluctance to go to bed was solely due to fear. If I could persuade anyone to accompany me until I was undressed and safely in bed, all was well. On one occasion when I was undressing on the landing, too scared to enter my room, what seemed to be a growl came from an adjacent room. I fled down the stairs screaming. It was a long time before I could be persuaded that the noise was due to the violent snoring of a child, who, unknown to me, had been put to sleep in the next bedroom, and not to some ferocious animal. There were many other incidents which accentuated the trouble, and it was not until I was nearly of age that fear ceased to dominate me. I still remember with gratitude our cook who allowed me to inveigle her into reading to me while I undressed. She was a remarkable character. Maid after maid gave notice because of her appalling temper, but as soon as they had left became her devoted friends. As a plain cook she was unrivalled, but what chiefly reconciled my mother to her was her devotion to us boys. No matter how late or unexpectedly we arrived home, a hot meal was forthcoming. 'Boys must be fed' was a governing principle in her life. It certainly suited us, and for her devotion to us my mother forgave all else. And there was much to forgive.

It was not until I was fifteen that I was allowed to see even a play of Shakespeare's, and then only one a year, because, as we were told, theatres were 'wicked' places best avoided. On the other hand 'parties' were encouraged. The most popular was the one given by the Jobbinses of Blackheath, because Mr Jobbins was a caterer as well as a confectioner, and the refreshments far exceeded what others could provide. Preparations for such parties were intense. The excitement was so great that when I had been carefully dressed up for my first Jobbins party in a little Lord Fauntleroy velvet suit with brass buttons, I managed to spill a whole pot of jam down it!

A family gathering was another great event at which over a hundred might be present. From the programme of one such gathering which I still possess, all my brothers and sisters appear to have performed for the entertainment of our relatives. Everyone was expected to take some part, either vocally or on the 'cello, violin, or even banjo. The standard was deplorable, but the audience appreciative. My only recollection is an inability to eat a meringue—an inability I have never overcome.

Between festivities of this kind, the state of our morals and our religious beliefs was under constant observation. The amount of moral instruction we were presumed to be capable of absorbing seems to me in retrospect simply staggering, and our faith had to be accompanied by good works. We were always collecting for the London Missionary Society or some other 'good cause'. On one occasion a prize of an enormous picture of the LMS ship *The John Williams* was offered to any boy or girl who collected £5. We all became champion cadgers, and I was one of the few who, with a sister's help, attained the goal, largely because of an enterprising invasion of the sacred precincts of 50 Upper Thames Street, where my wealthy Spicer uncles obviously felt that they must encourage such ardent missionary fervour.

No account of my childhood would be complete without a reference to our old family nurse, Mrs Smith, who played such a large part in all our lives. She worshipped the family, and it may truly be said she lived for us. We were her life. Deeply religious, of Irish origin, witty and full of fun, she was the one to whom we could always turn in trouble or emergency with certainty of finding instant sympathy or assistance. By the time I was a day boy at Blackheath she had already retired and lived in a room near Lee station, where I nearly always dropped in to see her on my way home. Needless to say there was always some attractive tit-bit awaiting the ever-hungry schoolboy. She was puzzled by the fact that I always bolted away immediately a train from town arrived at Lee station. When she questioned me, she was amused to learn that if you walked up behind the gentlemen and listened to their conversation, 'you often picked up a thing or two'. My desire to be well-informed evidently started early. I had at that time my own little printing press, but I have no recollection of using journalistically the 'news' thus obtained. My printing efforts were restricted by the size of the machine (a German toy) to programmes, labels, book plates, etc.

In the summer of 1894, when I was nine years old, my parents decided to celebrate their silver wedding by taking the whole family to Switzerland for six weeks. In these days the formalities and expense connected with such an undertaking would be forbidding, but in those more civilized times there were no formalities, and even a passport was a luxury. The English golden sovereign was itself a passport. As to expense, I should not myself believe it had I not recently come across my father's accounts which he always kept so meticulously, because the entire outlay for the ten of us, including the fares and drive from Aigle to Vers L'Église and a night in Paris, amounted to £118 for a six weeks' stay. The pension terms did not include afternoon tea, but we took the tea and a tea kettle with us and made it ourselves. All that was required was a little milk, and my first acquaintance with French was 'Voulez vous me donner un peu de lait, s'il vous plaît', because I was always sent to fetch it. We had a wonderful time, and it gave me a love of climbing (for the benefit of real mountaineers I should say 'a love of walking uphill') which I have never lost. I still prize the little album of photos taken with his old Frena camera with which my father later presented each one of us as a souvenir. One incident on the outward journey I am never likely to forget. My parents had taken an additional girl under their wing, so that there were eleven of us in a compartment with five seats on each side. What was to be done? 'Put young Stanley up on the luggage rack' was the advice of an elder brother, and up on the rack I went. But the joke was in the morning when it was discovered that I was the only one who had had a comfortable night.

Today parents with only one child find a holiday at the seaside an intolerable effort, but conditions were easier in the 'nineties, and the ten of us went away year after year, and always to a different place. Redcar, Pwllheli, Melice, and innumerable other places carry ineffaceable memories for those of us who survive, even if it be merely, as in the case of Melice, of my falling into a pigsty and having to be rescued from being consumed by the pig who seemed to regard me as an attractive morsel!

Throughout my childhood I had the great good fortune, which few children enjoy today, to have many brothers, not to mention two sisters, who had no hesitation in letting me know what a poor opinion they then had of me. Their admonitions, occasionally in writing, left me under no illusions about my many defects. It was altogether an admirable form of education, the more so as I apparently preserved a due amount of resilience. Perhaps fortunately, they have never felt it incumbent upon them to continue their efforts since I became an adult.

My eldest brother Edward (Ted), the popular Rotarian and Mason, late Chairman of Unwin Brothers Ltd, the century-old family printing firm, still continued to refer to me, however, as 'Young Stanley' when I was in my sixties. My doctor brother Will (I take them in order of age), the surgeon, the most genuinely *un*-mercenary man you could find, was much concerned about my mercenary instincts. On every visit to New Zealand it has been brought home to me how deeply and widely he was loved and respected. The third brother, Sidney, a schoolmaster turned farmer, had a hard life, through no fault of his own, tilling stony soil. The relief from it has probably added to the happiness he is enjoying in his retirement. My brother Cyril, who spent three years studying horticulture at Versailles, made beekeeping his career. His perfect French proved invaluable to the non-commissioned officers of the New Zealand regiment with which he served in the First World War. No French peasant woman could begrudge anything to a New Zealander who spoke fluent French and looked a little like a Frenchman. Unfortunately he was badly knocked about in the war, and died just before my father did. My craftsman brother, Bernard, who was only three and a half years older than me, worked for some time with the late Romney Green, making most beautiful furniture, some of the best specimens of which are to be found in Holland, where his superb craftsmanship was rightly admired. Later he worked with that musical genius, Arnold Dolmetsch, making old-time musical instruments. The clavicord which Mr Carl Dolmetsch uses today is one made by my brother.

As to my two sisters, Mabel, the elder, received an embarrassing number of proposals of marriage as a girl, all of which she rightly declined. Later, when on the staff of Bedales, she met and married Mr A. Moray Williams, with whom she had a most happy married life. She was an astonishingly sweet character—beloved by all who knew her. My younger sister, Ella, was afflicted with polio as a child, though it was not called that then, and it made her slightly lame. She abandoned her career as masseuse to look after my father in his old age. She spends her life thinking of others, and keeps all the members of our large family (of whom there are now about thirty in New Zealand) in constant touch with one another, because she never forgets any of them.

Dr Johnson maintained (1758) that 'good brothers make good sisters'. We certainly had two remarkably good sisters, but whether we brothers can claim any merit is another question. Anyway, I owe all my brothers and sisters more than I have ever been able to repay. It would be pleasant to write more about them, and to refer to their children, some of whom have already distinguished themselves, but this hardly seems the place.

CHAPTER 2

EDWARD UNWIN: 1840–1933

My father and mother were an interesting contrast. Both were deeply religious; both were typical Nonconformist Victorians. But my father was concerned with compliance with the outward manifestations of his religious feelings, and unduly sensitive to the opinion of his fellow Nonconformists, whereas my mother was guided by an 'Inner Light' which left her unconcerned with the opinion of others if satisfied that what she was doing was right.

At a time when 'spare the rod and spoil the child' was a household doctrine, Father, although he had six sons, never beat any of us. But he always wholeheartedly backed Mother, and their united front maintained perfect discipline. They doubtless had many differences of opinion, but they were relegated to the privacy of their bedroom and we were never conscious of them. In all matters, including our education, upon which I now know they had divergent views, they acted as one, and therein lay their strength.

My father inherited much from his maternal grandfather, William Mattingly Soundy, to whom the late A. R. Orage paid the following delightful tribute under the heading 'The Admirable Victorians':[1]

'I have too deep a respect for the Victorian character ever to make light of it, especially for my own generation that can afford to laugh at so little. Mr Strachey's "brilliant" essays, therefore, leave me laughing at him rather than with him. One is impelled to take him personally, and to turn the tables upon Mr Strachey with the *argumentum ad hominem*. As a set-off to the "brilliant" essays of Mr Strachey I have recently read on the loan of his great-grandson, the privately printed personal memoir of William Mattingly Soundy, who died in 1862,

[1] *Readers and Writers* (London: George Allen & Unwin Ltd., 1922), p. 63.

at the full age of 96. For 74 years he was a member of his local Congregational Church, and for 46 years he was a deacon. During nearly
the whole of that time he never missed a meeting, Sunday or weekday,
and was never known to be late, though he lived two miles from the
church. It is the round of a machine you may say, and there is no
wonder that the age was mechanical. But I think of the passionate
mainspring that kept a "machine" going for so long without a psychological breakdown. What an intensity it must have had! What a
character! If to love it is impossible, it is impossible not to admire it;
and since we truly live by admiration, hope and love, it is something
for the Victorians that they can still fill us with admiration. My own
generation (now past as a force) has provided the soul of the world
with nothing so fine.'

Father had just such a passionate mainspring and was equally
punctual. His devotion to Congregationalism, the London Missionary Society, the School for Sons of Missionaries, the Pastors'
Retiring Fund, and many other similar bodies was unbounded.
No personal sacrifice for their well-being was too great, and it
was due to his indefatigable efforts that the money was raised for
the purchase of Eltham College where the School for Sons of
Missionaries is now. 'If the Jews thought a tenth of their income
the appropriate amount to allocate to charity,' he used to say,
'a Christian ought to give at least an eighth.' He was never well-
off and we all of us often had to go without things, but the eighth
was a first charge on his income and never diverted from what
he called his charity purse. He thus always had money available
for any good cause, thereby acquiring the unfortunate reputation
of being a rich man, which he never was. No charity to which
he was a regular subscriber need worry to apply for his subscription—in fact, he rather resented it if they wasted money in
doing so—because he kept a special diary giving the precise date
and amount, and even after he was ninety and bedridden, saw to
it that it was forthcoming on the due date. I occasionally protested that in the case of some of the 'charities' he was merely
paying the salary of someone better off than himself, but it made
no difference, and I was instructed, as his executor, to pay a

further subscription to all of them on the due date during the year following his death.

His father, Jacob Unwin, the founder of the family printing firm of Unwin Brothers, likewise had much of William Mattingly Soundy's characteristics. The correspondence which followed his betrothal to my grandmother, Emma Soundy, some of which I have had the opportunity of reading, is remarkable for its complete unconcern with worldly problems and its absorption in the effect of marriage upon their spiritual well-being. My father was only two years old when his mother died, but she left the deepest impression upon him. He treasured endless letters of hers, and throughout life often spoke to me of her saintliness.

Jacob Unwin, although primarily a printer, was a publisher in a small way and the distributor of *The Youth's Magazine*.[1] He likewise died before my father reached manhood, but there were others to look after his well-being. He seems to have been a sickly child, and there are references to his 'being despatched at six years of age to the care of a maiden aunt at Burford to recuperate'. The fact that two elder brothers perished in a fire at Bucklersbury fifteen months before he was born seemed to haunt him throughout life. An account of the occurrence, in which a cat saved the lives of others in the house, appears on pages 64–5 of a little book *A Voice from Fire*,[2] and is the subject of a remarkable (and appallingly long) sermon at the Weigh House Chapel, Fish Street Hill, by that most famous preacher of those days, the Rev. Thomas Binney, reprinted in the Penny Pulpit Series under the heading *A Sudden and Signal Calamity Improved*.[3]

This tragic loss, which he felt deeply and often referred to, no doubt partly accounts for the fact that my father was timidity itself. He was capable of becoming nervously worked up even when travelling in a 'growler' (a one-horse closed-in cab), let alone in any faster conveyance. My mother, on the other hand,

[1] See *A Century of Progress: The History of Unwin Brothers Limited*, 1926.
[2] Thomas Ward & Co., 1840.
[3] Nos. 234, 235 and 236, May 30, 1839 (London: James Paul, 52 Paternoster Row).

was benignly placid. But the characteristic which surprised me most was my father's unbounded confidence in others. He was so good himself that he found it impossible to believe others were not actuated by equally good motives. He was so concerned that the other man should not be let down that he got the worst of any bargain. And I don't think that anyone could be more gullible. In later life I had over and over again to protect him from himself. One incident in my childhood stood me in good stead in later life. My father was approached by someone near Lee station who had run out of money and wanted his fare home. My father unhesitatingly produced what was needed. Later that day we encountered the same gentleman, still in Lee, being directed to the police station hopelessly drunk. Many years later, a man came one afternoon to my office with a most convincing story of his need to go to Manchester. I asked him whether he was quite sure that he really needed to go to Manchester, and that it was not merely the fare that he wanted. He was quite sure. I found that there was a non-stop train in an hour's time; would that suit him? It certainly would. I accompanied him to Euston, bought a ticket, took him to the train, and stood by the compartment door until the train moved out. Until the last moment he kept me uncertain whether his story was true, but the look of horror on his face when the train steamed out and escape was impossible told its own story.

There were occasions when my father's gullibility seriously affected the well-being of the family. In 1895 it looked as if the prosperity of Unwin Brothers could be relied upon, and he felt justified in buying a large house called 'The Mount' at Shortlands, which was then near the outskirts of London. It was a much more aristocratic neighbourhood and we all felt that we had gone up in the world. All the houses then stood in their own grounds of not less than an acre. Horses and cows grazed in the fields behind our house, and rooks nested in a nearby wood. In the front we had a picturesque view of Bromley Parish Church across the inter-vening valley, then green fields but now covered with small pre-fabricated villas.

Socially we saw and knew little of our neighbours except the few who happened to commute in the same part of the same train every morning, and even those we never met in any other connection. Between Shortlands and Catford on the way to town the train passed through an attractive estate which added to the feeling that we had moved into the country.

All might have been well had my father not called in an eloquent and enthusiastic Welsh architect. Obviously a few things needed doing, and central heating was desirable, but the architect persuaded him to add a new wing, with a bay window, and to have a completely fresh roof to the whole house. He declared also that a fresh roof was needed for the stables, but by that time the cost of the house had doubled and my father was too alarmed to accede. (As the stable roof was still serviceable forty years later, the urgency of its replacement was a little exaggerated.) What my father never realized was that it was in the architect's interest to persuade him to spend as much as possible, because every addition meant a bigger fee. When the builder's estimate was obtained, the architect pronounced it preposterous, and said my father would save money by having his own clerk of the works, and doing it on a cost plus a percentage basis. The workmen knew that when our house was finished they would be unemployed and spun the work out interminably, with the result that the final cost was much greater than the builder's estimate—to the architect's profit. The upshot was that my father had to raise a mortgage of £4,000 at 5 per cent. That mortgage dominated my father's life for about twenty-five years. The interest upon it, the rates upon such a large house, the central heating, the constant painting of no fewer than seven greenhouses, and the gardeners' wages absorbed the whole of the seven-eighths left of his small income, because immediately following the purchase of 'The Mount' Unwin Brothers' prosperity temporarily waned, their works at Chilworth were burnt to the ground, and they were confronted with the greatest difficulties. How often we children would have liked to dynamite those greenhouses when we observed the financial anxiety their upkeep involved, but my father clung tenaciously to them; he took immense pride particularly in his orchids, grapes and cucumbers.

At the same time frequent attempts were made, and much expense incurred, to sell the house. But no bid, even of the amount of the mortgage, was forthcoming, and as my father had not the wherewithal to make up the difference, we could not move.

Throughout all this trying time voluntary pensions were being paid to his old Unwin Brothers' employees to an amount in excess of his own income, and his charity purse was never raided.

During the First World War the mortgage was called in, and the astonishing solicitor then employed by my father fooled him into the belief that no gentleman would take advantage of the moratorium on mortgages for which provision had been made by Parliament. He even drafted a letter for my father to sign, waiving his rights, regardless of my father's statement that he could not find the money. Fortunately I saw it just as my father was about to sign, and immediately insisted upon the rewording of the letter in a completely contrary sense, and arranging for repayment by small instalments which I could help to find. From the foregoing the unworldliness of my father may be judged.

To art he paid homage in Victorian ways, and in particular by a yearly, almost ceremonial, visit to the Academy. We all set off by an early workmen's train, and breakfasted at 'Lockhart's' so as to be at the Academy before 9 a.m. when the doors opened. What memories 'Lockhart's' evokes; how grateful we often were to those primitive catering establishments for the working classes which were open at hours when no other sustenance could be obtained! To me they are indelibly associated with Queen Victoria's funeral, when my brother Cyril and I journeyed to London overnight in order to take up our stance at dawn on the Achilles statue, whence we had a superb view.

Although my father's knowledge of music was limited, he encouraged us all to learn some instrument, and himself regularly attended the Monday Popular Concerts in the famous St. James's Hall, where Charles Dickens gave the second series of his

'Readings' in 1861—a building in the Moorish-Alhambra style since replaced by the Piccadilly Hotel.

In the realm of literature, unless sermons be classed as literature, he was quite unreliable. Although he enjoyed the work of Charles Dickens he was not reconciled to novel reading in the young; it was not an 'improving' use of time. I have never forgotten his taking *Oliver Twist* away from me just as I had reached the exciting picture of Fagin in his cell, and giving me as an alternative Max Muller's *Chips from a German Workshop* (four volumes) and *Kingsley's Miscellanies* (two volumes) which an itinerant bookseller had foisted upon him as works of outstanding importance, but which he himself had never read. How I managed to wade through such arid stuff I cannot think, but I know that I conscientiously read all six volumes, inwardly cursing their authors! They stirred in me no interest in the origin of the Aryan tongue or the geology of chalkpits.

My father was desperately concerned about my spiritual well-being, and on the eve of my eighteenth birthday wrote me the following letter;

'My dear Stanley,

'Our mutual occupations are rendering anything like a quiet chat more and more difficult—yet one on paper has its advantages, and need not be omitted for any reason. So it affords me pleasure to take the opportunity of your birthday tomorrow to supplement what may be the hasty congratulation as I go off to town by the more sober and extended written thought, albeit it may trouble you a little to read it. First let me express my very hearty congratulations and good wishes for many happy returns of your birthday. It is very pleasing to me to see you contented and happy in your young business life and with every prospect of steady advancement. Moreover I believe you have sufficient ballast in the way of character to keep you from the allurements of the great city. All of which one is devoutly thankful for.

'But my thoughts went last Sunday eve a little deeper as I listened to Mr Nicholson's earnest pleading with his young people from Psalm 37, 31 and I was wishing you were there.

'Do you remember, in *Brothers and a Sermon* of Jean Ingelow,

My Father

My Mother

The Spicer
family
1903

the reproach the preacher desired should never come—"Old man, you told us not of this" and so on? And so, Stanley, lad, I feel I must tell you, for the love I have for you, my and your mother's earnest desire that the "ballast" you carry should be "the law of your God". I fain believe it *is* actuating your conduct. What joy it would give us to see you an avowed disciple! Nicodemus was a splendid fellow but with all his failings I admire Peter more.

'My morning reading took me to Deut. 4, 29, and I thought of you once more. If you still have to "seek" there is a gracious promise for you, but having "found" then comes following and I can speak from experience of the help it was to me to declare myself openly as a willing follower of my dear Lord and Saviour. Do we not owe it to Him? Think about this and if I can help you, let me.

'I was going to say, Forgive my filling up my letter in this way but I cannot. Jesus Christ has done so much for my life that I dare not keep Him from my chat with you tonight (12.15).

'Thank you for all the happiness you throw into our home circle, and with much love, believe me ever

'Your affectionate Father.'

I found it deeply embarrassing. I knew how grieved he would be if I declined, and hated even the idea of disappointing him. I was far too convinced by my mother's example of the value of the Christian way of life to want to make even a temporary break with home traditions as one of my elder brothers had done. On the other hand my religious convictions seemed to me too precious and personal a thing for public display and I had a horror of announcing them in the formal way my father desired. A deacon for whom I had an instinctive dislike took a hand and brought no little pressure upon me. But I temporized. About a year later, when I was in Germany and to please my father, I became (*in absentio*) a member of Bromley Congregational Church. I thus avoided the formalities I so much dreaded and my father was temporarily satisfied. I am still, and am likely to remain, a Nonconformist, but forms and ceremonies are of less importance to me than the 'Inner Light', and I have found myself increasingly in sympathy with the Quaker attitude to life.

Much later in life, when I was reading Lowes Dickinson's *The*

Meaning of Good, my father looked down at the book on his return from church, and remarked that if the last word had been spelt with one 'o' the book might have been more suited for Sunday.

Throughout our childhood playing cards were taboo, but when he was nearing eighty my father's views broadened; whist was approved; he took to the films with avidity and became a Charlie Chaplin fan. Sometimes he would admit a little shamefacedly that he had stopped at Catford on the way home to see the pictures.

His vitality right to the end was incredible. When just on eighty he climbed the Monument with two young kinsmen from Rhodesia, whom he was showing round London. When he arrived on top with his long white beard and rosy cheeks, a cockney girl who was resting exhausted on the parapet gazed at him in wonderment and exclaimed, 'Lor', if 'e done it I ought to be ashimed'. Later that day the three of them came to my office; the two young men were quite tired out and sank into chairs. My father, they said, was wearing them out!

Not long before he was ninety, my sister Ella, who looked after him, felt that it was time he reduced the number of his activities and suggested that I should use my influence. I said, 'Make a list and I will go over it with him'. She did so, and it contained twenty-three items. When confronted with it he said at once, 'Oh, this is not nearly all'. By the time he had completed the list it contained forty-seven different committee memberships, treasurerships, trusteeships, and boards of one kind and another. In his ninetieth year he journeyed to Scotland to fulfil his task as treasurer, of presenting the accounts at the Annual Conference of the Master Printers' Federation, as he had done since 1911. Even on his deathbed (aged ninety-three) he lived three weeks after the doctor had said he could not survive the night, in such perfect condition were both his heart and lungs.

He was a great soul, and when one looks back and thinks of the extent to which he lived and worked for others, it makes one feel very humble and inclined to echo the words of the cockney girl on the Monument—if he did it, I ought to be ashamed.

CHAPTER 3

ELIZABETH UNWIN (*née* SPICER): 1840–1921

James Spicer (1807–1888), Congregationalist and chief creator of the paper firm of Spicers, was a remarkable man, and not least in the number of his progeny. At a family gathering held in 1948 no fewer than one hundred of those present were found to be his direct descendants or married to them. His own immediate family consisted of ten—four girls, followed by four boys, and then two more girls.[1]

'Harts', his house near Woodford Green, with its two porters' lodges and mile walk round the grounds, must have been a wonderful home. Those were the days when the merchant princes of London could live in regal splendour, and James Spicer was one of them. Although I went to 'Harts' as a child, I was too young to enjoy its benefits like my elder brothers, who made my mouth water with their enraptured accounts of peaches and nectarines which they were permitted to eat if they had dropped, and left me lost in admiration of their skill in ensuring that the appropriate quantities did drop!

My mother was the second eldest, and although she had neither the stately presence nor masterful[2] personality of her elder sister,

[1] The eldest daughter (Mrs Martindale) has been vividly portrayed by Miss Hilda Martindale in a volume entitled *From One Generation to Another* (London: George Allen & Unwin Ltd., 1944), and there are attractive biographical sketches of the youngest daughter (Miss Charlotte Spicer) and the second eldest son (The Rt. Hon. Sir Albert Spicer, Bt.) in *Some Victorian Portraits* (London: George Allen & Unwin Ltd., 1948). A more detailed and most excellent biography of the latter is to be found in *Sir Albert Spicer, Bart.*, written by one of his sons (London: Simpkin Marshall Ltd., 1938). No life has, however, yet been written of another famous son, Sir Evan Spicer, Chairman of the London County Council, 1906–7.

[2] Her younger daughter objected to the adjective as denoting lack of femininity. I reminded her of George Meredith's words in *The Tragic Comedians* which are so applicable to my Aunt Louisa: 'You meet now and then men who have the woman in them without being womanized; they are the pick of men. And the choicest women are those who yield not a feather of their womanliness for some amount of manlike strength. And she is one; man's brain, woman's heart.' (London: Constable & Co. Ltd., 1904, p. 61.)

Louisa Martindale, she was probably in her own unobtrusive way the most remarkable character in a very remarkable family. I have certainly never met anyone with such deep underlying power. Unlike many short people, she did not make up for shortness of stature by even a hint of aggressiveness. In quietness and confidence was her strength.

Her father entrusted her with his cellar (for which he was famous), and at one stage with the instruction of the two youngest daughters, who, when they were white-haired, Mother still referred to as the 'girls'. Mother enjoyed the first task immensely, and to the end knew much about, and enjoyed, good wines, so that it was a real deprivation to her to discard her share of her father's cellar, which she and my father did when they became, on principle, and some time after their marriage, life-long abstainers. From that moment nothing alcoholic was kept in the house, and the one visitor (John Shrimpton, founder of the Homes for Working Girls in London) permitted a 'night-cap' had to bring his whisky with him.

Teaching her young sisters she never enjoyed, and it was a task she was ill-fitted to do except by example. In shrewdness, judgment, intuition, strength of character, she excelled, but intellectual power, which Goethe regarded as the least important attribute in a woman, she did not possess. That last fact led many to underrate a character at once so unspectacular yet so unusual. Visitors to our home, unless they possessed exceptional insight, would never have guessed the power that lay behind that serene and quiet little person who never asserted her authority. But there were some who realized it, and they found in her a source of unlimited strength. For my own part, I owe anything worth while in me to her. She had unbounded confidence in me, and that knowledge enabled me to take difficult decisions with an equanimity not otherwise attainable. In her mind there was never any doubt that 'All things work together for good to them that love God', and she had patience to abide the Lord's good time.

Her father took her many tours on the Continent, which, like the Ruskins, they made in their own carriage. She thus acquired a taste for foreign travel which she never lost. He was, I must add, a very Victorian father, and had decided views about the husbands his daughters ought to accept. He would, I am sure, have approved the Victorian dictum, 'Don't marry for money, but marry where money is'. Unfortunately for him his daughters, having strong characters of their own, had, and maintained, other views. The Unwin brothers, George and Edward, were members of the same Congregational church as the Spicers, and like Lizzie and Maria Spicer were Sunday School teachers, so that no exception could be taken to them on religious grounds (as I believe was later the case with a younger step-brother), but, alas! they were struggling printers, and impecunious. George, although barely twenty, had taken over the Jacob Unwin business on the latter's death; my father, Edward, had joined him later as a junior partner. It was hard enough for old James Spicer to accept George Unwin as prospective husband of Maria (his third daughter), but when the younger and still more impecunious brother, Edward Unwin, proposed to my mother, an elder daughter, it was almost more than he could bear and all the resourcefulness of the eldest sister, who was also devoted to my father, and others, was needed to secure his consent. Even so, onerous conditions were laid down before the engagement was permitted. In the end the two Unwin brothers were married to the two Spicer sisters, and their two families, of eleven and nine respectively, were thus doubly related. Both marriages proved intensely happy.

Although our Sundays may have been 'cabin'd, crib'd and confin'd', and theatres and playing cards were taboo, we enjoyed for those days remarkable freedom, and this, I think, we owed largely to Mother, who had the most absolute confidence in us all, and let us know that we had her confidence. She never found fault, but appealed to the best in us. Her capacity for making us feel ashamed of ourselves if we did anything wrong was remarkable. In the matter of sex education she was a long way ahead of her time. She was determined that we should be fully informed, and we were thus brought up with clear ideas of what was right and wrong in such matters, and with no unnatural inhibitions from discussing such problems. On one point she was insistent, and that was equality of the sexes. What was wrong for a woman could not be right for a man, and a man had no more (but no fewer) 'rights' than a woman. To the many religious people who in those days objected strongly to the imparting of sex information she had a complete answer. It was all in the Bible.

Again, as an outcome, I imagine, of her strong feelings about equality of the sexes, my mother felt that, as the person jointly responsible for the arrival of an infant, the father should take his full part. If the mother had the burden and pain of carrying and delivering the child, the least the father could do was to be present at the hour of trial to comfort and encourage the mother. My father was accordingly present at the arrival of all nine of us. If a man is going to prove a nuisance in such circumstances he is best out of the way, but whatever my father felt about it I would be sorry not to have been present at the birth of all my four children.

It is perhaps a strange thing to say, but knowing better than most men just really what it means, and being in many other respects a physical coward, I would have been quite prepared to take my turn of child-bearing were that possible. There is nothing more intensely satisfying than creation, and is there anything more noble we humans can create? No wonder, as the Bible says, 'she remembereth no more the anguish, for joy that a man is born into the world'.

The completely unobtrusive way in which my mother held her own was astonishing. We were an argumentative family, and Mother just listened silently. When we had exhausted ourselves, someone would ask Mother what she thought. Her reply showed that she had pierced through all the verbiage to the heart of the problem, and in a few quiet words she would pronounce a verdict which left us completely satisfied.

One evening I announced at supper that I had to go off almost immediately for a long business tour on the Continent, and jokingly asked round the table, including my father, whether they wouldn't like to come with me. After they had all declined,

Mother said quietly, 'You haven't asked me'. When I responded, 'Well, would you come?' she replied, 'Why not?' and that was the beginning of a wonderful series of yearly business journeys upon which she accompanied me to many places from Vienna and Budapest to Copenhagen. They always had to be achieved economically, but that did not disturb her in the least. She was the ideal travelling companion, full of zest, interested in everything, completely philosophical whatever happened. While I called on booksellers she would sit in some central square and knit, or merely observe the life around her. Between my calls I would dodge along and report what luck I had with orders, and she was as keenly interested as if her own well-being depended upon them.

What was more remarkable was her ability to sleep under any conditions whenever she wanted to, and for any length of time. As an illustration of the latter, I have known her come down at 3 p.m. ready to catch the 3.15 train to Beckenham to go to her bank. It took between seven and eight minutes to walk to Short-lands station, but Mother liked to allow ten. When she observed the time she would say, 'Oh! Just time for five minutes' sleep', put a newspaper over her head, and five minutes' good sleep she would have without any anxiety about waking up at the right moment. She *knew* she would wake up and she always did precisely when she expected. On one occasion we were travelling from Jena to Nuremberg, and to save both time and money decided to travel by a night train, leaving just before twelve, and arriving at Nuremberg at 4 a.m. I was full of anxiety that we should oversleep. Mother had none and went to sleep at once. At 4 a.m. she was as fresh as a daisy; I was tired out and did not observe her put her hat on in the semi-darkness.

After an early breakfast I started calling on the booksellers, and Mother agreed to walk up and down the pavement outside as we had planned to go up to the castle together afterwards. When I came out from my first call I found her in great distress. She said that while she was walking along the pavement a policemen came and spoke to her. When it was clear that she understood nothing, he had taken her arm and conducted her to the opposite pavement, and then as soon as she turned round escorted her back again. I at once questioned the policeman and found that, being very narrow, the pavements were 'one-way', so that walking up and down was *verboten*. But the joke came later. Up at the castle, after we had watched the donkey turn the wheel that pumps the water, I left Mother for a moment, and on returning found her once again in distress. A girl attendant had been looking most strangely at her and said something in German, which, of course, she had not understood. At that moment the girl arrived with a mirror, and Mother observed to her consternation that she had her hat on back to front! As I at once pointed out, her hat had been facing the correct way when the policeman disapproved the direction she was walking! Mother just loved amusing incidents of this kind, of which we had plenty on our travels, but the kind of thing she appreciated most was a Sunday morning in the Prater Allee in Vienna in the days of its glory. The parade of pair-horse open carriages, with liveried coachmen and footmen, driving at top speed one way, and walking their magnificent horses back the other, was most impressive. The entire aristocracy seemed to turn out and the attractive outdoor cafés were thronged with the élite.

Mother's interest in, and devotion to, the Royal Family were intense. She knew their precise relationship to all the ruling families on the Continent, and watched their movements as if they were those of her own children. And the arrival of a royal baby excited her as much as that of another grandchild. But when she read Lytton Strachey's *Life of Queen Victoria*, and learnt how the Queen had treated her beloved Gladstone, she admitted with a sigh that Victoria had really been very 'naughty'.

The fundamental difference between Mother and any other man or woman I have known was the completeness of her faith. No one I have met, save Gandhi, possessed as she did the faith that will move mountains. An example of the application of that faith will show what I mean. One of my elder brothers, for reasons which are in this connection irrelevant, had a most serious mental breakdown. Our own doctor and two mental specialists who were called in were unanimously of opinion that it was a type of insanity for which no cure could be anticipated, and that there was no alternative but to certify him. My mother merely smiled and said with complete assurance, 'He is going to get well and he is not going to be sent to an asylum'. Against most emphatic advice, given because of a tendency to violence, he was kept at home with a male mental nurse in constant attendance. The only person in our household who was not scared of him was my mother. His constant shouting and uncertain behaviour wore the rest of us out. After we had endured the prolonged nervous torture for about three months, my father and we others said that we could stand it no longer, and pleaded with Mother to allow him to be certified and sent away. Her immediate reply was: 'Very well, I will take him away. He is going to recover so that there can be no question of putting him away', and take him away by herself with the male nurse she did. Within another two months he had recovered sufficiently to be brought home again, and in the end he became completely well. Her faith had made him whole. On one occasion, when he was still in the violent stage, Mother visited him alone in his room upstairs. He rushed at her with the intention of throwing her out of the window, which, in view of her diminutive size, he could easily have done. She just smiled at him and said, 'You wouldn't do that'. The completeness of her confidence checked him. Recalling the incident later, my brother admitted that had she shown even a flicker of fear his threat would have been carried out. But Mother had no fear: 'Perfect love casteth out fear.'

Another incident comes to my mind which illustrates her unusual character. A fashionable lady from Bromley drove up in a carriage and pair in a state of great excitement to announce that her dressmaker, whom she had learnt Mother also employed, had locked herself up in her little room with several bottles of spirit and had not left the room for any purpose for three (it may have been four) days and nights; that she refused to open the door; was incoherent, and, as far as could be seen through the keyhole, was lying on the floor, and would Mother do something about it.

Why she came to Mother instead of tackling the job herself she did not explain. After she left, Mother said she was going down to see what she could do. I refused to let her go alone and accompanied her. As all the hammering on the door had had no effect, I decided that we must try bluff, and yelled 'Fire'. There was a slight stir, a figure dragged itself along the floor and turned the key. I have seen some filthy pigsties in my day, but they were pleasant compared with the sight that met our eyes! There on the floor in the midst of the mess was a black and indescribably dirty mass of humanity, sodden with urine and worse. The stench was revolting. After one glance Mother observed calmly, 'We cannot expect the other people here to deal with this; we must take her home'. I could only gasp. 'You had better get a cab', she said. The struggle to get that huge, sodden mass down the stairs (she was a big woman, quite 6 feet in height) is one I shall never forget because she was incapable of walking by herself. The cabman had a good deal to say about being expected to convey her, but we got her home. 'I can't ask the maids to give her a bath; I must do it myself', said my mother on arrival, and do it she did, after cutting away the mess in which the good dressmaker was embalmed, because 'undressing' was, of course, an impossibility. When the process was all over and the one-time garments had been burnt, Mother smilingly remarked, 'Well, she won't be able to leave the house now to get anything more to drink because she hasn't any clothes!' The fact that her detention against her will was illegal, and the knowledge that it might be necessary to nurse her through an attack of delirium tremens, left Mother unmoved. She had set her hand to the plough and there was no turning back; in our best spare room the dressmaker remained until she could be trusted to make a fresh start. Mother knew that she could be cured, and cured she was.

During the troublous times when Father was so worried about his inability to sell 'The Mount', Mother, who had no wish to be upheaved at the end of her life, used constantly to assert, 'You will have no difficulty in selling when the *right* time comes'. As always, her faith was justified. A year or two after her death, and

at the appropriate moment, Father received an acceptable offer
which enabled him to move to less expensive quarters.

Mother's fearlessness and readiness for anything new showed
themselves in many ways. No sooner were motor-cars invented
than she was all agog to try them, and as soon as I could afford it I
hired cars to take her for drives, so that I might share and enjoy
the thrill they gave her. Long before it seemed probable, she
frequently told me that I should live to fly, but that she was
afraid she wouldn't. When the Zeppelins came over during the
First World War nothing would induce her to take cover; night
or day she wanted to see them, and out she would go when others
sought shelter.

Like her elder sister, she had the strongest views about Women's
Rights, and they sometimes revealed themselves in curious ways.
My father had to include her income in his Income Tax return.
In so far as it concerned the revenue from the trust fund so
providently provided by James Spicer, the figures were available.
But in the course of years Mother had saved and invested a few
hundred pounds as a reserve for any emergency. That was her
money; it had nothing to do with anyone else. The law did not
compel *her* to disclose the amount (she was correct; it didn't), and
despite all his entreaties she absolutely refused to tell Father the
amount to be included in his 'return', and he just had to guess it.
The amusing part was that as Mother trusted me with her accounts
I knew the precise figure, and was able to give Father the comforting assurance that his guess was correct. The fact was that
Mother had no confidence in Father's judgment in financial
matters, and felt that the less he knew about her affairs the better.
Where we should have been without Mother's business acumen
I do not know.

Her interest in missionaries was profound. We must have
entertained hundreds, and often complete families, and for long
periods. We children often resented their intrusion into our
family life, but it made no difference. Mother's philosophy of
entertaining and hospitality was definite. She had a poor opinion
of entertaining people who could, and probably would, entertain

you in return, and we did practically none. But entertaining those who needed it and could do nothing in return was quite different.[1] That she would put herself out to do. When I was twenty-two, Mother having had only nine children of her own, more or less adopted two more. They were daughters of missionaries, and both were in too precarious a state of health to remain at school. They lived with us for years, completely recovered, and are both now happily married with children of their own. Later in life, when I spent eighteen months travelling round the world, I found that my parents, having no sins which could descend upon their children, had passed on the benefit of their virtues. Everywhere, even in the most distant places, I encountered missionaries, or more frequently the successful sons of missionaries, ready or anxious to help or entertain me.

Mother's dislike of any form of prevarication was intense. She could not abide any conduct which was not, as she would say, 'up and down straight'. Her unselfishness and thoughtfulness for others had no bounds. Although I was her Benjamin and, being for so long the only son at home, had become her mainstay, no tinge of possessiveness, let alone jealously, marred her relationship with my wife, to whom she was greatly attached. Did not the Bible say: 'Therefore shall a man leave his father, and his mother, and shall cleave unto his wife?', and to Mother the Bible was the word of God. I paid her regular visits (on Saturday afternoons after playing tennis at the covered courts at Dulwich) during the seven years following my marriage, and to the end she wanted to be satisfied that Mary approved, which Mary always did because she shared my devotion.

But Mother's thoughtfulness extended to those at whose hands she had suffered much. Just before her end she asked me to look after an aged employee who for many years had been a great trial to her and who was then an Old Age Pensioner of eighty, with, as it proved, quite a long life ahead of her.

One of the most touching tributes paid to my Mother after her death was from the working women of Shortlands, who wove an

[1] See Luke xiv. 22.

exquisite garland of flowers culled from their own gardens in memory of 'one they would never forget'.

Until her marriage, Mother lived in luxury; thereafter she was content herself to do without. She adored jewellery, but I can remember only one occasion when my father was permitted to give her any, because, as she would say, 'There are so many things more urgently needed'. When funds were low, as they often were, and I asked for anything, she would never say 'no'. She would answer, 'Just think whether you could not do without it and let me know tomorrow'. Well, there are few things that survive that test, and later in life I used teasingly to tell her that the most valuable lesson she had taught me was how to do without. It gave one such complete independence of material things.

A year before Mother died she was at death's door and I was summoned to her side. She was only just conscious, but was able to make it clear that she was ready to depart. I said to her, 'Mother, you simply must stay; we cannot do without you'. She paused, obviously reluctant to make the effort, and then said quietly, 'If God has more work for me to do here, I shall stay'. A year later when she had a further severe attack of pneumonia (she had been down on her knees mending a carpet the previous day) I was at Wernigerode in the Harz Mountains, staying at the Hotel Weisses Kreuz, where some years before she and I had had some happy days together. When I got back from a long day's tramp the post office had just closed, so that I did not get the telegram telling me of her illness until the following morning. I hurried back, but before I arrived she had passed on, relieved, I sometimes think, that I was not there to call her back again from the peace that passeth all understanding. I kissed that beloved face for the last time and walked out into the brilliant sunshine to look at the spring flowers in the garden, where my wife and I had so recently observed the ecstatic joy with which Mother walked up and down with our baby daughter Ruth in her arms. We had lost our first little girl, named after my mother Elizabeth Spicer Unwin, and Ruth was all the more precious to her on that account.

There was now nothing left for me to do except place a few forget-me-nots in those dear placid hands which had toiled so devotedly for others, conscious that her spirit remained with us, and confident that her unswerving faith that we should meet again must be justified.

CHAPTER 4

ABBOTSHOLME SCHOOL

The circumstances under which the Unwin family became early supporters of Abbotsholme are interesting. My three elder brothers were all educated at the City of London School, and on leaving had gone to Hanerau in Germany for a year to learn German, as all educated persons were supposed to do in those days. My third eldest brother, Sidney, was only 16½ when he returned and my father thought he ought to have another year's education. An account of a new school which was to be opened in Derbyshire that October appeared in W. T. Stead's *Review of Reviews*. The practical side of the programme attracted my brother, and my father decided to take him to see Dr Cecil Reddie, with the result that my brother was one of the first three boys there. As he was later on the staff, and I was Unwin 6, we had as a family extensive experience of Dr Reddie's virtues as well as of his weaknesses and idiosyncrasies. My elder brother saw him at his best, and says that he altered his whole outlook on life. At his best he was quite exceptionally good; by the time I came on the scene degeneration had set in. I should describe him as both a genius and a crank.

My start at Abbotsholme was not altogether auspicious. This is my brother-in-law, Gerald Brooke's, recollection of it:

'I remember very well a most modest little Stanley arriving for his first term at boarding school. He was a little younger than I was, so that I was then in a position to look down on him. . . . He had a great asset—a training in Nonconformity. He arrived with nature-form boots. This wanted some living down for a schoolboy, but he succeeded all right. He had a slogan about letting nature do its own work.'

Those 'round-the-corner' boots, as they were called, haunted my early schooldays, but they have left me with feet of the shape nature intended so that I have no regrets about them. Today they would cause little excitement because they were not very different from the popular Sir Herbert Barker shoe with its straight inner line.

Dr Reddie's[1] influence was intense and in the early days all to the good. He impressed upon the boys that man was a trinity—hand, heart and brain; that their time at school was planned accordingly—the mornings in the development of their brains, the afternoons to manual work, and the evenings to social activities and music culminating in chapel. The motto of the school was 'Glad Day, Love and Duty', and he hammered home the importance of service long before Rotarians were thought of, and 'Laborare est Orare' must be engraved on most Old Abbotsholmians' hearts. Hygiene was taught about thirty years before more conventional schools thought about it. Mind cleanliness as well as bodily cleanliness were emphasized, and sensible ways of sublimating sex instinct explained at a time when most literature on the subject was deplorable and in some cases injurious.

In the chapel services, readings were not confined to the Bible—and wisdom and religious experience of the ages were drawn upon. The death of Socrates, for example, was the subject of the reading on the Sunday before Easter to lead up to the death of Christ. Music played an important role in school life. Dr Reddie was undoubtedly a pioneer ahead of his time. Abbotsholme was the first of the 'new schools' (Bedales and Clayesmore followed), and many of his early ideas have been adopted by the public schools and are today accepted as commonplace. He emphasized that *e-duco* stood for lead out, not cram in. He had the greatest contempt for the mere memorizing of facts for examination purposes. 'Facts,' he used to thunder, 'facts can be got by any fool from encyclopaedias and works of reference; what matters is that you should learn to *think*.' And many were the ways in which he sought to achieve that end. He refused to allow games to

[1] *Reddie of Abbotsholme*, by B. M. Ward (London: George Allen & Unwin Ltd., 1934).
Cecil Reddie and Abbotsholme, by R. A. Wake (*The Times Educational Supplement*, June 6, 1958).

My Mother
and her
Sisters at
'The Mount'
1907

Lining up for Estate Work.   S. U. second from right

ABBOTSHOLME
1897–1900

The Last Load.   New buildings in background

become a fetish, and they were confined to, at most, two after-noons a week; the others were devoted largely to work on the estate. The grounds, including a mixed farm, consisted of about 240 acres, and there were always endless odd jobs to be done—it might be mending a fence or gate, creosoting some timber, tarring railings, digging potatoes, cleaning out a cowshed, or more often something quite unexpected. We lined up in the yard, and the master in charge picked on some elder boy, told him what needed doing, gave him a squad of smaller boys to help him and sent him off. Once on the spot it was the elder boy's duty to decide what tools or materials were needed and to delegate the small boys to fetch them. A little later the master would come round and ask how he proposed to tackle the job. If the answer was satisfactory he would say 'carry on' and return later to see what progress had been made. If the elder boy's proposal was bad, he would ask the smaller boys what was wrong with it and if they could suggest a better, and so all were kept on their toes and made to think. No boy who went through that training and discipline was easily intimidated by practical problems in later life. It certainly taught me much.

Dr C. P. Gunning, a contemporary of mine (later headmaster of one of the largest and most important schools in Holland), emphasized recently to me that we were not only encouraged to think for ourselves and not be regimented or swept off our feet by herd movements, but actually learnt to. In confirmation he cited an incident which I had long since forgotten, but which he said had made the deepest impression upon him. On Mafeking night, when as a Dutchman he felt isolated and miserable, I had gone up to him and pressed his hand and told him not to worry. I had read J. A. Hobson's *The War in South Africa* and realized that Britain was not necessarily in the right.

Some of Dr Reddie's own classes were astonishing. If the subject was hygiene we learnt a great deal about economics, and if we were supposed to be studying political economy the time was sure to be occupied with hygiene. On one occasion, in a state of fury at our incompetence, he broke the pointer across the table and said that if we did not learn to think and to take more pains we should end by blacking the boots of the Germans. This was way back in 1898, long before the Germans had attained the industrial supremacy that they had achieved by 1914. He described how they came over here, worked as volunteers in our factories, lived on the smell of an oil rag, picked our brains, and then with German thoroughness did the job better than we did. He certainly made an impression upon some of us; boot-blacking had no attraction for me—I had done too much of it as a fag for some of the prefects—and I determined not to fail for lack of *Gründlichkeit*. It was a great satisfaction to me in later life to do the very thing he praised the Germans for doing, and end by having the German translation of my book on publishing adopted as the text-book for the German book trade, and my description of their book trade organization accepted as authoritative.

Dr Reddie's appreciation of books was critical. In a Preface to his own book[1] he said 'he felt a growing conviction that words and books, less by quality than quantity, exert an exaggerated influence in our lives, producing new perils to body, mind and character. Reading means sitting. Reading words is not seeing Things. And the inordinate flood of printed matter that pours through, or at least over, the average brain, disorganizes steady thinking more seriously than even our modern chaotic life. But mankind has so long been fed on an Education through words, that men naturally reward the Phrasemonger more highly than the Doer.'

Although personally I owe Dr Reddie (or C. R. as we called him) quite a lot, there were others upon whom his almost hypnotic influence proved disastrous.

My first term (summer 1897) was miserable. I was a hopeless coward in water, and it did not help matters that on the first day I was made to jump off the diving board into deep water. It is true that there was a strong swimmer there to rescue me, but my confidence was insufficient to induce me to jump well out, and in

---

[1] *Abbotsholme* (London: George Allen, 1900).

consequence I cut my feet badly on the floitering stones of the river bank. Bathing was compulsory and every boy *had* to learn to swim. I was in such a state of terror that the last class in the morning was torture to me, unless to my great relief it was pouring with rain. A Scottish youth shared my anxiety, and in panic ran away after he had undressed. He sped along the river Dove and actually covered the half-mile to a main road before he was caught. As we bathed in a state of complete nudity the chase caused quite a stir. It was not until the end of term that I managed to pass the first easy test; I don't think my fellow sufferer ever did.

At that time I evidently looked as if butter would not melt in my mouth and that I had not got it in me to do anything wrong, whereas the fact was that I was too astute to get found out. I had come from a day school where 'swopping' and 'trading' were part of the daily life, but my brother Bernard maintained that anything so mercenary was out of keeping with both the Abbotsholme and Unwin traditions. There were the further complications that Unwin 1 was my form master (he had warned me that he would be stricter with me than with any others) and Unwin 4, a cousin, a martinet, was head boy and had given me a licking on my second night for slowness in getting into bed. I have never wasted any time in the process since. As I had not thereafter been 'caught' doing anything forbidden, C. R. was more than surprised when he told all those to stand up who had been helping themselves to fruit in the orchard, to find me among the first to do so. I had in fact organized some of the raids. He looked at me in astonishment, and said, 'Unwin 6. Well done, Sir! Sit down! Do it again!' to the intense amusement of the whole school. Thereafter I was christened 'plaster saint', and later, on the principle I suppose of poachers being the best gamekeepers, put in charge of the fruit room.

It was doubtless due to the idea that I was like Kipling's Tomlinson, incapable of doing anything wicked enough to take me to hell or good enough to justify entrance to heaven, that prompted some of the astonishing comments in my school reports—reports, by the way, so all embracing that they took some hours to digest, including as they did a sketch of educational ideals and an elaborate analysis of psychological steps in education. The form must have intimidated most parents—so formidable was it. This accusation of being a 'Tomlinson' led to my praying daily, as I did for years, not merely that I might have the courage of my convictions, but that I might have convictions. It has been suggested to me that those prayers were answered.

With my second term at Abbotsholme I found my feet and was intensely happy. Among other joys was the derelict miniature railway in the grounds of a nearby estate. It was trespassing to go there, but that did not deter us. With a select three or four others I founded the DBMR (what the initials stood for, Dove Bank Miniature Railway, was kept secret) to restore the line to working order. I appointed myself chairman, and with great prescience Charles Renold[1] managing director, and we restored it to such effect that we made the points as well as the signals work from the signal box, which they had never previously done. We had to maintain a constant look-out lest we were caught, and did so successfully until the end of one term when we had taken some others to show them our handiwork and a gamekeeper approached from an unexpected direction. Those on the school side of him ran away; I was in the signal box and could not escape. He told me to get down, and as we had only recently and illegally removed the padlock from the door I laboriously got out of the window as we had always done previously. But the gamekeeper had, alas! observed that the padlock had gone, and asked why I took the trouble to get out of the window now that the door had been opened. We pacified the keeper with assurances that as term was over we could not come back even if we wanted to, and he and we took our departure. However, we had our own back on those who had deserted us in the hour of trouble. We told them that the keeper had let us off, but that those who had run away

[1] Later Sir Charles Renold, Chairman of Renold Chains Limited and President of the British Institute of Management.

were to be reported unless they went back and apologized. They besought us to accompany them, but we refused. With their tails between their legs they set off, but before they had gone far the rest of us burst into laughter and called them back.

But apart from incidents of this kind life was far from dull in the Abbotsholme of 1897–99. Each term, for instance, brought with it a new foreign master, and what astonishing apparitions they seemed to us!

There was the broad and big-headed Herr 'B', whose first encounter with set 'C' no boy who was present is ever likely to forget. He stalked in with enormous strides, stood to attention in true German style, scowled fiercely at us, and then bellowed 'Zee parallel lines zay meet in zee endlessness'. He pronounced the last word as if it had but one syllable, and the class just looked at him in blank amazement, whereat he shouted it again as if addressing a regiment. The class gasped with astonishment; it felt it was confronted with an escaped lunatic. Observing that something was wrong, Herr 'B' strode to his desk, seized a dictionary and, putting his finger on the place, turned upon us in triumph and pronouncing it again as one word shouted, 'endless-ness—in-fie-nigh-tie!' Thereafter there was, I am ashamed to say, pandemonium. However, it was indelibly impressed upon our memories that parallel lines meet in infinity, though personally I cannot pretend to have derived great benefit from that particular piece of knowledge—which was all Herr 'B' ever taught us.

Then there was Herr 'S', who was as thin and cadaverous as Herr 'B' was big and boisterous. Herr 'S' had the most astonishing habit of pulling violently two or three times at his nose between each remark. At the conclusion of his first class he announced in the most doleful voice imaginable: 'I am no more' (downward tugs at his nose). 'Zee class is dissolved' (more tugs at his nose). 'You may do what you may.' The class certainly was dissolved . . . in laughter.

One feature of the school—unusual then, though common-place now—was the encouragement of reading. Apart from the school library, which was well used, it was compulsory for every boy to build up his own library by the purchase each term of what became known as a 'term' book for private reading. There was a wide list of 'approved' books, from which each boy could make his own selection, and I still possess volumes thus acquired, as well as a shelf full of Canterbury Poets and Scott classics, then issued, cloth bound, at 1s and 1s 6d respectively by the Walter Scott Publishing Company, whose publications, by some special dispensation, I was able to buy at half price. Moreover, the history masters encouraged us to read historical fiction, and I remember reading no fewer than fourteen of Scott's novels one after the other. I made time for reading in various ways, such as hurrying over changing after games or gardening, and managed to read other boys' 'term' books as well as my own.

With the growth of the school additional buildings were needed and they proved to be C. R.'s undoing. There is no doubt that the building operations were a terrible strain both upon C. R. himself and certain of his staff, to which C. R. himself contributed not a little by his idiotic refusal to speak to the foreman builder and his insistence upon dealing with the smallest query by correspondence. Every detail was taken with tragic seriousness, and even we boys could see that headmaster and staff were much 'on edge'. But we did not foresee that by the last week of term C. R. and one of his staff would be completely unbalanced mentally, with disastrous results for the school.

To us boys the construction of the new building added variety to our life; the unexpected was always happening. Classes had to be held in all sorts of weird places, and the cowshed (later the workshop and now a cowshed once more) was turned into a temporary dormitory. I was too interested in life in the 'cowshed' to be disturbed by ought else.

It would take too long to recount all our doings. We had a most imaginative dormitory captain in the person of Norman Wilkinson, subsequently famous as a scenic artist. The decorations of the dormitory left nothing to be desired, and when the parson at Rocester preached a sermon which consisted of the repetition of texts like 'It is better . . . higher . . . up' or 'They made light . . . of it', we pinned them up in holly leaves across the beams.

There were coke stoves at either end of the 'cowshed' and we used to fill an old wire basket with potatoes and roast them in the oven. Ghost stories were a popular feature, and I remember inventing one about a haunted bedroom in which the occupant found his hair being brushed just as he fell asleep. At the crucial moment a hair brush, which, unknown to most, I had suspended from one of the beams with staples and fine string, was let slowly down upon the head of the unfortunate boy at the other side of the dormitory. The excitement was intense when he announced, 'I say, fellows, there is a brush on my head!' Most of the boys shouted, 'What nonsense! Light the lamp and see'— but, of course, by the time they had done so the brush had been pulled out of sight.

Of our doings at 'The Lodge', where some of us slept during the building operations, and of the uses of incense when you are surreptitiously cooking sausages I must say nothing. While these things were happening serious troubles were brewing.

Haymaking was one of the features of school life. Classes were suspended until the last load was safely in. As a rule it was a happy time, but in the summer of 1900 something happened which upset C. R.'s balance. I have a vision of C. R. standing up after lunch and yelling something about *my* hay, and again *my* hay, and of a master intervening incoherently and being told to sit down.

But the ideas behind Abbotsholme survived. Years later—in 1927—after C. R. had perversely continued to run the school until there were but two boys left to be inculcated with his views upon the abolition of capital letters, something happened which I believe to be unique in the history of education.

A group of old boys (including some of the 'outcasts', as those who had left at the 'break-up' were occasionally called) persuaded C. R. to give in; to sell the school and estate to a non-profit-making company to be formed by them, and to accept an annuity on the condition that he did not come near the place again. This last stipulation sounds cruel, and it was a bitter pill for C. R. to swallow, but we knew our man and it was essential. No new headmaster would have a fair chance if C. R. had been free to interfere. Colin Sharp was appointed, and under him, and with its new constitution, Abbotsholme became more successful than ever before.

My education was much augmented in the holidays by my many elder brothers. One, a craftsman of genius, felt that it was good for my soul to help him in the workshop whether I wanted to or not. Another pressed the claims of gardening. Two elder ones were enthusiastic play producers, for whom I had to learn and play 'parts'. When they finally staged *The Taming of the Shrew*, Petruchio laid about him with his whip so violently that as one of the grooms I skipped around in real terror. There was no question of 'acting'. Years later, the elder of the two, my brother Will, did much to encourage amateur dramatics in New Zealand.

CHAPTER 5

SHIPPING AND INSURANCE

Even a term before I actually left Abbotsholme it was clear that, although I was still not quite fifteen, my father would not have the wherewithal to keep me there. The printing works of Unwin Brothers at Chilworth in Surrey had been burnt to the ground. All available resources, including the night-long efforts of the entire George Unwin family who lived next door, and many of their workpeople, had to be concentrated upon an endeavour— happily successful—to prevent the fire from spreading to a gun-powder works, where TNT was stored, only a few yards away.

The assessor of the insurance company treated Unwin Brothers most shabbily—in fact, so badly that when it became known people refused to have anything to do with such a company, and over the years they must have lost thousands of pounds' worth of business through the action of their assessor. The then Duke of Northumberland, Unwin Brothers' landlord, was both ruthless and callous. He could not prevent them rebuilding the works *precisely* as they were, but he could, and did, veto the slightest modification, even in the antiquated interior arrangements of the factory. My father and uncle made a special journey to Newcastle to plead with him, but although they had been good tenants for years, he refused even to see them. In this connection it is interesting to note that he had consistently objected to the erection of any better dwellings for their work-people, and even improvements in the existing cottages. In such circumstances it was folly to rebuild, and so, to preserve their business, my father and uncle had forthwith to acquire any premises that were immediately available. The best that could be found was a derelict paper mill at Old Woking, Woking—a choice that proved most expensive as expansion became necessary.

A shipping friend of my father's told me that if I wanted to help him I should start at once to earn my own living, and that if I agreed he would help me to get a job as office boy. Accordingly, armed with a pair of new kid gloves (bought before the disaster) and letters of introduction, I set forth. My visit to the Baltic Shipping Exchange, where I had the thrill of hearing members 'called' in a stentorian voice, proved fruitless, because Mr Sigismund Mendl much regretted that the vacancy for an office boy had just been filled; but my visit to a ship and insurance brokers in Crosby Square proved successful. The principal of this long since defunct firm looked at me and at my kid gloves, and then asked if I was prepared to sweep out the office every morning. I replied 'certainly' with such conviction that he appointed me at the prevailing wage of 10s od per week, though cleaning was not among my duties. When I look back at those days in Crosby Square I am filled with amazement. I was constantly out delivering letters and messages, and went daily to Lloyd's. I never walked if I could run, and learnt all the short cuts through buildings from one street to another. We sometimes worked incredible hours; mails had always to be caught, though letters were seldom signed until the last moment, and had then to be copied in an old-fashioned tissue letter book. If we missed the late fee post at the local office we had to go to the GPO, and if we missed that the Newcastle letters had to be posted on the train at King's Cross. We always started sharp at 9 a.m., however late we were the night before, and 3 p.m., not 1 p.m., was the closing time on Saturdays.

To other office boys I must have seemed a strange freak, clad as I always was (at the instigation of my parents' friend and prince of snobs, John Shrimpton) in a frock coat and silk hat—the more so because, owing to our liberal supply of them at home, I was able to follow Joseph Chamberlain's example and wear an orchid in my buttonhole! But there is no doubt that in those days it secured me attention at the counters of other offices which, clad more modestly, I might not have received.

My meagre pay was inadequate to provide, in addition to fares, the kind of luncheon desirable for a growing boy, nor were there in those days the facilities later introduced by Lyons and others. Large threepenny plates of lentil soup and penny macaroons are not an ideal diet, but a sixpenny dish of Cambridge sausages and chips which I once remember eating daily for six weeks, is not much better. The choice in those days for those with slender means was so restricted that bulk became the chief criterion; then at any rate one *felt* full. The results of such unbalanced diets could be observed in the wide prevalence of boils and anaemic countenances. But we were well off compared with the lean and cadaverous-looking bootblack who took his stand at the entrance to the Square. What he lived on, or how he survived, I couldn't tell. His emaciated condition horrified me. Most of his time seemed to be occupied in picking up stubs of cigarettes, and whenever I could collect any I dropped them near him. His was indeed a hard life. Things are better today, but life as an office boy, though not so hard as that of the boot-black, was certainly strenuous; not the slightest slip was allowed to pass. I entered into it with zest and learnt much that helped me later.

The firm acted as brokers for a fleet of twenty-three tramp steamers, the chief owner of which was my principal's eldest brother at Newcastle upon Tyne. With one exception they were a decrepit lot of ships, and not one penny was expended upon them which by hook or by crook could be avoided. Every day a sheet was prepared showing the position of each boat; but all day long telegrams poured in saying that one boat had passed Beachy Head, another had arrived at Cardiff, etc. My principal, referred to as 'Mr Charles', nearly always called out on his return from the Baltic, 'Where is the S.S. this or the S.S. that', and there was a scurry round the office for the latest information. We all saw the telegrams as they arrived, and I made a point of memorizing the positions so that when he called out I was able to tell him right away. It soon resulted in his turning to me not merely for such elementary information, but about points which had arisen in correspondence which I had noted when indexing the letter book. This had an awkward sequel. He entrusted me with all his confidential correspondence with his eldest brother at Newcastle with instructions to reveal its contents to no one. Now the correspondence was much of it incriminating; it often dealt with ways and means of evading regulations, even regulations for the safety of ships. It contained information which the secretary of the company, the head of the insurance department, and others would have given anything to know. It must have been exceedingly irritating to them to realize that I knew. They did their best to trick me into revealing the secrets, but in vain. Finally the most insistent one reported me for insolence. Mr Charles sent for me in great ire. Although he took me by surprise, I fortunately had the presence of mind to look him straight in the eyes and ask, 'Is silence insolence?' He gave a long drawn out 'Oh!' and then with a smile said, 'You won't hear anything more about it'. Nor did I until just over a year later when I handed in my notice.

The work of the chartering clerk, a vigorous and lively personality, always attracted me. It was his function to secure employment for idle ships, and to find available tramp steamers for those who wanted to charter them. It was also his job to act as intermediary for the sale or purchase of ships. On one occasion when he had written in response to an inquiry from a would-be buyer of a small tramp steamer that we had nothing to offer, I startled him by inquiring whether he had not over-looked the fact that in a circular he had discarded ten days earlier we had been offered a ship of the precise specifications needed. Thereafter we became firm friends, and he discussed his side of the business freely with me. About that time the second in command of insurance matters, the settlement of claims, average-adjusting, etc., left to take a more lucrative post, and I was offered the job. Although he was getting the good salary of £400 a year, and I was being paid only £1 a week, no rise was suggested and I was too proud to ask for one. The work interested me intensely and the settlement of claims when, for example, a barge was damaged by one of our ships, or some question of salvage arose, and the haggling that ensued gave full play to those mercenary instincts which my mother approved (as reflecting her father) and for which some of my brothers had such a profound contempt.

But these deplorable instincts had previously been indulged. My immediate chief, noticing an advertisement of a cheap phonograph, asked me to slip up to Hatton Garden in my lunch hour and buy him one. I found many people on the same mission. While waiting, I looked around and saw a notice 'Agents wanted'. When my turn came to be served, having observed what wonderful value the phonographs were for 6s 8d, I said that I wished to be appointed an agent and was prepared to buy a sample machine at once. As I had surmised, others in the shipping office immediately placed orders and my 'agency' was soon in full swing, particularly, of course, for the supply of records. I even opened an account with a firm in Bromley, but the margin of profit in that case was negligible, and the effort of carrying and delivering the goods considerable. From the cash and ledger accounts I kept at the time, and recently came across, I see that in the six months during which I ran the agency I made the princely sum of £5 in addition to a phonograph and more than a dozen records. It was hard work, but I notice in the accounts that it enabled me to buy a bicycle 'with Bowden brakes'. It was certainly a useful experience.

I had also started a small stamp business under the name of L. Winstan & Co. I had forms printed, suitably headed for sending out stamps 'on approval' and for display in small shops which collected a commission on any sales. But it needed more time than I could give to it and I never carried it very far.

It was also during this period that my mother entrusted her accounts to me, and left me to keep an eye on her investments. It was in the days before the nationalization of telephones, and her holdings included, I still remember, a small amount of 4 per cent National Telephone Company Debentures, because while still at school I had myself withdrawn £20 from the Post Office to invest in them, thereby stepping up my unearned income from 10s 0d to 16s 0d per annum.

Despite the long hours I was working, and the absence of any time to myself, I was expected to attend a boys' Sunday After-noon class which met in different people's drawing-rooms. So long as the class was conducted by its sprightly founder (Herbert George) it was just bearable, but when it was taken over by his heavy and dull successor it was intolerable. Looking back, I realize that I endured it solely because of the extent to which it would have grieved my parents had I refused. In any case in those days children were taught to obey their parents; what is more, they usually did.

About that time I was becoming more and more disturbed by the goings on of the two brothers at the shipping office, and as the one person who knew of their illegalities I felt that I was becoming an accessory after the fact. I had become increasingly conscious of the incompleteness of my education, and was determined that if I did nothing else I would improve my knowledge of languages. In any case, shipping as an occupation was the result of accident, not of choice. Accordingly, with my mother's approval (because I already realized that in such matters her judgment was better than my father's) I handed in my resignation. The result was disconcerting. The secretary of the company and the senior who had complained of my insolence came running to me to ask what they had done to upset me. To their obvious relief I assured them that they had nothing to do with my resignation. Would I make that quite clear to Mr Charles? To which I replied 'Certainly'. When I did so, he at once said, 'Then what will you take to stay?' I explained that it was now too late to discuss that because I had arranged to go to Germany, and we parted. I still have happy recollections of 'Mr Charles', who was uniformly kind to me and certainly meant well, but the elder and wealthy brother in the North was a thoroughly mean and wicked old man. What brought about the downfall of the company I don't know, but soon after the First World War it had ceased to exist.

Book publishing seldom takes one to the heart of the city, but one evening over forty years later, when I had been invited to dine at the Hall of a City Company, I found that I had half an hour to spare, and motored round my old haunts. At the dinner I was introduced to Lord Leathers, and mentioned that I had been visiting Crosby Square where I had started my business career. The following conversation ensued:

Lord Leathers: 'I started in Crosby Square.'

S.U.: 'I was at No. 6.'

Lord Leathers: 'I was at No. 6'!

S.U.: 'I was paid 10s 0d a week.'

Lord Leathers: 'I was paid 10s 0d a week.'

S.U.: 'I was on the second floor.'

Lord Leathers: 'I was on the first floor.'

And it turned out that we had been there at the same time.

My interest in insurance made me, while still an office boy, look closely into the respective merits of Life Assurance Offices before embarking upon a policy (which I still hold) for the large sum of £100. In those days there were no comparative tables of past results so I made one of my own of what I thought were probably the six or seven best companies. A few years later the *Statist* issued such a comparative table, and I was greatly rejoiced to find the company I had selected, and for which I had become an agent on my eighteenth birthday, was at the top of the *Statist* list.

When in 1950 I was invited to join the Board of the Equitable Life Assurance Society (a mutual company which employs no agents) over which, in their day, both my grandfather, James Spicer, and uncle, Sir Evan Spicer, had presided, I could not resist the temptation to return to my youthful haunts in the city. I enjoy the work immensely; the atmosphere is so entirely different that it is a pleasant relaxation from publishing.

Some people would regard it as chance—Mother certainly did not—but on the day my notice to the shipping company expired, my schoolmaster brother and I received an invitation to spend a week-end with my father's younger step-brother, T. Fisher Unwin. We had neither of us been previously thus favoured, and the invitation caused a stir. It was subsequently clear that I was sent for to be inspected; in brief, and in book trade language, I was 'on sale or return'. On Sunday night, after a thorough examination, in which his wife and her sister, Mrs Cobden Sickert, took an active part, I was apparently approved, and T.F.U., who was childless, asked me whether I would like to enter his business. My over-enthusiastic brother, who would not hear of my asking any questions as to what acceptance might lead to, was all for my giving an immediate and unconditional 'yes'. But my reply was, 'When I have had a year in Germany and six months in France, yes'. T.F.U. wanted me at once. Much argument ensued, and as I was adamant it was eventually agreed that I should have nine months in Germany forthwith and three months in France at some future indeterminate date. At that moment it may, I suppose, be said that my career as a publisher began, though it was not until a few weeks later after a previously arranged holiday tour through Surrey in a horse-drawn caravan that I left for Germany.

The Miniature Railway
Mr and Mrs George Unwin seated

ABBOTSHOLME

In the Dingle

At the Cottage window

My Family
1909

CHAPTER 6

GERMANY

In September 1903 the cheapest way to go to Germany was by
direct steamer from Harwich to Hamburg, so to Hamburg I went,
although my destination was 'Haubinda', a school related to
Abbotsholme in Sachsen Meiningen. The inadequacy of my
schoolboy knowledge of German was soon brought home to
me. I set out to visit an old family friend in Blankenese, and on
arrival asked for the Wedeler Chaussee. The reply was 'Ja!
Gerade aus' (Yes, straight on), and on I went. Each time that I
inquired, as I did with increasing frequency, I received the same
answer, until without realizing it I had reached Wedel six or
seven kilometres away. There I paused to rest. When I got up and
asked the way, 'Ja! Gerade aus', said the person, pointing in the
direction from which I had come. I had been in the Wedeler
Chaussee all the time, and the house I wanted was precisely
where I had started.

The most impressive thing about railway travel in Germany
in those days was the fatherliness of the guards. They would
have considered it a reflection upon their competence were
anyone to go astray; so that although the journey to Hildburg-
hausen, the nearest station to 'Haubinda', took all day and
involved endless changes, I was duly delivered there, but not
until 10 p.m.

At that moment my troubles began. I found there was no one
to meet me, though due warning had been sent of my coming.
I knew the school was some distance from the station, but did
not believe it the impossible journey the hotel porters tried in
broken English to explain. Hotels were not included in my
itinerary, and a hyper-conscientious feeling for the people who
I thought were expecting me at the other end, prompted me to
go on, with consequences which made a deep impression upon

the timid boy I then was. I reproduce the account of the incident I wrote years ago because it reveals so clearly the deep influence of my early upbringing—an influence that consciously and unconsciously has dominated my whole life.

'I was thoroughly tired with the long day's journey, but all went well for the first three or four miles till my lamp went out. My attempts to relight it proved futile and nearly exhausted my supply of matches. I remounted and was shortly cheered by the sight of a farmer's cart coming towards me. I spoke to the driver, but could neither get him to understand nor myself follow the extraordinary dialect he spoke. I thought of the printed heading and pulled out a letter from the school. He shook his head; he could not read. There was nothing for it but to go on into the darkness. A few minutes later the road entered a wood, and even the dark cloudy sky was no longer visible overhead. I felt the machine slipping away from underneath me and my brake seemed powerless to prevent it. Down I seemed to drop until with a sudden jerk and splash I found myself in water. A fairly deep stream crossed the road at this juncture, and once in it nothing was to be gained by turning back. The night was cold, and I realized that only by pushing forward was there any prospect of keeping warm.

'A sense of fear was arising in me. I passed through a village, but there was not a light to be seen nor a window open. I recalled my attempt at conversation with the driver and wondered what would happen if I disturbed one of those sleeping households. I pressed on with a wearisome monotony until I found myself brought gradually to a standstill and my cycle toppled over. I fell off to find myself in a ploughed field. A feeling of despair mingled with terror crept over me—and what despair, what terror, is there like a child's?

'I was some distance from the nearest habitation and had quite lost my way. I felt I must give up and spend the night in the fields and wait the dawn. I wondered whether in my wet condition I could possibly keep warm. Then with a sudden flash I realized I was on my knees. I was still holding up my cycle and remained where I had fallen. I proved for myself the truth of Meredith's words, "who rises from prayer a better man, his prayer is answered"; for it was with absolute confidence that I retraced my way and eventually found the lost road. Another mile or two brought me to a village and to my joy a light. It came from a little shop. The owner was jubilant; he had been out in his accounts and had determined to sit up till he had put them right. He had just found the mistake before I entered.

'Immediately I mentioned the school he showed me the road to take, warning me that I was little more than half-way. A few miles further on I was again in difficulties—the road branched into three. I clambered up the signpost, but could not read the names. (I found subsequently they would have conveyed nothing to me as I had not heard of any of the places mentioned.) I hesitated a moment, and then had no doubt as to which turning to take. In another few miles I was confronted with the same difficulty, though this time there were only two alternatives. I was certain that I had taken the right one, though I did not stop to dismount. I pushed on feeling sure I must be near my destination, but there were no buildings in sight. The road ascended and with some little difficulty I climbed to the top. I could just see a long spin downhill before me when I heard a slight hiss; my back tyre had punctured and I was brought to a standstill. A moment of despair was followed by an exclamation of surprise, for behind me I caught a glimpse of a large white building some quarter of a mile from the road I had traversed. It could only be the school, and with a glad heart I retraced my steps. I soon found the gateway I had missed and walked up to the front door; it was wide open though no lights were burning. I entered, but could obtain no response to my calls. It was evident from a glance at some of the rooms that the building was not occupied. I walked upstairs. There were beds in plenty, but not one was made up. I noticed a light in some outbuildings; apparently someone must be astir despite the late hour. Presently the light was put out and a man approached. I endeavoured to explain in broken German who I was. "Then you are English. I am the English master here", he replied, to my unspeakable relief. "You have come too soon; there must have been some mistake; term doesn't begin till next week. I'm the only one here; if I hadn't been so fearfully ill all the evening you would not have found me up at this hour."

'Next day I made some inquiries as to the road along which I had come. I found that any of the other turnings would have taken me miles away from my destination.

'I also discovered a curious thing. It was only at the spot where my bicycle punctured that the school could be seen from the road. Ten yards further it passes out of sight and the road winds on another eleven miles before reaching a village.'

'Haubinda' was a German edition of Abbotsholme. Dr Hermann Lietz, its founder, visited Abbotsholme, wrote a book about it entitled *Emlohstobba* (Abbotsholme spelt backwards), and was so convinced of the soundness of Dr Reddie's educational methods that he founded a series of *Land-Erziehungs-Heime* (country educational homes) with Abbotsholme as their model.

I went to 'Haubinda' as a paying guest and was free to attend any classes I chose, to work on my own, or in fact to do what I pleased. My enthusiasm to learn German was such, and my time so short, that I resolved at the outset to avoid speaking a word of English, even to English people, so that I might as soon as possible start thinking in German.

I rose with the boys at 6 a.m., went with them and Dr Lietz for the morning 'run' before the first breakfast, worked on my own at German grammar for three hours or so before the second breakfast at eleven, then attended some class where there was likely to be a good deal of question and answer, and thereafter either returned to German grammar and translation exercises, or found someone ready not only for an hour's conversation, but willing to correct my every error.

The person who helped me most was an old lady, mother of one of the staff, to whom I went most afternoons. She made me read German plays, poetry and stories, and corrected not merely my pronunciation, but the slightest mistake with intonation. In the evenings I mixed with the boys, attended the chapel service, and usually did more grammar before going to bed. No one could have worked harder, and towards the end of term when there was snow on the ground and it was freezing hard, working on my own involved sitting in my little unheated room in an outbuilding with a dressing-gown over my clothes and swathed in blankets. But I was well rewarded for my efforts when at the end of term I went for a glorious fortnight's holiday to Jena ('du mein liebes Jena') and found that I could converse without difficulty.

As the crow flies, Coburg is not so far from 'Haubinda', and in those days it was such a famous place that I longed to visit it. A study of maps and time-tables showed that a footpath through a forest would take me to a wayside station on a branch line, whence I could get a fourth-class return ticket to Coburg for 70 pfg. It meant a long walk, and as my total cash resources were Mks 1.50 left little margin for other expenses. But by starting at daybreak, raiding the school bakery, stuffing every pocket with rolls to keep me going for the day, it could just be done. A visit to the old castle cost 50 pfg; 15 pfg went on chocolate to supplement the rolls, and 15 pfg on a picture postcard to my mother, who I knew would be thrilled to learn that I had visited Coburg. The trip was a great success, and was a first lesson in economical travel, of which I had unique experience before leaving Germany.

A bookseller in Jena was willing that I should work with him as a 'volunteer', and it would have been an ideal arrangement, but unfortunately T. Fisher Unwin insisted upon my going to Leipzig, where I had no friends. Now Leipzig was the right place to go to work in the office of one of the Kommissionäre round whom the vast book trade organization revolved, and this I did subsequently, but curiously enough was not the ideal spot for general retail bookselling—possibly because so many of its inhabitants were 'in the trade'. However, a most respected and centrally situated firm, the J. C. Hinrichsche Sortiments Buchhandlung accepted me as a 'volunteer', and there I worked for no pay for three and a half months from 8 in the morning until 8 at night, Saturdays included. They wanted me to work part of Sundays as well, but I was able to say with truth that my parents would have the strongest religious objections. I may add that I was most grateful to my parents for their objections!

Hinrichs were theological publishers as well as booksellers, and their connections were thus largely theological. But it was an exceedingly well-run shop and set a standard which few Anglo-Saxon booksellers manage to attain. The service they gave was remarkable. Their regular customers actually saw and handled in their homes every new book in their particular field or branch of knowledge, and people are so reluctant to part with books on their own pet subject if they are any good that the results were gratifying.

The German book trade organization was in those days, and up to 1914, the finest and most complete that the world has ever known, or is likely to know in any foreseeable future. The destruction of Leipzig in the Second World War, and its subsequent occupation by the Russians, almost entirely disrupted it. Before 1914, and even later, the most important job in any bookshop handling German books—and that meant the shops of many countries besides Germany—was to go systematically through the *Börsenblatt*, the *daily* book trade paper. It did not usually contain a great deal of text, but it had all the many official notices, and above all the detailed advertisements and announcements of that day's new publications. Each issue contained sheets of standard order forms for each new book announced. To miss a single issue of the *Börsenblatt* would be to miss the publications of that day because those announcements represented the chief and sometimes the only link between the publisher and the bookseller. Travellers were a later, and by no means universal, innovation. At Hinrichs the proprietor would indicate with a blue pencil what was to be ordered, and it was then my job to fill in and cut out the order forms which went with any other orders in one envelope to the orders clearing office. The details of the elaborate organization are to be found in the first three editions of *The Truth About Publishing*.[1] When the books arrived, those for which we already had orders were, of course, at once invoiced and despatched; but they formed a small part. The large part was the business the bookseller himself set about securing. I played a minor role in this because it was my job to see, for example, that Professor Dr Kisch was sent for inspection every new book on his branch of theology, and if he did not return it within 'x' days to see that it was charged to him. Customers who were not thus privileged to have books

[1] London: George Allen & Unwin Ltd., 1926-29.

sent to their homes received a printed form on which it was merely necessary to add the title of the new book they were being invited to call and inspect. This last involved very little trouble, yet what a small proportion of Anglo-Saxon booksellers tackle this part of their bookselling systematically. Many say that they have not time, oblivious of the fact that it does not take many seconds to write the names of the potential customers on a slip of paper and tuck it into the book. The most junior assistant should then be able to copy the title of the book on to the printed form and complete the address.

Working as a 'volunteer' is far from unusual in European bookshops. Booksellers' assistants on the Continent would not consider themselves adequately trained unless they had had experience in bookshops in other countries and had a sufficient knowledge of three or four other languages to handle (that does not necessarily mean read) books in those languages. Never a month goes by without my firm being pressed to accept a 'volunteer' from abroad. Some of these 'volunteers' are now heads of important continental publishing and bookselling businesses. When as President of the International Publishers Congress in 1938 I arrived in Leipzig, a young Dutch publisher, who had worked a few years before as a 'volunteer' in my office, came up and said that as he had motored from Holland he had his car with him and would like to act as my chauffeur during the Congress. He was a wise young man because he learned much thereby about everything that was going on. Again, when my wife and I visited the Stanford University Press in California, a man rushed out to open our car door and to give us an enthusiastic welcome, and to my surprise I found another 'volunteer' who had become the Assistant Manager of the Press and had never forgotten the happy time he had spent with us in London.

I was always conscious during my time in Leipzig of the determination of the young continental bookseller to master his job in the way my old headmaster extolled. It was brought home to me again when in 1931 I was invited by a group of young German publishers to return from my visit to the Leipzig

Book Fair via Heidelberg to talk to them about British book trade organization. To my surprise over a hundred turned up, some of them from towns thirty or forty miles away. Equally impressive is the pride they take in owning, as well as reading, all the best literature about their life's work.

I wanted to return from that visit to Heidelberg by air from Frankfurt, but Fritz Schnabel, the head of the League Publications Department, who met me at Heidelberg, had persuaded my wife that it was too risky. I protested that it was not so dangerous as travel (at that time) by French railways. Unfortunately I proved to be right, and I learnt how unpleasant a railway accident can be. The train in which I travelled left the rails, the stoker was killed, the engine-driver badly injured, and my particular coach was telescoped right up to my compartment.

Before that accident I slept peacefully in a *wagon-lit*; now if the train is badly jolted over some points I wake with a start and live through that unpleasant episode again.

One incident during my time at Hinrichs I shall never forget. The otherwise uncommunicative clerk who sat next to me suddenly turned upon me one day, and without the slightest provocation, announced, 'You English have only three great writers: Shakespeare, Bee-ron and Vilder'. This was a little much for me. Shakespeare, yes of course, I replied, but we have greater poets than Byron, and as to Vilder I have never heard of him. He dashed across the shop muttering 'Vilder, Vilder', and triumphantly produced a copy of *De Profundis*. Byron's exalted position in German eyes will be readily appreciated by anyone familiar with Goethe's enthusiastic tributes to him in his *Conversations with Eckermann*,[1] but that Oscar Wilde should be placed upon such a pinnacle, as he still is in Germany today, is less understandable.

The hours of work at Hinrichs left little time for amusement. Moreover, on only two occasions could I put my hands upon the ninepence necessary to secure a seat at the opera. In fact, so short of money was I in those days that by the time I had

[1] Everyman's Library, No. 851.

paid my board at the Pension in the Augustus Platz I could afford a penny cup of afternoon tea at the automatic restaurant next door on only one day a week. My parents were unaware of my impecunious state, and I was far too conscious of their financial worries to enlighten them. On the other hand, I pined for a week-end at Jena, and much wanted to visit Berlin. Ingenuity accomplished both. I learnt that for the week-end of the great Leipzig Fair bedrooms were at a premium. I therefore asked my landlady whether, if I packed up all my belongings and vacated my room for the Saturday and Sunday nights, she would share the benefit with me. She jumped at the idea, and I secured my fourth-class return ticket to Jena, and a few pennies to spare.

Berlin was a more difficult problem. I wrote to my uncle, said that I proposed visiting Berlin, and inquired whether I could do any business for him there, and, if so, would he contribute towards the expense. I reckoned upon his sending at least £5 if he sent anything, and that £5 would, if need be, pay my fare and a week's board. He sent £3 and a programme of work for a fortnight! This was indeed a challenge, because I was far too proud to tell him that I hadn't another penny, and I felt that somehow I must 'make good'. The fare was 12s od, so that I had £2 8s od, for a fortnight's living expenses. I was fortunate enough to secure an inexpensive garret in a Hospiz in the centre of Berlin; bought bread, cheese and sausage by weight and ate them in my bedroom, and indulged (as one could in those days) in halfpennyworths of milk. My chief task was the exceedingly difficult one of persuading Berlin booksellers to buy English books for cash when they were accustomed to buy even German books 'on sale or return'. I soon found that it was necessary to do some quick thinking if I was not to be shown the door before I had started. It was essential to begin by agreeing about something, so my opening gambit was to ask whether it would not be absurd to suggest that a German bookseller should buy English books other than 'on sale or return'. Obviously they could not disagree. It was then for me to demonstrate that my case was the exception that proved the rule. It was uphill work, but in the course of the fortnight, during which I called upon every bookseller of the slightest importance, I sold over £120 worth of books so that my uncle got good value for his £3, and I could not help thinking how much better off I should have been on the usual 10 per cent commission basis. But there were other tasks besides calling upon booksellers. Austin Harrison, then Reuter's Correspondent in Berlin and later editor of the *English Review*, had contracted with my uncle to write a book on Germany, and the manuscript was long overdue. I was instructed to see him and collect it. But I could not collect what did not exist. He frankly admitted that he had not written a line of it. The journey to the suburb where he lived cost money I could ill afford, but it was far from fruitless. He asked me whether I would like to dine with him the following night. Would I not? Perhaps I would care to go to a theatre? Would I not? Dinner at the best restaurant in Berlin and stalls at the opera were gifts from the gods to an ill-fed impecunious youth, and I am never likely to forget that evening. I arrived back at Leipzig with 10 pfg (one penny) in my pocket.

Life in my Pension on the fourth floor of the Augustus Platz was not without incident. I have a horror of drunks, for whom unfortunately I appear to have a magnetic attraction, so that when I heard what appeared to be a drunken brawl in the passage outside my room at two in the morning I laid low until the landlady hammered at my door and appealed to me for help. I found that a mad drunk student was successfully endeavouring to heave a very sober theological student out of the window, and had got him as far as the sill. So mad was he that he invited me to assist him in the process. This enabled me to approach him from behind, pull him over backwards, and release the other man. After which the two of us proceeded to sit upon him. This had a sobering effect. He spoke of his mother, burst into tears, and complained of thirst. I sent for water, and after he had had a drink, spilt the balance over his head. This produced hysterical laughter; he had never been in such a funny predicament in all his life. With difficulty I got him to his bedroom, and my last vision of him was seated on his bed trying to read his Bible, which he was holding upside down.

Although I had had only seven out of the covenanted nine months, my uncle pressed for my immediate return. I countered by suggesting that I should do another business trip for him first and would he contribute to the cost. My visit to Berlin had been so successful from his point of view that I hoped he would come up to the scratch with something more substantial. He did. He sent £10, but with it was a most carefully prepared itinerary.[1] It provided for my travelling via Dresden, Karlsbad, Marienbad, Franzensbad, Prague to Salzburg, Innsbrück and Lake Constance. It covered every place of any importance in Switzerland from Constance to Geneva, then took me to Basel and to innumerable towns on the Rhine down to Cologne.

My heart sank when I discovered that if I visited the maximum places per day the trip could not be accomplished in less than a month, and I could have wept when I found that a third-class Rundreise ticket available by cheaper slow trains would cost £5 12s od, leaving me with but £4 8s od for a month's board, lodging and living expenses. Could it, or could it not be done? It was clear that a shilling a night was all that I could afford for a bed, and that once again I must buy my food by weight and eat it where I could. Subject to that it was just practicable, and I set out. But Karlsbad in the height of the season was a depressing place for a youth in search of a room for one shilling, and the trouble was accentuated by lack of funds with which to leave my belongings in the railway cloak room. With a heavy bag of samples in one hand and luggage for a month in the other, I tramped the less salubrious parts of Karlsbad in a vain endeavour to find accommodation, until I finally collapsed

[1] Years later I learnt from the German publisher who was a 'volunteer' in my uncle's office that he had prepared the itinerary with Teutonic thoroughness with the thought (mistakenly) that I was the wealthy son of the house, and he was determined to make the young b—— do some hard work!

from exhaustion in one of the main streets. I prayed for guidance, and it came in the form of a spotlessly-clad white-haired peasant woman. She had such a motherly face that I turned to her for help. Could she tell me where I could find a bed for a shilling? She looked me up and down, and, being apparently satisfied, said that by chance she had a room in a neighbouring side street which I could have for a shilling.

At Prague I had my first experience of anti-German feeling. I was met in one bookshop with a blank stare when I started to talk German; I then tried French without success, and finally explained that I was English and knew no other languages. 'Oh, if you are English', the bookseller responded in faultless German, 'we will certainly speak German.' I was later to have a similar experience in a post office in Budapest. I had arrived at Prague late on Friday night, and had planned to spend the Sunday travelling by slow train to Salzburg, but I had provided so much sustenance to my hungry bed companions on the Friday night that I could not face a return to them. Furthermore, I could save the shilling my bed would cost me by joining a slow train at 7 p.m. and sitting up all night five a side on hard wooden seats. As my companions on the journey were smoking long Bohemian cigars with straws down the centre, and insisted upon keeping the windows closed, my relief on arriving at Salzburg midday Sunday was considerable. In Prague it had been wet and miserable; in Salzburg there was a blue sky and warm spring sun. In those happy days a notice outside the station pointed the way to a modest little Gasthaus, whither I went. Had they a room? Yes, would I like one for sixpence or ninepence? Ninepence, I proudly replied. A study of the menu showed that I could afford two boiled eggs—a most welcome change of diet. When thereafter I walked across the meadows and climbed up to the enchanting castle which dominates the valley, the reaction from what I had been through was so great that I could dance like little Pippa and sing, 'God's in His heaven, All's right with the world!'

My return journey through Switzerland naturally took me

to Zürich, and to this day I cannot walk down the Bahnhofstrasse to the shores of the lake without recalling my first arrival there in the evening, and my weighty decision that a row on the lake, costing the large sum of sixpence, and a roll of bread and small piece of chocolate to fortify me, were more to be desired than a substantial evening meal. From Switzerland I went down the Rhine and returned to Leipzig with fourpence left out of my £4 12s od just in time to make my first acquaintance of the Easter Book Fair. I was the guest of T. Fisher Unwin's Kommissionär. With him I attended the Sunday banquet which started at 2.45 and ended at about 7.15 p.m. There were endless courses and speeches of inordinate length between each. Toasts were constantly drunk, but as I was a total abstainer one and all refused to drink them with me. It was embarrassing for a mere boy, as I still was, but I took it good humouredly and stood my ground. Following the dinner, we adjourned to one beer-cellar and wine-cellar after another, Eckerleins, Auerbach, and I don't know how many others, meeting different groups in each until 3 a.m. I was glad to make my escape. The sequel next year was amusing. The Kaiser having meanwhile announced that toasts might be drunk in water, bookseller after bookseller, publisher after publisher came from all over the banquet hall, insisting that they must drink every toast with Herr Wasser-Trinker (Mr Water-drinker), and this continued throughout the long years I attended the Easter Book Fair. On most occasions I was the only representative of the English-speaking world, and at that time T. Fisher Unwin was probably the only British publisher carrying stock in Leipzig, and, under my supervision, making full use of the German book trade organization.

The day before I was due to leave Germany, I had my first encounter with a German policeman. I had rescued my bicycle from where it was stored, and had committed the unpardonable offence of riding it down the Grimmaischestr. In fact, before the policeman had finished with me he discovered that I had broken five different regulations. Where was my 'Schein', he demanded, to which I replied in English that I did not know what he meant. I had in fact no idea that a bicycle licence was obligatory. When he kept repeating 'Schein' I produced my passport, which in those days was a sheet of paper headed with the Royal Arms, nine-tenths of the printed matter on which consisted of the late Marquis of Lansdowne's innumerable honours and titles. It was clear that they impressed the policeman, though he could not make head or tail of them. He stood to attention, instructed me to go straight to the Police Station to acquire a 'Schein', and impressed upon me that I must walk there and on no account mount the bicycle until I had a 'Schein'. As I was leaving Germany the following day, and in any case had not the wherewithal to pay for a 'Schein', I am afraid that I merely walked until the policeman was out of sight and then rode my bicycle home.

Although my uncle had pressed for my premature return, he announced as soon as I got back that he would not be ready for me to start with him for another three months. Fortunately I was able to make good use of the time working at my father's printing works, then just behind Ludgate Hill station. I went through all departments, worked in the composing room on the Navy List, learnt precisely how long it takes to make corrections in standing type, and much else that proved invaluable to me as a publisher. My lunch times I usually spent in the Visitors' Gallery of the Law Courts nearby, and learnt much about legal procedure which not only interested me but has often proved of value to me in my career, and enabled me on more than one occasion to act successfully as Counsel in mock trials.

But the three months were soon up and it was now time for me to bring my preliminary training to an end and embark upon publishing itself.

CHAPTER 7

T. FISHER UNWIN: 1848–1935

Of the many peculiar characters to be found in the British book publishing world of the 'nineties, T. Fisher Unwin was in some ways the strangest. Tall, handsome, bearded, with a floppy yellow tie, physically as straight as a dart, a keen mountaineer, he was wonderfully good company out of office hours. But in business he was a different person. His apprenticeship to publishing was with Jackson, Walford & Hodder (the predecessors of Hodder & Stoughton), where he seems to have had a wide experience of all sides of the work.

He had printing and publishing in his blood on both sides. His father, Jacob Unwin, founder of the Gresham Press, published books by Dr Binney and other famous Congregational divines. His mother belonged to the Miller family,[1] who were printers, publishers, booksellers and authors in the same way as the Chambers of Edinburgh, whom, indeed, they preceded with a cheap magazine very early in the nineteenth century. This *Cheap Magazine* (as it was actually called) is referred to by J. M. Barrie in *Auld Licht Idylls*. It was issued at the low price of fourpence, and twenty years before *Chambers's Journal* was started it was being sold all over Scotland, also in London and in various districts of England, with a circulation of between 12,000 and 20,000 copies a month.

When T.F.U. (as he was always called) decided to start on his own account in 1882 he bought the small business of Marshall Japp & Co. of Holborn Viaduct. The price he was to pay after a period of six months was one thousand pounds, but within that period he had made enough out of the concern for it to pay for itself and so did not have to find the money.

---

[1] See W. J. Cowper, *The Millers of Haddington, Dunbar and Dunfermline: A Record of Scottish Bookselling* (London: T. Fisher Unwin, 1914).

In 1884 he moved to 26 Paternoster Square. On a door opposite his private office at No. 26 appeared the name of Alfred Harmsworth (later Lord Northcliffe), and there in a small room *Answers* was born.

When I joined T.F.U. in September 1904 he was installed at 11 Paternoster Buildings, and had already embarked upon the 'Story of the Nations', a library of historical works which was the first of several series of books he projected. Many distinguished historians contributed to it. The business was then still a small concern, but it had already acquired a considerable reputation for discovering promising authors. This was due in part to an interesting venture—the 'Pseudonym Library', a series of eighteenpenny paper-bound volumes which introduced to the world a number of brilliant new writers, such as 'Lanoe Falconer', author of *Mademoiselle Ixe* (praised by Gladstone) and 'John Oliver Hobbes'. W. B. Yeats, 'Vernon Lee', 'Ralph Iron' (Olive Schreiner) and 'Ouida' were other contributors to the series. The 'discoveries' were Edward Garnett's and W. H. Chesson's, but to T. Fisher Unwin must be given the credit both for employing them and acting upon their advice, as well as for appointing T. Werner Laurie as his manager. T.F.U. always believed that if a book had quality it would make its way, whether the author was known or not.

But discovering and nursing young authors is not the same as making money or securing their gratitude. It is apt to be in fact a most disheartening process, because it is so often the publisher who reaps where other publishers have sown who makes the money and is a fine fellow in the eyes of the author. It is doubtful whether during at any rate the five years following their first publication, T. Fisher Unwin made any money out of a tithe of his more important discoveries. He certainly made none out of the publication of the early work of Joseph Conrad, George Moore, John Galsworthy (under the Pseudonym John Sinjohn), H. G. Wells, H. de Vere Stacpoole, W. B. Yeats and many others, and up to the time I joined him his profits, when he made any, averaged about £600 or £700 a year. But

The Two
Young Men

Ploughing
with fourteen
donkeys

Cyrus, Bulawayo
our headquarters
in Rhodesia

My Wife

that does not prevent authors, who, on their own admission, owed everything to his encouragement, from criticizing if not abusing him because in cases where the risk of loss was considerable he did not feel justified in adding to it by paying royalties until he had recovered part of his outlay. Take as an example the following extracts from Mr Somerset Maugham's *The Summing Up:*

'I wrote two short stories which together, I thought, would make a volume of a size suitable for this collection[1] and sent them to Fisher Unwin. After some time he returned them, but with a letter asking me if I had not a novel I would submit to him. This was so great an encouragement that I immediately sat down and wrote one.'

It was called *Liza of Lambeth*, and was at once accepted by T. Fisher Unwin, though it is doubtful whether at that time any one of the old-established publishers would have dared to issue it. This is Somerset Maugham's reaction:

'Fisher Unwin was hard on his authors. He took advantage of my youth, my inexperience, and my delight at having a book accepted, to make a contract with me whereby I was to get no royalty at all till he had sold so many copies; but he knew how to push his wares and he sent my novel to a number of influential persons. It was widely, though diversely reviewed, and Basil Wilberforce, afterwards Archdeacon of Westminster, preached about it in the Abbey. The Senior Obstetric Physician at St Thomas's Hospital was sufficiently impressed by it to offer me a minor appointment under him, for soon after it appeared I passed my final examinations; but this, exaggerating its success and determined to abandon the medical profession, I unwisely refused. A second edition was called for within a month of publication, and I had no doubt that I could easily earn my living as a writer. I was somewhat shaken when, a year later, on my return from Seville, I received a cheque from Fisher Unwin for my royalties. It amounted to twenty pounds.'

Now at the time that payment was made, although Mr Maugham, as will be observed, had received other incidental but important

[1] The famous Pseudonym Library (referred to previously) of which T. Fisher Unwin gave an interesting account in *M.A.P.* (*Mainly About People*) April 2, 1910.

benefits, it is doubtful whether, in view of the smallness of the editions in those days (1,500 copies), and his expenditure on 'pushing his wares', T.F.U. had himself made £20 out of the transaction.[1] Wherein then lies the 'hardness'? Where *at that stage* was the margin for generosity? The agreement provided for a royalty of 12½ per cent after 2,000, 15 per cent after 4,000, 20 per cent after 6,000, thus ensuring the author the full benefit of the subsequent success which he is presumably still enjoying.[2]

Mr Maugham continues:

'Fisher Unwin pressed me to write another much longer book about the slums. He told me that was what the public wanted from me and prophesied that it would have, now that I had broken the ice, a far greater success than *Liza of Lambeth*. But this was not in my ideas at all. I was ambitious. I had a feeling, I do not know where I got it, that you must not pursue a success, but fly from it; and I had learnt from the French to set no great store on the *roman regional*. I was no longer interested in the slums once I had written a book about them, and I had indeed already finished a novel of a very different sort. Fisher Unwin must have been dismayed when he received it. . . . Luckily for me Fisher Unwin refused to give me the hundred pounds I wanted for it and no other publisher would have it at any price.'

Now the importance of all this in any study of publishing problems is that a competing publisher who steps in after the market has been diligently prepared by a colleague has a flying start, and thus appears in the eyes of the author as the better publisher. Furthermore, having incurred no preliminary expense, he has a margin for generosity.

Here is another striking example. My firm published seven volumes of essays, plays, etc., by Stefan Zweig, on all of which

[1] Mr A. D. Marks who was T. Fisher Unwin's trade manager at the time reminds me that *Liza* was published at 3s 6d, not the usual 6s as was the custom in those days, so that the royalty on the 500 free copies amounted to less than ten pounds.

[2] This did not prevent George H. Doran, the American publisher, who ought to have known better, writing in his *Chronicles of Barabbas* (page 144): 'T.F.U. paid Somerset Maugham £25 *for all rights* in *Liza of Lambeth*', and going on to say, 'It discouraged Maugham from writing as a profession'.

we lost money. We did so, confident that one day he would produce something more readily saleable. But when he wrote his first popular book he was badly in need of 'dollars', and without reference to us sold the English language rights to an American publisher. The book was successful, and the publisher who secured the British rights who had at that time done nothing to establish the author's reputation, and whose bid included goodwill built up by us, not merely reaped where we had sown, but secured the reputation of being the more effective publisher.

In a recent history of a famous publishing house, the author commented upon the number of distinguished poets in their list. Had anyone inquired how many of the poets those same publishers had launched on their careers, and how many they had 'acquired' after the poets' reputations were established, the answer would have been startling.

However, I have no wish to exaggerate the seriousness of the problem, let alone to malign my colleagues, distinguished or otherwise. My concern is to demonstrate that in the last resort it is the public, not the publisher, that determines what it is practicable for a publisher to pay authors; that a young firm launching the work of newcomers is taking a considerable risk and has no margin for generosity unless and until the sales give it to him, and that such firms may deserve encouragement rather than abuse. The test to my mind is what each of the two parties is getting out of the transaction. If a publisher has lost money on launching an author, he is not mean merely because the author has not made money.

I certainly do not set out to defend T. Fisher Unwin against a charge of meanness, because he was on occasion terribly mean. But he was often treated unfairly by authors who at their start owed everything to him. As an exception to prove the rule, there was the case of Arminius Vambery, an early author with whose book Fisher Unwin had an unexpected success, who never ceased to extol his virtues and the fact that he had made him two payments over and beyond what the agreement had provided.

My first job at 11 Paternoster Buildings was invoicing, seated facing the tall counter to which authors and other callers came, and at which the booksellers' collectors 'called over' (that is read out the titles of the books they wanted). Beside me were A. J. Thieleman and H. B. Ringham, both of whom took subsequently to the road and became most successful publishers' representatives. Behind me sat the energetic trade manager, Mr A. D. Marks, later director of The Quality Press, with what then seemed to me an incredible knowledge of the past as well as the present publications of the firm. In those days it was a crime to answer a book 'not ours' if it was—thirty years ago. Wrong answers were an unforgivable sin. But I soon took on other tasks. I had a spell 'on the road', and thereafter Marks and I plunged into an export drive with the slogan 'Advance Information' in large type at the head of all the circulars. Today this is commonplace; in 1904 it was a novelty. We were at the highest pitch of enthusiasm and took infinite pains to build up our export business.

In that connection I early took over the sale of American editions, American and translation rights, and overseas serial rights. This brought me into close contact with visiting American publishers whom my uncle insisted upon my interviewing in his presence while he continued to dictate letters.

T. Werner Laurie, who had been T.F.U.'s manager, had just started on his own, so that I never worked with him, but though we never met we maintained the most cordial relations throughout his career and he often consulted me on Publishers Association matters. He was evidently a strange character—'a combination of rake and religion', to quote Mr A. D. Marks's description. 'He and George Moore wrote risky stories for a racing journal called *The Hawk*, and as a sideline Laurie himself wrote sermons and sold them to parsons at 7s 6d each.' Shortly before his death he assured Mr Marks that they were very good sermons and that he thought many of them might be in use today.

Another predecessor of mine at No. 11 was G. K. Chesterton,

who however left no mark on the business beyond some very good and amusing drawings in the margins of the ledgers and on the walls of the one and only lavatory, whither he was reported to have had a habit of retiring to compose poetry. Edward Garnett had left, and had been replaced by Will H. Dircks, who had previously done valuable editorial work for the Walter Scott Publishing Company, publishers of 'The Canterbury Poets' and pioneers in the reprinting of the classics.

But the two characters who stand out most vividly in my memory are the illiterate production manager, Anderson, a one-time machine minder who knew a lot about printing, and the hypersensitive, highly intelligent, frail little Clement Miles,[1] who attended to MSS and did most of the minor literary work of the office. Unlike the rest of us, Anderson had the poorest opinion of Miles, who occasionally failed to pass on information, and I have never forgotten him shouting up the speaking tube to Miles following one such instance, 'Here am I, all in camera, left to me own emergencies'.

T.F.U. who in such matters was exceptionally wise, felt it essential that I should keep contact with booksellers at home and abroad. Accordingly three times a year I visited Oxford and Cambridge, the 'ground' reserved for me. It was indeed an invaluable experience and brought me into touch with some outstanding booksellers. I am never likely to forget the late B. H. Blackwell, who seemed to know our back-list as well as I did, and knew precisely what he could or could not use. Nor shall I forget the late hours I worked writing out the orders I secured and my regrets that I was not working on a commission basis but merely on an allowance of 12s 6d, later 15s od a day to cover my hotel and other expenses. 'Entertainment' did not figure as an item in the petty cash dockets of those times, at any rate not in the Fisher Unwin business. If one was ever foolish enough to want to invite an author to lunch (as I was) it was at

---

[1] A pleasing account of his remarkable qualities will be found in *M.A.B.* (*Mainly about Books*) of March 1918. The article ends with these words: 'It's no exaggeration to say that he was far the best man I ever met, so transparently honest and unselfish, so true to his own ideals and so unsparing of himself.'

one's own expense. I still remember my anxiety lest Captain (now Major) David H. James, who had just returned from the Siege of Port Arthur, would choose such expensive items from the menu that I should have to forgo my own lunches for the rest of the week. As I never allowed myself more than eighteen-pence my concern was understandable. However, James took in the situation and was as modest in his requirements as he is over his own achievements, so all was well. We became lifelong friends, and later I could laughingly assure him when he lunched with me that he need not study the cost as closely as he did on the first occasion.

Each year I went to the Easter Book Trade Fair at Leipzig— the Cantate Messe—held on the fourth Sunday after Easter, and with my uncle's encouragement took the opportunity of 'travel-ling' part of the Continent. They were strenuous trips because, to make them worth while, much had to be crowded into a short time. But in this way I acquired a unique knowledge of conti-nental booksellers and their requirements. But even before that time I remember receiving a letter from Hodder & Stoughton asking me to drop in because there were some matters about the continental book trade they would like to discuss with me. My uncle, to whom I showed the letter, was most indignant, and I was instructed to send a curt refusal. Today exchange of information between publishers is a commonplace. It is indeed in danger of being abused. There have been days when my secretary has told me that I had devoted as much time to giving information and advice to my competitors as to my own affairs.

With the growth of the Fisher Unwin business, I was deputed to look out for larger premises, preferably near Charing Cross. Just as we were hesitating about Chandos House (subsequently occupied by Eustace Miles' Restaurant and later by Chatto & Windus), No. 1 Adelphi Terrace, at one time the quarters of the Arundel Club, became available, and its lovely riverside position and historic Adam architecture led us thither. This gave us the opportunity—which I seized—of transferring our bank account to Coutts and thus emphasizing our improved financial status.

7. Frähr Erwein

T.F.U. had a flat on the top of No. 3 so that after the move he virtually lived on the premises. His energy was colossal; it was amusing to see him trot (literally 'at the double') along Adelphi Terrace between No. 1 and No. 3 on his way to or from lunch. His overcoat was always flung loosely over his shoulders, his top hat on the back of his head and his arms full of books and papers. He believed in combining business with pleasure. He was full of ideas, particularly for making further use of his own past publications in some new form. He could never believe any series was finished and made constant attempts to revivify it. The title of one of his steadiest sellers, *How to be Happy though Married*—much used as a wedding present—was his invention. His pet subjects were mountaineering and Free Trade, and nearly all the best books on those subjects published at that period will be found to bear his imprint. Unfortunately there was then but a small market for them and those who have subsequently reprinted his many standard works on mountaineering have made more money out of them than he ever did.

But there was much else of interest in his list and we never lacked excitement of some sort. John Oliver Hobbes (Mrs Craigie), one of his 'specials', was not the first author to live beyond her means, but not all have indulgent American fathers to help extricate them from their financial difficulties. Her practice was to secure payment ahead of delivery in the form of bills at three, six, nine and twelve months. These were accepted by T.F.U. on the definite understanding that they would not be presented until the MS of the new novel was forthcoming. The bills were, however, forthwith discounted by Mrs Craigie, and when they fell due, which they invariably did *before* the author had completed her work, there was a hurry and scurry to produce the wherewithal to meet them. It was my task to see Mr John Morgan Richards (Mrs Craigie's father), a most charming American, who in various forms found what was needed until a fresh bill could be drawn and discounted to repay him. The procedure had not enhanced T.F.U.'s credit with his first bankers and was an additional reason for making the change.

The first three novels by H. de Vere Stacpoole, *The Doctor*, *The Bourgeois*, and *The Lady Killer* were all failures. With *Crimson Azaleas*, over which he had much assistance from our 'readers', the tide began to turn. But it was with *The Blue Lagoon* that he enjoyed his first and biggest success. He was a charming person; very tall and thin, with a slightly Irish accent. At that time he frequently called at Adelphi Terrace. The fact that he was not always sober was disturbing to one as strictly brought up as I had been, and it was a great relief to me when the lady he subsequently married successfully took him in hand. *The Blue Lagoon* provided some of the many instances I have encountered of people seeing evil where none existed. We received an indignant letter from a clergyman, among others, protesting at our publishing a book glorifying incest. They had all overlooked the fact that the children were unrelated, but had been brought up *as* brother and sister. In such a hurry are some people to suspect others of wrong-doing that one cannot help wondering whether they themselves have guilty consciences.

As a pro-Boer T.F.U. outbid all competitors to secure the publication of Kruger's Memoirs. As an enthusiastic supporter of the Aborigines Protection Society he welcomed the opportunity of issuing *Red Rubber* by E. D. Morel, a work which secured much-needed reforms in the Congo. As himself a Reformer, he took a special pride in a series called The Reformer's Bookshelf, which included besides *The Life and The Political Writing of Richard Cobden* (his father-in-law), the Lives of such distinguished figures of the times as Charles Bradlaugh and George Jacob Holyoake. A volume members of the staff were never allowed to forget was *The Hungry Forties*, edited by his wife, Mrs Cobden Unwin.

Other names which immediately spring to my mind are Annie Besant the theosophist, Wilfrid Scawen Blunt, poet, Arabist, breeder of horses, and, above all, Olive Schreiner, known best, of course, for her *Story of an African Farm*. For *Trooper Peter Halket of Mashonaland* he paid, if I remember correctly, £1,500, the recovery of which, in view of the fact that the book contained fewer than 25,000 words, was a considerable feat successfully achieved by printing fewer than 100 words per page and thereby turning it into a conventional 6s od novel. It was a childhood ambition of mine to meet Olive Schreiner, but when I went to South Africa in 1912 she refused to see me, confusing me in some way I think with T.F.U. whom for some reason she disliked. However, her brother, the Hon. W. P. Schreiner, to whom I showed her offensive letter, made up for my disappointment by his great kindness to me, and later, quite by accident, I found myself at *the* South African Farm which inspired her book.

One of the curious businesses of those days, of which G. Bell & Sons and T.F.U. were the chief exponents, was the handling of so-called Colonial editions of the novels of publishers who found it simpler to sell, say, 500 or 1,000 copies of their new fiction in the form of flat sheets at 1s od (or in the case of an unknown author at 10d or 11d) per copy than to deal with this overseas business themselves. The purchaser then bound the sheets in paper covers for sale to Colonial (Dominion) booksellers at 1s 6d, or in cloth at 2s od. The margin of profit was small, but the extra turnover was in those days so welcome that competition to obtain new books for Bell's and Unwin's Colonial Libraries was keen. The bindings were plainness itself, but the demand for picture jackets which eventually led to the supply of the home edition to overseas booksellers brought this particular phase of publishing to an end. But the reduced price for Colonial editions persists to this day, though the justification for it is no longer there.

Those, too, were the days of 'Unwin's Library'—an attempt to compete with Tauchnitz by 'running on' an extra 2,000 copies and binding them for sale on the Continent to the public at the equivalent of 1s 6d in either marks or francs, and to foreign booksellers at nearer half that price. Today the mere paper on which the books were printed would cost more than the finished article in those days.

When I take from my shelf some of the cloth-bound books

we published at 2s 6d, such as John Morley's thousand-page *Life of Richard Cobden*, and Villari's *Life and Times of Machiavelli* which was even longer, I can but marvel and wonder how we managed it. In many cases the shorter volumes in a series had to pay for the longer ones. I still remember that when with great *éclat* we reissued the works of Mark Rutherford at 1s 0d cloth bound (the binding alone would cost more than that today) the *Autobiography* and *Deliverance* had to cover the deficit on *The Revolution in Tanners Lane*.

It is no wonder that the balance sheets of the smaller publishers of those days were such depressing reading. The margins upon which competition drove them to work were almost non-existent and their turnover negligible. I recently had occasion to look through the accounts of Swan Sonnenschein for the period 1904–1910 when they were producing many important books, some of which are still selling. Their average yearly turnover was only about £14,000.[1]

As far as T.F.U. was concerned, his profits were pleasantly augmented by the sale of cheap edition rights, which was my speciality, and in the last year I was with him his accountant asked me how T.F.U.'s share was to be dealt with because it exceeded the figure to which the valuation of copyrights had been reduced.

Among leading authors whose early work had been published by T.F.U.—at a loss—was, as I have said, H. G. Wells. In 1908 most publishers who had issued his books had large unearned advances rather than profits to show for their foresight in recognizing genius, and Wells was unable at that time to find a publisher in Britain or the U.S.A. willing to advance more than about £200 on account of royalties, whereas he had had £750, and even in one case, so keen had been the competition, £1,000.

At what proved to be a favourable moment, I had suggested to T.F.U. that he should send one of his conventional letters to Wells saying that 'he would welcome the opportunity of publishing some further work from his pen'. The reply that came

[1] See Mumby: *From Swan Sonnenschein to George Allen & Unwin*, page 48.

startled him. It was to the effect that Wells had completed the first 40,000 words of a novel entitled *Ann Veronica* which, if T.F.U. would commit himself at once, he could have 'lock, stock and barrel' for £1,500.

That was indeed an invitation to gamble, and the sum was much more than in those days T.F.U. had readily available. He would at once have dismissed the proposal as preposterous, but I pressed him to ask to see the instalment, which committed him to nothing. When it arrived it was obvious that the novel had great possibilities, and I persuaded a reluctant T.F.U. to plunge. On financial matters, though I was then only twenty-three, he invariably followed my advice. I said that our acceptance must be subject to two conditions:

(1) that we should have permission to make ruthless 'cuts' for serialization.
(2) that payment should be made in three instalments of £500 each.

To the first Wells readily agreed; he had tried and failed to place the serial rights and never thought that we should succeed. The second point was adjusted by the deduction of £30 towards the cost of borrowing the money, of which Wells was in urgent need, and the contract was quickly signed. Within a few days, however, came a pathetic letter to the effect that the translation rights ought to have been excluded as they had always been his wife's perquisite. We reminded him of his own phrase 'lock, stock and barrel', but nevertheless conceded the point.

It was now my task to demonstrate as quickly as possible to a nervous T.F.U. that my advice was sound. Immediately we had the complete typescript I consulted C. F. Cazenove, a literary agent with journalistic experience, about placing the serial rights. He agreed that if all but the love story were eliminated it should be possible, and at once set about the drastic blue-pencilling necessary. Hultons bought the rights for £400. I then did something which I should not have done but for the hurry to get T.F.U. his money back. I told Harpers that we had bought the copyright and that they could have it for the USA for a cash payment of £525. With some hesitation, because at that time Wells's sales in the States were small, they accepted. It must have been one of the best bargains they ever made.

T. F. U.'s anxieties were temporarily at an end. When, however, the book appeared in 1909 it was denounced in the *Spectator* (then under St Loe Strachey's editorship) as 'a poisonous book'. Poor T. F. U.! At No. 3 he had to face the furious indignation of his wife that he should publish such a book, and at No. 1 smiles of contentment that 'The *Spectator's* attack had made *Ann Veronica* a best-seller, and uproarious laughter over J. A. Hobson's comment when the Manchester Public Libraries banned the book, that "if the sun ever shone in Manchester the Watch Committee would probably prosecute it for indecent exposure" '.

In due course the author, who had shown no sympathy in connection with over-payments made and losses incurred by T. F. U. in relation to his early work, clamoured for royalties. In other words he expected us to gamble on the basis heads the author wins, tails the publisher loses. He had boasted that no publisher had made any money out of him. With *Ann Veronica* we broke that record.[1]

The publication of novels always played an important role in the Fisher Unwin business. The public had become accustomed to look to him as a discoverer of new talent, and his 'First Novel Library' attracted many promising new authors. In addition, he organized one of the first prize competitions for novels by new writers. Manuscripts poured in, and the two readers who reported upon them were kept hard at it. Among the manuscripts was one by Ethel M. Dell, which showed great promise but was unsuitable for publication as it stood. It had, in fact, been declined by eight publishers. Suggestions for its improvement were made over and over again; Miss Dell worked away patiently under tuition until eventually *The Way of an Eagle* emerged in its present form, when all of us were confident that we had a best-seller.

---

[1] On the whole question of the outright sale of copyrights see *The Truth About Publishing*, pp. 63–64, in the 4th, 5th and 6th editions.

Often in a publishing business there is *hope* that a best-seller has been discovered; it is seldom that there is a feeling of complete certainty. With *The Way of an Eagle* not one of us had any doubts.

Between January 1912 when it was published, and 1915, twenty-seven printings, each larger than the previous one, were produced and sold under the advertising slogan 'The novel with an ugly hero'. So substantial were the sales of Ethel M. Dell's novels that there came a moment when T.F.U.'s auditors reported that they were responsible for half the then very large turnover of the firm.

One novel we published with no little success, *The Canon in Residence*, by Victor L. Whitechurch, influenced my life because it aroused an interest in winter sports which I have never lost. Although my yearly holiday was confined to a fortnight, without even an extra Saturday morning thrown in, I decided to devote a week of it to seeing for myself what Switzerland was like in winter. It was a long way to go for such a short time. My mother, who had also read *The Canon in Residence*, and was equally curious, accompanied me, and we went to St Moritz, which she had visited as a girl when it was necessary to drive over the Julier Pass. We arrived at the end of the season, when the sun was so hot that skating was permissible in the mornings only, but in time to see the Grand National on the Cresta Run. We enjoyed every moment, and from 1909 onward I took the whole of my fortnight's holiday in winter, but at Lenzerheide, not St Moritz.

My first visit to Lenzerheide was disastrous, but it was a disaster out of which amazing good was extracted. I went on that occasion with my schoolmaster brother to join another schoolfellow, Gerald Brooke, at the Kurhaus, one of the first of many winter sports hotels run by Dr Lunn. On arrival at tea-time, after the long cold drive in open sleighs from Chur, Gerald Brooke announced that plans had been made for a wonderful excursion on the morrow. Ten of us were to go on two bob-sleighs to Tiefenkastel, take the train thence to Thusis and visit the Via Mala. We little knew what was ahead of us. The bobs were of the most antiquated type, steered by a rope in the front, with rope stirrups for one's feet, and a brake which applied on both sides simultaneously and was thus of no help with steering. As the road approaches Lenz, the gradient increases. We went through the village at top speed, yelling to the inhabitants to get out of the way, and I remember wondering why even 'mad Englishmen' should be permitted to behave in such an outrageous fashion. On we went, down the main road, at ever-increasing speed until we came to a corner we couldn't take and 'crashed'; but as it was in soft snow no one was any the worse. We picked ourselves up and went on again. Just as the road approaches Tiefenkastel it takes a hairpin bend. There is (or was) a narrow bridge at the bend, and to our horror we noticed as we approached it that there was a horse sleigh drawn up on it. We leant over and tipped the sleigh up on edge and just managed to swerve by, but were going too fast to complete the turn and crashed into a big oak post. Our steersman was knocked senseless and fell back on to my brother's knee which was pinioned by the stirrup; he in turn fell back on to a heavy girl with a huge camera on her back, who collapsed with all her weight on to my equally pinioned knee. The brakesman at the back was shot scatheless into the snow. The steersman recovered in due course from his concussion and was dancing that same evening, but my brother and I could scarcely stagger the hundred yards or so to the station, and with difficulty got into the train. By the time we reached Thusis we were unable to get out without assistance and quite incapable of walking to the Via Mala. By the time we got back in the evening we were both in great pain with knees double the normal size. And that was all the winter sports I got on that occasion and it was my holiday for the year. It was so dull remaining in bed, that after we had endured it for a week, Gerald Brooke hired the sitting-room of an inn frequented by commercial travellers whence the rink could be seen, and took us there on a toboggan every afternoon. What fun, we thought, to have this little inn to ourselves next year with a party of friends. 'Why not let us do it?' said I. We sent for the proprietor, and discussed the project with him. He was enthusiastic because in winter he had no guests beyond an occasional commercial traveller. We examined the accommodation, not overlooking the drains, and discussed the kind of diet we should need. The proprietor promised to bottle a generous supply of fruit for us, and Gerald Brooke undertook to ship out tea and coffee from bond. We prescribed what courses we were to have at each meal, and stipulated for the inclusion of afternoon tea, and coffee after meals to be included in the pension price so as to avoid 'extras'.

As soon as practicable after our return I went into the problem of 'party rates' for the tickets, and the provision of sleighs from Chur. Finally, when all the costs were known (£12, everything included), we sent a circular to a few select friends, the last paragraph of which read as follows:

'There is no danger of over-stating the merits of Lenzerheide in winter. While London lies fogbound, Switzerland basks in sunshine, and it is at Lenzerheide that skating, ski-ing and tobogganing are to be enjoyed under ideal conditions.'

The response was immediate; we filled the sixteen beds available in the hotel, and arranged to secure beds out for four others. The conditions of that time would not be regarded as 'ideal' today, certainly not by the ladies who were expected to ski in long thick tweed skirts. The mere rumour that one of our party when on a climb involving frequent kick-turns, had temporarily removed her skirt to do them in comfort in knickers, caused consternation in the more fashionable hotels, and led to our party being regarded as complete 'outsiders'. There were no such things as ski-lifts and few of us had skins so that climbing was hard work and we certainly earned our runs down. The rink was dominated by 'English' skaters, with their oranges, who begrudged us international style skaters even odd corners in which to practise. There was no doubt about our unpopularity with the visitors at the other hotels, and we did not lessen it by challenging them collectively to an ice hockey match and soundly defeating them. The musical as well as sporting standards of our party were high; it included some excellent singers whose accompaniments I greatly enjoyed playing. There was happily no doubt about our popularity with the local people. The bar at our little inn was their chief rendezvous and we got to know many of them. Our doings are recorded in the three issues of the *Lenzerheide Chronicle* written and illustrated by members of the party, edited by me, and privately printed in limited editions of about thirty copies each.

T. F. U. was one of the founders of the Johnson Club, as well as of the National Liberal Club. Socially he could be most pleasant. He was a charming host both in his beautiful top-floor flat at Adelphi Terrace and at his home at Heyshott—Richard Cobden's birthplace; but as an employer he was intimidating. He was as jumpy as a cat on hot bricks and wandered about the office tapping every desk or obstacle he passed with a long pencil, and singing 'yes' in a deep voice and repeating it immediately an octave higher. This would continue until he finally came to a halt at someone's desk, when with a quick movement he would lean over the unfortunate individual and mutter quickly, 'Anything for me?' As we had most of us been summoned to his presence by bell, when we were supposed to take any queries to him, the answer was usually 'No, Sir'. But we were conscious that he had taken in precisely what we were doing and were kept very much on our toes.

No one could be associated with T. F. U. without being conscious of a power behind the throne. His wife, Jane Cobden Unwin, daughter of Richard Cobden, was indeed a forceful personality, but highly emotional and unreliable in her judgments. Her enthusiasm for such causes as Women's Suffrage, the Protection of Aborigines, anti-vivisection, was unbounded. Invitations to lunch at No. 3 were 'royal commands' that had to be obeyed, but they were disconcerting occasions if for any reason (usually political) the feelings of 'The Jane' had been aroused. One was apt to be greeted with a tirade as if one was personally responsible for what she disapproved. But it was unwise to assume that she would hold the same views two days running. Her anger knew no bounds when on one occasion I expressed sympathy with a cause she had espoused only a day or two before. I suffered much at her hands, though she, too, had a genuine streak of kindness in her. She was capable of real affection and was devoted to T.F.U. (despite her disapproval of some of his publications!). Her sister, Mrs Cobden Sickert— a more balanced personality—was often secretly helpful to me. Secretly, because the jealousies of the Cobden sisters made it inexpedient that 'The Jane' should ever be aware that I had visited her sister in Buckingham Gate.

T.F.U.'s fiery loquacious Irish town traveller, J. H. Crane, and the four or five most important people in the firm, were summoned to a weekly conference to discuss MSS on offer to us of which favourable reports had been received. Much naturally turned on the sales possibilities of the books, and on occasion my knowledge of the continental market turned the scale.

One hard battle which I fought and won looks ridiculous in the light of today. The Methodist Book Company of Toronto had published *The Songs of a Sourdough* by Robert W. Service, and their representative, Mr Walker, gave me the refusal of the rights. I was enthusiastic, but was in a minority of one. The others were too obsessed with the difficulty of selling poetry. Finally I persuaded them, rather reluctantly, to allow me to import 250 copies in sheets at sixpence per copy on the plea that if it were a 'flop' the loss would be negligible, but that if I was right we should have secured a best-seller, which we did. The conference method has its points, particularly if it is merely advisory, but I doubt whether the best publishing businesses are ever built up by committees; they will usually be found to be the creation of one man.

In my early Adelphi Terrace days I decided to work after office hours for a degree at the London School of Economics which had just been founded, but as I had not matriculated this was a formidable undertaking. It involved evening classes in

London and getting to my home at Shortlands in Kent in time to go to bed, which in any case I was doing on our 'conference' evenings. I persisted until my family intervened, and on health grounds insisted upon my giving up the attempt. Instead I was persuaded by my parents, much against my inclination, to give up one and often two evenings a week to helping to run a social club for the youths of Shortlands. My parents were concerned that I was doing nothing for others; 'faith without works is dead'. The fact that I was doing an almost excessive amount for T.F.U. did not count. One most useful relaxation I did allow myself. I joined a Debating Society in which two of my cousins were interested, and took an active part in every debate. I owe much to the practice I thus obtained in marshalling facts and stating a case, and can still remember my enthusiastic defence of the theories of Henry George. I was always a fast walker and in those days made it an unwritten law never to let anyone pass me. On the one occasion when I found myself in real danger of being left behind and had to quicken my already fast pace I discovered on turning down Adam Street from the Strand that the man who had thus extended me was Bernard Shaw. He was then living at the other end of Adelphi Terrace and it was always a joy to see the vigour with which he walked. It was not until much later that I got to know him.

About this time I received a telegram from a Russian friend of my family—an inspector of roads—reading 'Send hansom cab'. I knew that he had set his heart upon possessing one because he had said so when he had stayed with us, but the message was none the less startling, and in fact slightly intimidating. As it happened, finding and buying a hansom cab which had been in private use and was in good condition proved comparatively easy. The problem was to get it to Gorodok (via Danzig). With most horse-drawn vehicles the shafts can, if necessary, be removed, but not so with a hansom cab. It would be easier to pack the Lord Mayor's Coach. In the end the packing-case cost more than the cab, and the freight more than the case. But the cab was safely delivered and my friend inspected his roads driving it himself with two horses, tandem fashion, much to the joy and entertainment of the local population.

Early in 1907 T. F. U. suggested that I should make a trip to the USA for him, and I at once agreed on the understanding that, on this occasion, I should not have to consider expense.

I went to the States full of eager expectation. I expected to find the Americans efficient and rapid and anticipated learning much. I was sadly disillusioned. They did not seem to me nearly as efficient as the Germans, and although there was constant talk of hustling, there was astonishingly little of the thing itself. But the publishers were all most charming to me, and I did a great deal of profitable business. It must be remembered that this was 1907 and the pace was much more leisurely then than now. The over-heating of the hotels and offices gave me frequent attacks of nose-bleeding. On one occasion I had returned to the hotel to clean up and had put out a supply of clean handkerchiefs, but in my anxiety to keep my next appointment left them behind. When I was half a mile from the hotel another attack came on and I found that I had nothing but a pair of kid gloves with which to assuage it! I tore back to the hotel with the blood pouring down like the oil in the 133rd psalm even to the skirts of my garments and leaving a trail behind me. Before I reached the hotel I had a chain of small urchins following me, who evidently thought from my appearance that at least I had had my throat cut.

A luxurious journey in a drawing-room car from Toronto to Chicago was marred by the failure of the car attendant to clear my luggage through the customs and it was held up at Detroit. Time and time again I called at the depot at Chicago for it until I became a well-known character there. When it finally arrived it was at once put on an open truck. I refused to be parted from it again and drove up to the Auditorium annex, Chicago's biggest hotel, seated upon it.

Law publishing is quite out of my line, but a director of Callaghan & Co., law publishers, sought me out immediately he learnt that I was a grandson of James Spicer, whose coachman his father had been and who as a child had known my mother. He had started as a traveller and had done so well for the firm that he had become a director. He wanted to give me the best steak that Chicago could produce, and was obviously delighted that an opportunity had presented itself for him to be host to a member of the family with which his had so long been associated. Once again I benefited from the virtues of my ancestors.

About the trip itself T. F. U. had at that time little to say, but about three months later when I was in hospital he wrote: 'Since you have left I have had time to grasp and know the results of your USA journey. Certainly it was a great success from every point of view—direct and indirect—so good we begin to wonder when and how it may be repeated.' From anyone else this might mean little, but for T. F. U. to commit himself to such a statement was remarkable.

As an employee, T. F. U. had apparently had no holidays, and he regarded any holiday as a 'concession'. My business trips on the Continent and to the USA had been so profitable, and we were taking export business so seriously that it was considered desirable that I should visit South Africa, Australia, New Zealand and the Far East to secure first-hand knowledge of those markets. Every detail of the trip had been thought out and agreed, and the arrangements for my departure made, when, in a fit of excessive conscientiousness, I said to my uncle that, apart from the fact that I had not been too well, there were so many of my family in those countries who would expect to see me, that I should like to feel that I could take in all three weeks' instead of the regulation fortnight's holiday. The fat was in the fire; all the bookings were cancelled rather than he should concede the extra week, though no one could have known had I without permission taken an extra day here and there during the course of fifteen months' travel.

Just before the cancellation of the world tour, on an occasion when I had been unduly provoked, I had mentioned to T. F. U. that he had never fulfilled his undertaking to allow me to go to France for three months to work at French. The reminder had rankled and he suddenly decided that instead of the world tour I was at once to have three months in France. The Paris–Lyons Railway had issued a prospectus extolling the merits in winter of Briançon which they said boasted two skating rinks. On the strength of it I went to their Terminus Hotel, to find it unheated, myself the only guest; one small rink, the private property of the officers of the garrison, the other a village puddle covered with sticks and stones! Naturally I protested, but there was little the hotel manager could do except secure me permission to use the officers' rink when they were not using it, and this he did. But I wrote vigorously to the PLM, and suggested that the least they could do was to give me a free pass from Briançon else-where, and with this suggestion they complied, though not until I had left for Corsica. In 1908 Corsica was comparatively little frequented, apart from Ajaccio, where people of all nationali-ties seemed to congregate. At one large dining-table at the hotel I found people from all over Europe, including an English professor, his wife and daughter. For the most part German was spoken, with French of course to the waiters. I joined in freely with the conversation, but had no occasion to speak English. At breakfast next day I found myself seated at a small table with the Professor's daughter, who spoke to me in faultless German. When I found that she was English I asked in German whether it would not be more appropriate for us to speak English. 'Can you?' she replied. She then revealed that, after I had left the dining-table the previous evening, they had dis-cussed my nationality, and that the only country which no one had suggested I came from was England.

My efforts to make myself as fluent at French as at German were frustrated, because, before I had completed even two of my three months, I was summoned home by my uncle to act as chief witness in a libel suit. As the original publisher of S. R. Crockett, T.F.U. was naturally anxious to publish another novel by him. His recent books had gone to the buyers of the serial rights, James Clarke & Co., of *The Christian World*. When, therefore, Crockett's agent, the late A. S. Watt, offered us the book rights in a new novel entitled *Me and Myn*, we accepted it with alacrity. We were unaware that James Clarke & Co. had an option on Crockett's next novel. When Clarkes saw our announcement, they naturally protested. Crockett's reply, which was embodied in a letter from A. S. Watt to Clarkes, was to the effect that he regarded our book as 'a light collection of stories about stamp collecting' and not a novel at all, regardless of the fact that it had been sold to, and contracted and paid for by us, as a novel. Clarkes forthwith reproduced in the trade press the statement they had received from A. S. Watt. The effect was instantaneous. Booksellers from all over the country telegraphed and wrote cancelling their orders for our book on the ground that they had bought it as a novel and had no use for a volume of short stories. One cancellation even came from Lourenço Marques.

It was most unfortunate that I was abroad when all this happened because I knew the Clarkes, and would have found some way of avoiding litigation, at any rate against them. But Mr John Nayler, T. Fisher Unwin's manager, took the view that, as the publishers of the libel, Clarkes were the people to be sued, an opinion with which the solicitors concurred.

We had published a book on International Law by F. E. Smith (later Lord Birkenhead) written incidentally not by him but by a barrister named Sibley, and partly for that reason, but also because of his great reputation, F. E. Smith had been briefed by the time I got back, and the case put down for hearing. T.F.U. himself was in too nervous a state to attend the court (he retired to Brighton for the period of the proceedings) and I was summoned to deputize for him. F. E. Smith, who could barely be persuaded to look at the book about which the case was being brought, nevertheless felt it essential to define a novel. When I protested that you could not define a novel, he brushed me aside and made me repeat parrot fashion his definition that a novel was a story with a hero and heroine, etc. When in the witness box I trotted out this definition, Justice Lawrence (Long Lawrence), who up to that moment had been half asleep (he did go completely to sleep for a brief period later in the trial) suddenly turned upon me, and in a gruff voice said: 'Have you never heard of "a novel without a hero"?' (meaning, of course, *Vanity Fair*), but I was so startled and tongue-tied that if he had asked for my mother's name I could not have given it! Sketches of proceedings in court were permissible at that time, and the next day there was one of me with the caption 'Publisher who had never heard of Thackeray'.

Altogether I was in the box for the best part of two days— an ordeal for a young man of twenty-three. The defendants had two excellent counsel, Colam, then a most able junior, and Dickens, KC, a bully who did his best to terrify me. On one occasion in a hectoring voice he shouted, 'Yes or no; will you answer my question?', to which, to his chagrin, I answered, 'No, I am here to tell the truth', because his question was one of the 'Have you stopped beating your wife?' variety. At another stage I appealed, successfully, to the Judge against Dickens's bullying.

But despite F. E. Smith's painfully superficial eloquence, the case went against us. The Judge thought that Crockett and Watt ought to have been in the court, not the Clarkes. Our solicitors wanted us to appeal, and were bitterly disappointed when I advised my uncle against it. The case had already cost £1,000, and that was enough. From the outset it had been as clear to me as to the Judge who the really guilty parties were.

Following the departure of Mr John Nayler, who nominally took over Werner Laurie's position, the virtual control of the business drifted more and more into my hands. T. Fisher Unwin made a practice of ascertaining my opinion on any and every transaction before announcing *his* decision, always making it very clear that it was *his* decision, though in fact he never failed to follow my recommendations. Apart from trade matters, the bulk of the correspondence was dictated by me, though every letter was signed (often unread) by my uncle.

In the same way, people who asked for me, on the telephone or in person, were put through or shown up to T.F.U., and I was then summoned to his room. It was all part of his desire to emphasize that everything was done by him personally, which though inconvenient, did not at first disturb me. But later it reached incredible and ludicrous lengths.

But working for T. Fisher Unwin was a discipline in more ways than I have indicated. I don't remember the precise date it started, but I began to be troubled with intense abdominal pains. Scarcely a month went by without my being worried by them. Our family doctor, a doctor cousin and a Harley Street specialist all diagnosed the trouble as appendicitis. The last even wrote to T.F.U. emphasizing the risk I should be running were an operation delayed. But T.F.U. would not hear of it; he knew better; appendicitis was a new-fangled complaint and I just wanted to be in the fashion. Time off for an operation? Absurd! He would send me to his doctor, and he would soon put me right. Accordingly round I went to a GP in Bloomsbury. He had evidently been told that I had a bee in my bonnet and 'imagined' that I had appendicitis. Accordingly, he patted me on the back and in a soothing tone said, 'Soon put you to rights— just a little opening medicine—soon put you to rights'. And accordingly I was given a mild aperient to take every night. Needless to say the treatment had no beneficial effect; the attacks went on just the same.

Two I shall never forget; one on a night journey with my mother from Venice to Milan. I was in such agony, and the vibration of the train was so unendurable that, just after midnight, we got out at Padua. Alas! it was the one night in the year when hotel accommodation was just not to be had. We wandered about and it was after 4 a.m. before we managed to get even one room (a huge one) between us. The other was the day I arrived in New York in March 1907, after an exceptionally bad crossing. On both occasions I just starved, endured the pain, and waited for the trouble to subside. But after this second experience it was clear that it was unsafe for me to travel until my appendix had been removed, and on my return my family insisted upon another specialist being called in. He pronounced in favour of an immediate operation and T. F. U. had to give way. But he stipulated that my period of convalescence after the operation must be considered as my holiday for the year. Which it was. The surgeon said that it was remarkable that I had survived so many attacks and that I might at any moment have had a fatal one.

All this sounds incredible. People today find it unbelievable that an employer should have such power over an employee, just as an employer of those days were he now to come to life would feel about the abuse of power by trade unions in the reverse direction. The pendulum has swung. Then the employer laid down the law; now the trade unions do so. My position was in any case a peculiar one. I was supposed to be enjoying a great privilege in being taken into my uncle's business with the possibility (many would have said probability) of being his successor.[1] To defy him would have involved a break. I always hoped to satisfy him. Commercially I did so. I held an unqualified power of attorney to act on his behalf in relation to the business and had been steadily obtaining effective control. Was it the moment to part company? No similar opening was then even on the horizon. Later when I was in a much stronger position and the break did come, most people thought that I was reckless.

About this time the business expanded rapidly. I was able to secure the agency for the sale of the Ordnance Survey Maps, and through my personal Leipzig connections the agency for Baedeker Guides. I had, in fact, a completely free hand in connection with all contracts, provided I preserved the convention that my uncle had negotiated them, even though towards the end of my time nothing would persuade him even to give a quotation to an American publisher without reference to me.

When, owing to threatened heart trouble, his doctor pressed him to go to Italy for three to four months, I was left to run the

---

[1] Actually he was my father's younger step-brother. The fact that he disapproved of my father influenced his attitude to me and made it unlikely that I should inherit anything.

business for him. During his absence I was able to acquire and resell a lease with a clear profit to him of over £500, the cheque for which I handed to him on his return. There was no 'Thank you'; merely a muttered 'I suppose it's all right'. In fact, the more I succeeded in building up the business the more difficult my position became because his jealousy of me increased. And it showed itself in a policy of pinpricks, which for a long time I took philosophically, but which in the end became unbearable.[1] The fact that I took all the responsibility but never had any credit did not worry me, but to be constantly snubbed and treated like a naughty child was another matter. A few instances will suffice. A cousin who had been at school with me arrived home from Nigeria and dropped in to see me; I had not asked him to do so. T.F.U. found out that I had spoken to him for five or six minutes, rang for me, and cursed me for wasting the firm's time. The fact that I constantly and of course gratuitously worked after office hours counted for nothing.

I used to spend occasional week-ends with relatives at Haslemere[2] where my craftsman brother, Bernard, was at that time working with Romney Green, as he later did with Dolmetsch. My brother and I jointly owned a tandem on which we went long rides together on the Sunday. The first train on Monday morning was due at Waterloo at eight minutes to nine, and by sprinting across Hungerford Bridge I could get to Adelphi Terrace punctually at nine. But on Monday mornings the train was often two or three minutes late, with the result that, however hard I sprinted, I arrived about two minutes after time. The opportunity was at once seized by T.F.U. to reprimand me in the presence of others, and he carried it to such lengths that I eventually asked permission to be three minutes late on

[1] Since that was written I have come across a letter from T.F.U.'s senior country representative in which he said: 'I admired the quiet way you took T.F.U.'s manner to you. I fear I could not have had the same tact.'

[2] On one such week-end when attending a crowded amateur performance of a Gilbert and Sullivan opera I stood up in the interval, looked round the hall, and (why, I cannot explain) said, 'I believe my future wife is in this audience'. My relatives laughed. It was not until years later that I first met her and then discovered that she had been.

the Monday morning whenever I went to Haslemere. He would then inform every member of the staff, including the office boy, that I had been given permission to be late, and all this at a time when I was the holder of an unqualified power of attorney to sign for the firm!

An American publisher and I had spent an hour one afternoon standing in T.F.U.'s office while he remained seated at his desk. The American publisher had bought several books, and on leaving said that he would drop in next morning with the formal shipping instructions and particulars of his imprint. He did so, and was shown up to the waiting-room adjoining T.F.U.'s office, and thither I went in ignorance of the fact that the office boy had omitted to comply with the regular formula of notifying my uncle. The American publisher was an old friend, and after handing me the shipping instructions paused for a few minutes' talk, during which I heard T.F.U. approaching the door between us on tip-toe. He peeped through the crack, but could not see who the visitor was. Pitter-patter he went to the other door, which he cautiously opened a crack, but again without satisfaction. Back he went to his desk, and bells started ringing. When at long last he discovered who was in the waiting-room he strode across his room, flung wide open the door, drew himself up majestically, and announced: 'I'm here. I believe I'm the head of the firm.'

Much as I loved my work, and proud as I was of the successful way in which the business was being built up, I began to find the constant pin-pricks unbearable, the more so as I had no certainty about the future. Accordingly I gave a month's notice to terminate my association with the firm at the end of the year. My uncle paid no attention to my resignation until I went to say good-bye to him on December 31st, when he doubled my salary to induce me to stay. The same thing happened a year later, but on the third occasion I decided that, whatever he paid me, I could not remain as an employee. From an uncertain £600 or £700 a year the profits had grown to a very certain £6,000 or £7,000 a year, and as there was no question of my inheriting the business the more I built it up the more I should have to pay for it.

I made my position clear in the letter of resignation, and this time my uncle sent his accountant to see me. The accountant knew what I had done for the business, and approved the terms I laid down, which provided for the business to be turned into a private limited company, of which T. Fisher Unwin was to be Chairman and I was to be Managing Director. The capital was to be largely in the form of preference shares which T.F.U. would hold. I was to have the right to buy one-third of the ordinary shares forthwith, and another third in the event of his death.

But when I examined the Articles of Association drafted by his solicitor, Sir George Radford, I found that T. Fisher Unwin was appointed Governing Director and that the Managing Director was to do what the Governing Director told him. Still worse, that if ever I left him I was neither to start a publishing business on my own nor accept a post of any kind in any other publishing business. We now know, as the result of a subsequent decision, that such a restriction has no legal validity; but at the time it was thought otherwise.

Despite Sir George's remonstrance that I was a young man in a hurry (I was twenty-eight and had been in business more than a dozen years) and my Uncle Howard Unwin's assurance that I was a fool because the ripe apple was about to drop into my lap, I adhered to my resignation. I have often smiled over the phrase about 'the ripe apple', because I should have been well over sixty by the time it finally dropped!

On the day after I had said good-bye to Adelphi Terrace I felt like Bunyan's Pilgrim when the heavy burden rolled from off his back. The relief was so intense.

As to the Fisher Unwin business, I prophesied that for two years, thanks to Ethel M. Dell, the profits would increase and that thereafter there would be a steady decline. The prophecy was fulfilled and about ten years later the business was losing money. T.F.U.'s financial position was such that in 1926 he was glad to sell out to Ernest Benn Ltd. in exchange for an annuity for himself and his wife. Both lived to a ripe old age and drew their annuities for many years beyond anyone's expectations.

The transfer of the business to Benns left me free to comply with the Baedekers' wish that I should once more handle their guides. I had refused so long as the agency was in T.F.U.'s hands; it was so much more essential to him than to me. Victor Gollancz's hasty visit to Germany to secure an assignment of the contract to Benns was thus fruitless. But the transfer to me brought its complications. Ernest Benn Ltd. had agreed to take over the staff of Fisher Unwins, but now pointed out that with the loss of the Baedeker Guides some of the staff would be redundant. T.F.U. approached a cousin, who in turn approached my father, to find out what I could do to help them. I replied that if he himself asked me I would gladly take over three members of the old T.F.U. staff, many of whom were well known to me; but that if he was so determined to go to his grave harbouring ill-will against someone who had never done him a bad turn that he did not want to have anything to do with me, it was difficult to help him. This evidently startled him because I am glad to say that he relented and approached me direct. Subsequently my uncle took the initiative in proposing me for membership of the Reform Club; called upon me at Museum Street, and invited my wife, son and myself to tea at his country home, so all ended well.

To complete the story, I ought to add that two other nephews who followed me each in turn left him. They were succeeded by a great-nephew, Philip Unwin, who was transferred with the rest of the staff to Benns, but, having no future there, came to me, and is now a most active director of George Allen & Unwin Ltd.

When I left in 1912 the business of T. Fisher Unwin had world-wide fame; today it is nearly forgotten. I often wonder how it would have developed had not his jealousy of me made it impossible for me to remain in charge of it. He was in some ways a great, and most certainly a remarkable publisher. Mr

A. D. Marks, who worked for him before, while and after I did, writes:

'My impression of T.F.U. was that he was a lonely man who did not like loneliness. His sense of humour was only slightly developed. He could never understand how he antagonized people yet he was doing it all the time. Some temperaments were at once irritated by his pose. A good deal of that pose was caused by a highly nervous disposition. I am sure he felt he ought to be the most popular man in any company, but he never was.

'In business, his ability to avoid a decision was considerable. I have been with him when people have just got up and walked out. This attitude became really acute in his later life. An attempt between the late J. B. Pinker and myself to bring T.F.U. and Conrad together again after many years, resulted in Conrad threatening to throw him out of his own window. Incidents of that kind multiplied, and as the years went on he developed an inordinate jealousy of everybody and everything. Some of those jealousies were petty in the extreme and really pathetic, and now perhaps they are best forgotten. They seem rather sad anyway and some of them almost incredible.

'If you could get down under that awful crust of his you would find him human and capable of deep emotion. I experienced this when his brother Buxton died and I, small callow youth, crept into his room to ask if there was anything I could do. He just burst into tears.

'I mention these incidents to show that he could be, and was, human.'

That seems to me a very fair summary.

CHAPTER 8

A WORLD TOUR

April 1, 1912, was one of the happiest days of my life. The nightmare of working for an exacting and jealous taskmaster was over. I was for the first time as an adult a free man and captain of my soul. The relief was incredible and my wife recalls my ecstasy. We were not then even engaged, and I dared not propose because I had made up my mind that immediately I was free I would visit overseas markets to fill the most important gap left in my publishing experience, and to embark upon matrimony at that moment would have wrecked my career. I did the next best thing. I suggested to my prospective wife's father that her brother should accompany me on my world tour, and so it was arranged.

As a child I frequently told my old nurse that I was determined to travel round the world. When on one occasion she asked me where the money was to come from I appear unhesitatingly to have answered, 'I should sell my stamp collection'. I still have the collection, but even at today's valuation its sale would not take me very far. Fortunately I had saved enough to cover the comparatively small amount needed in 1913.

I had not forgotten my old headmaster's lessons about the methods of the Germans, and my determination to travel was reinforced in my office boy days by a speech of King Edward VII, then Prince of Wales, emphasizing that if we wanted to hold, let alone to increase our export markets, we must study our customers' requirements on the spot. It was an exhortation I have never forgotten, and there are now very few parts of the world in which I have failed to call in person upon any bookseller who was selling, or could be persuaded to sell, British books. It has already taken me four times round the world. The study of foreign markets fascinates me and the fact that 55 per cent of my firm's turnover is represented by export sales demonstrates, I think, that my travelling has not been altogether in vain.

Before embarking upon the first world tour I had given much thought to the route to be taken. I wanted to cover as much territory as possible outside Europe and North America, which I had already visited. South America I felt must wait for another occasion. Accordingly we went first to South Africa, thence to Australia and New Zealand and home via the South Sea Islands, Philippine Islands, Hong Kong, Shanghai, Tsingtau, Japan, Singapore, Penang, Colombo, Egypt, and Algiers. My companion and I had relatives or friends at most places so that the journey in its social aspect was almost a royal procession. But as that is fully described elsewhere[1] there is no need for me to dwell at length upon it here. Immediately my uncle heard of my plans he pressed me to travel for him, but this I declined to do. I had no wish to give up my hard-earned freedom.

The trip was one of the best investments I ever made. Today, with the facilities for flying, many publishers visit the Dominions, but in 1912 no principal of any publishing house had the first-hand knowledge of overseas markets which I acquired. It was in many ways an advantage that for the first time I was unhampered by samples, and had nothing (except perhaps my personality) to sell. I was able to explain to booksellers that my sole mission was to study their requirements and learn all I could about our overseas markets before starting on my own—adding, with a smile, that it was up to them to see that I did not go empty away.

As I was the first publisher to take the trouble to cover the whole ground systematically, the booksellers' enthusiasm over my visits was unbounded, and I learned far more than would have been practicable had I been occupied in selling them my uncle's wares. I took most careful notes and compiled a card index (which I still possess) in which I included not merely such obvious things as the importance of the shop, the kind of books they bought, through whom they bought and shipped them, the

---

[1] *Two Young Men see the World,* by Stanley Unwin and Severn Storr (London: George Allen & Unwin Ltd., 1934).

quantities they could use, etc., but the names of any partners or directors, and, what was most valuable, personal impressions or personal information they gave me which would help me to recall them and their shops years later. As a result, whenever I had occasion to correspond with one or other of them I found myself able to write to a man whose personality I could recollect. This acquired for me the reputation of having a quite incredible memory. I still remember the amazement of a New Zealand bookseller whom I reminded, about thirty years later, that when I called upon him he had said that he felt like Job because he was suffering so badly from boils. Alas! most of the many friends I made on that trip have long since passed on—T. Maskew Miller of Cape Town, George Robertson of Sydney, George Whitcombe of Christchurch, to mention but one famous bookseller in each Dominion.

It was at Cape Town that I had my first impression of Dominion bookshops—other than in Canada—and it left me overjoyed. Maskew Miller, Darters, and Jutas, then near one another in Adderley Street, were all huge judged by English standards, and carried magnificent stocks. It must be remembered that before the days of air mail two months might be needed to replenish supplies, unless they were so urgently wanted as to justify a cable. Naturally the shops in the smaller towns—and I visited practically every one south of the Zambesi—were not on the same scale, but the standard almost everywhere was astonishingly high. South Africa is well served in the matter of bookshops, and it is not surprising therefore that, in proportion to its comparatively small white English-speaking population, it is one of the British publishers' best markets.

The five months spent in covering South Africa were peculiarly happy ones. The descendants of Robert Moffat, the missionary to whom my family is related, were at that time spread all over the country, and as many of them had used my parents' home as their headquarters in London, hospitality and help of all kinds were everywhere forthcoming. Our experiences included such diverse things as a long talk with General Smuts (who was born on the same day as my eldest brother), ploughing with a team of fourteen donkeys (with the foals running alongside some of them), and sleeping under the stars on sun-baked earth in the vicinity of the Zimbabwe ruins. Despite the many advertisements of special facilities and excursions to enable tourists to visit the Zimbabwe ruins, there were none at that time the moment one left the railway at Umvuma or Selukwe. There were many hindrances, but of these the posters said nothing. The conditions were in fact so appalling that my companion and I wrote a long letter to the *Bulawayo Chronicle*[1] describing them, so that others should know what to expect and not be led to undertake the journey under false pretences. Soon after the publication of this letter, the much talked of railway was extended to Victoria, and today one can unhesitatingly recommend tourists to visit Zimbabwe. There are few such unforgettable places.

We were most reluctant to leave South Africa, and I always wanted to return, despite the unpleasant political atmosphere from which it is so difficult to escape. So far I have managed to do so only once, and then for an all too brief stay.

Our first port of call in Australia was Adelaide, where an ancestor of my companion, a brother of Joseph Rayner Stephens, the Chartist, was the first colonist to set foot on South Australian soil. For me it was the home of that distinguished Australian author, William Hay, the merits of whose work, which I published, though immediately acknowledged in Britain were not recognized in Australia until after his death. When Australians assert, as they are so fond of doing, that British publishers are prejudiced against Australian writers, I cite William Hay as one of the many instances where it was the Australian public, not the British publishers, who displayed prejudice. He and his wife entertained us with old-world courtesy at his home, 'Mia, Mia', at the foot of the Mount Lofty Range and gave us a foretaste of that boundless Australian hospitality which we encountered everywhere.

I am always glad that we did not content ourselves, as most

[1] October 1, 1912.

people do, with visiting the capital cities of Australia, but took the unusual course of travelling from Adelaide by boat up the River Murray to the irrigation settlement at Mildura, and thence through the Mallee country to Melbourne, where we took the opportunity of visiting Gippsland.

The bookshops in Australia were as gratifying as those in South Africa, but were not then so widespread because of the excessive concentration of the population in the capital cities. Since those days the market has developed enormously and there are many secondary towns of importance.

From Melbourne we went through Tasmania, which pleased us immensely, on our way to New Zealand, where we landed at the Bluff at the south of the South Island. This gave us the opportunity of going 'the finest (as well as the wettest) walk in the world', from Lake Te Anau to Milford Sound, which I so fully described in *Two Young Men see the World*. At that time the only other way of reaching Milford Sound was by sea. Today a road through a long tunnel gives access to it by car, but it is a poor substitute for a walk through fairyland.

We covered New Zealand very thoroughly, and there must have been few bookshops upon which I failed to call, as I have done twice since, though they are widely spread over both islands. Before my visit three of my elder brothers had emigrated to New Zealand so that I felt very much at home there, and was fortunately able to take time off to see a great deal of the life of that delightful country as well as its beauty spots. At Mount Cook I ran into Freda Du Faur, the first woman to make the complete traverse of Mt Cook. Her *Conquest of Mount Cook* was one of the first books I published after my return and the first of a long series of mountaineering books which I have issued since. It was at Christchurch that I learnt from George Whitcombe about the importance of a reprint of that classic work, Pember Reeves's *The Long White Cloud*, for which I made arrangements about a year later. It was the beginning of a close and valuable connection with New Zealand authors—poets, economists, historians, climbers—which has developed from year to year ever since.

We had planned to return to Australia from Auckland—the north of the North Island—direct to Sydney, but in those happy days you could change your plans at the last moment and didn't have to ask anyone's permission to go anywhere—if you avoided Russia. Accordingly, when we learnt by accident that there was a boat leaving from Auckland for Sydney via the Friendly Islands, Samoa and Fiji, we seized the opportunity to visit these delectable spots. I cannot pretend that there were booksellers to be visited in Nukualofa, Haapai, or Vavao, but there was much else of interest, including the Tongan land system. At Apia we were able to visit Robert Louis Stevenson's old home and to climb up to his grave. In those days that particular Samoan Island was a German possession and Stevenson's house was occupied by the German Consul, who most kindly let us visit it. In Fiji, which in some respects we found less attractive, there were booksellers to visit upon whom I have since called again on two occasions.

We arrived in Sydney just in time to witness the electrification of the signalling on the railway, which had been carried through by my cousin, Cyril Byles, with whom we were staying. Today it is a commonplace; then it was an event, and the transfer from one system to the other—the most difficult part of the procedure—was carried through without a hitch.

We made our way north via Brisbane to what was then German New Guinea, and called among other places at Rabaul, destined to become so famous in the Second World War. Our boat touched at many islands, including Maron and Yap, before landing us at the Philippines, where the mixture of three completely different civilizations fascinated us. The dilapidated Catholic churches and the absorption of the populace in cock-fighting still stand out in my mind even more, I am ashamed to say, than the bookshops, of which there are several of some size. I suspect that my forgetfulness of the bookshops is due to the fact that a discriminatory tariff gave the United States a virtual monopoly of the market. When Americans complain, as they do so frequently, about 'discrimination', I always want to ask, 'Why did you set us such a bad example?'

I am not a prophet, but during the Second World War an American who evidently thought I was, drew my attention to the following passage from my book,[1] which I had long since forgotten:

'The heights of Corregidor bristle with armaments of the most modern kind; the fairway is mined, and the whole place, besides being impregnable, carried sufficient supplies of food, ammunition and water to shelter fifteen thousand Americans and Europeans for ten years. At least this is what an American told us as our ship passed by. Our glasses enabled us to admit that this *might* be possible, and that it *might* take the Japanese guns—for the Japanese are admitted to be the next conquerors of Manila—a long time to subdue the island fort. But the most likely thing for the Japanese to do would be to turn their attention upon Corregidor last of all and reduce the stronghold from the superior heights of the main island.'

Which, as my American correspondent pointed out, is precisely what the Japanese did, though I am sure they did not require my assistance to do anything so obvious.

Hong Kong and Shanghai, at both of which we were entertained by sons of missionaries who had often been entertained as boys by my parents, and were contemporaries of mine at the school for sons of missionaries, were both important centres for British book distribution. At Shanghai a visit to 'The Commercial Press', then the largest and most important Chinese firm of publishers and booksellers, proved fascinating. I shall never forget my luncheon at their printing works—subsequently destroyed by the Japanese. I sat with a dozen or more directors and managers at an enormous round table, in the centre of which was a huge round dish of all the delicacies to be eaten with the boiled rice, with which we were all plentifully supplied. Each of my hosts helped himself with his chopsticks to one item from the centre dish, which he forthwith consumed, then each in turn selected (with the same chopsticks) what he regarded as the choicest morsel and placed it, with a deferential bow, in my bowl. It was the greatest honour they could pay me, and I tried to comfort

[1] Op. cit., pp. 450–1.

myself with the statement once made to me by my chemistry master at Abbotsholme, 'the chemical composition of saliva is the same the world over'.

The German port of Tsingtau, now once again under Chinese control, was a most interesting example of town planning, because what was a fishing village a few years before had become the sixth most important Chinese port. The general planning was typically German; broad avenues planted with trees, and magnificent government buildings were to be seen in every direction—everything had been thought out, everything possible done in the way of sanitation, water supply, street lighting, etc. Although the experiment was never completed, enough was done to teach many lessons, but whether the Chinese profited from them is another question.

Japan had always been such a particularly good market for British books that I was most eager to go there. The Maruzen Book Store in Tokyo, which used to carry the finest and most representative stock of any bookshop in the world, was destroyed by earthquake shortly after my visit, but another and finer building was soon erected in its place. I was so impressed by the Maruzen Company and what they could do for the George Allen & Unwin type of publication that on receipt of the news of their earthquake disaster I took an unusual step. I cabled my sympathy, and showed it in a practical form by telling them that the payment of the current quarter's account could wait their convenience, and that I would give them a year's credit on any order they cared to send us to replenish their stock of our publications. It was a gesture they never forgot, and we had no cause to regret it though it strained our then most meagre resources.

The invasion of China and consequent depreciation of the yen had already hit Japanese booksellers badly before the Second World War, and of course during, and for some time after, the war British books were virtually unobtainable. But the Japanese have such an insatiable thirst for knowledge, and such a love of British books, that in the long run nothing will stop their acquiring them.

After the Second World War, when Maruzen had yet again to rebuild their premises, we were happily able to make another gesture indicative of our confidence in the future of this most remarkable concern. By chance I was there at the time. It was early in October and only one-third of the twelve-storey building was even partially built. When I asked how soon it would be completed Mr Tsukasa, the President, confidently replied: 'We shall be in for Christmas'. When I retorted: 'You mean next year?' he smiled and said, 'No, this Christmas'. I looked up at the skyline and observed that the workers carrying bricks and cement were all doing so at a jog-trot. It was clear that there were no restrictive practices in connection with bricklaying or building in Japan. Mr Tsukasa's forecast proved correct.

There are two ways of seeing something of such a country as Japan. There is the way of the conventional tourist who patronizes European hotels and is conducted from place to place in luxury; and there is the way of the unconventional man who prefers to leave the beaten paths and to tramp wherever the spirit moves him, putting up at wayside inns and living as far as possible as a Japanese traveller would live.

European hotels and motor-cars are the same the world over, and though they are both extremely comfortable and convenient there is no need to journey to Japan to make use of them. So my companion and I chose the way of the tramp, and this may justify mention of a few of the things which struck us in those far-off days before the First World War.

I was fortunate in having at Kobe an old friend, Major D. H. James, to whom reference has already been made, who was born in Japan and spoke Japanese like a native. He undertook to start us on our way, so that for the first two or three days we had some guidance and were able to learn the ropes. When once the routine is mastered, life in Japanese inns can be most pleasant and interesting, as well as entertaining, though unless you have been brought up to sit on the floor like a tailor that part of the proceedings is exhausting. Then I must admit that having eaten rice for breakfast, rice for lunch and rice for the evening meal for six weeks I have never wanted to be confronted with rice again. Fortunately I learnt one sentence in Japanese—'I like my fish cooked', which was an intimation not merely that we expected some fish, but that we did not want to eat it raw. It is of course no use expecting any privacy in Japanese inns, not even in the bathroom, through which people may pass freely. A hot bath at sunset is a regular feature of Japanese life. In the old days, and even in 1913 in the country districts, the *né-san* attended to the guests' needs in the bathroom as elsewhere. I am not likely to forget my companion's and my own surprise when she insisted upon scrubbing our backs, which she did with as complete nonchalance as if she were scrubbing the floor. To Westerners this lack of privacy is alarming, but the Japanese think nothing of it and are surprised that anyone should see anything unusual or immodest about it. Certainly no one seemed to be one penny the worse, and it served to show how much these things are a matter of convention, for curiously enough a few things that to us are quite ordinary, such as some of our dances, the Japanese think immodest. Who can confidently say that we are right and they are wrong? I certainly could not after a Japanese had asked me whether I thought anything improper was likely to happen in a bathroom through which people passed, and then inquired whether improper feelings were not more likely to be aroused by a 'bunny-hug'—the then popular Western dance.

A Japanese inn is one of the cleanest places imaginable, for there is precious little in it to get dirty; you take off your shoes before you enter. But the same cannot always be said of Japanese bedding. Although such creatures are not supposed to exist in polite society, experience of eighteen months' travel demonstrated that there is no part of the world that is absolutely immune from parasites, and in particular fleas, and they—to my friend rather more than to myself—were the one real source of discomfort of which we had to complain.

During the course of an evening it is no uncommon thing to hear a strange cry out in the street, and this emanates from a blind masseur or masseuse announcing that he or she is prepared to massage you from head to foot for the not exorbitant sum of sixpence or possibly a shilling. In Japan massage is a monopoly of the blind, who instinctively develop a unique sense of touch.

Inability to understand or speak Japanese did not prove any great difficulty. When you once know what is expected of you, very little conversation is necessary. We knew about how much *chadai* (tea money) to give, and we got over the difficulty of the indecipherable hotel bill by sheer bluffing. We knew approximately what it ought to amount to. When it arrived we examined it critically and gave a paper note of over the amount, so that change would be called for. We looked at the bill again, counted the change most carefully, and nodded our approval, assuming, as practically always proved to be the case, we got about what we expected. As far as railway travelling is concerned, the English or American tourist had in 1913 an easy time, for all the names of the stations were in English as well as in Japanese. In case of difficulty, quite a large percentage of the stationmasters knew at any rate just a little English. The carriages for the most part were like the inside of a tram, that is to say the seats ran down the sides, and it is amusing to a European the way the Japanese remove their footgear and squat on the seat itself, sometimes with their back to the centre corridor, enjoying the view.

Refreshments were obtainable in those early days at prices that seemed to us absurd. In England we thought nothing, even in 1913, of paying fourpence for a pot of tea. The usual charge in Japan on the railways was a penny, and, unbelievable as it sounds, the pot and cup were thrown in. For the most part people just left them behind or threw them away as we might the bag in which a sandwich was served, but I kept one of mine and still have it. If a penny procured you the teapot as well as the tea, you can imagine the charge for the tea was infinitesimal. The luncheon baskets served on the trains called 'bento' were most tastefully packed; some of them consisted of layers of rice between seaweed in the shape of sandwiches.

On one occasion we asked one of the temple priests what

was the chief difference between the two principal religions of Japan, the Shinto and the Buddhist. He replied that there was very little—the Buddhists were vegetarians and the offerings consist of fruits and vegetables, but (with an envious glance at the priests outside the Shinto temple not far away) they get fish as well.

Our walking tour in Japan took us to many beautiful places and I looked back to those weeks of unalloyed pleasure for forty years with a longing to return. Above all I wanted to revisit Nikko and its temples, and walk once again up the fascinating valley of the Daiya Gawa to Lake Chuzenji and on to Lake Yumoto, which was the turning-point of our travels. Thereafter we were homeward bound. But, alas! when I did so forty years later, what a different place it was! Nikko was crowded with tourists and one had to queue to visit the temple. Chuzenji was no longer the peaceful lake where we had put up for the night on our way to Yumoto. Today, as in so many other countries, it is necessary to go further afield to escape from the madding crowd, and for that, on my second visit, I had no time. Moreover, nearly everything is as expensive as earlier it had been the reverse. The American occupation had changed the standard of living for European visitors to the towns. But much that is fundamental remains unchanged.

Our homeward journey in 1913 was via Nagasaki, Hong Kong, Singapore, Penang, Colombo. But for the most part they were just stepping-stones en route where we paused long enough to see the booksellers. In Egypt we rode camels for the first time on our travels, and visited one of the Pyramids and the Sphinx. But our funds were exhausted and we had to hurry on and be satisfied with a brief glimpse of Algiers. It is difficult to believe it today, but those eighteen months of travel cost me just under £400. It must of course be remembered that in many parts of the world I had no hotel bills and that in Japan we lived astonishingly cheaply. Much more important, we needed no passports, let alone visas, and there were no currency complications; the pound sterling took one everywhere. It was unnecessary to ask any official's permission; we just took tickets to wherever we wanted to go, and we did not have to queue to get them. What a contrast with today when to make a tour through Asia it is necesssary to fill in over forty forms, provide endless photographs, spend a fortune on visas, for some of which one has to wait interminably, and crave the permission of the Bank of England for currency! Even to make a tour of the West Indies I recently found that I had to fill in endless forms to get from one island to another. The world was more civilized in 1913.

Why I should have had this lifelong passion for travel I find it hard to say. I suppose that it is in my blood because my mother adored travelling and was the member of his large family whom my grandfather most often selected to accompany him on his continental journeys, in the days when it was done in a carriage and pair. In any case, the moment I get into a boat train for Harwich or Dover, whether it is to embark on a business trip or a winter sports holiday—still more, when I board a ship taking me farther afield—I feel like a dog let off its chain, ready for anything. The release from routine, the complete break in my thoughts, because the work I have left behind is immediately forgotten, the prospect of plunging into an entirely different atmosphere all contribute to the thrill which with me is perennial. Curiously enough, although aeroplanes take me farther and quicker, and I am now compelled to use them, they do not give me quite the same feeling—somehow the romance is missing.

When as a child I said that I wanted to see the world I meant the whole world, and not merely a few fragments of it. I wanted to see all the countries whose stamps I had collected. My sister reminds me that at the end of my first world tour I wrote to her 'I know now, that whatever is in store for me, life will be more full of meaning than it would ever have been had I not seen so much of the world'. Today there are not many countries left which I have not visited, and I have enjoyed every minute of my many journeys, whether they were in the tropics or in the far north, whether they were for business or pleasure, because strange as it may sound to some, my business is my pleasure. It has in fact been my life, and my passion for travel has contributed to its success.

* * * *

I returned in December 1913 from my journey round the world to find that my parents had themselves, at the age of seventy-three, just set off with my younger sister to visit my three New Zealand brothers. It was a disappointment to miss them, but I consoled myself in a way which met with their approval. I did immediately on my return what I had wanted to, but could not do, eighteen months before, I became engaged to my companion's sister, with whom I had kept in close touch throughout our wanderings, but not until her decision had been delayed a few hours as a gentle protest at the length of time she had been kept waiting. My interview with my father-in-law, Rayner Storr, with whom, as I used laughingly to tell my wife, I fell in love before I fell in love with her, ought, in view of my impecunious state, to have been embarrassing, but was far from it. He was then, as always, a perfect dear. He said that he approved of what I had done to complete my publishing experience and had entire confidence in my future. It was now for me to justify his opinion of me. Having demonstrated that I could build up a business for someone else, I felt sure that I could do it for myself.

CHAPTER 9

A FRESH START

My plan was to find a bankrupt concern and buy the assets so as to have something to sell to cover the immediate overheads. When, therefore, on January 1, 1914, within a week or two of my return, a receiver was appointed to wind up the affairs of George Allen & Co. Ltd., an ideal firm from my point of view, I felt that providence was very much on my side. But not for long. I found that the receiver, a chartered accountant, had no knowledge whatever of publishing, and took William Allen's stock valuations at their face value.

Now Ruskin's friend, George Allen, who started at Orpington in 1871 to publish his books, was an able man as well as an expert engraver, but the two sons and the daughter who inherited the business in 1901 were not of the same calibre. Furthermore, in Ruskin's lifetime Ruskin's books sold themselves; the Allens merely had to hold back the impatient crowds of would-be buyers. But when Ruskin sales began to fall off, and the Allens embarked upon general publishing, they were confronted with a very different situation. They made beautiful books, but the public did not clamour for them. Profits proved elusive. Trouble was staved off by various means. They bought the assets of the Bemrose London publishing business in 1909, making payment by long-dated bills, and augmented their immediate cash needs by remaindering much of the Bemrose stock. They amalgamated with Swan Sonnenschein & Co. (founded in 1877), who were likewise weak financially.[1] The lean kine swallowed the lean kine, but neither grew any fatter. It was not a case where two minuses make a plus, and in consequence the evolution of George Allen & Sons into George Allen & Co. Ltd., following the amalgamation in 1911, soon saw the new company short of capital. But the

[1] Though enterprising enough to advertise on the front page of the first issue of the *Daily Mail*.

results were not such as to tempt an investor. Obviously they must be improved. What easier way than to pretend that the stock was worth more than it would in fact realize? An advertisement that an old-established book publishing house has an opening for a partner or director with capital will always bring scores of inquiries. That of George Allen & Co. Ltd. was no exception. Solicitors and accountants were duly employed by the would-be investors. The balance sheet and accounts looked excellent, and had not the stock valuation been certified by the managing director, William Allen? What was the value of the opinion of solicitors and accountants on that item? How could they know that there were cases where the stock had been written up in value instead of down? The capital was forthcoming; more directors were appointed; more debentures issued, but the company became more, not less, insolvent.

A glance at William Allen's valuations, upon which the receiver was relying, showed me that it was useless to prolong my first interview with him. I smiled and said, 'I will come back and see you in three months' time, when you will have a more accurate idea of the value of the assets. Please make a note in your diary.'

But it was an embarrassing moment for me because I hadn't three months to spare. I wanted to settle down to work at once. It was necessary for me therefore to look elsewhere. Alfred Nutt had died, the retail side of the David Nutt business had been sold to A. G. Berry, but the publishing side was available and I received a letter from Mrs Alfred Nutt—a French lady— suggesting that I should become her publishing manager. I don't think that I have ever encountered anyone so suspicious. The negotiations were interminable, but led nowhere. As soon as I looked like coming to terms with her solicitor she threw him overboard on the ground apparently that I was in some mysterious way in league with him. I would then start afresh, but as she could never finally make up her mind what she wanted, nothing ever came of the negotiations. Meanwhile the publishing business, or what was left of it, was rapidly fizzling out.

At the expiry of the three months I telephoned to the receiver of George Allen & Co. 'Yes, do please come along,' he said, 'I have been waiting for you. You were quite right about the stock valuation; it was absurd. If I can get 20s 0d in the £ for the debenture holders I shall be satisfied. There will obviously be nothing for the shareholders or ordinary creditors.' To all of which I replied: 'Now we are talking business; I doubt whether you will get 20s 0d in the £ for the debenture holders, but you may well get something near it. I will make a detailed valuation.' And this I proceeded to do, item by item, including stock, bound and unbound, stereo plates, blocks, moulds, copyrights, original illustrations, office furniture, and even Martin pottery, of which there were specimens. But equally important, I did what no other prospective buyer apparently did. I made a detailed valuation of the liens, of which there were many, because every printer and binder to whom money was owing naturally claimed a lien (or mortgage) on any stock or plant held by him. An offer for the assets free of lien—the usual method—means that the receiver has to pay off all the liens, which reduces the value of the offer by that amount. Now it at once occurred to me that this might be a case where the amount of the liens would in some cases exceed the value of the stock, etc., upon which the liens were claimed. My systematic investigation revealed this; in fact there was one lien of £1,000 upon stock which I should not need for several years, and worth at most £25. I therefore determined to make my bid subject to lien, which meant that the whole of the amount offered would be available to the receiver, whereas from all other offers the amount of the liens would have to be deducted. Moreover my method saved the receiver endless trouble—a point to which no receiver would be blind. I was not therefore surprised to hear that my bid was accepted, nor to learn later that a competitor's offer would have been several thousand pounds better had it been made more intelligently.

I was naturally delighted, and set about raising the substantial amount of money involved, provisional promises of which I had previously secured. But when the receiver, having accepted my offer, made no further move and weeks went by, I became disturbed. When I questioned him, he admitted that the debenture holders would not ratify his acceptance, and as my offer did not quite secure them 20s od in the £, he was powerless to compel them. They could themselves make a better offer without having to find a penny, because it merely involved in their case taking money out of one pocket and putting it in another. I was in a quandary. I badly wanted the business, but it was impracticable to outbid the debenture holders if they were determined to hold on to it.

Who were they? and were they qualified to run the business? were the two questions I at once put to the receiver. The answer was a colonel who had been a director of Swan Sonnenschein, a solicitor, and a man who had trained to be a solicitor, both of whom had recently bought directorships in the Allen business. They were certainly not qualified to run it, he said, and if they were wise they would get me to do so for them. He offered to see what could be done.

The final terms to which I agreed were onerous, and involved my taking great risks. On the other hand, they necessitated my raising far less money. In brief, the debenture holders were to retain their debentures in full; to hand over the business to a new company, George Allen & Unwin Ltd., with a nominal capital of £5,000 of which they were to have £2,000 shares allotted to them gratis, and I was to be permitted to acquire £1,800 for cash. I was also to find cash to buy out some smaller debenture holders and provide working capital.

It will be seen that all the money I found was immediately subject to the debenture holders' mortgage, and that collectively they had a majority holding. It was Hobson's choice as far as I was concerned. I had already had the humiliation of being 'out of work' for six months, and I knew that this was the ideal business from my point of view, as indeed it proved to be. Moreover, I had merely to convince one of the debenture holders that I knew what I was about to have a majority. To protect myself, I had to stipulate for a life appointment as Managing Director, because otherwise, having got my money, they could refuse to re-elect me as director. This involved giving them the same status, and four Managing Directors for such a small craft was indeed over-loading the ship. All I could do was to make provision in the Articles that the Managing Directors' remuneration should not exceed £300 per annum each unless the directors voted unanimously to the contrary. This self-denying ordinance proved to be our salvation, because the two solicitors, if I may so describe them, started agitating for increased remuneration before we had even started making profits, and were most annoyed when I insisted that the claims of the staff who were 'sweated' must come first. The irony of the position was that my fellow directors did not really need the money, whereas it involved my receiving as a married man a fraction of what I had earned as a bachelor.

The statement that the staff was 'sweated' was no exaggeration. There was none on a salary basis. The senior member was paid £4 per week and the next highest paid was the Production Manager who received £2 10s 0d. A married man in the warehouse had £1 13s 0d with which to support himself, his wife and child. The last had tried in vain to get a better post elsewhere and his pleas for even a trifling increase had been turned down. The total wage bill for the entire staff was less than £20 a week, yet when Friday came even that paltry sum could not be found and 'our Mr Ellard' had to hurry to Charing Cross Road with a bag full of books to sell them as second-hand to make up the missing amount. Needless to say I saw to it that the financial position of all these long-suffering people was improved as rapidly as our means allowed. The married man referred to completed over fifty years' service with the firm, and eventually retired on a pension of considerably more than the pay he was getting when I first encountered him. His knowledge of the Swan Sonnenschein back-list was infallible and we still miss him.

Early in July 1914 (before Serajevo), when these negotiations were taking place, most people assumed that wars were a thing of the past; people were too civilized for anything so stupid.

The formalities took some little time to complete, and the company was registered at Somerset House and we formally took possession of the business on August 4, 1914—the very day of the declaration of the First World War. But after over six months of unemployment, during which some people began to wonder whether I had not been foolish to give up my managerial position with my uncle, I had fulfilled my ambition to have a business of my own, and it was for me to see what I could do with it, war or no war.

The outbreak of war had reduced the value of the assets we had bought by about a third on the very day we started. The turnover, which even during the receivership, when nothing was being published, had always remained at over £1,000 a month, dropped to a few hundred.

A fine old Australian bookseller, George Robertson, whom I had met in Sydney, wrote me:

'It is a great thing to bear your yoke in your youth. If you can stand a knock-out blow on the day you start you will take whatever else comes to you in life with perfect equanimity.'

(I had reason to recall that remark when in the Second World War I lost one million four hundred thousand books with one bomb.)

The outlook was indeed depressing, but there is no evil out of which some good cannot be extracted if you look for it. Our competitors all had capital locked up in autumn lists of publications produced for quite other conditions. We had no such commitments or preoccupations. We could concentrate our attention upon what the changed circumstances called for. For example, we rushed out M. Philips Price's *Diplomatic History of the War*, at the end of which we bound the various Governments' white, red, blue and yellow books, with which they were only too happy to supply us gratis with copies for the purpose. Austin Harrison hastily produced a best-seller for us entitled *The Kaiser's War*, and confident that it would eventually be wanted I put in hand a reprint of Kant's *Perpetual Peace*.

But our time in the first weeks was taken up with moving. The Allens had signed a lease for their premises in Rathbone Place, which provided for the rent rising every three years—a thing we could not contemplate. As we had merely bought the assets from the receiver we were entitled to remove them, and were under no obligation to take over the lease. But quick action was needed. Among the premises available was 40 Museum Street, and a derelict warehouse immediately behind it, but unconnected with it. Museum Street was such an ideal address for a publisher that we decided to move thither, but it was essential to connect it with the warehouse behind. They were separated by a narrow passage, to which there was no access of any kind, and to which apparently no one made claim. All we had to do was to cut a doorway into it from either side, and this we did. But to roof the intervening space would have connected the two premises in contravention of LCC regulations, and our architect said it could not be done. But the moment an architect says something can't be done, or can only be done in one way, it is time to bring a little imagination to bear. I demonstrated that the space could be roofed without connecting the premises, and so it was until the premises were rebuilt.

The speed of the move necessitated quick decisions, and one of the most disastrous was given by my solicitor colleague, who authorized the pulping, with much unwanted junk, of all the Swan Sonnenschein correspondence. Now Swan Sonnenschein published J. M. Barrie's first book, *Better Dead*, the early work of George Bernard Shaw, George Moore's *Confessions of a Young Man*, and many books by Karl Marx, including *Capital*. We thus lost invaluable autograph and historical material. It is most tantalizing to read in the old letter books, which we still possess, the letters addressed to Bernard Shaw by Swan Sonnenschein, and have to guess at Shaw's more entertaining part in the correspondence. It is almost painful to contemplate the amount the Bolsheviks would have paid for all those Karl Marx–Engels letters.

An important section of the existing turnover of the firm was Church of England business. Bellars's *Before the Throne* was, for example, one of our best-sellers, and we had inherited through the

Bemrose connection a department for supplying Church Door Notices, Offertory Forms, Churchwardens' Account Books, etc., which we could not afford to neglect. This compelled us, against my inclinations, to be cautious about the kind of books we accepted for our early lists. The books with which we started would tend to label us. What we did a year or two later would by comparison have no such effect. Now it is astonishing in life how frequently the most attractive proposals come one's way at the moment when it is impracticable to accept them. Within a few months of our start we were offered, probably at the instigation of Austin Harrison, then editing the *English Review*, three manuscripts which we wanted to accept and would have unhesitatingly accepted eighteen months later, but which represented too startling a departure from the then character of our publications to accept at the very outset. It must be remembered that the attitude towards books was much more squeamish and puritanical in 1914 than it has been since 1918. The three books I recall were George Moore's *The Brook Kerith*, Caradoc Evans's *My People* and Thomas Burke's *Limehouse Nights*. We were so impressed by the last that we at once commissioned him to write *Nights in Town*, which we published with success, and gave him a job in our office to tide him over temporary financial difficulties. He was the fastest typist I have ever known.

The first novel we published was *Rain Before Seven* by Eric Leadbitter. It had been declined by ten or twelve publishers, but our readers thought it showed promise. We persuaded the author to put a good deal more work into it, as the result of which it was greatly improved. Although the sales remained modest, its reception was almost startlingly good. After the publication of a later novel, on which at our suggestion he had also put in a good deal of additional work, an enthusiastic reviewer described the author as a second Thomas Hardy. This we knew would be too much for some of the big fiction publishers who had declined the author's first book, but would unquestionably feel that a second Thomas Hardy must be 'acquired' at all costs. On the expiry of our contract we were invited by the author's agent to make an offer for the author's next three novels. We knew that whatever offer we made, one of the big fiction publishers would go one better, so we decided to make them pay handsomely for the privilege of 'acquiring' our author. His earlier books, all published on a royalty basis, had earned very close upon, but not quite, £100 each. We offered 'advances' of, I think, £250, £300 and £350 respectively—anyway much more than was justified, but, as we had anticipated, the agent persuaded a big fiction publisher to outbid us. The next book—probably too hastily written—was a flop, and years later I learnt had earned little more than £80. This experience demonstrated the unwisdom of depending upon fiction for one's livelihood and confirmed the desirability of building up a more solid list. It also gave me a contempt for the practice of 'acquiring' a competitor's author by outbidding him— a practice I have consistently avoided. I have on the other hand more than once secured a book by offering less. I remember one instance when an author brought me the actual offer received from another publisher, and asked whether I would pay more. My reply was: 'Surely you don't expect to get my services as cheaply as you can those of my competitors? My service is outstanding, but it is not cheap. The best is seldom the cheapest.'

But in all these matters, authors and most agents are wiser than they were forty years ago, and recognize that the amount of the advance payment is not the only criterion. When the boot is on the other leg and I am selling to an American or foreign publisher, I regard the status and efficiency of the firm as of greater importance than the size of the initial payment.

One of my earliest tasks when we settled in at 40 Museum Street was to realize as much as possible of the dead and unsaleable stock. Anything which could readily be disposed of had gone, and often at absurd prices if cash was urgently needed to pay the week's wages and there was no money at the bank. Upon the success with which I could tackle this difficult problem much depended. My unique knowledge of overseas markets proved of inestimable help as the following instance will show.

Among the stock was an unsuccessful series of supposedly

popular technical handbooks for which no remainder buyer would make an offer, and as the 12–14,000 copies took up a lot of space I was urged by the then head of the trade department to have them pulped. 'Give me two months', I replied, 'and I will sell them, because there is one overseas customer who could use them.' I sent this one and only man a sample set and said that he could have the lot at eightpence a copy provided he cabled his acceptance. I felt sure that he would pay ninepence or tenpence, but could not afford to risk a refusal because it was important to me to demonstrate to the staff that I knew my job, and at eightpence I knew that my customer could not fail to be tempted. To the surprise of the staff the cabled acceptance arrived as I had anticipated. That one order paid for the whole of my world tour.

The staff was so accustomed to directors who knew nothing whatever about their job that it took them some weeks to acclimatize themselves to dealing with someone who knew a great deal more about it than they did. It was a shock to me, for example, to be solemnly informed that review copies were sent out ahead of publication. I thanked my informant and said that had always been my practice throughout my publishing career. In view of their past experience it was really difficult for the staff to believe that a director might know what he was directing.

The disposal of some of the surplus stock called for imagination, which is often lacking in the book world. There was a huge stack of an attractively produced sixpenny paper-bound edition of Gray's *Elegy*. No bookseller could be persuaded to offer even 10s od for the lot, and once again I was told that 'pulping' was the only method of disposal. I replied that nothing would persuade me to pulp a nice edition of a classic, and if the booksellers wouldn't or couldn't help us we must as a last resort seek our own channel of distribution—that obvious right of the publisher which booksellers so bitterly resent. I slept over the problem and on the next day wrote to the vicar of Stoke Poges and offered him the lot at a penny a copy, pointing out that visitors to his church would welcome the opportunity of refreshing their memory of the poem on the spot, and that even if he sold the copies at half price it would yield a pleasant margin for church funds. He accepted by return. The copies were soon sold and he wanted more, which of course I could not supply. The disposal of all this accumulated stock put us in funds to finance new publications, and also gave me an insight into the methods of my predecessors. I was confronted with a series of plays for children published at sixpence which I could see at a glance would cost at least that amount to produce. When I asked what they cost to manufacture I was told that they sold very well. I said, 'Yes, but what do they cost to produce?' and received the reply, ' "X" buys them 250 at a time at half price'. When finally I succeeded in ascertaining their cost, it proved to be ninepence for the first edition and five-pence for reprints, so that the more copies they sold the more money they lost!

At the first board meeting following the formation of the company we decided the respective functions of the four direc-tors; the policy to be adopted in connection with the acceptance or rejection of manuscripts, and the allocation of the directors' rooms. Colonel Dalbiac, a charming man, who having longer experience of publishing always backed me, was elected chair-man. He expressed a wish to do the authors' accounts. (He was immensely proud of the speed with which he did them; the fact that they were so inaccurate that they had to be done again was not revealed to him.) The fully qualified solicitor (C. A. Reynolds) was appointed secretary, and in theory undertook the correspon-dence. The other director (E. L. Skinner) stipulated that adver-tising should be in his hands. All trade matters were left exclusively to me.

It was clear that our views were so diametrically opposed that we should never agree about the acceptance of manuscripts. I therefore urged that the sole criterion must be whether or not the undertaking would pay its way, because we could not afford to endow each other's failures, and this was agreed. It was also understood that we should each of us be responsible for the correspondence, production, etc., in connection with the books we introduced.

There were only two good private offices on the first and second floor respectively. As the colonel was only doing book-keeping he was relegated by the other two to the top floor. To their surprise I contented myself with a cubby-hole on the ground floor, whence I could see every visitor who called. Both of the other two wanted the first floor office, and were left to fight it out.

Now as I arrived at 9 a.m. and my colleagues did not put in appearance before 10 a.m. I saw all the correspondence, and as I was responsible for the introduction of about 90 per cent of the new books the actual running of the business soon drifted largely into my hands. Moreover the colonel was almost immediately called up, and a little later Skinner secured a post in the War Office, first as a lieutenant and then as a captain. I was thus left with Reynolds, my most difficult colleague. He was indeed a strange person. A senior member of the warehouse staff had to spend from nine to ten every morning tidying up his room, and polishing the little bronze nude ladies with which his desk was littered, regardless of the pressure of any other work. How expensive a luxury he was may be gathered from the following. We were offered for publication at about the same time *Married Love* by Marie Stopes and a novel by an attractive girl, whom Reynolds had interviewed, dealing with homosexuality and conscientious objection. I saw at once the sales possibilities of *Married Love* and pressed for its acceptance. Reynolds wanted to accept the novel. I examined it and felt sure that in the then state of public opinion we should be prosecuted if we published it. I warned Reynolds of the danger, to which he replied that if we could not publish the novel we could not publish *Married Love*. I remonstrated that marriage was a legitimate and normal thing, whereas homosexuality was illegal and a perversion, but he remained unmoved. If I would not consent to the firm publishing the novel he would not consent to my accepting *Married Love*, and our joint signatures were needed to an agreement with authors. I was so certain that in *Married Love* I had a best-seller that I endeavoured to get myself proved wrong about the novel. I sent the typescript to that most experienced and broadminded editor, A. R. Orage, to whose assistance in those difficult days I shall ever be grateful, and asked him whether I could possibly publish it, mentioning that to do so would secure me the rights in another book which was a certain best-seller. His reply was unhesitating: 'You cannot publish this novel; you will be prosecuted if you do.' Both manuscripts were accordingly declined. When the authoress of the novel called, Reynolds telephoned to me that as he had told her that we should probably be accepting the book, he would like to give her the name of another publisher to approach, and would I suggest one. I replied that in view of the subjects dealt with I did not think that any publisher would consider it; the only man who might conceivably do so was C. W. Daniel. The sequel was interesting. Daniel accepted the novel, was prosecuted for publishing it, and sentenced to three months' imprisonment or £460 fine (to which latter, having a guilty conscience for having mentioned his name, I contributed). Of *Married Love* more than a million copies were soon sold.

Building up a publishing business under such handicaps was not easy, and in any case the ship had too many captains. At that moment (July 1917), however, the authorities decided that they could not continue to grant both Reynolds and myself exemption from military service. I was at that time a pacifist. As such it seemed to me essential to do whatever I could conscientiously do. Accordingly I served from an early stage in VAD LONDON I,[1] under Sir James Cantlie, and passed not only the usual examinations in First Aid, Home Nursing, Hygiene, but advanced exams in all three subjects.

As a member of VAD I, I was automatically summoned by telephone about five minutes ahead of any general air-raid warning so that I might immediately report for duty at our headquarters in Regent Street. As I was always 'at call' I remained in uniform, and was thus able to reach Chalk Farm tube station before it was besieged by people taking shelter. Our flat was at the top of a tall building, and it was far from pleasant for my wife

[1] See *The Work of V.A.D. London I.*: Edited by Stanley Unwin (London: George Allen & Unwin Ltd., 1920).

that I should have to desert her whenever there was a raid. It was the kind of thing to which most of us got accustomed in the Second World War, but was new and therefore more terrifying in 1915.

VAD I had many interesting tasks. When the King had an accident in France, VAD I was called upon to meet him at Victoria and put him to bed in Buckingham Palace (incidentally insisting upon his having a new bed). When a Zeppelin was brought down at Potters Bar, it was VAD I that was first on the spot. But the most unpleasant task was rescuing the survivors —many already half-dead—from what were then *John Bull's* premises. The building was totally unfitted to be a shelter, but people had crowded into the basement, and when the building caught fire machines crashed down from upper floors and pinioned many of them. Because of this, some were in fact drowned in the flood of water, used to extinguish the flames, which steadily mounted up in the basement. The mixture of printer's ink with the water made everybody and everything black. We were hard at it all night, and it was an experience I am never likely to forget.

I always spent two nights a week at our headquarters, the Polytechnic, Regent Street, and at least one afternoon a week acting as porter at Charing Cross Hospital. This last interested me intensely because it was my duty, with a colleague, to collect patients from the wards and take them to and from the operating theatre. We were suitably clad to remain in the operating theatre if we wished to do so, and in fact were sometimes needed there. On one of the first occasions the surgeon was dealing with a broken leg and the two portions of the bone were overriding, and we had the strenuous job of extending the leg while the surgeon fixed a silver plate to the sides of the two pieces. My colleagues and I had ample evidence before he had finished of the respective strength of leg and arm muscles. The surgeons were nearly all contemporaries or students of my elder brother, W. H. Unwin, MD, BS, FRCS (a Charing Cross man), and put themselves out to show me anything specially interesting, and I must at one time or another have seen operations upon every portion of the human frame. The skill and surgical cleanliness of the surgeons varied greatly. Some of them I would have trusted to do anything with me; others, thought highly of by the public, I should not have wanted to operate upon my little finger. I imagine that any theatre sister would feel the same.

Reynolds claimed before the tribunal that he was fully competent to run the business by himself, but unfortunately for him his medical classification was B1 whereas mine was B3 and the tribunal said that they wanted him. Just as the army call-up came he secured as a solicitor an appointment as lieutenant in the Navy, and spent the rest of the war somewhere in Southern Ireland decoding telegrams.

Censorship, like many other things during the First World War, was incredibly stupid. There was a secret list of books and periodicals which it was prohibited to export. For some inexplicable reason, Lowes Dickinson's *The European Anarchy* was placed upon it. Why, still puzzles me. By accident I learned that many cases of books destined for Japan had been detained and opened so that one copy of this 'dangerous *anarchist* [sic] literature' (as the inspector described it) might be extracted. But the most startling case was that of the *Polish Review* which, with the approval of the Foreign Office, and largely, if not entirely financed by the British Government, was edited by Zaleski, later Foreign Minister of Poland, with the assistance of J. H. Harley. The *Review* was produced and published by us. Of one issue Zaleski was particularly anxious that 250 copies should be sent to the Polish Information Service in New York, and in accordance with his instructions we posted them. When they failed to arrive Zaleski accused us of failure to send them, and refused to take our word that we had done so. We agreed to duplicate the order and to register every package, but those copies likewise failed to arrive. To every inquiry about them the Post Office remained evasive until I threatened to take action. They then admitted that the copies had been handed to the War Office, who had destroyed them. Years later I ascertained that a reactionary Pole—Dmowski, a political enemy of Zaleski's, had told Field-Marshal Sir Henry Wilson in Paris that it was a bad thing for such a journal to be circulated, and that the Field-Marshal had sent instructions to the War Office to have it included in the secret list of books and periodicals which it was prohibited to export. Here then you had one Government Department financing a periodical which a second Government Department handed to a third to destroy at the instigation of a Polish refugee in Paris, and no one could say or do anything about it. Fortunately in the Second World War the censorship of books was carried through intelligently and worked without a hitch.

With the death of Sir Charles Seeley (Colonel Dalbiac's father-in-law) his holding of £6,000 debentures came into the market, and I assumed (correctly) that the Public Trustee would welcome an offer for them. In view of the fact that a year or two previously the assets of the company had been insufficient to cover them in full they were not an easily marketable security. But to me they were worth more than the £4,000 which, with the help of my bankers, Messrs Drummond (my one and only over-draft), I paid for them. I knew that the interest would be regularly paid and would cover both the interest and amortization of my loan. Furthermore, I had every intention of redeeming the debentures as soon as our resources permitted. This purchase strengthened my position because I now became the largest debenture holder as well as the largest shareholder.

My difficulties in building up the business were greatly accen-tuated by the fact that we had no paper ration and had to buy in the open market whatever we could obtain—and what dreadful stuff some of it was and what a price! To be sure of getting the offer of anything available I let it be known to the leading stationers that I would put aside whatever I was doing to see their representative whenever they had anything to offer; that I would give an immediate decision, and furthermore pay cash. There were times when we paid as much as 1s 7d a pound for paper greatly inferior to what we could have bought at 2¼d before the war. In brief, as in the Second World War, paper was Priority No. 1.

CHAPTER 10

EARLY DAYS OF
GEORGE ALLEN AND UNWIN LIMITED

Among the first visitors to call on the firm in August 1914 were Dr Eden and Mrs Cedar Paul. They had escaped from France where they had been living a nomadic existence with all their belongings in a little hand-cart which they wheeled about. They were penniless and starving, and called to collect £10 which was owed to them in connection with a translation made for the late firm. In the circumstances the news that the 'Receiver' had not even a penny in the pound for the old firm's creditors was catastrophic. Their case was so pathetic that I was asked by one of the staff if I would see them, which I did.

When I heard their story I said, 'The first thing is to give you something to eat, and we will consider what is to be done after that'. I found them most interesting, and it was the start of a lifetime's friendship with Dr Eden Paul (a son, by the way, of Kegan Paul, the famous publisher). I was then myself too impecunious to be of much help to them financially, and the outbreak of war had given my firm a temporary 'knock-out', but we advanced £10 on account of a translation of Hamon's *Bernard Shaw: The Twentieth Century Molière*, upon which the Pauls were engaged. It was a good book, but it did not enjoy a great sale, and I am sure that we should not have accepted it at that juncture but for Eden Paul. I have long since lost count of the number of books he translated for us thereafter.

The Pauls were not the only refugees from the German invasion. Belgians poured in and it was a problem to find accommodation for them. There was a large empty house at Shortlands near where my parents lived which was turned into a temporary hostel for them. I served on the committee responsible for their welfare, and night after night called in to see how they were getting on and to pour oil on the ever-turbulent French/Flemish waters. The two sections never had a good word to say for each other. However, I managed to establish pleasant relations with both sides, and was very proud when, four months later, I received a unanimous letter of appreciation of my services and their congratulations upon my marriage.

At that time everyone was talking about Treitschke, the German historian, who, it was maintained, had a large responsibility for Germany's chauvinistic spirit and thus for the outbreak of the First World War. A young man working for the brothers Jarrold who was full of ideas, pointed out to me that, despite all this talk about Treitschke, there was nothing about him in English. The brothers Jarrold, he said, were too unenterprising to do anything about it themselves, but if we would co-operate and they got the printing, he was sure that they would feel differently. I agreed, and we started upon a short life of Treitschke and included with it some of his more notable essays, all translated by the Pauls. We issued it under the title *Treitschke: His Life and Works*, and made quite a success of it. We followed it up with a volume *Germany, France, Russia and Islam*, and at that point I wanted to stop. But an American publisher, Robert McBride, persuaded my friend at Jarrolds that we ought to publish a translation of Treitschke's *History of Germany*, a gigantic undertaking in seven large volumes. I at once pointed out that long before the translation and production could be completed the intense interest in Treitschke would have waned and that the British sales would not cover a fraction of the enormous cost. But McBride was persistent; he would underwrite the venture by ordering 1,500 sets for sale in the USA. I was still dubious. We obtained references from the States demonstrating that McBride's partner, Nast, was a man of substance and that we could not go wrong with such a guarantee behind us. I was still unhappy and stipulated for £100 on signature of the contract, and payment for each volume by three monthly bills so that each volume should be paid for before the next was shipped. The first two volumes were duly delivered, but by the time the third arrived in New York,

McBride was failing to meet his obligations. Mr Nast had ceased to be a partner and we were indeed in trouble. The Pauls were well ahead with delivery of the translation, for which we paid as each instalment was completed; a further volume was almost ready for despatch and yet another in type. We had burnt our boats and could not go back. The British sales were as insufficient as antici-pated. McBride did not appear to be worth powder and shot, and meanwhile warehousing charges for the third volume which had reached New York were mounting up. We were in a sorry plight and in no position to face such a disaster. McBride offered to take 600 sets at a rather higher price provided we would take back 500 each of the first two volumes and cancel his liability in respect of the two additional volumes, bringing the work up to date, which at his instigation we had commissioned W. H. Dawson to write. There was no alternative to acceptance, but the resultant loss was a strain upon our then meagre financial resources which I am never likely to forget. It was a handicap from which it took quite a long time to recover. We were not helped by the fact that the cost of paper was rising to what were then fantastic heights, and that a subsequent shipment of 600 copies of one of the volumes was torpedoed on its way to the States, thus leaving us, after we had replaced them, with 600 imperfect sets which had not even a 'remainder' value. Years later McBride called with complete assurance and wanted to do business with me again, but I declined. History apparently repeated itself in 1950; but it was another British publisher who had losses to write off on that occasion.

During 1915 I was invited to publish a collection of Lord Curzon's speeches with an introduction by Lord Cromer. We accepted the manuscript and at once put it into type. We invited Lord Curzon to prepare a descriptive paragraph for our announce-ment list, which he did. Most authors err on the side of modesty which, as the announcement is the publisher's, is unnecessary, but Lord Curzon made no such mistake. He described himself as 'a leading statesman and one of the foremost speakers of the day'. When the page proofs were complete and we were ready to go to press, he telephoned that it was essential that an additional speech should be included. I demurred, but, as he was so insistent, gave way; but no sooner were the proofs of the further speech sent to him than he telephoned that on no account must it be included. It was vital that it should not. A glance through the speech revealed the reason for his anxiety. It condemned coalitions; in less than forty-eight hours he was a member of one. I thus knew before anyone outside cabinet circles what was in the wind, but kept it to myself.

As we had had no wish to include the speech or to omit it, it seemed reasonable to pass on to Lord Curzon the printer's charge for setting it, and the item, about £5, was accordingly debited in due course to his share of the profits. When the book was ready he said that he particularly wanted members of the Cabinet and certain Librarians to have a copy with *his* compliments. As he had already had a double allowance of author's free copies, it seemed to us that these further presentation copies should be charged to him on the special terms upon which authors are entitled to buy their own books. The amount involved was again about £5. Lord Curzon's indignation over these two items was fantastic. Night after night he must have sat up to write us in his own handwriting about them. At first we saw no reason to give way, but there came a moment when we felt that it was not in the national interests that in war-time a Cabinet Minister, and a leading one at that, should be burning midnight oil and devoting his energies to a dispute over two such paltry sums. The late Mr Curtis Brown, the literary agent through whom the payment had to be made, agreed with me. I suggested that we should each give way on one item and that Lord Curzon could decide which it should be. Mr Curtis Brown said that he was sure that he could secure a settlement on that basis, and he did. But it did not prevent Lord Curzon from raising the question again when the next account was rendered.[1]

[1] This will not surprise anyone who has read Lord Derby's letter to Bonar Law quoted by Lord Beaverbrook in his *Men and Power 1917-18* (London: Hutchinson, 1956).

Lord Cromer was most impatient about the book's appearance. He called the day the book was finally passed for press. I pointed out that it had still to be printed, bound, sent out to the Press for review and 'subscribed' to the booksellers before it could be published; that this would take not less than three weeks, and could not efficiently be done in less. He solemnly assured me that his publishers only took a week. I am afraid that he over-estimated my credulity.

As will be gathered from my experiences with these two distinguished people, a publisher's lot is not always the happy one it is supposed to be. On the other hand, I must give Lord Curzon credit for being a most excellent debt collector, second only to Archbishop Velimirovich. During the First World War I published several books of special interest to the Serbians, of which they purchased five hundred copies. They were better at ordering books than at paying for them. When the Archbishop, an impressive figure with a long flowing beard, called to express appreciation for what I had done for his country, I told him of our fruitless endeavours to collect payment for the books we had supplied. His indignation was unbounded. In my presence he at once spoke to some official at the Serbian Legation. I could not understand a word, but his torrential eloquence was impressive—and effective, because before noon the next day more pound notes were being counted out over our counter than we had ever seen in the place before, and the debt was cleared. But history repeated itself a year or two later when there was no Archbishop to help us. It is not permissible to sue a Foreign Embassy or Legation because of their extra-territorial status, so in despair I turned to Lord Curzon, then Secretary of State for Foreign Affairs. About a week later an official from the Legation was busily counting pound notes over our counter.

We encountered no such trouble with the Czechs, who were always most punctilious, and it was during the First World War that I began to publish for both the first two Czech Presidents and started my happy relationship with what later became Czechoslovakia. The first book of Masaryk's was his *Spirit of Russia* (two volumes), translated from the German by Eden and Cedar Paul, and the first by Beneš was *Bohemia's Case for Independence*. Masaryk called once or twice at Museum Street (he was living in Hampstead at the time) and I was immediately impressed by his personality. No one could fail to be—he was so transparently good and so obviously wise; one instinctively felt it a delight to converse with him. Alas! in publishing, those authors one loves to see call all too seldom; it is the bores who are constant in attendance.

With Beneš, one was conscious of a quick, subtle, clever mind; but it is unfair to compare anyone with Masaryk, who was one of the greatest men of our time. Another Czech, Karel Čapek, for whom I subsequently published so many books, was a charming man. Following his death I wrote as a postscript to *The Cheat* an account of my relationship with him. The opening and closing sentences speak for themselves:

'There are few authors, living or dead, from whose works I have derived more enjoyment than I have from those of Karel Čapek. On that ground alone it was a great satisfaction to be his English publisher. . . . Were I asked what were the features about him which impressed me most forcibly I should answer—his simplicity, his vitality, his uncanny intuition, and psychological insight. On my office desk I have always in front of me some words I hastily copied down when reading the typescript of his novel, *An Ordinary Life*. They are as follows—

"God, how simple is the prescription for a happy life; to do what we have to, out of love for the thing."

I loved publishing for Čapek and it certainly brought me happiness to do so.'

But I must return to 1915.

One of my greatest satisfactions in taking over the George Allen list was that it automatically made me the publisher of the late Professor Gilbert Murray's superb translations from the Greek. Among our early publications were a revised edition of his own play, *Carlyon Sahib* and his little volume on *Stoic Philosophy*. Subsequently we published many more translations for him, as well as a volume of *Essays and Addresses* and a book on foreign policy. He had had an unhappy time with our predecessors, and although we had no responsibility for their debts we felt justified in his case in assuming liability for part of them as soon as we were in a position to do so. One of the happiest moments of my life occurred a year or two later when he sent me a postcard reproduced below in facsimile:

Yatscombe, Boars Hill.

FROM GILBERT MURRAY, 82 Woodstock Road, Oxford.

What a very interesting list your autumn announcements make! If I had any money I wd. buy them, & if I had any time I wd. read them, all.

His visits to the office were a joy and full of interest to me, lit up as they always were by his wit and delightful sense of humour. Although the description may seem inappropriate to a Rationalist he represented to me what a Christian *ought* to be. His intrinsic goodness, his nobility of mind, his indefatigability in the cause of peace, were an inspiration to anyone who had anything to do with him. His generosity is exemplified by a letter he wrote to me years later saying that it had been 'a great pleasure to him in our fairly long and entirely untroubled business relationship to feel his publisher so much one at heart with him'. It is that kind of relationship which makes publishing so very much worth while.

Another author whose books it was a pleasure to 'inherit' was Edward Carpenter. He had been connected with Dr Reddie at the start of Abbotsholme so that I had already heard much about him. He had been treated so badly by our predecessors that he was at first most suspicious of the new firm. But we voluntarily recouped him part of his losses, and as an old Abbotsholmian I was soon able to establish the friendliest relations with him. He was one of the first visitors my wife and I entertained when we secured a little flat at the top of 'The Grange', Maitland Park, in 1915, some three or four months after our marriage in December 1914. I still remember our nervousness as host and hostess, but it was quite uncalled for. He was both simple and charming, and had a most pleasing sense of humour. Thanks to our handling all his books, and thus being able to make one sell another, and to list them all together, we were able to build up his income for him most agreeably. He was always most appreciative of what we accomplished for him right up to the last years of his life, when unfortunately he lost his memory and was apt to blame us for doing something he had instructed us to do only the day before. His delightful autobiography, *My Days and Dreams*, reveals a beautiful character and tells the strange adventures of his most famous work, *Towards Democracy*, the early editions of which were printed at his own expense and shifted from publisher to publisher—on one occasion by himself on a dray. I had a battle royal with the authorities at Scotland Yard over his book *The Intermediate Sex*, but as it is described in full in *The Truth About Publishing* under the heading 'Censorship', there is no need to repeat that amusing and instructive story here. It was a great satisfaction to me to be able to produce to Sir Basil Thomson, the Chief Commissioner, when the battle was over, the wonderful testimonial given to Carpenter on his seventieth birthday, with its array of signatures of distinguished authors and public men.

Teixeira de Mattos, whose translations of Maeterlinck we had taken over, brought me a translation of *The Path of Love* by that most famous Flemish author, Stijn Streuvels. Teixeira was certain that his work would 'catch on' in England, but although we experimented with a further book it never did. Why, it is difficult to say.

The fact that I had become Ruskin's publisher did not bring me the pleasure and satisfaction I had anticipated. The entire stock and the electroplates and blocks were the property of the Ruskin Literary Trustees, and we merely had a modest commission on the sales. All would have been well had they maintained the stock of at any rate the more saleable titles. But replacements, owing to the enhanced price of paper, would have absorbed a large part of the proceeds of sales. They accordingly decided to postpone reprinting any volumes until after the war. The result was disastrous. We could not supply the books most in demand, and at the end of the war, as they had in the meantime treated the sales as 'profits', or at any rate as income, they were unwilling or unable to find the substantial amount needed to build up the stocks again. As a result, although we advanced money to enable one or two books to be reprinted, we have never been able to supply complete sets of Ruskin's works in either crown 8vo or pocket size. They were, and are now, available only in the huge 38-volume Library Edition. The then trustees could not have 'killed' the sale of Ruskin's works more effectively had they been his worst enemies instead of his literary heirs.

In his early days a publisher is almost desperately dependent upon personal connections and recommendations. My circle of friends was at that time very limited, but the few in a position to be of assistance were most helpful. One recommended the late R. C. Trevelyan, the poet and brother of the historian, to come to me, thereby starting a lifelong friendship. In course of conversation I mentioned that it was my life's ambition to publish for G. Lowes Dickinson, and Trevelyan brought him along. Dickinson was at that time paying frequent visits to the British Museum, and to my joy made a practice of dropping in to see whether I was free for lunch. Those many talks we thus had together were among the greatest pleasures of my life. He was interested in a symposium which Charles Roden Buxton was editing, and that came my way and brought with it a lifelong connection with both Charles and Noel Buxton. The symposium brought me into contact with others, and the fact that I was ready and anxious to publish for the then unpopular minority soon became widely known. Romain Rolland's *Above the Battle*, to which Arthur Clutton Brock paid such a glowing tribute in *The Times Literary Supplement*, came to me in C. K. Ogden's excellent translation, as well as books by John A. Hobson, L. T. Hobhouse, H. M. Hyndman,

J. M. Robertson, Camille Huysmans, Emile Vandervelde and J. Ramsay MacDonald, to mention but a few.

My chief trouble over this otherwise pleasing and rapid development of the business in the direction I desired was that nearly all these publications were wholeheartedly disapproved by my two solicitor fellow directors. (The colonel was in Salonika and out of the picture.) Now every agreement called for the signature of a second director, and under the decision of the board I could secure their signatures only if I could demonstrate that the publication would be profitable. This presented me with untold difficulties and called for much ingenuity on my part to ensure in advance that we should not lose money even if we did not make much. It was a discipline which few publishers I imagine would wish to undergo, but from which I certainly benefited, though it seriously hampered my activities. Fortunately the unpopular minority supported us and in those early days even if we did not make much money we made no losses.

Perhaps the most unpopular was Bertrand Russell, articles by whom were appearing in American magazines, such as the *Atlantic Monthly*. They were so brilliant that I wrote expressing the wish to publish for him. It was thus in June 1915 that I first heard from him. He said that he had written various articles on the war and matters arising out of it which he would be glad to publish as a book, adding—

'I fear, however, that you might find too little patriotism in my opinions—though I doubt if there is less than in Price's *Diplomatic History of the War*.[1] If you think it possible that that would not prove an insuperable objection I should be glad to . . . send the articles for your inspection.'

With the arrival of these articles, which became *Principles of Social Reconstruction*, my colleagues' cup of misery overflowed. They felt that I was going too far, and it was not easy to demonstrate to them that it would be a money-maker whatever my own 'hunch' might be. Fortunately I had an inspiration. I knew that

---

[1] Which we had just published.

they had the greatest respect for Professor J. H. Muirhead, editor of our Library of Philosophy. 'Let us', I said, 'send the typescript to him and abide by his judgment.' They unhesitatingly agreed, but to their chagrin his verdict was as follows:

'I have read the most of Russell's *Principles of Social Reconstruction* with the greatest possible interest. It is a brilliant book and I congratulate you on having the publication of it. Parts of it, especially the part on marriage, will give rise to a great deal of discussion, possibly even opprobrium, but people ought to be sufficiently familiar with the point of view and it is one that has to be faced and reckoned with. The central problem that is raised—the place of institutions, family, state, church—is a vital one, and it is of quite extraordinary interest to find William Godwin's polemic against them revived in so brilliant and up-to-date a fashion. . . .'

It is thus to Muirhead, to whom I was so indebted in other ways, that I owe the privilege of publishing for Bertrand Russell. Later Muirhead, much as he disagreed with Russell's philosophy, welcomed the opportunity of including *An Introduction to Mathematical Philosophy* and *The Analysis of Mind* in his Library. The former was largely, if not entirely, written in prison, during which period I had many enjoyable visits from Bertrand's elder brother, the then Earl Russell, famous for his insistence upon being tried by his peers when charged with bigamy—a procedure long since disused. Lord Russell was rightly determined that his younger brother should be properly treated in prison and was not prepared to stand any nonsense from anyone. On one occasion, to my intense amusement, when I mentioned that 'blank' at the Home Office was the man to see about some privilege he wanted, he replied: 'Blank! Oh, he was my fag at Winchester and will have to do what I tell him.' I don't believe that Russells are ever intimidated, though Bertrand pretends he was as a boy by Gladstone. When we reprinted *Principles of Social Reconstruction*, which we soon had to do, I delighted its author by printing on the jacket Lord Cromer's verdict, 'A thoroughly mischievous book'.

I was much helped about this time by A. R. Orage, editor of

The New Age, than whom no one was doing more to assist and encourage young authors of promise. Hilaire Belloc, in the course of his eloquent dedication of his book, *The Free Press*, to Orage, described him as the pioneer of the Free Press in Great Britain, and the *New Age* as the only paper in which the truth with regard to our corrupt politics, or, indeed, with regard to any powerful evil, could be told. As the result of Orage's introduction, I published (under the pseudonym 'Edward Moore') what must I think have been the first work of Edwin Muir, *We Moderns*, as well as books by such then influential writers as Ramiro de Maeztu and A. J. Penty. Whenever I was in doubt about a manuscript I knew that I could confidently turn to Orage for advice. On October 19, 1922, I wrote to him:

'You must not shake the dust of London from off your feet without receiving some word of regret from me—some indication that you will be missed—some expression of gratitude for your never-failing kindness and help.

'Book Publishing (particularly when chiefly concerned with the propagation of new ideas) is not a bed of roses; and your frank recognition of the difficulties and readiness to give the benefit of your judgment made the day you first came to Museum Street a memorable one. . . .'

He was a real friend in need and I regretted his retirement to Fontainebleau to sit at the feet of the Armenian philosopher-mystic Gurdjieff, who had established his 'institute' there. Gurdjieff's disciples and pupils (of whom Orage became one) were subjected to a severe and sustained course of physical, mental and psychological exercise and training designed to promote self-knowledge, intellectual firmness and subtlety. The place was conducted somewhat on the lines of a monastery, and Gurdjieff's methods were so drastic as in some cases to drive his pupils beyond the limits of their endurance. The hour I spent with Orage at Fontainebleau was one of the most depressing of my life, and I cannot say that I thought, either then or later, that Orage's personality gained by his experience there. On the other

hand, it is a fact that he went to America shortly afterwards in
order to raise funds for the 'institute' by expounding Gurdjieff's
ideas, and I do not know that he ever regretted having submitted
to the influence of that remarkable man.

A letter I received from Orage in July 1930—one of the last—
gave me great pleasure. It read:

'Your catalogue is so attractive that I wish I were starting life as a
reader all over again. Your list is a liberal education.'

From such a critic this was praise indeed.

Another source of authors was the acquisition of books from
three small publishers, Howard Latimer, Max Goschen, and
Stephen Swift, all of whom dropped out almost before they had
got going, so easy is it to start publishing but so difficult to 'make
good'. This secured me books by Benedetto Croce and Strindberg,
Sorel's *Reflections on Violence*, Flecker's *King of Alsander*, Jules
Romain's *Death of a Nobody*, and the early work of Sir J. C.
Squire.

When I undertook the publication of *The Making of Women* by
A. Maude Royden, Eleanor Rathbone and others, I little suspected
that the energetic and efficient editor of that volume, Victor
Gollancz, was destined to become a competitor and that it was to
be the one and only occasion I was destined to be his publisher.
But my experience of him left me in no doubt that, when he did
start on his own, where others might fail he would certainly
succeed.

Conscientious Objectors were most stupidly handled during
the First World War, and I published several books on the
subject. By far the most famous was *I Appeal unto Caesar* by
Mrs Henry Hobhouse, with an introduction by Professor Gilbert
Murray, and impressive 'Notes' by the Earl of Selborne, Lord
Parmoor, Lord Hugh Cecil and Lord Henry Bentinck, a book
about which John Galsworthy wrote in *The Observer*: 'This little
book has stirred me deeply. I urge one and all to read it.' Thousands
wished to do so, but so great was the wartime prejudice on the
subject that many booksellers refused to stock or even handle it.

Over a thousand people came to our office to secure a copy. The book was referred to in Parliament and in the end thousands were sold, but it was an uphill fight with the book trade which I have never forgotten. Throughout I had the wholehearted backing of its indefatigable author (mother of Stephen Hobhouse, whose cause she espoused), one of the famous Potter family and sister of Beatrice Webb.

Just over four months after the start of George Allen & Unwin, my wife and I were married on my birthday at Lyndhurst Road Congregational Church, Hampstead, by Dr R. F. Horton. In the vestry afterwards I had laughingly said to him, 'You ought to write your autobiography'. To my joy he did so. When it came to discussing terms he put me on the spot in the most charming and disarming fashion. He said: 'I leave it to you; I know that you will offer me whatever is fair.' Well, he got a higher royalty than he would have obtained through any bargaining. The book was an immediate success. Following its publication Dr Horton wrote to me, 'It is one of the greatest blessings of my life that you led me to write a record which has helped so many people'. But there was a curious sequel. In the course of a most sympathetic reference to his friend Arnold White, whom he had visited in prison, Dr Horton said what a shock it had been to observe the 'arrow marks' on his clothing. Arnold White brought a libel action against us on the ground that the 'arrow marks' indicated penal servitude whereas his was only a short sentence—a fact which Dr Horton had clearly stated. Nothing Dr Horton could say or do would pacify him. He was determined to secure 'damages' from us, though the references to him were so charming that he had not suffered in any way. It was very worrying, and I did what I have done with success on other occasions, went to sleep saying quietly and confidently to myself, 'I shall wake up with the solution'. As is often the case, it was a simple one. I woke up with the idea that I should search out the solicitor who had prosecuted him. I did so (with my own solicitor's concurrence) and handed him the correspondence. After looking it through he smiled and said, 'You won't hear anything more from him'. I didn't, but Dr Horton received a bitter letter of complaint that his 'cruel publishers' had set 'his old tormentors' upon him.

On another occasion when we had published a book for a provincial branch of a London charitable organization, the Preface to which, unknown to us, the London Head Office disapproved, we received a writ for libel. We at once offered to reprint the offending page, or to do anything within reason to put the matter right. But nothing would placate the offended parties, who seemed bent on litigation. I took the problem to bed with me and woke up with the idea that a certain charitable trust had probably given financial assistance to both the branch and the head office of the organization. I accordingly telegraphed to the secretary of the Trust to ask whether he approved of two organizations his Trust supported using their funds for litigation. He most emphatically did not, and within a few hours of his having the facts we were being urged by the solicitors who had previously refused to listen to us, to settle the matter amicably by doing the very things we had previously offered and they had declined even to consider.

Libel is a nightmare to publishers, and many of the actions brought might properly be described as gold-digging operations. They are far too often settled out of court because if the plaintiff is a man of straw from whom the costs cannot be recovered that may in some cases be the cheaper course. But, thanks to the publicity given to this particular form of racket, imaginary sufferers no longer get away with damages as easily as they did.[1]

In 1917–18 much thought was being given to after-war problems and we published a book under that title in which most distinguished people collaborated. It was a great satisfaction to me that, among innumerable other works on the same theme which we issued, two *The Framework of a Lasting Peace* edited by Leonard Woolf, and *A Proposal for the Prevention of Future Wars* by Viscount Bryce and others proved particularly useful when the

[1] The Defamation Act, 1952, makes that form of activity far less attractive.

League of Nations Covenant came to be drafted. I was desperately concerned about the nature of the peace to be concluded, and was one of the delegation which went to Lansdowne House in 1917 to thank Lord Lansdowne for his courageous letter in the *Daily Telegraph* advocating the opening of negotiations. I feared the consequences of the hysterical mood into which the populace was being worked up by the Northcliffe press. One of my own brothers who had come over from New Zealand to serve in France was so indignant with me for going to Lansdowne House that he could scarcely bear to speak to me. But not many years elapsed before he frankly admitted that he was wrong and that it was a tragedy that Lord Lansdowne's advice had not been followed. When I visited Germany again soon after the end of the war with Canon Streeter and some others it was more than ever clear to me that if the German people had realized in no uncertain fashion that the occupation of Belgium was the one obstacle that stood in the way, we might have had a negotiated peace. It must be remembered that although Ludendorf (through Hindenburg) had almost unlimited power he was not an absolute dictator. The Reichstag was still functioning and could have acted had pressure been exerted. There must be few who today would have the temerity to suggest that the world would not have been better off had peace been negotiated in 1917 on the basis of German withdrawal from Belgium.

Looking through our lists of this period I am struck by the number of titles we managed to issue despite our acute difficulties with paper. A few, such as Woolf's *International Government*, George Lansbury's *Your Part in Poverty*, which had a big sale, and *A Century of British Foreign Policy* by G. P. Gooch and J. H. B. Masterman, were produced by independent organizations and merely issued by us. Some, of course, like the little book by Hilaire Belloc on *The Free Press* to which I have already referred, did not call for much paper, but there were many big philosophical books. The explanation, of course, is that it was possible then to print quite small editions of 1,250 or even sometimes 1,000 copies and yet make the undertaking pay its way if the entire edition was sold. How one sighs for those conditions in which the publication of scholarly work was so much less difficult than it is today!

I cannot let the name G. P. Gooch pass without recording the quite astonishing amount of encouragement I received from him. He went out of his way to show appreciation of what I was trying to do, and on one occasion when Arthur Henderson was Foreign Secretary and we three happened to meet at a reception given by Ramsay MacDonald at 10 Downing Street, he told Henderson that few people had done so much for the League of Nations and the cause of peace which he had so much at heart as I had done. Lowes Dickinson once commented upon Gooch's incredible learning. It is only exceeded by his modesty and generosity. I owe him much more than he could ever realize.

Many curious things happen in publishing. Here are three which occurred about that time. We had a considerable stock of sheets of the crown octavo edition of *Praeterita* in three volumes, for which there was no demand. We hit upon the happy idea of printing fresh title-pages, re-christening the book *The Autobiography of Ruskin*, with the word 'Praeterita' underneath. It sold out immediately.

We had a considerable stock of an art book in two volumes which was quite incredibly good value at £3 3s od the set but booksellers would not buy it at £2 2s od nor the public at £3 3s od. We changed the price on the jacket to £3 3s od per volume, i.e. £6 6s od the set; told the booksellers that they could sell it at half price and pay us £2 2s od. The stock just melted away. There was no change in the price either to the booksellers or the public. Everyone was pleased and both booksellers and public clamoured for more copies than we could supply.

I noticed that one or two of our publications, of which the first editions were still in print and available to any bookseller at our trade counter, were being sold by antiquarian booksellers at a premium. I did not realize at that time what a big gulf sometimes separates the new and secondhand booksellers and was so puzzled that I arranged for copies of the books to be put up for auction. To my surprise booksellers bid more than the published price for them. Thereafter our representatives were at last able to persuade booksellers that those titles were worth stocking.

But all these examples of strange ways of selling books fade into insignificance compared with what Mr Haldeman-Julius tells of some of the things he has learned of American people in the course of selling them one hundred million books at five cents apiece.[1]

For some reason which I cannot pretend to explain, world wars stimulate an interest in Russian literature. We did our part in ministering to that demand. We published, for example, translations of Kuprin's *The Duel* and Goncharov's *Oblomov*. With the last book we got into trouble. How it came about I do not know because 'fiction' was my colleague's preserve, but he arranged for it, or at any rate allowed it, to be abridged—a quite unforgivable treatment of a classic. We were quite thoroughly and properly trounced, and I am glad to be able to add that I made amends by subsequently publishing a complete version of that masterpiece (a favourite book of mine) and arranging for its eventual inclusion in Everyman's Library. We also took over from Maunsel & Co. of Dublin 'The Modern Russian Library', which included works by Chekhov, Kuprin, Dostoevski and Ropshin.

Towards the end of the war I was sent for by the first Lord Leverhulme, who as a Congregationalist had long known my father. He handed me a huge pile of pamphlets and leaflets and said he wanted to make a book of them. Apparently whenever he gave an address or speech, as he frequently did, he had it printed. A glance told me that there was endless repetition and I said: 'You can't print this as it stands; it will need editing.' 'Aye,' he replied with a good Lancashire accent, 'that's what I want you

[1] *The First Hundred Million*, by E. Haldeman-Julius (New York: Simon & Schuster, 1928).

159

to do.' I was a trifle taken aback because I had not at that time had much journalistic or editorial experience, but I said that I would study the problem. As I left he said: 'Name your fee and make your proposition for publishing. Remember, I shall want a lot of copies.' Thus it came about that *The Six-hour Day and other Industrial Questions* by Lord Leverhulme was edited by Stanley Unwin. It was a terribly long job, and to this day I regret that I was so modest about my editorial abilities that I merely charged a fee of £25. I am sure Lord Leverhulme would have thought more of me had I made it £250. However, it was a profitable publication, and I was able to arrange for it to be separately printed and copyrighted in the USA.

One incident I shall never forget. He sent us a cheque for 2s 6d for a book he wanted or had bought. The cheque was 'dishonoured' and returned marked 'no assets'. It must be unique for a bank to treat a millionaire in such a fashion and for such a paltry amount, but then banks do curious things. In connection with 'Sondermarks', a temporary German currency, the Bank of England once credited my firm with 1s 11d and said that their charges for doing so were 2s 6d. As a matter of fact I have a high opinion of the Bank of England, but a very poor one of the big five. But that is another story.

Apart from a shortage of paper the war handicapped us in many ways. The stock we had purchased was stored by many different printers and binders. The fact that their and our records show that they held it did not ensure that it could be produced on demand. In some cases it had been moved from one warehouse to another and nobody knew precisely where it was; in others the warehouseman who could put his hands upon anything wanted had been 'called up'. The binders in particular were desperately shorthanded and had to avail themselves of any assistance they could get. One firm especially could never find anything we wanted. This continued for a long time until the manager of the bindery got suspicious because when he went to look himself he experienced no such difficulty. The explanation was simple, though it is hard to believe. They discovered that the warehouseman they

At Thorpeness
with
David and Ruth

Lady Unwin with Rayner

With David
in Germany
1931

Walking

Skating

Taking his degree

Tennis

had appointed could not read. In many cases the stock was found long after the possibility of selling it had passed.

Soon after the war was over, paper slumped in price overnight and a new era for publishers started. Those, like myself, who thought paper prices would do the same after the Second World War were bitterly disappointed.

CHAPTER II

AFTER THE FIRST WORLD WAR

After the end of the war when all three directors returned, I was able to demonstrate that in their absence I had built up the business so satisfactorily that their shares (for which they had paid nothing), as well as their debentures, were now fully covered by assets; that as they had received half pay from the firm as well as full pay from the Army or Navy, I had been by far the worst off, and that in the circumstances the vote of even a token bonus to me of £50 for what I had accomplished would be a pleasant gesture. But, although I pointed out that with a family coming and no other source of income it would mean a great deal to me; that, in view of the fact that I owned about half the shares, about half the bonus would in effect be paid by me, and less than £10 would be borne by Skinner—the colleague I approached—he would not hear of it. He preferred to 'muzzle the ox that was treading out the corn'. But when I told him that I did not feel justified in carrying on as we were, and that either Reynolds or I must go, he had no doubts about my value to him and persuaded Reynolds to sell out to me, for which assistance, to my surprise, he subsequently demanded £100. The departure of Reynolds materially eased the position, and incidentally gave us more much-needed space for our growing staff.

When we settled in at 40 Museum Street we hoped that the address would be permanent. It came as a shock therefore to learn one day in 1919—less than five years from our start—that the whole of the block in which it is situated between Little Russell Street and Gilbert Place was to be put up for auction, first as a whole, then if need be in lots, and that as an outcome our lease might be terminated. Lot 1 contained not merely 40 Museum Street and 3 and 4 Gilbert Place, of which we were in occupation, but 40a Museum Street (a laundry), 41 (a hairdresser), and 26, 27

and 28 Little Russell Street (tenements). It was a question of b
or being turned out, but the last thing we wanted to do at
moment was to lock up money in buildings. We bid up to £9,
for Lot 1, but at £9,750 it was knocked down. A few days later
we learned from one of the owners (a syndicate which had
acquired the property from the Duke of Bedford during the
Lloyd George budget scare) that it had been withdrawn at the
auction, and would we come and see him about it. When I did
so, I explained that we had gone as far as our resources warranted.
He replied by asking me an intriguing question. If, in view of the
then high prevailing rate of interest, he could demonstrate that
it would pay us better to buy at his (higher) price on his terms
than implement the bid we had made, would that interest us? I
replied, 'Certainly, if you can convince me of anything so
surprising'. The proposal was that, although we should buy at
once, the actual transfer should not be completed until some years
hence, and that in the meantime on half the purchase money we
should have the benefit of the exceptionally low interest rate to
which they themselves were entitled, and that apart from £2,000
down, the balance of the other half could be paid by yearly
instalments. From our point of view this was such an ideal
arrangement that we gladly agreed to pay the higher price. Once
again good had been extracted from evil. It seemed a disaster
that we should be compelled to buy, but it proved to be just the
reverse—in fact the best investment the firm ever made.

It is always interesting to a publisher to recall how he came to
publish books that proved steady sellers, or in the jargon of the
trade 'bread and butter lines'. I had heard a great deal about
Dr Fort Newton, who, with Maude Royden (for whom I had
published), occupied for some time the pulpit at the City Temple,[1]
but it was from my eldest brother, Edward Unwin, himself an
enthusiastic mason, that I learnt that Dr Fort Newton had written
a book entitled *The Builders*, of the deepest interest to masons and
likely to be used for presentation to initiates. Our predecessors
had published masonic works by Dr Albert Churchward, so that

[1] July 1916 to November 1919.

The Builders was in keeping with our list, and I had no hesitation in securing it, and we have been selling it ever since. In fact, the strength of the Allen & Unwin business lies in the number of such books on a wide variety of subjects that are in steady demand. One such, originally published by George Allen, of which we are particularly proud, is Hilaire Belloc's *Path to Rome*. Libellous statements appear from time to time to the effect that George Allen bought the copyright for a song, whereas the truth is that he paid what was then a substantial sum on account of royalties, and the author had a royalty on every copy sold from that date until his death.

Another steady seller which we acquired in the 1918–19 period was *The Life of Francis Place* by Graham Wallas (Professor Muirhead's brother-in-law). Its original publishers had allowed it to go out of print and we were proud to reissue it, even though it had to be on paper of which we were ashamed, and to publish subsequently other work by that most gifted teacher.

This incident brings to mind a number of outstanding books by Čapek, Laski, Russell and others which we have similarly taken over and reprinted two or three times—one of them had even been remaindered by its original publisher with whom it had been a complete failure. In this, as in many of the other cases, the book was an isolated one in the particular publisher's list, whereas we had many books by the same author. As I have often had occasion to point out, you cannot maintain a fire with a single piece of coal.

An author for whom I was particularly pleased to publish about that time was Margaret MacMillan, who convinced me (though I did not need much convincing) of the overwhelming importance of nursery schools and the outlet that they give to the child's creative instincts, the thwarting of which is responsible for so much juvenile delinquency. *Education Through the Imagination*, as one of her books was called, and not through mere memorizing of facts, appealed to me. Some years later we came to an agreement with Dents, who had published some of her work as well as a number of books by Lowes Dickinson, by which they took over all our publications by Margaret MacMillan and simultaneously assigned to us those they issued by G. Lowes Dickinson.

The 1918–19 period was a most active one for us in many fields—volumes of poems by Richard Aldington, R. C. Trevelyan, plays by Romain Rolland, Miles Malleson, St John Ervine (the last taken over from Maunsel of Dublin, from whom we also later acquired the works of J. M. Synge); in the field of philosophy *The Metaphysical Theory of the State* by L. T. Hobhouse, for whom I was particularly proud to publish; books by Bertrand Russell, Sir Hector Hetherington, John H. Muirhead, Clement C. J. Webb; and *The New Psychology and its Relation to Life*, a pioneer work by A. G. Tansley which went through edition after edition. In the field of politics there were new books by Mrs Sidney Webb, H. N. Brailsford, Vernon Bartlett, Walter Lippmann, Israel Zangwill, not to mention Trotsky's *History of the Russian Revolution to Brestlitovsk*. The typescript of Trotsky's book was brought to me by Litvinoff, whose wife was the daughter of Sir Sidney Low whom I had known in my Fisher Unwin days. It was shortly before Litvinoff's arrest at Golders Green, and I was approached by an official from Scotland Yard who wanted to know from whom I had obtained a work of Trotsky's. I inquired under what authority such information was demanded—under what section of what Act, adding that if I was merely being asked to oblige some doubtless praiseworthy civil servant it was quite a different matter. After due inquiry the official reported that it would be much appreciated if I could help his chief, to which I replied that they should have the information on the following day—by which time Litvinoff was in Copenhagen.

The Russian Revolution brought us a spate of books, many of which we published. The first, and one of the most successful, was Arthur Ransome's *Six Weeks in Russia*.

Here I should like to digress to place on record my view that it was deplorable that instead of leaving Russia alone, watching the gigantic experiment upon which she was embarking, and learning what was to be learnt from it, either positively or negatively, we intervened and without adequate justification backed Denikin and Koltchak. Our action in so doing contributed to Soviet suspicions which have dogged our relations ever since. Had we refrained, would the revolution have necessarily taken the extreme and deplorable course it has? As another outcome events were not studied objectively; only the books that took extreme views sold—anything balanced was stillborn. The public wanted to be told that the Russians were either angels or devils.

In conformity with our policy of maintaining an open forum, we published books giving both points of view. This had an amusing result. At the moment when the Harmsworth Press was running a violent anti-Soviet campaign, we published on the same day two books on Russia—one pro- and the other anti-Bolshevik, and the *Evening News* praised what from that paper's point of view was the wrong book, though, as the reviewer correctly said, the better one.

There were at that time many socialist organizations about whose activities I made a point of keeping myself informed. It was through one of them, the British Socialist Party, that I secured the publication of Lenin's *The State and Revolution*, of which *The Times* said 'a remarkable little book . . . may be regarded as a kind of *vade mecum* for the true Bolshevik'. We published many other books on the Russian Revolution, notably *The Practice and Theory of Bolshevism* by Bertrand Russell, in which Russell foresaw so clearly what was coming that the book could be reprinted without change twenty years later.

About that time I was much preoccupied with the problems of American copyright, or rather absence of copyright, and at the suggestion of A. R. Orage wrote an article on the subject which was subsequently issued as a pamphlet.[1] It was my first attempt at writing for publication, and I still remember how impressed I was by the many small changes Orage made in my text every one of which was an obvious improvement. It was 'editing' at its best, and I learnt much from it.

[1] *Literature and The United States* (London: George Allen & Unwin Ltd., 1919).

I followed it up at the request of Leonard Woolf with an article in *The International Review*, and at the suggestion of C. K. Ogden by one in *The Cambridge Magazine*.[1] I pointed out that little printing was secured by American printers as the result of the manufacturing clause in the American Copyright Act, and added: 'What is a few hundred pounds' worth of printing to the USA? Is not a good name to be chosen rather than much printing?' The article closed with these words:

'In the preamble to the League of Nations Covenant we are invited by President Wilson "to promote international co-operation"; in the matter of copyright, the nations of the world have been setting America an example of international co-operation since 1886. Even in 1919 it is not too late for America to amend her ways.'

It was not until thirty-six years later that she did so.

The most important new author, for whom I first published in 1919, was unquestionably Arthur Waley. His translations of Chinese poems had been appearing in *The Cambridge Magazine* and I wrote to him enthusiastically about them. He was at that time working in the British Museum and at once dropped in to tell me that unfortunately the day before receiving my letter, he had left the typescript of his *170 Poems* with Constables, but that he would prefer to have me as his publisher. What were we to do? Today I think I should have said, 'You can withdraw your MS because Constables have not yet had time to examine it or incur any reader's fee', but at that time I was so desperately concerned that nobody should be able to question the correctitude of my professional conduct that I said, 'We must wait their decision, but there is no reason why, if Constables make you a satisfactory offer (which they did), you should not at once explain that you could not give them an option upon further work because it would be going to George Allen & Unwin'. And that is what happened. Accordingly, in 1919 we issued his *More Translations from the Chinese*, and later, by arrangement with Constables, most of the *170 Poems* were included in a complete volume of *Chinese Poems* which we publish.

[1] *Copyright in the U.S.A.*—February 22, 1919.

The year 1920 was full of excitement and good things for George Allen & Unwin. It started appropriately with a volume of Centenary Studies of *Ruskin, The Prophet* by John Masefield, Dean Inge, C. F. G. Masterman and others; *The New Outlook* by Lord Robert Cecil (as he was then) and *The Forerunners* by Romain Rolland. With the last we had an unforgettable experience. We had arranged with an American publisher to print 1,500 copies at the same time as our own edition, and to ship them to him in the form of sheets with his imprint on the title page. The binders to whom the sheets were delivered were given in writing the correct instructions and were supplied with the appropriate invoices and consular certificate. After the shipment was well on its way, the binders informed us that by a mistake *bound* copies had been shipped. We immediately informed the American publisher, who in turn advised the American Customs of the error, and asked for permission to substitute invoices which included binding. But although *we* had drawn attention to the mistake and the cases had not been opened, the American Customs ruled that because the invoices and consular certificates had passed a certain desk, replace invoices were not permissible, and that in view of the misdescription of the goods they had no alternative but to inflict a penalty which amounted in sterling to £525. They added that the penalty was automatic; there was no appeal, no redress. The American Chamber of Commerce in London moved heaven and earth to get the case reconsidered, but in vain. We suggested that as the whole consignment was worth only £175 it should be dropped into the Atlantic, but that alternative was denied us. The American Customs insisted upon their pound of flesh. Every American I consulted agreed that it was monstrous that we should be fined for a mistake to which we ourselves had drawn attention, and some years later the Act was amended. But the £525 has never been refunded.

Just before this time I had started publishing for the London School of Economics and the Fabian Society. In connection with the latter I had many interesting discussions with Sidney Webb (later Lord Passfield), some of whose books I published. The agreement which I negotiated with him was on the lines beloved by Bernard Shaw. The Fabian Society produced their own publications at their own expense, put our name on the title page, and left us to attend to their sale and distribution outside their own membership. The connection was for us at that time a valuable one and introduced me to such authors as G. D. H. Cole, but it is doubtful whether the commission on sales which Sidney Webb thought adequate remuneration for the use of a publishers' imprint and his services as a distributor covered even half an efficient publisher's overhead expenses. It certainly yielded no profit.

To me by far the most exciting work it brought us was Tawney's *Sickness of an Acquisitive Society*, which they produced in red paper covers for sale at 2s od. I started reading it one Saturday night and continued while wheeling the pram with my eldest boy up Haverstock Hill and Rosslyn Hill on Sunday morning on my way to the Heath. I was so immersed that I paid little attention to the pram and its occupant, and it was a miracle that the babe was not tipped out. I was in fact so excited about the book that I bought copies to give to people to make it better known and get it talked about. Our enthusiasm was unbounded, and we soon sold out and clamoured for further supplies from the Fabian Society—supplies which were not forthcoming. My feelings can be imagined when I learnt that, without our being told, let alone given an opportunity to make a bid, the rights had been sold to G. Bell & Sons Ltd. But book publishers have to learn that they are not expected to have feelings.

As a firm we prided ourselves on publishing what would interest people tomorrow. In the field of ideas we wished to lead rather than to follow. Our predecessors had published the first translation of Karl Marx's *Capital* and the first translation of a work by Freud, *The Interpretation of Dreams*, which at the time were courageous things to do. Similarly, we published the first book on the League of Nations; the first book on The National Trust; the first book on auto-suggestion, Baudouin's *Suggestion and Auto-Suggestion*, which introduced Coué to the English-speaking world, and too many other books to mention individually. At the time we issued the book on *The League of Nations* it was regarded by many as a pro-German activity—one famous London bookseller (now dead) threatened to throw our representative out of his shop. I protested and told the bookseller that the movement would be blessed by the Archbishop of Canterbury within a twelvemonth—which it was.

The interest aroused in Coué by the publication of Baudouin's *Suggestion and Auto-Suggestion* was so great that we decided to send someone to Nancy to watch Coué at work and to write a popular book on *The Practice of Auto-Suggestion*. At the recommendation of the Rev. Ernest Charles of Malvern Link, an old friend of the family who read manuscripts for us, we selected C. Harry Brooks, then a young man, who is now better known as Cyrus Brooks, the literary agent and translator. Of the book which resulted we must have sold close upon a hundred thousand here and the same number in the USA, and the English edition still sells steadily, as, of course, does Baudouin's standard work.

During the same period I had the excitement of publishing new books by Lowes Dickinson, Freud, J. A. Hobson, Gilbert Murray, H. W. Nevinson and Bertrand Russell, to mention but a few outstanding authors. Canon Barnett, who called upon me in connection with his book on *The Perils of Wealth and Poverty*, much impressed me by his insistence that in the welfare state the saying 'God loveth a cheerful giver' ought to be 'God loveth a cheerful taxpayer'—a view which I try to remember on January 1 when sur-tax becomes payable.

One publication deserving special mention is *Terrorism and Communism* by Karl Kautsky, of which we were able to issue an English translation because of my personal knowledge that we could sell more than half of the first edition in Japan. One Japanese bookseller cabled for a thousand copies immediately on receipt of a letter from me announcing it.

Finally, there were two books which got me into trouble—one with Sir Archibald Bodkin, Director of Public Prosecutions, and the other with G. Bernard Shaw. The first was *A Young*

Girl's Diary, translated from the German and prefaced by a letter from Freud which begins:

'This diary is a gem. Never before, I believe, has anything been written enabling us to see so clearly into the soul of a young girl during the years of puberal development.'

Now when I say that my Victorian mother had read a set of proofs of the book with interest and approval, it will be realized that there could be nothing 'obscene' about it. There was in fact nothing in the book read *as a whole* 'calculated to deprave and corrupt those whose minds are open to such immoral influences, and into whose hands a publication of this sort may fall' to quote the ridiculous hundred-year-old definition of Chief Justice Cockburn, the validity of which was never tested in a higher court, and has been superseded in America by Judge Woolsey's enlightened and masterly judgment in the *Ulysses* case. But there was one entry, essential to the whole because it so influenced the girl's later life, which describes what the child had seen from a top floor window in a bedroom opposite. From that moment the child's mind was obsessed by what appeared to her as the cruelty of a big man to a small woman. On that isolated entry in the diary Sir Archibald fastened, and I was summoned to his presence.

I went armed with letters from leading medical psychologists and educationists, emphasizing the importance of the book, but they were brushed aside. 'Filth, my dear Sir, filth', shouted Sir Archibald, as he grew more and more purple in the face and repeatedly banged his fist upon the table. Fortunately I kept cool and asked him whether the medical and educational professions ought to be deprived of a work they regarded as of outstanding value and importance. He said, 'No, but the book is not fit for the general public'. When I then asked him how this discrimination was to be achieved, he said that the book should be clearly marked for sale only to members of the legal, medical and educational professions, and that this should be clearly explained to the booksellers. I replied, 'May we assume that if we had done that you would have no grounds for complaint?' He agreed. I then took the wind completely out of his sails by assuring him, as I could, that we had done all that and more. I was able to point out that every invoice had a printed label affixed reading—

'This psychological study is intended for the use of members of the educational, medical and legal professions only.'

'In that case,' said Sir Archibald, 'how was it that my policeman was able to buy a copy in Charing Cross Road?' I pointed out that we had no knowledge that the particular bookseller was ignoring the condition of supply. 'Well,' responded Sir Archibald, 'I shall not prosecute, but in future you must obtain the name, address and occupation of the bookseller's customer before supplying the book.' I inquired whether this condition was to apply to booksellers on the Continent, to whom copies of the original work and other translations were freely available, and who did not regard the work as 'wicked'. Sir Archibald agreed that they might be exempted and allowed responsibility for their own morals or lack of morals.

These rigid restrictions and our refusal to supply soon got us into difficulties with distinguished people who considered themselves very much aggrieved. One such letter from a Lt.-Col. ——, CMG, together with the writer's record (taken from *Who's Who*), I passed on to Sir Archibald, whose reply as follows can be allowed to speak for itself:

'In my opinion, to sell a copy to your correspondent, Col. ——, would not be a breach of the arrangement and undertaking comprised in your letter of the 13th April on the ground that Col. —— appears to be a person really and bona fide interested in such topics to deal with which is the alleged object of the book. I agree that you might quite properly exercise a limited discretion as to the circulation of this book amongst persons similarly minded to Col. ——, as to whom you are satisfied that they have a real and bona fide intellectual interest in the subject-matter of such a work.'

About six months later my then colleague sent Sir Archibald a cutting from *The Lancet* of September 17, 1921, the most relevant portions of which read as follows:

'There has recently been a change of attitude towards the discussion of sex matters. . . . In this connection the need for education of the adolescent is fully recognized; further, it is well known that withholding sex information from the child results in that information being acquired in fantastic form from unclean sources. Few people deny this, but custom is strong. . . . *A Young Girl's Diary* . . . shows us what happens on the child's side of the barrier. . . .

'If the power of taboo will allow us to admit that we also were the victims of the conspiracy of silence there is very little, except a "Peeping Tom" episode, that would not be acknowledged as having happened to many of us in childhood. . . . The most thought-provoking thing in the book is a publisher's slip limiting its "study" to members of the educational, medical and legal professions. It is not easy to understand why parents belonging to trades or other professions should not read it.'

Attention was specifically drawn to the last sentence and the suggestion made that we might be allowed a little more discretion.

The Lancet review roused Sir Archibald to even greater fury. His reply was most revealing, and it is a pity that as it is marked 'Confidential' I am debarred from reprinting it. It left one with the impression that he had become doubtful whether even the *medical* profession could safely be entrusted with such a 'disgusting' book; there could certainly be no question of allowing us even a limited discretion.

I have described this incident at length because few appear to realize the troubles which beset a publisher who is thinking of tomorrow when confronted with officials whose ideas are firmly rooted in the past. It is no new problem. How many of the present generation, I wonder, are aware that before the First World War a publisher ran grave risks if he even mentioned the existence of venereal diseases in a book intended for the general public? Going a little further back, but not so many years before that, the condemnation of the unfortunate Vizetelly for publishing English translations of the works of Zola was unqualified. According to the most sober papers of the time he was 'justly' punished, 'his sentence was merited'.

Who today would defend the unpleasant and bitter things said of Grant Allen for writing *The Woman who Did?* Our ideas in these matters change from generation to generation, and the foolish judgments of Lord Eldon proscribing the works of Byron, Shelley and Southey are a warning, as Judge Augustus N. Hand pointed out, to all who have to determine the limits of the field within which authors may exercise themselves.

'Dirt for dirt's sake' is a workable definition of obscenity. The intention of the writer, and the effect of the work *as a whole*, not upon a child, but 'on a person with average sex instincts'— *l'homme moyen sensuel*—must be considered in any test of obscenity. People who want to bring children into the test overlook the fact that normal children are uninterested in, and incapable of understanding things far beyond their own experience which in a book may sexually excite an adult. Children left unrestricted access to a library of sexology would remain uncorrupted unless elementary information had been wrongly withheld from them and they had been led to believe that there was something mysterious about sex which adults were hiding from them.

As to *A Young Girl's Diary*, I am glad to be able to add that some years later, when the question of reprinting the book arose, the Home Office agreed that the condition imposed by Sir Archibald might appropriately be waived.

My trouble with Bernard Shaw was of a very different character. We had published two books about him, and lost money on each, when a third came our way, *The Quintessence of Bernard Shaw*, by H. C. Duffin. It was a good book and we told the author so, adding that as we had lost money on both the previous books on Shaw we regretted that we must decline his. The author then asked us what we estimated the loss would be, and whether if he contributed the amount involved we would publish the book. We replied that if he was definitely willing to lose £75 we would go ahead, and arrange the royalty on such a basis that he would get at least half his money back in the unlikely event of our selling the first edition of 1,000 copies. He accepted. An offer to Bernard Shaw to show him the manuscript before it went to the printers brought the following characteristic reply:

'Dear Mr Stanley Unwin,

'I cannot imagine why people who want to know what I have to say to them should ask a policeman instead of coming direct to me. However as I have written a Quintessence of Ibsenism I suppose I cannot complain of someone else writing a Quintessence of Shavianism.

'I will not take the responsibility of reading the MS as it might perish by some accident in my custody and leave me under perpetual suspicion of having done it on purpose. But if you care to send me a set of proofs to this address (I shall be here until the 20th) I may be able to glance through them and correct one or two of the more outrageous errors in matters of fact which most of my commentators fall into.

'I am much obliged to you for offering me the opportunity.

Faithfully,

G. BERNARD SHAW.'

The proofs were duly sent; Shaw thought highly of the book and returned the proofs heavily annotated. Naturally both the author and we wanted to include the annotations though they would have involved considerable expense for typesetting, re-make up, etc. Shaw's reply to the author's request for permission was to ask to see the agreement. The author sent it to him without apparently mentioning the circumstances under which it had been arranged. Shaw did not at that time know me and obviously suspected the worst. He agreed to the inclusion of the annotations provided we refunded the £75 but nevertheless paid the abnormal royalties designed to reimburse the £75 and were content with a five-year licence. We went into the matter most closely, but found that by the time we had paid for the re-make up, etc., even if we printed a larger edition we should lose money on every copy sold if that quite abnormal scale of royalties was applied. And in those days it was a luxury we could not afford, so the book appeared without Shaw's annotations.

The sequel was interesting. Some years later (in 1929) when

Shaw was recommending people to sell his letters while the going was good, I chanced to notice an entry in Hodgson's catalogue:

'Lot 467 Shaw (G.B.) A Series of 3 Autograph letters and one typed letter (each with envelope), also 2 postcards connected with the publication of the "Quintessence" referring to the agreement, the Society of Authors, the American rights and royalties, written between 11th January and 25th August, 1920.'

I hastened to Chancery Lane and found, as was to be anticipated, that the correspondence referred to me and was libellous. It ended with a postcard, the last paragraph of which read as follows:

'Why, oh *Why* did you throw all that good money to the sharks? It is all very capital for them and for me; but for you!—well, it can't be helped, d—n it.'

The following correspondence ensued:

18th June, 1929.

'Dear Mr Shaw,

'I have just been examining some letters and postcards, written by you to Mr H. C. Duffin, which are now on view at Hodgsons and are to be sold on Thursday.

'You are entitled to think I am a "shark", and that I "take every possible advantage of an author". You are, I imagine, privileged to say as much as you do (and more) in *private* letters to Mr Duffin. But I should be surprised to learn that the law permits you to authorise the sale of your libellous remarks by public auction, with the consequent publicity this gives to my customers, the booksellers—not to mention the public at large.

'I think you would find it very difficult to "justify" your statements about me in a Court of Law, but that is, I hope, an irrelevant question, because I refuse to believe that you had, or at any rate have, any wish or intention to injure me. You have on several occasions shown me a courtesy and consideration (notably in connection with my book, *The Truth About Publishing*) which you would hardly have extended to a "shark".

Bertrand Russell, OM

Gilbert Murray, OM

John H. Muirhead

G. Lowes Dickinson

Lancelot Hogben

Harold J. Laski

Sir S. Radhakrishnan

Arthur Waley, CH

'The first step is clearly for Lot 467 to be withdrawn from the sale, and we have telegraphed and written to Mr Duffin to this effect.

'I think you will agree that the next move is with you. Obviously the matter is urgent, and I am accordingly sending a copy of this letter to you, by express registered post, to Ayot St Lawrence, in case you happen to be there.

Yours sincerely,
STANLEY UNWIN.'

19th June, 1929.

'Dear Mr Stanley Unwin,

'I am very sorry. I was on the point of wiring Duffin and Hodgson when my secretary rang up from London to say that Duffin has withdrawn the letters. The present mania for relics (prethumous) is a terrible nuisance to me. My letters fetch large sums; and I have no power to prevent their sale. I can prevent multiplication of copies, as the owners possess only the material sheet of paper; but I cannot prevent the exhibition of the sheet in an auction room for inspection by purchasers. It seems to me, however, that such exhibition must constitute publication as distinct from infringement of copyright, and that a libelled person therefore has a remedy against the auctioneer or his principal or both.

'At all events your protest has, I am glad to note, proved promptly effective.

'I always tell young authors who consult me that publishing is a gamble in which the publisher, who must make one best-seller pay for several duds, must take every advantage he can obtain, and that it is up to the author to take care of himself. That, I think, is sound.

'Of course, I had forgotten all about my counsel to Mr Duffin when I said he could sell my letters; but I certainly did not mean to absolve him from all discretion in the matter.

'Shark is a generic term, used without malice. But it shouldn't be thrown about in public.

'I greatly regret the annoyance the incident has caused you, and crave your forgiveness for my share in it.

Faithfully,
G. BERNARD SHAW.'

'Dear Mr Shaw,   20th June, 1929.

'Thank you very much for your most courteous letter. I felt sure that you had forgotten what you wrote, and that your action was prompted solely by a generous wish to benefit Mr Duffin.

'I do not agree with you that a publisher *must* take every advantage he can obtain, but I do agree that the author should take care of himself and join the Authors Society.

'When you wrote your letters I am sure you did not realise that we had stated in writing to Mr Duffin (through his agents) that, in view of the fantastic price of paper and the costs of production generally which were then still rising, it was in our judgment impossible for his book to be made to pay, and that if he contributed towards the cost, as he offered to do, he would only get about half his outlay back even were the entire edition of 1,000 copies sold. I have just re-read the correspondence and do not see how the facts could have been put before him more clearly. Actually the production (owing to rising prices) cost us even more than we estimated, and the gross proceeds of the sales have not to this day covered our out-of-pocket expenses for printing, paper and binding. . . .

'Thanking you once again for your charming letter—which I do not propose to sell!   I am,
                                        Yours sincerely,
                                        STANLEY UNWIN.'

I made no claim for 'damages', but I did claim possession of the libellous letters and postcards which I have before me as I write.

My next encounter with G.B.S. was in connection with one of the first series of Broadcast Talks, *Points of View*, edited by G. Lowes Dickinson. All the six speakers except Shaw signed the agreement submitted to them by Curtis Brown. In a letter to Lowes Dickinson confirming his refusal Shaw described it as 'a mountainous absurdity' that any publisher should say that a collection of essays by him (Dickinson), Dean Inge, H. G. Wells, Sir Oliver Lodge, J. B. S. Haldane was not good enough without him, and at the conclusion of his letter said:

'all the broadcasters are, like yourself, personal friends of mine; and far from disregarding their interests I am leaving more money to be divided between them in royalties'.

If Shaw had been the last speaker in the series his statement might be justified, but unfortunately he was the first and the subsequent speakers referred to his talk, which made the volume (which I had contracted with the other speakers to publish) an incomplete work—a point upon which reviewers naturally fastened.

The first time that I met Shaw in person I told him bluntly that he had treated me very badly. He pulled himself up and said, 'How so?' I recalled these two instances, gave him the miserable sales figures of the incomplete broadcasts, and told him that Duffin had eventually recovered the whole of his £75 in royalties, though the process had taken many years. Shaw's reply was, 'Well! you and I were wrong and Duffin was right'. It is quite clear that Shaw was wrong, but I have only his word for it that I was.

From that moment onwards Shaw went out of his way to show me courtesy and consideration. On a later occasion when I wanted to include one of his broadcasts in a symposium, he said, 'Will this do?' and proceeded to write:

'Pursuant to our conversation of yesterday I hereby authorise you to print and publish my recent broadcast on freedom in the projected BBC collection of Series of Talks on that subject; and I undertake not to raise any question of author's fees as between us unless and until the number of copies printed exceeds 7,500 copies.'

and at another time, when we were discussing his 'Whither England?' broadcast, he ended his letter with the kindly words:

'I should of course have no objection to your very public-spirited imprint.'

I noticed in the *Manchester Guardian* of August 19, 1929, Sir Edward Elgar's statement that Bernard Shaw's Music Criticisms ought to be republished, and that he (Elgar) would like to edit them. I drew Shaw's attention to Elgar's remark and added that 'it would be a thousand pities for material so calculated to arouse intelligent interest in music to remain buried in the files of

The Saturday Reviewer or elsewhere. This provoked a postcard reply:

'I shall have to get these old things together for the long delayed Collected Edition of my works; But God forbid that I should waste Elgar's time on the editorial drudgery.'

Towards the end of 1933, Shaw included Edward Carpenter's 'England Arise!' in his play *On the Rocks*, and, without any reference to us, had a gramophone record made of it for the purpose. In accordance with instructions from one of the Carpenter literary trustees, I drew Shaw's attention to the copyright infringement, pointing out that the music as well as the words were by Carpenter; that as the song was actually sung in the course of the play, there was presumably a question of performing right, as well as the mechanical rights, about which we had been in correspondence with the Gramophone Co. Ltd. There was also the right to reprint the words in the play when it was published in book form. The trustee felt that, in view of the probable continued use of the words and music, a substantial payment should be made, but added that as both he and Shaw were members of the Society of Authors, it was appropriate that the Society should be consulted concerning the appropriate payment. Shaw's reply was characteristic:

'I enclose the result of my inquiry, which I addressed to HMV as a better mark for it than the Society of Authors. Between ourselves I have no doubt at all that my use of "England Arise" is well within the limits of "fair quotation", which are familiar to me as a much quoted—not to say pirated—person; but as you think that the copyrights are not too lucrative, we had better arrange for a ten guinea fee, which will be good business for the executors.

'It is not possible nor desirable to put an acknowledgment in the program, as it would imply that the record is on sale by HMV. This is expressly excluded in the form of receipt which I have drafted. The record is quite unsaleable, as it gives forth a great deal of cheering and street disturbances with the unemployed bawling the tune in unison in all sorts of dialects. I have of course given the song as Carpenter's in the book.'

The suggestion of 'fair quotation' was, of course, nonsense, but as the trustees authorized us to accept the proferred fee, the affair ended happily, with best wishes for the success of the play.

A letter in July 1937 suggesting that it was high time a collection of his letters should be published brought the following amusing answer:

'There are some billions of letters of mine in existence. Some thousands of them have been purchased and kept by Gabriel Wells, who has often proposed to publish collectors' editions of them. But as this would have involved my reading them, and I'd rather have died, they await my death and the action of the Public Trustee who will inherit them. I am delighted to learn that you have a very large sum of money to gamble with; but I doubt whether it would be really friendly to let you. I am grateful all the same.'

At one time or another I had the privilege of introducing distinguished people to him such as Walter Rathenau, of whom I shall have more to say later, and Asgeir Asgeirson, at one time Prime Minister and later President of Iceland, and it was at a lunch given to the latter I first met Mrs Shaw. Following her death I wrote to Shaw:

'My dear Bernard Shaw,

'You will be receiving more letters than you can cope with. Nevertheless I feel I must let you know how much you are in my thoughts and how much I feel for you. It is indeed strange that you and Sidney Webb should have lost your wives—and such wives— so soon after one another.

'When I lunched with you and Mrs Shaw a few years back I had the privilege of sitting next to her. Later that afternoon someone asked me what had impressed me most about that delightful occasion, and I replied without a second's hesitation "Mrs Bernard Shaw". In view of my overwhelming regard for you, could there be a greater tribute to her personality? What a wonderful companion you have had. But please don't let her loss discourage you, because your voice and clear mind are still as greatly needed as ever. The youngest old man I ever met was ninety-nine, so that you have time ahead of you.

Yours most sincerely,

STANLEY UNWIN.'

To this Shaw replied:

'She always assumed that I was the attraction, even when I was clearly the detrimental; and it pleases me greatly when I get fresh evidence that she was wrong. So your letter is right on the spot.

'It all came off quite happily.

G. BERNARD SHAW.'

One incident at that luncheon I shall never forget. Shaw was talking a lot of nonsense about Mussolini and Mrs Shaw turned to me and said, 'Do you agree with him?' I shook my head. 'Neither do I', she said.

CHAPTER 12

THE NINETEEN-TWENTIES

During my Fisher Unwin days and thereafter, I was a member of the National Liberal Club, which has a most excellent library. But in the First World War the premises were requisitioned and the club was moved to Victoria Street. When I found that owing to its distance from Museum Street I had not visited it for a whole year, I resigned. I thus welcomed the opening of the much more conveniently situated 1917 Club. In *Remembering my Good Friends*,[1] Mrs Mary Agnes Hamilton writes that it was

'planned to be a point of rapprochement for Liberal and Labour people who felt the same about the war. Its actual birthday coincided with the first Russian Revolution. This tremendous event acted like a galvanic shock. At last, something good had come out of the war. Indeed we felt inclined to go about quoting Edmund Burke on the French Revolution—"How much the greatest event is this that has happened since the beginning of the world, and how much the best!" '

In its early days it was a most interesting place. The premises, No. 4 Gerrard Street, left a good deal to be desired; we fed in the basement on bare wooden tables; the diet was austere, but astonishingly good in relation to the modest prices charged. All the Left Wing intellectuals were members; at lunch time the place was usually full of distinguished people, including many Allen & Unwin authors, such as H. N. Brailsford, C. Delisle Burns, Charles Roden Buxton, Seymour Cocks, G. D. H. and Margaret Cole, G. Lowes Dickinson, Gerald and Barbara Ayrton Gould, J. A. Hobson, Pethick Lawrence, E. D. Morel, H. W. Nevinson, Arthur Ponsonby, Bertrand Russell. Nearly all the future members of the first Labour Government including, of course, Herbert Morrison, were members, besides many younger people destined

[1] London: Jonathan Cape, 1944.

to become famous such as Krishna Menon, Leslie Plummer and John Strachey.

'In its heyday [writes Mrs Hamilton], there was no ceremony and not much manners. Everybody talked to everybody. The "stars" coruscated freely at lunch time; after lunch, a big circle would gather round to hear them talk—above all, to hear MacDonald.'

Those present will not forget Ramsay MacDonald's arrival there from Buckingham Palace after his appointment as Premier.

But, as Margaret Goldsmith reminded me, one of the most striking features of the Club was the lack of respect for famous names. The waitress Gertie once asked Ramsay MacDonald 'not to sit down at the high table of which he was not a member, as the members of the table wouldn't like it'.

Although Left Wing politics predominated, the interests of literature, music, science and the drama were well represented. As examples, George Orwell, Francis Meynell, A. L. Bacharach, Harriet Cohen, Dr H. Levy, Harold Scott were members. That distinguished actress Elsa Lanchester, with her flaming red hair and her startlingly unusual costumes, was quite a feature of the Club. It must, however, be admitted that many who, though politically to the Left, were conservatives sartorially, were sometimes shocked by her departures from convention.

Mr J. E. Parley recalled in the *News Chronicle* an amusing incident:

' "Some 30 of us", he writes, "mostly young men with long hair and young women with short, were in the lounge when the door suddenly opened to disclose the commanding figure of Mrs Hamilton.

' "With one sweeping glance round the room, she barked, 'Ah, nobody here!' and was gone. How right she was!" '

Although it was a good place, and well run in its early days, it degenerated sadly and in less than fifteen years had ceased to be.

Mention of the 1917 Club brings to my mind Dr Walther Rathenau, who achieved miracles in maintaining German supplies during the First World War when his country was so effectively blockaded. He was indeed a remarkable man—a rare combination of contradictions—a philosopher, yet a man of action; a multi-millionaire, yet a keen socialist. He shrewdly criticized what he termed 'official socialism', and was the prophet of a utopia which was to embody all that was best in the socialist vision. He was the leading spirit in the AEG, the huge German electrical combine; but as a philosopher he looked beyond the problems and the conflicts of the hour.

When he arrived in London in 1920 for the first time after the end of the war he was very nervous. Some of the best hotels were still refusing German guests, and he admitted that the friendly reception I had given him, first on the telephone and then at my office, came as a great relief. When I offered him the alternative of lunch at the Savoy or a primitive meal at the 1917 Club he unhesitatingly accepted the latter. First-class hotels and restaurants, he said, were no treat to him, but the 1917 Club sounded unique. I arranged for a number of people to meet him and we had a most enjoyable time. It was the beginning of a warm friendship. I published an English edition of his book, *In Days to Come*, which I found most interesting; but I still remember the retort of Eden Paul, who translated it, when I asked for an index, 'You can't index a fog'. When in the late spring of 1922 I visited Rathenau in Berlin, he gave me the option of a dinner party in my honour or an evening meal with him alone in his villa at Grünewald. I chose the latter. I found him highly cultured, incredibly well informed and charming, and the evening passed all too quickly.

A few weeks later the world learnt with surprise and horror that this man, who had served his country so well, had been assassinated. Those were the early days of violent German anti-Semitism, of which we were all to learn so much later. Men of Rathenau's calibre are rare, and it was a loss Germany could ill afford. Like many great men he had a remarkable mother, and on my next visit to Berlin I took the opportunity to have a talk with her about her distinguished son.

Another remarkable, but much less pleasant, author I encountered in 1920 was Major C. H. Douglas, who captivated so many people in such diverse parts of the world with his economic theories. He came to me at the instigation of A. R. Orage, himself a whole-hearted convert to the 'Douglas Credit Theory' as it came to be called. Because Douglas's ideas seemed to me to have something in common with J. A. Hobson's views upon 'Under-consumption' with which I had long been impressed, I approached the typescript, *Economic Democracy*, with special interest and promised to read it personally. Unfortunately, before there had been time for me to do so, I collapsed with a most acute attack of influenza. Douglas could not wait for me to recover; he called at my home and demanded to see me. As I was running a high temperature, my wife (rightly) refused. Thereafter he kept asking her on the telephone whether I had completed the reading of his book. At that time I was running the business single-handed and my absence from the office presented difficulties. Although I was still far from well, my doctor agreed that, provided I went by car both ways, well wrapped up and stayed less than an hour, I might go to Museum Street. Somehow Major Douglas got wind of it and was awaiting my arrival. Without any 'by your leave' he followed me to my room and demanded an immediate decision. I reminded him that I had been too ill to look at his work, and that he could see for himself that I was still not well enough to do so. As he persisted in demanding a decision there and then, I handed him his typescript.

But that was not the end. He took it to Cecil Palmer, who became his publisher until he failed, whereupon Major Douglas returned to me with the suggestion that I should take over his books on the terms he had obtained from Cecil Palmer. I explained that the royalties Cecil Palmer had contracted to pay, but had not in fact paid him, were uneconomic. As he was not prepared to modify them we again parted company. And history repeated itself. He turned to another small firm which accepted his terms, but soon went into liquidation. It was a wonderful illustration of the truth of my old dictum: a 10 per cent royalty that arrives the day it is due is better than a 20 per cent royalty that is never forthcoming.

My reference to John A. Hobson's 'Under-consumption'

theory prompts me to point out that he anticipated Keynes, who in the great depression of the nineteen-thirties arrived at similar views.

In an article in *The New Statesman*[1] on the centenary of Hobson's birth, G. D. H. Cole wrote:

'He was among the half-dozen most upright men I have ever known, and also, I think, among the half-dozen ablest and most congenial. For to me at any rate what is commonly known as the Keynsian was much more the Hobsonian revolution in economic and social thought.'

In a letter to Cole, Keynes expressed his sense of the injustice meted out to Hobson. An honorary degree would have been an appropriate recognition of the injustice, but though I did my utmost to secure him one it was not forthcoming.

It was about this time that I wrote to D. H. Lawrence, expressing my readiness to publish a small book for him on the Education of the People. Nothing came of it, but I had the satisfaction of learning later that my approach and obvious interest in his views on education had greatly cheered him at a time when he was much depressed.

On December 1, 1920, I took over The Swarthmore Press Ltd. Philip Burtt, late Passenger Manager of the North Eastern Railway, an ardent Quaker, had acquired the publishing side of Headley Brothers and planned to build up under the imprint of The Swarthmore Press a business not unlike mine but with a more definite Quaker Pacifist background—a most difficult undertaking. He was a fellow member of the 1917 Club and we were most friendly rivals. His unflagging cheery optimism about the results he was achieving alarmed me. It was too good to be true. I repeatedly asked him whether he was *sure* that his stock had been depreciated adequately, and the invariable reply was that it had been drastically dealt with. Unfortunately, when the showdown finally came, he found that, like so many publishers before him, he had deceived himself and that his stock would not fetch anything like the figures at which it stood in his balance

[1] July 5, 1958.

sheet. He could have put the company in liquidation and avoided any personal liability, but being the good Quaker he was he saw to it that the creditors were paid in full out of his own pocket. When I drew the attention of two or three of the bigger firms to the sacrifice Philip Burtt was making to pay everyone in full they were so impressed that they voluntarily waived a portion of their debts.

The purchase of The Swarthmore Press helped me in two ways. It added many interesting authors and titles to our list including Ramsay MacDonald's beautiful memoir of his wife Margaret MacDonald, The Christian Revolution Series, the Swarthmore International Handbooks, and some attractive books on gardening and dairying, and it also gave me an alternative imprint. I sold all the assets to George Allen & Unwin, but kept the company in being so that I could accept for publication at my own risk books of which my colleague Skinner disapproved. A case occurred almost at once, Romain Rolland's book on Gandhi. Either a book by Rolland or one on Gandhi was objectionable in Skinner's eyes; the combination of the two was altogether too much for him to swallow and it appeared (with considerable success) under The Swarthmore Press imprint. But that was many years ago and the company has long since ceased to function.

Another firm that grew up at the same time as The Swarthmore Press and with which I became connected was Maunsel & Co. Ltd. of Dublin, who published for A.E., Synge, St John Ervine, and other distinguished Irish authors. At first we acted as their selling agents, but eventually, when they failed to make ends meet, we took over much of their stock and some of their agreements and thus became the publishers of the plays of Synge and St John Ervine.

As the publisher of Freud's *Interpretation of Dreams*, it was natural that I should have the privilege of publishing his *Introductory Lectures on Psychoanalysis*, which still enjoys a steady sale and also be granted the selling agency for the International Psycho-Analytical Press which was set up at that time. Unfortunately the agency did not last many years, because, in accordance with my practice of maintaining an open forum, I ventured to publish a book critical of Freud. That was a heinous offence and the agency was forthwith transferred elsewhere—by no means the only instance where insistence upon freedom to publish conflicting points of view has cost me dearly. In that connection I am always glad that I had the courage to publish at that period *Under the Searchlight: The Record of a Great Scandal* by Violet Douglas-Pennant. The facts are simple. Miss Douglas-Pennant, who had a most distinguished public career, was invited by the Air Ministry in April 1918 to become Commandant of the WRAF (Women's Royal Air Force) and was appointed on June 18, 1918. On August 16, 1918, she asked General Paine's leave to resign Commandantship as a protest against certain irregularities. On August 17th her resignation was refused by Lord Weir and General Paine on the ground that her services were too valuable. Ten days later she was summarily dismissed by Lord Weir and Sir Auckland Geddes on the strength of secret 'serious' information provided by two subordinates (temporary women war workers) which was accepted without inquiry, and never investigated and never disclosed. Miss Douglas-Pennant was never allowed to know of what she was accused. It was another Dreyfus case, and because it happened in war-time the people responsible thought they could hush it up. The wrong was never righted, but its exposure was beneficial.

I was, I imagine, the first British publisher to visit Germany after the war. I did so both on business and (later) as a member of the party which went in April 1922, under the late Canon Streeter's leadership, to study conditions over there. Our Governmental handling of the situation immediately following the end of the First World War will not stand investigation. It was redeemed only by the heroic determination of the Quakers to feed the starving German children. Both trips were in their respective ways peculiarly instructive. I found that during the war the Germans had developed the offset process (photolithography), describing it under such trade names as 'Manul', 'Rodardruck', etc. Its great possibilities were obvious and I immediately used it to bring back into print books such as Hare's *Walks in London*, of which we had neither plates nor blocks. We enjoyed a clear run of nearly two years before the process was developed in England and used by our competitors. The prejudice against anything 'Made in Germany' was at that time so great that I adopted the phrase 'Printed in Saxony' which aroused no such deep-seated emotions, and continued to do so until the American Customs expressed ignorance of the existence of such a place as Saxony and decreed that the wording did not conform with their regulations. I have never forgotten, when Germany was suffering from acute inflation, having to instruct our bankers to pay C. G. Röder of Leipzig for one of these reprints 739,000,000,000 Marks, which before the war would have represented more than the total German National Debt.

When I was in Berlin, my good friends the two partners in Dietrich Reimer, the geographical publishers, showed me a book on Egypt. The text was unbelievably dull, but the coloured illustrations were superb. 'Give me a quotation for 3,000 sets of those illustrations on paper suitable for mounting', I said. 'But what about the book?' they replied. 'I am not interested in the book; forget it', I said. They were anxious to do business and complied. The illustrations cost me little in sterling and I commissioned someone to write a popular book on Egypt to go with them. The result was an attractive book full of coloured illustrations issued at a popular price. It sold so well that we had to replenish our supplies of illustrations. A competitor who envied me such a quick-selling line said that he had worked out the cost and I must be losing money on every copy I sold. He was left more than ever puzzled when I assured him that the book carried an unusually large profit margin. I cite this merely as an instance of the diverse ways books may come into existence, and of the use of imagination in business. Another instance on the same trip was the sight of Felix Meiner's *Selbstdarstellungen*, which led to my commissioning the volume on *Contemporary British Philosophy* in the Muirhead Library, in which all the then leading British philosophers summarized their beliefs.

The visit with Canon Streeter was intensely interesting. We interviewed endless prominent people. Of all those we saw the man who most impressed us was Ernst Troeltsch, whose *magnum opus* on *The Social Teaching of the Christian Churches* I subsequently published by arrangement with the Sir Halley Stewart Trust. Troeltsch was in every way a big man. He was open, frank, well informed, and made no attempt to excuse or defend, as many others had done, things which from a Christian point of view were indefensible.

One of the greatest joys of the kind of publishing I have attempted is the personal contact into which it brings one with really great people. My connection with C. F. Andrews (to whom I shall refer later) and Selly Oak College brought me into association with Albert Schweitzer, whose lectures, *Christianity and the Religions of the World*, formed Volume 3 of the Selly Oak College Series which my firm published. To know Schweitzer is to love as well as to admire him. Oddly enough my first conversation with him was due to his need of a hair-cut and his inability to describe in English his precise requirements. I offered to accompany him to act as his interpreter and to ensure that it was done in the way he wished. With that little incident our friendship started, and I have been in touch with him ever since, and had the very great privilege of publishing his two volumes of autobiography—*Memoirs of Childhood and Youth* and *My Life and Thought*.

The outbreak of the First World War had produced many hastily conceived regulations about aliens. One of the sufferers was Dr Oscar Levy, editor and proprietor of the English translations of the complete works of Nietzsche. He had long been resident in England, and it was so absurd that he should be turned out that I took up the cudgels on his behalf. This provoked a statement in *The Times* of September 27, 1921, as follows:

'*Expulsion of a German Scholar.* The Home Secretary has sent a letter to Mr Stanley Unwin, replying to his protest against the expulsion of Dr Oscar Levy under the Aliens Restriction Amendment Act 1919.

'Mr Shortt, after explaining the provisions of the Act, states: "Dr Levy, being of German nationality, is a 'former enemy alien' within the meaning of the Act, and his residence in this country before the war does not except him from the statutory provisions. He left this country of his own accord in January 1915, and when in April 1920 he desired to return, in order, as he represented, to transact business with his publisher, he was allowed to land for a period of three months on that 'special ground'. Subsequently temporary extensions of time were granted to him, *having satisfied myself* at first on the ground that his business with the publisher was not finished, and, later, on the strength of medical certificates as to his state of health. In August of this year, having regard to the long extensions already granted, and having satisfied myself that the state of his health could not prevent him from travelling, I came to the conclusion that there were no longer special grounds, within the meaning of the Act, on which I could renew for any further period the temporary permission, and I had to tell Dr Levy that he must make immediate arrangements to leave the country." Mr Shortt adds: "So far from using my powers against Dr Levy, I have used such limited powers as are conferred on me by this Act to make the utmost possible concessions in his favour". '

I am far from being a Nietzschean but I felt so indignant about the whole affair that as a gesture to Dr Levy I offered to advance, free of interest, the whole of the cost of reprinting the complete works for him and to credit him with the whole of the proceeds of the sales, less a commission which did not even cover our overhead expenses. It was a gesture which later I was given some cause to regret, but that aspect of the matter is best forgotten. The whole of the sheet stock was destroyed in the 'Blitz', and as it was Dr Levy's property and not ours we could claim no compensation. The bound stock was soon exhausted, so once again the complete works are unavailable. I offered to reprint some of the volumes on a royalty basis, but the offer was declined.

When I asked Arthur Waley one day what he was going to do next he replied that he would like to translate a novel by Lady Murasaki, *The Tale of Genji*, written in the days of King Canute in early Japanese which a modern Japanese could no more read than could the average Englishman read Anglo-Saxon. He added that it was so long—six volumes in Japanese—that no publisher could be expected to commit himself to its publication in English. 'Is it a really outstanding work?' I inquired. Waley's quiet reply: 'Oh yes, one of the two or three greatest novels ever written', startled me. 'Well then', I said, 'we must find a way of doing it', and there and then our plans were laid to carry through the venture on a basis which kept the risk of loss to reasonable dimensions. I had implicit faith in Waley's judgment, but it was not until he delivered the first volume that I realized what a gem he had brought us. His translation is so superb that it has a steady sale in Japan where it is read by many in preference to versions in modern Japanese.

Among strange authors whom I have met I should certainly name Robert Briffault. We had published his first book, *The Making of Humanity*, with some success; his second book, *Psyche's Lamp*, with less, when he brought me his *magnum opus*, *The Mothers*. He warned me that it would involve more 'corrections' than an ordinary book, but agreed that if I allowed him £150 instead of about £50, which would then have been the normal amount, there would be no trouble. To this I consented. When the correction bill exceeded £250 I voluntarily offered, in view of the importance of the work, to double the correction allowance and make it £300, but made it clear that beyond that we could not go. Corrections and additions continued to pour in. Protests were met with the statement that he would disown the book were they not made. A trebling of the allowance did not satisfy him and eventually he incurred a personal liability of about £600 which he had not the wherewithal to meet. Years later, when in America he became a best-selling author—of books critical of Britain—the editor of one of the most famous New York publishers wrote me a letter to the effect that it was disgraceful— nay, monstrous—the way I had treated Briffault in the matter of corrections. I gave the editor the facts, and asked him whether he could name an American publisher who would have behaved with greater forbearance. To that letter no reply, let alone an apology, was forthcoming. I mention the incident in order to suggest the desirability of checking the facts before swallowing *all* the statements made about publishers' wickednesses.

In 1940 there remained 500 sets of the three volumes, from which some profit might eventually have been derived, but the stock of two volumes was destroyed by enemy action, leaving us with 500 unbound copies of an odd volume. At quite disproportionate expense 500 each of the two missing volumes have been replaced, thus making the important work available again. In fairness to Briffault I must add that he had (at any rate until he went to America) a sad and difficult life and accomplished his work under most trying conditions. I find the following letter to Dr Briffault in my file:

'I was extremely sorry that I could not find any justification for adding (even temporarily) to the amount of your indebtedness to my firm. But that does not preclude me from doing something personally. Although it is not as much as you need, I hope the enclosed cheque may be of some slight service to you in your financial difficulties. The question of repayment is entirely optional, as I have no wish to add to your debts, and the amount will not be regarded as such by me.'

From this it will be seen that it is only the American editor, who ought to have known better, about whom I feel a trifle bitter.

Harold J. Laski was a model author. It was early in 1925 I think when he walked into my office with the enormous typescript of *The Grammar of Politics*. I was so impressed that I took the typescript home with me that same evening, and he had my acceptance almost in a matter of hours. I don't think he ever forgot the rapidity of my decision at that rather critical moment in his career. From then onwards we published practically all his books; one which went elsewhere 'as a sacrifice on the altar of an old college friendship', as he said, subsequently returned to us. His one weakness was reluctance to give that last revision and polish to his typescripts from which they would have benefited, and I have often wondered whether it would not have been in his interests had I stipulated for a final revision, including the deletion of repetitions and the all too frequent use of some particular word like 'penumbra', before accepting *The Grammar of Politics*. Had he lived, we should have had a revised edition, because he was at work upon it. Publishing for Laski was a real pleasure, and I always enjoyed his visits and his stories, whether true or almost too good to be true. I don't remember ever having any unpleasantness or difficulty with him during our long association, and he apparently approved of me, for in one letter he described me as 'an ideal publisher to deal with, for you relieve the author from care', and in looking through his books I noticed one inscribed in his neat little handwriting: 'To Sir Stanley Unwin, the best of publishers'. Two brief notes from him I particularly treasure; one in acknowledging receipt of a cheque sent with an account of sales said 'it made him feel that a good publisher is "Embalmed and treasured up on purpose to a life beyond life" '; the other reads: 'Your cheque pleased me, but your letter pleased me more'.

Two incidents also I recall which gave me peculiar satisfaction. In 1932 Laski had written something which indicated that he felt that in some constitutional problem the King had shown bias, or was inadequately informed. I felt sure that Laski was wrong. The one man who could put him right was Lord Wigram, who to my personal knowledge took infinite pains to be fully informed of all conflicting points of view and to ensure that any advice he gave was scrupulously correct. Lord Wigram most kindly agreed to meet Laski, and the three of us had tea together on the balcony of the Reform Club. It amused me that we should meet there, because only a week or two before Laski's nomination for membership had been withdrawn because of the outcry it aroused. The meeting was a great success. Laski was immensely impressed, and Lord Wigram wrote to me from St James's Palace:

'Many thanks for an interesting talk with Professor Laski, whom I much enjoyed meeting. He was so much more understanding than I had expected and we had many points in common. I shall read his articles and books with increased interest now that I have met him.'

The other incident was in 1946. I had occasion to inform Laski that negotiations for a Serbo-Croat translation of *Liberty in the Modern State* had been terminated because he had fallen from favour with the Yugoslav authorities, and that 'the matter must be considered closed unless', as the Central Office of Information wrote, 'Mr. Laski changes his views about Communism or a change takes place in the Yugoslav regime'. Laski replied:

'In the course of a very long experience of publishing books I have had no letter that gave me so attractive a moment as the one you sent me from Belgrade. On a wet and gloomy day it really is a source of joy.'

When I received the typescript of Trotsky's *Where is Britain Going?* I found myself in a quandary owing to the virulence of his attacks on Ramsay MacDonald. Now I lived near MacDonald, and his wife was a distant relative of my father. It was MacDonald's practice to leave his home at 7.20 every morning (you could set your watch by the time of his departure) regardless of all-night sittings, late dinners or other considerations, for a walk—the same walk—on Hampstead Heath. He was accompanied by a fellow Highlander, Dr James Bonar, descendant of the hymn-writer and author of *The Philosophy of Political Economy* in our Muirhead Library of Philosophy. I frequently joined them. Bonar was a good old-fashioned Liberal, and they sparred unceasingly. Whether because I was a relative of his wife, or because he knew that I had no journalistic proclivities, MacDonald was most outspoken with us and I learnt much about the background of events, how much it meant to him, for example, to secure Sir William Jowitt as Attorney General. The only note I ever made of those conversations was after the Stresa Conference. It reads:

'Musso: "Do you still believe in Socialism?"
'J.R.M.: "Yes, more than ever, and what about you?"

'Musso: "Yes, I do too. Governing under a capitalist regime has more than ever confirmed me. You cannot trust the capitalists—they always cheat".'

Well, cheating was a subject upon which Mussolini could speak with authority.

On one such walk I asked MacDonald whether he would regard it as an unfriendly act if I published a virulent attack upon him by Trotsky. 'On the contrary,' he replied, 'go right ahead, whatever he says about me. Attacks from that quarter are a compliment.'

One of the most interesting and best-informed journalists I ever met was a Czech, Robert Saudek. His hobby—I think he might have said profession—was graphology. He came to me with an enormous typescript on *The Psychology of Handwriting*, which I am afraid I received with much scepticism. I did not believe that it could be scientific. He did not at that time know me, so I handed him a specimen of my writing. The long analysis (in German) which he sent me was startling in its accuracy and the reasons given were convincing. It is too long to reprint, but anyone who knows me would agree, for example, with the following paragraph taken from the middle of it:

'His urge towards a pregnant clarity, towards the avoidance of the possibility of misunderstandings, is always awake in him, and this for two reasons. First, because he is sedulous to avoid any misunderstanding which may lead to the wasting of time, and because he is above all anxious to avoid waste of time. Secondly, because all his activities are directed towards the simplification of function, towards the avoidance of complication. Just as his speech is terse and pregnant, so his simplified letter forms (in handwriting) show only the essential framework without needless flourishes. His handwriting is free from fussiness, for fussiness is disagreeable to him.'

But he produced much other evidence and satisfied me that there was more in graphology than I thought. We published the book and its sequel, *Experiments with Handwriting*, and could have sold more but were handicapped by the fact that all the specimens of handwriting were produced by him in Holland (in connection with foreign editions) and in war-time we had no access to them. Saudek loved to secure my undivided attention, and with astuteness succeeded in doing so on at least one day each year. He knew of my enthusiasm for tennis and invited me to Wimbledon. He fetched me at my office and the understanding was that I was entirely at his disposal except when games were actually in progress. I always chose the last Friday and thus saw in his company the famous match Gregory and Collins against Allison and Van Ryn, about which it might almost be said that the result turned on a net cord shot. Collins's volleying and Gregory's service and smashing were superb.

But Saudek was helpful to me in other ways. He helped me to establish my unique Czech connections and he told me about *All Quiet on the Western Front* within a few days of the appearance of the first instalment in the *Vossische Zeitung*. In a sense I knew about it too soon. But as it is an instance of the strange concatenation of circumstances which may result in one publisher rather than another securing a best-seller the story is worth telling.

Immediately Saudek told me about the book I wrote to Ullsteins for it. They knew me well because I called upon them on all my frequent visits to Germany. Back came the reply that they had not complete proofs but that they should be sent me as soon as they were available. When they were ready for despatch, the man at Ullsteins who had promised them was either ill or out of Berlin—I forget which. A set was sent to their London correspondent. Under ordinary circumstances that would not have mattered because he would have brought them in to me. But we had recently declined a book of his on the British Labour Movement on the very proper grounds that it was written for a public outside Britain—the reason which equally understandably led Putnams to accept it for the USA. Now as Ullstein's correspondent was visiting Putnams about his own affairs he left the proofs with them. Almost as soon as he had done so he heard from Berlin that the book was to be offered to me. But it was too late; Putnams had immediately accepted it.

Knowing about a book too soon may be as bad as hearing

about it too late. Hitler's *Mein Kampf* is a case in point. I studied it when it came out and unhesitatingly turned it down. Who would have read it if Hitler had not attained power, and at that time his chances of doing so appeared to be remote.

Spengler's *Decline of the West*, however, I heard about at the right moment, and it has been a steady seller ever since. But the negotiations were not without their tribulations. Spengler wanted to dictate who should undertake the translation. The man he had selected was an Englishman who had taken his degree at Cambridge, so that there was no ground, Spengler asserted, for our not complying, adding that we could not have the rights unless we did. We agreed in principle, but subject to the proviso that we should see and approve a specimen chapter. When it arrived it proved to be hopeless. It turned out that the man in question had lived in Germany about fifteen years and his English had become almost Teutonic in its construction; hence Spengler's confidence in its accuracy. It took him quite a long while to agree that we were better judges of English than he was. But in the end all was well. The translation finally made by C. F. Atkinson was superb.

The year 1926 was a peculiarly happy one for me because it saw the publication of so many books in which I had a deep personal interest, such as President Masaryk's autobiography, *The Making of a State*; Lowes Dickinson's *International Anarchy*, upon which he had been so long and so arduously engaged; my favourite book of Bertrand Russell's, *On Education: Especially in Early Childhood*; Radhakrishnan's *History of Indian Philosophy*, the beginning of my friendship with that most remarkable man. Then there were new books by G. D. H. Cole, J. A. Hobson, Karel Ĉapek, Richard Aldington, H. S. Altham's standard *History of Cricket*, and many more than I can enumerate here. Next year in the best-seller class was Emil Ludwig's *Napoleon*, the first of his books to be translated. Its reception by the book trade was interesting. 'What! Another book on Napoleon? Take it away' was the almost universal response. The subscription (that is, pre-publication) sales were almost nil, and nothing we could say would persuade booksellers that there might be an acceptable new approach to the subject. In a few weeks they were clamouring for more copies than we could supply, because it was a big book and paper of that size (small royal octavo) has to be specially made.

This was another demonstration of the fact that, had I listened to booksellers' advice, excellent as it is in relation to the past, I should long since have been out of business, because nearly all the books out of which we have made most money they would have condemned had they been consulted. And this brings me to my own book, *The Truth About Publishing*, issued about the same time. My colleague, who was all in favour of the publication of the book, would not risk one penny of the firm's money on it, and I had to publish it at my own expense. When confronted with the first copy Denny, the famous bookseller in the Strand, laughed at the idea of anyone wanting such a book. But he had to send to our counter for more than a dozen during the first week after publication and it has gone on selling ever since. Almost within hours of its publication, my well-informed fellow publisher, Swan Stallybrass, came to tell me what a b—— fool I was to teach my competitors their job, an idea that made me laugh. I thought I had made it clear that the book was written to show authors that there was nothing mysterious about publishing, but that it was an exceedingly exacting job. In so far as publishers read it, I anticipated criticism and corrections. To my surprise it was immediately accepted as a kind of 'Publishers' Bible' (Jonathan Cape's phrase) and to my great satisfaction it was immediately translated into German and adopted as a text-book. Its sales were gratifying, but what was much more so was the status it gave me in the publishing world, not merely at home but abroad. F. N. Doubleday, then a dominating figure in American publishing, wrote to invite me to visit him, so that he might sit at my feet. Actually we sat together in a high speed car, the condition under which by that time he found conversation most agreeable.

Doubleday's invitation was only one of the many pressing me

to go to the States. I am very fond of Americans, but I have an intense dislike of American Government red tape and formalities, not to mention their Customs. It is doubtless mere prejudice on my part, but I object to being treated as a potential criminal, cross-examined as such, and having my fingerprints taken. In consequence, though I have probably travelled more extensively than any of my competitors, I have allowed twenty years to elapse between each of my visits to the States. Officialdom once passed, everything is delightful, but what officialdom and what Customs! Volumes would be needed to recount all the ingenious methods by which they discourage imports. Here is an example. In July 1934 the US Customs suddenly levied duty on the cotton content of books imported into the USA. The tax amounted to $·04995 per pound of cotton, so that the duty on fifteen or twenty cases of books might amount to at most two or three dollars. But the labour and expense involved in computing the amount were formidable.

On my arrival in New York, I found that my book had aroused astonishing interest, and I was invited to lecture at Columbia University on 'International Book Distribution'. In Canada, a month later, I had the distinction of being the first British publisher to be made an honorary member of the Toronto Board of Trade.

Now it must be remembered that almost up to that time I had been, except in the eyes of a minority, a semi-outcast in British publishing circles. Had anyone had the temerity to put me up for membership of the Garrick Club, for example, I should have been immediately blackballed. The change in attitude following the publication of *The Truth About Publishing* was as remarkable as it was agreeable.

This enhanced status encouraged me to write to Lord Beaverbrook suggesting that the *Evening Standard* might devote some space to news and reviews of the latest books. At that time not one of the three evening papers devoted any measurable space to literary affairs, and I ventured the opinion that these papers underestimated the public interest in reading. Beaverbrook immediately replied that he would discuss the matter with his editor, and Arnold Bennett's appointment followed, and with it the startling effect of his first review upon the sales of Feuchtwanger's *Jew Süss*, which up to then had lain dormant.

At this point I must temporarily leave publishing to dwell upon another aspect of my life.

My parents were always pressing me to undertake some religious or charitable work. I was (and still am) a Trustee of the Friendly Almshouses, a charity which must in one respect be unique. Throughout its existence, since it was founded by my great-grandmother, it has been managed by her descendants on the female side. They have included, besides her daughter, six grand-daughters, three great-grand-daughters, one great-great-grand-daughter, and a member of the sixth generation is now its chairman. I had also allowed myself to be appointed a member of the Governing Body of the County Secondary School at Battersea, which took up time during office hours which I could ill spare, and was not best pleased, therefore, when I found myself nominated—at my father's instigation—a trustee of the Congregational Pastors Retiring Fund. The claims were many, and the claimants needy. Each case had therefore to be studied with care. One of my responsibilities was the signing of the half-yearly cheques for the annuitants. It made a lasting impression upon me that my father was able to sign 200 cheques while I struggled with 100. Since those days I have often had occasion to envy him that ability.

It was a relief when it was decided, early in 1923, to hand over the fund to the Congregational Union, though it led curiously enough to my becoming a trustee, and eventually chairman, of the Sir Halley Stewart Trust. A special meeting had to be called at which all the leading lights in the Congregational world were present. Mr (later Sir) Halley Stewart, a sturdy old independent, pointed out that in the original trust deed there was provision for 'independents' who were not necessarily accredited Congregational Ministers, whereas under the new dispensation there would be no such provision. Speaker after speaker opposed him. They thought that they could outvote him, but he warned them that their victory would be short-lived (as it proved to be) because he would appeal to the Charity Commissioners. I ventured to say that, much as they might dislike it, Sir Halley was right. Sir Halley and I—the oldest and youngest persons present—were in a minority of two—even my father voted with the majority. My action made a deep impression upon Sir Halley, who had just founded a most interesting charitable trust. The deed had been completed and the trustees appointed, but he nevertheless insisted that provision should immediately be made for an additional trustee—to wit myself. He was a most remarkable man and lived to his hundredth year. He was mentally alert right to the end, and in his receptivity of new ideas the youngest of all his trustees. He wanted me to accept the chairmanship in his lifetime, but I refused so long as his son, Sir Percy Malcolm Stewart, was available.

Later in 1923, at an Annual Meeting of the Congregational Union, someone criticized the management of the Publications Department and said that it needed completely reorganizing by a publisher like Stanley Unwin. My father at once assured the meeting that there was no difficulty about securing my services. I was not a little disturbed when I heard that I had been thus committed. The moment I investigated the position it was clear to me that the only hope of making a success of the publishing and bookselling side of the organization was to make it completely independent. I therefore laid down the most stringent conditions and made it clear that unless they were complied with my services would not be available. I stipulated for the formation of a limited company which I christened the Independent Press, to which the assets of the publishing and bookselling side of the Congregational Union should be assigned at a valuation to be agreed by me; that although the Congregational Union would be the sole shareholders and would have power to sack their directors, neither the Union nor their Finance Committee were to have any say in the management of the company, which would be free to build up its own reserves out of which to finance developments, etc. I hoped that my conditions would be declined and that I should be relieved of a task I had not sought, but they were accepted, and I received a categorical assurance *in writing* 'that the Trading Department would be encouraged to use a large part of its profits for the purpose of development'.

I accordingly valued the stock, and later formed the company which developed into a pleasant and profitable business. But after a lapse of years the very trouble arose which I foresaw and against which I thought I had guarded the Independent Press. The Finance Committee decreed that the entire profits must be paid to them in the form of dividends, and any money needed for the development of the Company, or to meet the increased costs of paper, printing and binding, must be borrowed from the Union. When I protested against this flagrant breach of a written agreement, the Committee took refuge in the statement that the agreement (which I produced) had not been 'minuted'. The incident confirmed my distrust of committees, and particularly religious committees. There are, of course, exceptions, but all too frequently they behave in a way that each individual member of the committee would be ashamed to do. I resigned my Honorary Directorship, and have had nothing to do with the Congregational Union since that date, though I remain an independent and a Nonconformist.

One of the first actions of the Sir Halley Stewart Trust was to found a series of lectures, and the first was on *Science and Human Progress* by Sir Oliver Lodge. From the outset Sir Halley made it clear that it was his special wish that any publications connected with the Trust should be issued by my firm, so that Sir Oliver's book became the first of many Sir Halley Stewart publications with which I have been connected. Bishop Gore's lectures, *Christ and Society*, followed and gave me the opportunity of knowing that saintly and remarkable man. He had been very devoted to Professor George Unwin, author of *Gilds and Companies of London*, and I think a little of George Unwin's mantle must have descended upon my shoulders, so quickly did Gore single me out amongst the Trustees.

It was about this time that T. Fisher Unwin sold his business, and, as mentioned in the chapter about him, I was able to send a postcard to Hans Baedeker saying, 'I am now free to take on the agency for your Guides'. From that moment I once again became the British publisher of those famous red guides, of which an American publisher once said to me, 'I would rather have an out-of-date red Baedeker than an up-to-date Guide in any other colour'.

The closing years of the 'twenties brought me into contact with that remarkable man Hjalmar Schacht. No one without experience of a runaway inflation such as Germany endured can have any conception of what it means. The speed of the depreciation of the purchasing power of what had been before the war one of the most stable currencies was in the end incredible. A housewife might find that the price of some commodity she wanted had risen beyond her means in the brief time occupied in going home to fetch her purse. The only thing to do with money was to spend it before it became valueless. The book trade found that it could not change published prices quick enough. The expedient adopted was to leave the price unchanged and announce each day by how many thousands it had to be multiplied. I still possess a note for 50 million marks which, when I acquired it, was worth a halfpenny, but in a short time was less valuable than the paper upon which it was printed. There was one note which was the subject of much wry humour; if folded in one way it displayed the portrait of an enormously fat German, and in the reverse way a painfully thin and cadaverous one. 'Before and after inflation' was the comment. It paid to borrow money almost regardless of the rate of interest because in a matter of weeks, if not days, it could be repaid in almost worthless notes. Schacht, whose book on *The Stabilization of the Mark* I published, brought an end to this disastrous situation. The mark, which in pre-war days was worth a shilling, had dropped to one-billionth of its value. He created through the Reichs Bank the position—1 billion paper marks (i.e. a million million) $= 1$ gold mark $= \frac{10}{42}$ dollar, and by a voluntary ratio of conversion, which rested on no legal basis of any kind, a Rentenmark, which was taken as equal to this gold mark. Before long, shops were asking for these Rentenmarks in preference to paper marks, so relieved was everybody in Germany to escape from a worthless inflated currency.

But Schacht's financial wizardry went further. He proceeded to make agreements with other countries (e.g. Yugoslavia) to buy their produce and raw materials at above world prices, much to the satisfaction of their primary producers. But simultaneously the countries had to contract to buy, to a corresponding amount, manufactured articles from Germany, which (except for such things as aspirins) had at that time only limited supplies for disposal. The effect was to make the countries which entered into such agreements disagreeably dependent upon Germany, whose recovery they were involuntarily helping to finance.

Some years later I ran into Schacht by chance at Lenzerheide, and was surprised to find that, unlike many Germans, he had a considerable sense of humour. When I asked him how he liked working for Hitler, he replied that working for a Dictator had the great advantage that you got things done without endless talk.

Reference to Schacht reminds me of my correspondence about him with J. M. Keynes, who said that though he agreed with him on some points there were, he was afraid, some rather serious differences between them on issues which were likely to be part of his subject-matter in *The Stabilization of the Mark*.

In the course of the correspondence I had told Keynes how interested I had been in the figures of production costs of Marshall's *Official Papers* and Malthus's *First Essay on Population*, which he had circulated as Secretary of the Royal Economic Society, and said how important I felt it was to secure a better understanding on the part of the public and authors and book-buyers in particular of the basis on which prices of books have to be calculated. The outcome was an invitation to a fascinating luncheon party at 46 Gordon Square, at which Mrs Keynes (Madame Lopokova) was our hostess. The guests were Hubert D. Henderson (the then editor of *The Nation and Athenaeum*),

Leonard Woolf (the Literary Editor) and myself. The subject of our most lively discussion was the public's attitude to books. Keynes's summary at the end of our talk was masterly, and laid the foundation of a series of articles in *The Nation*,[1] subsequently reissued by The Hogarth Press in booklet form under the title *Books and the Public*. It is a symposium still worth reading. To publishers, one paragraph in particular of Keynes's economic analysis of what he described as a profoundly unsatisfactory situation was comforting. He wrote:

'For a long time I was in the habit of maintaining that the fault lay with the publishers. I have become convinced that they are not the guilty ones. The fault lies, first and foremost, with the public—with their wrong psychology towards book-buying, their small expenditure, their mean and tricky ways where a book, the noblest of man's works, is concerned.'

This was the verdict of the man of whom Bertrand Russell wrote:

'He had the sharpest and clearest intellect I have ever known.'

There were other continental authors besides Schacht for whom I was then publishing. Even to mention their names would create a catalogue, but one man stands out, as he always did wherever he was, Fridtjof Nansen. Not all men who have great physical courage (as Nansen had) are endowed with equally great moral courage. I was at the League of Nations Assembly during the Corfu crisis, and saw for myself the way his personality shone out. I saw something of his indefatigable humanitarian activities, and took pride in publishing such works of his as *Armenia and the Near East* and *Through the Caucasus to the Volga*: relief work among the suffering populations of the Near East. Would that there were more such men alive today.

Before passing on to the nineteen-thirties, there are two matters (apart from those referred to in the chapter on The Publishers Association) to which I devoted much thought in the early 'twenties that call for mention.

[1] February–May 1927.

In October 1923—that is before the company had been in existence ten years—I decided that the senior members of our staff, all of whom had been long in the employment of our predecessors, should have some share in our increasing prosperity. Accordingly, we set aside each year a capital sum which was allocated to the more responsible long-service employees. It was a free gift and the conditions were as follows:

Interest was to be paid half-yearly at a rate dependent upon the prosperity of the firm. A minimum of 5 per cent was guaranteed, but in practice it was never less than 10 per cent nor less than the dividend upon our Ordinary Shares. It was often more.

The whole of the capital sum allocated to a member of the staff was payable at his (or her) death, or on retirement. It was thus a free insurance policy as well as a small but growing investment in the firm.

At the start, the 'Staff Fund', as our plan was called, was far from enthusiastically received, but as the capital and dividends increased the advantages became apparent, and some of the older members of the staff benefited most substantially from it. Years later it was superseded by a contributory pension scheme for all except those too old to participate in it.

In the autumn of 1925, following the death of the first Lord Leverhulme, his house, 'The Hill', on Hampstead Heath was put up for sale. I had long felt that the close upon three acres, which are connected with the garden of 'The Hill' only by a bridge, should form part of the Heath. I approached the late Sir Howard Frank (the estate agent) about the possibility of acquiring it for the purpose, and both he and the second Lord Leverhulme were most co-operative. They agreed to sell the land separately provided the property had not been sold as a whole in the meantime.

Unfortunately I was not in those days financially in a position to sign the contract first and then make an appeal, so I at once set about collecting the promises which would enable me to make the purchase. This involved great effort, endless letters and personal interviews, but by January 1926 I had over £6,000, and hoped soon to be justified in signing a contract.

But alas! at that moment the unexpected happened; a buyer was forthcoming for the property as a whole, and the opportunity to make an attractive addition to the Heath vanished. Months of hard work were 'love's labours lost'. Fortunately, however, the opportunity recurred in 1957—on much more advantageous terms—and the London County Council, with the co-operation of the adjacent local authorities, wisely availed itself of it.

CHAPTER 13

THE NINETEEN-THIRTIES (I)

Many people call themselves Christians, but few approach success in living up to Christ's teaching. C. F. Andrews—Charlie Andrews as he was affectionately called—was one of the few who came near to doing so. Born in Newcastle in 1871, the second of a large family—a delicate child who would have died of a rheumatic fever in his sixth year but for his mother's devoted nursing—he early displayed an ability to win scholarships. After twelve years of close connection with Pembroke College, Cambridge, some of which were spent at the Pembroke College Mission in South London, Andrews felt a 'call' to India, where in 1900 Bishop Westcott, under whose influence he had come, had died of cholera. Accordingly, at the age of thirty-three, Andrews set his face to the East and joined the Cambridge Brotherhood in Delhi, and from that moment devoted his life to India. He saw no inconsistency between his sympathy with India's desire for national self-expression and the belief in the essential beneficence of the British connection in which he had been brought up. His campaigns against racial exclusiveness and social injustice were continued without intermission. He was not only a saint and a pioneer; he was also a Christian statesman. He was Christlike in action as well as appearance, and it is not surprising that Gandhi was devoted to him. He certainly took no thought for the morrow, but I sometimes naughtily thought that it was fortunate for him— in this wicked world—that others, occasionally at any rate, did so. He came to us unheralded with a friend's manuscript and was being asked, in accordance with routine, to leave it when my then secretary—one of the missionary children my mother more or less adopted—observed him and at once came to me to say that there was someone at the counter whom she instinctively felt I ought to see. How right she was! I took to him at first sight and we became firm friends.

His work for India took him to all parts of the world, such as Africa and Fiji, where Indians lived and worked. A Norwegian scholar dubbed him 'The wandering Christian', and the title pleased him.

> 'A wandering Christian I,
> A thing of shreds and patches',

he commented, in apt misquotation of *The Mikado*. 'Nothing is so insipid in the historical records of saintly men', he once wrote, 'as to read about their superlative and superhuman excellencies without any counter-balance of their human weaknesses.' Andrews, who had a delightful sense of humour, was full of lovable human foibles. He loved Indians and Indians loved him. Gandhi said he was love incarnate. No man did so much to help Indians and the English to understand one another. It is difficult to exaggerate how much the friendly relations between our two peoples is due to Charlie Andrews.

I owe many of my special publishing connections with India, as well as my warm feelings for the people of India, to him. He edited three volumes of Gandhi's writings[1] largely based upon Gandhi's autobiography, and it was through him that I came to publish Rabindranath Tagore's *Letters to a Friend* and other work by that distinguished poet. But for Andrews I should never have met Gandhi, and the meeting was an unforgettable experience. To be known as Charlie Andrew's friend was to have an entry into Indian hearts. His death, when it came, was a blow. I look back upon our long connection with the happiest memories, and am glad to have been instrumental with the assistance of our mutual friend, the late Agatha Harrison, in arranging for a worthy biography of him[2] by Bernarsidas Chattervedi and Marjorie Sykes. It finishes with these words: '*The Life of Christ* (which we were to have published) had never been written; it had been, most faithfully, lived.'

[1] *Mahatma Gandhi: His Own Story; Mahatma Gandhi at Work; Mahatma Gandhi's Ideas* (London: George Allen & Unwin Ltd., 1929–1931).
[2] *Charles Freer Andrews: A Narrative* (London: George Allen & Unwin Ltd., 1949).

Another author for whom I had the deepest respect—as well as sympathy in his domestic afflictions—was Jacob Wassermann, for whom I published more than a dozen books during the nineteen-thirties. Edward Crankshaw compared him with the great Russians and wrote that 'to claim that a man so little known in England should be regarded as the equal or the master of these is to invite every scepticism; nevertheless I beg to advance this claim'. Arnold Bennett was of the opinion that Wassermann was one of the biggest of modern writers, and seemed to find difficulty in selecting sufficient superlatives to describe the magnificent sweep of *Christian Wahnschaffe* (*The World's Illusion*) which another reviewer stated was 'one of the greatest works of fiction of this or any other century'. In a letter to Geraint Vaughan Jones, author of an interesting and thus far unpublished biography of Jacob Wassermann, Thomas Mann described Wassermann as 'a great story-teller who was deeply and honestly concerned with the problems of humanity' and referred to his art as 'a tremendous mixture of virtuosity and sacred seriousness'.

Wassermann is largely forgotten today. Nevertheless, I still think some of his books, particularly *The World's Illusion*, *The Maurizius Case*, *Etzel Andergast* and *Joseph Kerkhoven's Third Existence* are outstanding; they are certainly written with deep feeling, and will one day, I feel sure, come into their own again.

Although we published more translations of novels by foreign authors than probably any two other English publishers put together, my firm has never specialized in fiction—possibly the most speculative of all forms of publishing. One novel which we had translated from the Swedish raised what is for publishers an interesting question—one which is now, I am glad to say, regarded in a more rational light. The book had been out some time in Sweden, but no film producer had evinced the slightest interest in it. When it was available in our English translation, its film possibilities were realized and £2,000 was paid for the film rights. In book form the novel was not a success and we lost about £150 over its publication. At that time it was considered wicked for a book publisher to make even the most trifling claim to a share in the film rights. Here was a case where a publisher's out-of-pocket expenditure had made possible a sale of the rights for £2,000. Could anyone maintain that an allowance of one-tenth of that amount to the publisher would be inequitable, let alone wicked? It would at any rate have covered the cost of securing the sale. The test is surely whether or not a service has been rendered. The same point often arises in connection with the sale of book rights. If, for example, we publish an English translation of a book that has long remained untranslated, applications for translation rights at once arrive from all over Europe. The fact that we have thought the book worth translating, still more the fact that it can be examined in English instead of in some less familiar language, stimulate the inquiries.

The early days of 1930 were enlivened for me by the dispute of H. G. Wells with my old enemy G. Herbert Thring, then Secretary of the Society of Authors, whom Wells referred to in a letter to me as an intolerable little ass.

At Wells's request I 'tastefully printed', to use Mr Thring's expression, 175 copies of a pamphlet entitled *The Problem of the Troublesome Collaborator*. It was headed 'Private and Confidential' and most of the copies were distributed by Wells to leading members of the Society of Authors. I was, however, authorized to retain a few for sale at a high price to first edition collectors and dealers like Gabriel Wells, to cover the cost of production.

Thanks largely to the intervention of Bernard Shaw, peace was eventually made, and I published a sequel entitled *Settlement of the Trouble between Mr Thring and Mr Wells: A Footnote to the Problem of the Troublesome Collaborators*, for private circulation only among those who received the previous 'pamphlet. Wells was most outspoken in his denunciation of Thring and quoted with approval the statement I had made in the preface to the third edition of *The Truth About Publishing* about the Society of Authors' (at that time) narrow and litigious point of view.

Thring's attitude to publishers was quite unreasonable because he assumed that even the most reputable firms must *ipso facto* be incapable in any circumstances of acting from a decent motive.

He attacked Wells as if he were a disreputable publisher, and naturally the sparks flew. Much heat was engendered and both parties were singed by it.

In the course of one of my walks with Ramsay MacDonald, he spoke most highly of Walter Lippmann, then at the beginning of his career. I naturally pricked up my ears and soon thereafter published Lippmann's *Preface to Morals* and other works. This is yet another example of the way 'Chance' may lead one to be the first to approach a future author of distinction before everybody wants to publish for him. But there are other ways. From the moment I took over The Swarthmore Press I became the publisher of the yearly Swarthmore Lectures. When Sir Arthur Eddington, himself a Quaker, consented to give the lecture *Science and the Unseen World*, we were handed a 'best-seller' on a plate. Then, again, as the publisher of the Muirhead Library of Philosophy, it was natural that I should get into touch with John Dewey, most of whose books (though not all) we imported from the USA. Despite his great prestige, his books never enjoyed a large sale in Britain, but we were never left with stock on our hands. We had merely to wait until the books went out of print in the States and then, with the American publisher's consent, supply American booksellers in urgent need of copies.

The publication of philosophical works seldom yields their authors, or publishers, much profit. Fortunately, as I pointed out in *Publishing in Peace and War*,[1] the authors of learned works may sometimes be rewarded in other ways, as I was reminded by a Professor of Philosophy, the sales of whose masterpiece had taken thirty years to cover the printing bill. The day after he had received a cheque in respect of 'profits' he called to tell me that it was an amusing coincidence that the first payment should have reached him on the very day of his retirement from the professorship which the publication of the book had secured him. The patient publisher had been out of pocket for thirty years without any comparable recognition of his part in such uncommercial activities.

[1] London: George Allen & Unwin Ltd., 1944.

This brings me to Williams & Norgate, a firm which in its day had been famous for the publication of philosophical and theological works. It had for years been going steadily downhill, and when a receiver was eventually appointed in 1928, he invited us to make a bid for the remaining assets. The turnover had dropped to a derisory figure, but the imprint still carried weight, and had an historic interest and value. It was not, therefore, a case for absorption into my own business, but for running as an independent company. My motives for buying were mixed. I like building up derelict book publishing businesses and demonstrating how it can be done, but there was the less admirable motive—the irony of my becoming the owner of the business of the man who had kept me out of the Publishers Association when my own firm was founded, and who had treated me with contempt. There was, however, a third reason at the back of my mind. The ownership of Williams & Norgate might prove to be of assistance—as indeed it was six years later—in enabling me to part company with my colleague Skinner.

We took over with the assets Mr Stanley Dunk, of whom I cannot speak too highly, and at first allowed Williams & Norgate to be run from 38 Great Ormond Street by the late B. N. Langdon-Davies and Mrs Manus, in conjunction with the Labour Publishing Company and the firm of Noel Douglas, whose assets Williams & Norgate later acquired. There was at that time a theory that there was a fortune to be made out of the publication of Left Wing literature, but most of those who put the theory into practice were soon disillusioned. The name Noel Douglas was derived from the second Christian names of the two chief persons concerned, B. N. Langdon-Davies and G. D. H. Cole. I attended the office daily, and put in much overtime building up the business. Langdon-Davies did not prove himself as successful a publisher as he later did a bookseller, and it was a relief to me when the business was moved into our own building at 28 Little Russell Street, and Langdon-Davies took his departure to Corsica.

Before the six years were up, we had turned the corner, had

greatly increased the sales, and were making a steady £1,500 a year or thereabouts. To build up a book-publishing business it is essential to plough back the profits. My chief difference with my colleague Skinner was that he was always pressing to draw more out of the Allen & Unwin business. Eventually I said to him bluntly, 'If you are dissatisfied, why not sell out?' The terms to which I finally agreed were onerous. I paid him hundreds per cent above the par value of the ordinary shares in George Allen & Unwin which had cost him nothing; a salary for ten years in compensation for loss of office, and sold him the Williams & Norgate business for about half of what it had become worth.

One incident in connection with the sale taught me something I am not likely to forget. An agreement recorded in the minutes of two companies, and signed by both parties as correct, has, in the absence of specific mention of some 'consideration' no legal validity. Both Professor Renier and I wished to exclude his book, *The English: Are They Human?* from the transfer. Skinner agreed that when the stock was exhausted the rights should revert to the author and myself, and the fact was recorded in the minutes of both companies. Nevertheless, when the time came, although he did not dispute the correctness of the minutes, which he had personally signed, he refused to part with the rights, and thanks to this legal technicality I had no redress.

However, to gain freedom almost any price was justified. From that moment the firm leapt forward. Immediate decisions could be made about everything, and I could please myself as to what I published or refrained from publishing.

I had been intensely interested in the League of Nations since its inception, so that when my friend, the late Fritz Schnabel, the translator of the German edition of *The Truth About Publishing* and head of the League Publications Department, pressed me yet again in 1930 to undertake the agency for the sale of their publications I succumbed, and we started on July 1st. It was a thankless task, particularly if one attempted, as we did, to effect the sales through booksellers and not direct to the public. The difference between the 40 per cent we were allowed and the discount we gave the booksellers was totally inadequate to cover the huge amount of detailed work involved. It was essential to have a well-educated man with knowledge of the League's vast array of documents in charge, because the agency was in effect an inquiry office. It was not unusual for an hour to be spent looking for a document that did not exist except in the inquirer's imagination, or one that, when found, cost sixpence. However, it gave me an insight into that maligned League organization, which towards the end was much more efficient than the United Nations ever seems to have been, and I had an excuse for attending the meetings of the Assembly, which I did on several occasions and found deeply interesting—the more so because I had freedom to attend committees, etc. On the other hand, when I was approached by UNO, I felt and showed no enthusiasm for the agency, and was glad to see the burden passed on to the broad shoulders of H.M. Stationery Office.

I am often asked why my firm has not an American branch. It is seldom realized what a big and difficult undertaking it is for a British publisher to start, or rather build up, a publishing business in New York, or for an American publisher to do so in London. Jonathan Cape and Alfred Knopf tried their hands at it about the same time. Both were exceptionally successful in their own countries; neither would, I think, pronounce his transatlantic experiment a success. Knopf, I imagine, felt sure that methods which had proved so outstandingly successful in the States could not fail if applied to Britain. But the conditions are completely different. Publishing businesses are run as extravagantly in New York as they tend to be economically run in London. In consequence overhead is an even more formidable item in America than it is in Britain. The extravagance takes many forms—three people where we should make one suffice; palatial offices where we should make do with more modest accommodation; a high powered salesman to get big subscription orders from a few big wholesalers who would buy the books in any case were there a 'run' on the book (and would expect surplus stock to be credited were there not), and who anyway merely execute the orders that come to them and can do little to 'create' sales. But, of course, the greatest difficulty is distant control. Few firms have the good fortune to find a George P. Brett to build up a business for them as he did for Macmillans in America. Nothing could persuade me ever to try to become an American publisher. I mention the Knopf experiment because, when the London office was finally closed down, we bought the remaining assets and took over some of their agreements, thereby adding further interesting items to our list.

Instead of locking up money in a New York branch and probably losing it, I used our resources to build New Ruskin House, 28-30 Little Russell Street, a project which had long been delayed by our action in letting at a nominal rental of £60 per annum each, on the understanding that they would be vacated at any time at a month's notice, the three derelict houses destined to be pulled down. The first War Rents Restriction Act unexpectedly gave the tenants permanent possession; entitled them to call upon us to do repairs, and enabled them ere long to let individual rooms for more than we got from a whole house. We planned to carry the building through to Museum Street, but were stopped first by the War Rents Restriction Act, then by the Second World War and the restriction on building following the war, and later by the whole area being 'designated'—in brief frozen—as described in Chapter 15.

After Skinner's departure, the major handicap to the development of my business was our production department. We had inherited our Production Manager from George Allen & Co., who in turn had taken him over from Bemroses when they acquired their publishing business. He was thus one of our oldest employees. Technically he was in many respects well equipped, but he had two major defects. He had no memory and no typographical sense. An ever-increasing tendency to imbibe more than was good for him did not help matters. It was a time of unemployment; he was too old to get another comparable job, and I felt that to sack him, even with a substantial payment, would be to put on the street an employee of nearly forty years' standing, which I was not prepared to do.

One day his chief assistant, to whom I had counselled patience, came to me in despair and said 'How long, O Lord, how long?' I replied that if you did what you felt to be right, Providence had a wonderful way of solving such problems. I little suspected what would happen. A few Saturdays later, on May 7, 1932, he did not turn up. When he failed to do so on the Monday, we sent to the address he had given us only a week or two previously, but it proved to be one he had left years before. A woman rang up to inquire about him, and I immediately sensed that it might be his landlady. My surmise proved to be correct, and she told me that he had left his room on Friday night with only a spare collar and handkerchief, and she had seen nothing of him since. About an hour later the police called to arrest him. Although he lived by himself in an inexpensive room, and was well paid, he consistently refused to pay his income tax. On a previous occasion we had advanced the money to save him from arrest, but had made it clear that we should not intervene on any future occasion.

From that moment he disappeared without a trace. We suspected suicide, but we were mistaken because two years later one of our staff saw him in the distance in Holborn. About 1948 we accidentally learnt of his death (aged over 80) in a secondhand bookshop where he had been working. His departure relieved us of a most irksome responsibility, to be quit of which we would gladly have paid out a considerable sum, and enabled us to maintain better typographical standards.

One of the curious features of the kind of businesses I was endeavouring to build up was the way biographies would dominate the list one year and science or economics other years. It is, of course, partly chance, but fashion comes into it. The public gets deeply interested at one moment, let us say, in currency problems, or psycho-analysis, and a flood of books arises on those subjects, many of them second-rate and ephemeral. On such occasions a publisher who maintains a standard observes books appearing which he has turned down as definitely not good enough. And the trouble is that the second-rate spoils the market for the good. Fortunately it does not do so permanently, and those best-informed book-buyers, the librarians of the Public Libraries, have an uncanny knack of separating the wheat from the chaff.

But some of the most interesting or amusing books fall into no class. Curiously enough I had to go to Germany to learn about that distinguished Spanish author, Ortega y Gasset, whose famous book, *The Revolt of the Masses*, we published (translated, of course, direct from the Spanish), and to Holland for that most entertaining work, *Drop Your Foreign Accent*. I defy any Englishman, let alone a foreigner, to read at sight at a reasonable speed the doggerel which appears at the end of that book,[1] without blundering, yet it is in straightforward English.

> 'I will teach you in my verse
> Sounds like corpse, corps, horse and worse.
> It will keep you, Susy, busy,
> Make your head with heat grow dizzy,
> Tear in eye your dress you'll tear.
> Queer, fair seer, hear my prayer,
> Pray, console your loving poet,
> Make my coat look new, dear, sew it.
> Just compare heart, beard and heard,
> Dies and diet, lord and word,
> Sword and sward, retain and Britain,
> (Mind the latter, how it's written)
> Made has not the sound of bade;
> Say, said, pay, paid, laid, but plaid.'

It continues in a similar vein for many pages.

It is an interesting and comforting fact that an outstanding book in any field always forces its way through, even though the process is slow. A good example is Lloyd C. Douglas's first and most famous novel, *Magnificent Obsession*. It appeared unheralded in Chicago under the imprint of a little-known firm; it made no sudden stir, but people started talking about it. The steadiness of

[1] *Drop Your Foreign Accent*, G. N. Trenité (London: George Allen & Unwin Ltd., 1932).

its sale impressed me, and it must have been about two years after its first publication that we sent for a copy and at once accepted it. It has sold steadily ever since. Unfortunately my then colleague Skinner, who regarded fiction as his special preserve, unwisely turned down Lloyd Douglas's second book, and all his subsequent novels have been published by Peter Davies, who accepted the book we declined.

Another novelist who interested me about that time was an Icelander, Halldor Laxness, and the circumstances under which I came to know him were unusual. However much a publisher may love authors, he needs an occasional rest from them, or at any rate from manuscripts. When I am on holiday my staff is not supposed to divulge my whereabouts; a holiday is no holiday if one is pursued with business. But by some subterfuge an author ascertained one year that I had gone to Wensleydale and forthwith followed me there. He wanted an immediate decision about his manuscript. He got it. Happy relations with such an author would soon be impossible, and unless the relationship is pleasant, the sooner it is severed the better, regardless of the profitability of the author's work. A year or two later, when I was worn out and quite abnormally tired, I decided, in view of that earlier experience, that Iceland was the place for me. There was then no air service, no telephone and no letters could reach me until I was on my way back. I retired to a farm on the Borga Fjord with an old school friend, and had the most mentally restful time imaginable. I say mentally restful advisedly because sitting on the back of an Icelandic pony mile after mile is not physically restful if you are not used to it, and during the first few days my seat was so sore that I could not sit down and I was too tired to stand up. However, that soon passed and I returned to Reykjavik with a new lease of life. There I found a message from Asgeir Asgeirson, the Prime Minister, later President, whom I had met earlier in London, suggesting that I should spend a few days at Thingvellir as the Government's guest and before doing so be shown some of Iceland's geysers and waterfalls in the company of Iceland's leading author, Halldor Laxness. We had a delightful day together, and as an outcome I published *Salka Valka*, which was Howard Spring's choice as an *Evening Standard* Book of the Month, and *Independent People*, which was a Book of the Month in the USA. In 1955 he was awarded the Nobel prize for literature, and I was made a Knight of the Order of the Falcon.

But there was another outcome of that visit to Iceland. At that time Great Britain was still represented by an Icelander at Reykjavik, and in view of the strategic importance of the island, and the interest the Nazis were taking in it, I felt that it was imperative that a British career consul should be appointed. Furthermore, I did not feel it was helpful to our prestige that the entrance to the sub-Consulate at Akureyri was through a broken and dilapidated gate which badly needed a coat of paint. Immediately on my return I got in touch with a friend at the Foreign Office about the appointment of a British representative, and offered to pay for the repair and painting of the gate if the Foreign Office vote was unequal to it. The gate was repaired and painted, but I received a message from an official in the Northern Department that I would not get a career consul appointed except over his dead body. I replied that I should be sorry to be responsible for his death, but that I was not going to let the matter drop, and I didn't. A career consul was fortunately appointed well before the outbreak of war, and some years later I heard that the obstructive official was still alive.

Iceland, so long linked with Denmark, reminds me of a translation from the Danish, *Uncle Give Us Bread* by Arne Strom, which aroused Sir Winston Churchill's interest. The book gave a sad picture of the Danish author's experience of life in Soviet Russia, and Mr Churchill, as he was then, wanted to know if I could vouch for its authenticity. I could only reply that the Danish publisher assured us that it was authentic, but that I had myself never met the author. My own belief is that it was at least 90 per cent true, but that there was no evidence that the same conditions necessarily obtained outside the particular corner of Russia in which the author lived and worked. I was interested to notice when referring to *Uncle Give Us Bread*, that in the same year as we issued these translations from Icelandic and Danish, we published translations from German, Swedish, Russian, Hungarian, Czech, Turkish and Flemish. I wonder if there is any other publisher who can equal that record in such a short space of time. Probably not. But then I do not know of any other publisher (since Heinemann's death) who has regarded the international interchange of literature as an outstanding part of his life's work. It is a tradition we have continued. No other house could, I believe, point to such a number or variety of translated works, and we can claim since the Second World War to be in the lead in introducing the best of *French non-fiction* to the English reader, a quite new development. It is a two-way traffic as far as we are concerned, and we maintain a department solely occupied with the sale of translation rights.

Like most Anglo-Saxons, and the more so because of my international connections, I was horrified at the outbreak of persecution of the Jews in Germany. In the summer of 1933 an important German official and the London Correspondent of a leading German newspaper to whom I protested, both deplored these Nazi activities; both said they were powerless, but would be grateful if I could put my views in writing, which I did. The letter reached influential circles, but nothing could curb the Nazis' blind hatred of the Jews.

In the course of my wanderings abroad in the mid-thirties, I had occasion to visit Vienna, and naturally called upon the Phaidon Verlag. When I observed what excellent work they were doing and realized that it would immediately end if Hitler marched in, I urged the proprietor, Dr Horovitz, to get out. He seemed to think that he had plenty of time. Now I had noticed that Jewish publishing firms in Germany became 'Aryanized' if purchased by non-Jews. I therefore asked the head of the Nazi publishing organization whether if *I* bought a Jewish publishing business that would Aryanize it. He said that if my pedigree was in order it would. As I was able to produce the Unwin family tree, showing no trace of Jewish blood, I asked him if he would put that in writing. Yes, he would, and did. Armed with that assurance, I bought all Dr Horovitz's stock. Everything was done correctly. Although I did not personally find the money, I remitted it to Vienna, and the stock became legally my property though at that stage no announcement was made.

A year went by and I kept urging Dr Horovitz to leave Vienna. I pointed out that when Hitler marched in, which he would do without warning, it would be too late. Dr Horovitz thought that as all the stock was in my name all would be well, but I drew his attention to the fact that he still owned the copyrights and the goodwill in the name Phaidon. A further agreement was hastily improvised, and Dr Horovitz came to London to put it through. He had only got as far as Holland on his way back when Hitler marched in. Within a few hours a Commissar was sitting in the Phaidon office in Vienna. He called for particulars of the stock, and refused to believe that Dr Horovitz did not own any. He wrote immediately to all the printers and binders, only to learn that for about a year it had been the property of George Allen & Unwin Ltd. Had they paid for it? Yes, the bank records showed that they had. The disappointment of Nazi art publishers who had thought they would acquire the business for a song was great.

For the purposes of my own business, I had pointed out to the Nazi authorities that there was a demand for George Allen & Unwin publications in Germany, but that German booksellers could get no sterling with which to pay for them. If I accepted payment in marks, I inquired, could I use those marks to produce English books in Germany? The answer was yes. I was now equipped to come out into the open. I drew attention to the fact that I had Aryanized the Phaidon Art Books, and asked for the promised authority to sell them in Germany, where, as Jewish publications, they had been prohibited. The demand caused consternation and infuriated the Nazi art publishers, but could not be denied. Stipulations were made that we should paste our name over that of the Phaidon Verlag, with which we, of course, complied. The next step was a careful, very formal, four-page advertisement in the *Börsenblatt* (the official German book trade paper) announcing that we had acquired the business and that our

The Ripon Hall Conference, 1934. S. U. seated between G. B. Bowes and Basil Blackwell

With Basil Blackwell

With Lloyd George at Churt, International Publishers Congress, 1936

With Ramsay and Malcolm MacDonald on Hampstead Heath, 1929

Kommissionär in Leipzig would deal with orders. Order forms for the books which were in stock were included and booksellers were encouraged to say which Phaidon titles they would like reprinted, and to indicate, though without committing themselves, the approximate number they could use if the desired volumes were reprinted. The result was impressive. The pent-up demand for these forbidden books was such that, with the exception of one or two small lines which never had been popular, the entire stock was sold for cash within forty-eight hours. The next step was to use that vast accumulation of marks as rapidly as possible to produce editions in English, and, as that was a comparatively slow process, to put in hand reprints of the most needed German editions. And that was the start of the Phaidon Press.

Meanwhile the Nazi authorities were busy trying to find some flaw in our purchase agreements. Long-distance telephone calls to Dr Horovitz's secretary at the Phaidon office in Vienna when the Commissar was out, kept us informed about what was afoot. One sentence in a letter of instructions from the lawyer at Nazi headquarters in Berlin amused me. It read: 'Streitigkeiten mit Herrn Unwin sind nicht erwünscht.' (Disputes with Mr Unwin are not desired.) The explanation was simple; I was President of the International Publishers Association; the next Congress was to be held in Leipzig and Berlin in the summer of 1938, and they probably feared that I might not turn up to hand over the ivory gavel of office to my German successor.[1] When the time came for me to go, I accidently ran into the Nazi lawyer in Berlin who had been handling Phaidon affairs. When he heard who I was he scowled and muttered, 'You were too clever for us'.[2]

All went reasonably smoothly with the Phaidon publications until war broke out, leaving 10,000 sets of the coloured illustrations for the *Van Gogh*, which were on their way to us from Austria, just on the wrong side of the Swiss frontier. The text and monochrome illustrations were already in our possession. At a

[1] See Chapter 22, page 413.
[2] In September 1945 I learnt that I was in the Gestapo 'Black List' of persons to be arrested immediately had the Germans invaded Britain.

later stage, when the dollar shortage was acute, we pointed out to the competent authorities that if they would authorize us to bribe the Nazis (through Holland) to release the illustrations, which were useless to the Nazis, we could forthwith complete the 10,000 books and sell them to the USA. A modest figure was agreed, the arrangements made, and the bribe about to be paid when the Nazis marched into Holland. Eventually it was decided to make fresh coloured illustrations in England. They were actually on their way to the bindery when our binder's warehouse was bombed and among the many million books destroyed were all but 1,500 of the 10,000 sets of the text and the monochrome illustrations of the Phaidon *Van Gogh*. We now had two large supplies of coloured illustrations, but only 1,500 sets of the rest of the book. Such are the incidents of war.

Throughout all this period everything had to be done in my firm's name, and the title pages bore the sole imprint of George Allen & Unwin Ltd. Dr Horovitz and the genius who collaborated with him, Dr Ludwig Goldscheider, kept completely in the background, though they were in fact solely responsible for the editing and production of the books.

But as soon as Hitler was safely out of the way, Dr Horovitz naturally wanted to come back into the picture. Our name was no longer to appear as publishers on the title page, but what mattered more to us, there was to be no explanation even in the book trade papers of the sudden change. Furthermore, the commission on sales was reduced to a figure which left no profit to my firm. Finally, when I was in New Zealand, Dr Horovitz gave notice to terminate the agreement. He was too much indebted to me to make the relationship pleasant for him. I had no regrets because he was so exacting. I had achieved what I had set out to do; I had rescued a most remarkable art publishing business from Hitler's clutches, and that was all that mattered. As it happened, it was providential that we parted with the Phaidon Press when we did because the warehousing and packing of Phaidon art books takes an inordinate amount of space and packing materials, and our warehouse, which had not grown like our turnover, could not have coped effectively with the masses of *Kon-Tiki* which followed a month or two later had the benches and gangways been blocked by Phaidons.

But I must go back to 1936 to that famous book, *Mathematics for the Million*, the name of whose author we had not at that time permission to disclose. When I sold the Williams & Norgate business I specifically reserved in the contract the stock and rights in the books by Lancelot Hogben. They were learned works which had enjoyed no profitable sale, but I had accepted them with options upon his future work because those whose opinions I respected assured me that he was a genius who was bound to make his mark. When one day he brought us an enormous MS (nearly 2 feet high) we received it with eager anticipation, and I was not surprised when my colleague, C. A. Furth, who was the first to examine it, pronounced it as quite outstanding and all of us who looked at it agreed with him. Our feelings can be imagined, therefore, when the author told us that, though we were entitled to the book under our contract, he had no wish for us to publish it. All his friends had insisted that ours was the wrong firm for a popular book and that he must unquestionably go to publisher 'X'. That put us in a quandary. I realized that we were dealing with a genius who might be temperamental, and that to stand by the contract was to say goodbye to any happy or permanent relationship. I decided to take a chance, and said, 'If publisher "X" declines the book, is it quite definite that we can have it?', in reply to which the author gave me the desired assurance. I banked upon the publisher being intimidated by the size of the typescript, the algebraical symbols, the rough diagrams, etc. (There were no nice Horrabin drawings then; they came later. It was Hogben who realized what a difference they would make.) My judgment proved correct; the typescript came back. Hogben was chagrined; we were delighted. Unfortunately his friends turned upon publisher 'X', who thereupon asked to see the typescript again, and Hogben wanted us to comply. I demurred. Hogben was insistent. We were back where we were. It was a case for quick thinking. 'If it is to go back,' I said, 'will you agree to its being conditional upon it being a joint publication?' Yes, he would. I banked upon the condition being unacceptable. The typescript came back with a note from the publisher that if it had come without strings he would, on second thoughts, have taken it, but that there was not enough in the undertaking to warrant a joint publication. He added, 'the idea, I take it, was that the book might be printed in a very large edition and handled for a very big market, . . . but I do not at all see a public for a book of these dimensions'.

We thus became the publishers of *Mathematics for the Million*. It called for very special and imaginative handling. The tendency to regard large-scale newspaper advertisements as the only, or even as necessarily the most important, form of publicity, is mistaken. It is an easy, though expensive, thing to fill large advertisement spaces, but it would not have secured for *Mathematics for the Million* the huge sales achieved by quite other methods. An entirely different technique was called for to keep such a book talked about, and it may be of interest to enumerate a few of the many plans worked out and carried through. As a start, every post-primary teacher of mathematics had a personal word from me, drawing his (or her) attention to the following letter from H. G. Wells:

'Thank you for sending me *Mathematics for The Million*. I've read it with care and a continually increasing interest and admiration. With its rather startling cover and its extraordinary freshness of approach it is not the sort of book one judges rashly.

'I've taken time to think it over. *And my deliberate opinion is that it is a great book*, a book of first-class importance, *and that it should be read by every intelligent youth from 15 to 90 who is trying to get the hang of things in this universe. . . .*'

But every sort of person interested in mathematics was separately considered, and use was made of other opinions equally enthusiastic, from Bertrand Russell, Sir Percy Nunn, Julian Huxley, John Hilton and A. J. Rowse. A note was added at the end to the effect that we had asked the recipient to read a great many opinions but that we had omitted as many, also important, equally enthusiastic. Finally, we emphasized how amusing the book was.

The statement in *Branch Banking* that mastery of its contents would vastly improve the efficiency of all bank staffs, and that Branch men should everywhere have the book available, was followed up. The whole field of accountancy was carefully studied. There was probably no direction in which mathematics plays a prominent part that was not pursued. The RAF, which found the book invaluable, was not overlooked. Some of the leaflets used mentioned that those who had an inferiority complex would find that *Mathematics for the Million* removed it painlessly. All were most carefully thought out and designed, and some of them are reproduced in my book, *Best-Sellers: Are They Born or Made?*

Suffice it to say we had a very contented instead of a dis-gruntled author, and one who had no regrets that, despite the advice of his friends, we had published his book. Fortunately we were able to issue it under the author's own name, because, by the time it was ready for publication, he had been elected a Fellow of the Royal Society, and no one could suggest that he was merely a popularizer. As the book was intended for the million, the author quite naturally wanted it issued at the lowest possible price. But it was a most expensive book to produce. Hogben most generously, and, as it proved, wisely, volunteered to reduce his royalty if we would cut our margin and publish the book at 12s 6d instead of 16s od or 18s od, the normal economic price. It meant relying upon reprints for any profits. We agreed, and his action certainly put the book within the reach of many who would otherwise not have secured it. It was a great satis-faction to us, therefore, to be able, ere many months had passed, to reciprocate by sending him a considerable sum over and beyond the reduced royalties due to him.

Our relations were of the happiest. My staff were instructed that Hogben was always right, and that if there was anything that troubled them they must come to me. In due course our Production Manager showed me a formidable bill for 'corrections' and said, 'What do I do about this?' Now I happened to know that 'corrections' had been a bone of contention in connection with an early book of Hogben's issued by another publisher, so I replied: 'Work out the figures, show the amount for which the author is formally liable under his agreement, and ask him what you are to do about it. Tell him that I have instructed you to do whatever he thinks reasonable.' Hogben's immediate reply was that his account could be debited with whatever *I* thought was reasonable in the special circumstances. May I hasten to add that there are not many people with whom it would be expedient to act in this fashion.

As I am dealing with Hogben, whose early Nonconformist background was not unlike my own, and whom I therefore understood better than some, I will skip a year or two and come to *Science for the Citizen*. It was an enormous typescript—bigger even than *Mathematics for the Million*. Libel and copyright infringements are always at the back of the experienced publisher's mind, so as I turned over the pages and came to the section on Biology, I recalled that Hogben had years before published a small text-book on the subject, the copyright in which had been acquired by the publisher. It had become out of date and was out of print. Nevertheless I foresaw trouble if any use had been made of it. Hogben assured me that he had not even looked at the book for years and my mind was set at rest. I was therefore not a little surprised to receive, within a day or two of publishing *Science for the Citizen*, a solicitors' letter complaining of infringement of their client's copyright. They admitted that the wording was not identical, but the order in which the subject was treated and even many of the phrases used were the same. There was no doubt that it was legally a technical infringement. What had happened was soon clear. Hogben had in both cases made use of his lecture notes. Although the infringement affected only a few pages, the damage could be fairly substantial because of the size of the edition we had printed. We worked out the figure with our lawyers and offered slightly more for the purchase of the copyright in settlement of the whole affair. As the copyright was of no use to the publisher so long as Hogben refused to revise the book, the offer was accepted. We paid the price and made Hogben a present of the copyright. His response was characteristic. He forthwith revised the book, and allowed us to treat the sum we had paid as an advance on account of royalties, thus enabling us to recover our outlay and giving us a saleable book into the bargain. Both *Science for the Citizen* and *Mathematics for the Million* still sell merrily, and revised editions appear from time to time.

Under the stimulus of Professor Hogben, my colleague C. A. Furth, who had taken charge of the educational side of our business, felt that a change in biology text-books was long overdue, and in fact inevitable. Until 1936 they were based upon the frog; it was considered indecent to relate them to the human frame. Richard Palmer, a biologist, strongly agreed with Furth on this point and we commissioned him to prepare a text-book for us under the title *Living Things*. When, as we anticipated, it became obligatory to base instruction on the human frame, ours was the only existing book that did so, and it has gone on selling ever since. Before that happened, the Science Mistress of a Ladies' College wrote to say what an excellent text-book it was, and how gladly she would use it were three diagrams omitted which would upset her committee. We told her to wait, and a year later she wrote that in view of the changed syllabus she no longer had any anxiety.

In October 1936, soon after our success with *Mathematics for the Million*, we contracted with Professor Julian Huxley for a popular book on Evolution. Few books can have achieved such a complete metamorphosis in the course of their writing. It started as a short crown octavo volume suitable for publication at about 7s 6d, but when the proofs were returned to us they had been so heavily corrected, and so much material had been added, that there was no alternative but to start afresh and completely reset the book as a large crown octavo volume to be issued at about 12s 6d. Professor Huxley took this new set of proofs with him to the States, and while there decided to enlarge the scope of the work with the result that we had to set it yet again, this time as a demy octavo volume to be published at 25s od. It was not until September 1942 that it was finally published. It was then immediately recognized as a standard work, and sold so well that neither author nor publisher had cause for discontent. In fact, the evolution of this small popular book into a standard work on Evolution benefited all parties, including those who bought it. By 1956 there had been six impressions.

The mistake of publisher 'X' in declining *Mathematics for the Million* is one we can all of us match. Edward Crankshaw had urged us not once but again and again to put our money on Georges Simenon. We were deterred partly no doubt by the fact that an American publisher had issued translations of six of his detective stories, and had abandoned his contract during the financial crisis, and that three of them issued over here by Hurst & Blackett were unsuccessful, but primarily it was their awkward length that made us hesitate. Routledge stepped in and signed an agreement for *Disintegration of JPG* in March 1937, and it was an absolute failure. They lost quite a lot of money on it. At that point our decision looked wise. But Routledge knew better because in March 1939 they signed an agreement for twenty-six novels with Simenon, and most sensibly published two stories in a volume. It proved a most profitable transaction and we realized what a 'himalayan blunder' we had made. I wish it were the only one I could recall. Publishing fallibility is, however, such a prevalent complaint that I am philosophical about it, except when my error is due (as in Simenon's case) to not acting upon my own principles.

I have always maintained that if it was by a recognized authority, and was the best on the subject, my firm would publish any book regardless of whether it was particularly in our line or not. One of my best friends among publishers thought he would put me to the test. He rang up to say that he had been offered a book on the Biochemistry of Malting and Brewing which wasn't in his line; would I like to publish it, adding that it came within my definition of the best book on the subject because it was the joint work of the chemist at the Tuborg

Brewery in Copenhagen (one of the finest, if not the finest brewery in the world) and the Professor of Brewing at Birmingham, the only British University, he believed, with a course on brewing. He was, I think, a little surprised when I accepted it for publication right away, with the comment that if people were going to drink beer they had better have it pure. We have sold three editions.

About the same time I was offered *Thoroughbred Racing Stock* by Lady Wentworth. Now I know nothing about horses or racing, but it was not difficult to ascertain that Lady Wentworth was one of the greatest authorities on horses—particularly Arabs—in the world. We accepted the book, and the subsequent volume, *The Authentic Arabian Horse*, without hesitation. Both now fetch a premium, and revised editions are in preparation. Books such as these require intelligent and individual treatment, but, subject to that, are less speculative than many books which some publishers would accept with greater confidence.

The third book to appear in the same season as the best of its kind is one of my favourite publications, *The Hobbit*, by J. R. R. Tolkien, a professor of English Language and Literature at Oxford. Now Allen & Unwin have never published many children's books, but those they do issue, such as the Père Castor Wild Animal books, are mostly outstanding. *The Hobbit* easily heads the list. My younger son, as a boy, must have read it eight or nine times, so absorbing did he find it. Many years were to elapse before the publication of its sequel—not addressed to children, though they will enjoy it—*The Lord of the Rings*, in three large volumes.

Such books present no insuperable problem to their publisher, but that cannot be said of *Germany's Air Force* by Otto Lehmann-Ruessbueldt which I issued about that time. It revealed the precise details of the secret rearmament upon which Hitler had embarked. I felt like a Cassandra because, despite endless effort on my part, letters to Members of Parliament, to editors and many prominent people, I could not get any attention paid to this timely warning. The Government of the day accepted

Hitler's assurance that the book was all lies, and the irony of it is that we now know, as I was confident at the time, that every statement in it was true. It is astonishing how anxious we were under the Baldwin–Chamberlain regime to believe what the Nazis told us.

Ford Madox Ford was a name I had known since my childhood because as Ford Madox Hueffer he published a volume in T. Fisher Unwin's Children's Library which I possessed, and in its heyday was editor of the *English Review*. He had a great influence on many writers of his time. Joseph Conrad, for example, learned a great deal about the management of the English language from him. But his own books, despite their unquestioned merits, did not enjoy a really remunerative sale. When, therefore, I heard from one of his many enthusiastic admirers that some financial assistance would help him I was interested. It ended in our publishing all his last books, including *The March of Literature*. It is doubtful whether, until possibly the very end of his life, he got the recognition that his work deserved.

Another writer we backed at that time (enthusiastically introduced to us by Edward Crankshaw) was René Béhaine. Ford Madox Ford wrote:

' "For many years now—for ah, how many!—M. Léon Daudet and I have cherished one belief. It is that René Béhaine is the most remarkable living novelist. Flaubert said that if France had read his *Education Sentimentale* she would have been spared the horrors of the *débâcle* of 1870. One may say of M. Béhaine that if the world would read his books—his one immense book in many parts—the world would be spared its next Armageddon—because it might know France."

'Conrad spent the whole of his writing life in trying desperately to find a new form for the novel. He used to say that the writing of novels is your one occupation for the proper man, because with the novel you could do anything . . . provided always that you had your New Form. M. Béhaine, who has something akin to Conrad's smouldering and passionate contempt for the imbecilities of common humanity, has, without any of poor dear Conrad's writhings as to form, consummately given the novel at least a new status. There is about his writing not so much a smouldering contempt as a passionate austerity. Beside it, as if on a height giving on to the whole world, you view a usually imbecile and almost always disagreeable humanity. But when you have read Béhaine you will know France.

'And knowledge of France is the sensitive spot of the Western Hemisphere. Sooner or later in your life you will find yourself fighting either to preserve or to destroy France. That has been the fate of humanity with almost exact regularity every half-century since first the hordes of Brennus thundered down, through the Gaul which is France, to the sack of Rome and the destruction of a mighty civilization.'

Despite this glowing tribute which forms the beginning of a twenty-page Preface to *The Survivors*, despite the outstanding merits of Mr Crankshaw's translation, it proved impossible to secure Béhaine adequate recognition, let alone a remunerative sale. We followed up the publication of *The Survivors* with two further novels, *The Conquest of Life* and *Day of Glory*, but they were complete failures.

Fortunately the publication of a translation of the *History of Europe: From the Invasions to the Sixteenth Century* by the Belgian historian, Henri Pirenne (1862–1935), covered our losses on Béhaine. It gave economic, social and religious factors a place as prominent as that given to political events in the development of national history. The late Eileen Power's enthusiasm for Pirenne secured it a wonderful send-off and it soon established itself as a standard work. How it came to be written is an interesting story.

Pirenne was arrested by the Germans in Ghent in March 1916 and deported to Germany, the idea being that by such intimidation the other professors at Ghent University would be induced to resume their lectures, for they had refused to continue during alien occupation. He was interned first at Krefeld and then at Holzminden, where he gave courses of lectures to other internees on economic history. Many attempts were made to force the Germans to release him by American professors, President Wilson, Alfonso XIII and the Pope. He was therefore offered a chance to live in any German university city he might choose.

He refused to take advantage of this and was forcibly transferred to Jena in August 1916. In January 1917 he was deported to Kreuzberg (near Eisenach) and it was there in the Gasthof zum Stern that he began the work, first conceived in Holzminden, which became his *History of Europe*. He began on March 23, 1917, and was interrupted on August 8, 1918, when he had got as far as 1550.

On his return to Belgium he became involved in his huge *History of Belgium*, and the *History of Europe* got no further. Nevertheless his volume on *Mohammed and Charlemagne* (which we also published) is a partial development of the *History of Europe*. It is interesting to note that the *History of Europe* was published exactly as written in Germany—it was never re-read or polished.

CHAPTER 14

THE NINETEEN-THIRTIES (II)

I am not a genealogist, but I have always been deeply interested
in my forebears, and have encouraged those members of the
Unwin clan genealogically inclined by printing the results of
their researches.

The latest family tree—an enormous affair—starts with Thomas
Unwin of Steeple Bumpstead, who died in 1566, and shows a
long connection with Coggeshall, where Unwins owned the
farm with the largest tithe barn in Essex.

Our family likeness is evidently pronounced. I was seated in a
South African railway carriage when a man who had passed up
and down and looked in, stopped and said, 'Excuse me, but I
think you must be an Unwin because you are so like a man of
that name whom I knew some years ago'. It turned out to be a
cousin whom I should not have thought I was particularly like.
But similar incidents have recurred at other times and places too
frequently to be a matter of chance. In what precisely the physical
likeness consists—whether in the shape of our heads or what—I
don't pretend to know.

The most distinguished member of the family was undoubtedly
Professor William Cawthorne Unwin, FRS, who not only said
that Niagara could be harnessed, but, when challenged, harnessed
it. I was glad, therefore, when his life was published, though
sorry that we were not called in to sell it until it had been privately
printed and partly distributed. He must have been a most inspiring
teacher, because whenever I have run into any of his pupils, as I
have done in many parts of the world, their eyes lit up at the very
mention of his name. The culminating honour of his career came
to him in 1921, when he was unanimously awarded the first
Kelvin Gold Medal—

237

'as being in the opinion of the Presidents of the Principal Engineering Societies—after considering representations from the leading engineering bodies in all parts of the world—the most worthy to receive this recognition of pre-eminence in these branches of engineering with which Lord Kelvin's scientific work and research were most closely identified'.

The speech he made following the presentation of the medal by the late Earl Balfour, reprinted on pages 161–2 of his *Life*, gives an interesting picture of the development of engineering.

In December 1924, in recognition of the great services he had rendered over sixty-seven years, he was accorded the unusual distinction of Honorary Membership of the Institution of Civil Engineers, usually reserved to Heads of States, prominent statesmen, etc. Even in his ninety-first year his interest in engineering still continued, and his knowledge was up to date. Although he had long since retired, his advice was sought about 'methods of measuring pump discharges by means of sharp-edged weirs' nine months before his death on March 17, 1933, in his ninety-fourth year. His funeral service was held at Kensington Chapel, Allen Street, where he had worshipped for many years, being, like most Unwins of his generation, a Nonconformist. The range of his engineering knowledge was quite exceptionally wide, and lest it be thought that his interests were limited to engineering it should be added that he was a keen mountaineer, photographer, fly-fisherman, and an 'Old Vic' enthusiast. He had such a remarkable power of concentration, that when considering a technical problem he could be completely unconscious of all surrounding disturbances, and even a brass band in the street outside would not interfere with his train of thought.

I sometimes think that but for his premature death at the age of forty, after an operation, J. D. Unwin, PH.D., Head of Cambridge House University Settlement, might have challenged Cawthorne Unwin's pre-eminence, though, of course, in quite a different field. In 1914 he was to have gone from Shrewsbury School as a Classical Exhibitioner to Oriel College, Oxford, but went instead into Kitchener's army. During this war service he was twice wounded, and was awarded the Military Cross. Instead of returning to Oxford after the war, he spent some years in Abyssinia. But academic life called him, and in 1928 he was elected Fellow Commoner Research Student of Peterhouse, Cambridge. His research work was concerned with anthropology. His principal work, *Sex and Culture*, a massive volume published by the Oxford University Press, appeared in 1935. Later we issued his *Hopousia*, a fascinating book with a silly title, which I could not persuade him to change. In addition to this specialized work, he found time to publish a brochure, *Notes on the Unwin Family*, and to do a piece of research work at the request of the Home Office on the subject of the imprisonment of debtors, the result of which appeared in book form in 1935.

But as the excellent obituary notice in *The Times* rightly stated, his most lasting contribution is on anthropological subjects. The work entailed considerable research in the customs of primitive peoples; he attempted to relate the degree of culture to the intensity of sexual prohibition. He had made for himself, from a tremendous array of evidence based upon an analysis of eighty widely separated tribes, the discovery that societies manifested what he called 'social energy' in proportion as they approached to absolute monogamy. If this correlation is proved by further research to be true, then an important discovery has been made in the relationship of sexual restraint to culture, and J. D. Unwin will take his place among the discoverers in social anthropology. At the time of his death he was engaged upon a volume which was to be supplementary to *Sex and Culture*. In the course of a tribute to him which appeared in *The Times* a correspondent justly said: 'From his writings alone one might have seen his industry, sincerity, open-mindedness and intellectual courage, without realizing the charming, human man beneath. For he had a modesty and reserve not easily to be penetrated.' Certainly he was a great scholar, and one with original ideas, who could undoubtedly have made a name for himself had he lived.

Curiously enough, years later, his brother, Lt-Col R. H. Unwin, DSO, who was in the Canadian Army and had nothing to do with books, a most able man, was put in charge of the reorganization of the German book trade in the British Zone of Occupation after the Second World War, ably assisted by my fellow director (Major) C. A. Furth, MBE, who put at his disposal the knowledge of the continental book trade gained with Allen & Unwin.

In the early BBC days at Savoy Hill, the then Department of Overseas Trade was allotted some small amount of time each week, and, presumably because of my special interest in the export market, and in particular the continental book trade, invited me to give, on December 17, 1930, a ten-minute talk on 'British Book Distribution throughout the World'. It was my first experience of broadcasting, of which I have done so much since in all parts of the world. It was on that occasion that I coined the phrase 'Trade follows the Book', the truth of which is now generally recognized.

One of the problems connected with broadcasting, which it is not easy to solve, is the publication in book form of symposia. If a series of talks is given by a dozen different distinguished authors, who is the publisher to be? The authors cannot all choose their own publishers, and if, as happened in the 'Points of View' Series described in an earlier chapter, the key speaker to whom all the others refer does not want his script published in book form on any terms, book publication may be rendered impracticable.

Having been personally confronted with the difficulty, I devised a way round it. I prepared an agreement (which, if I remember rightly, I got approved by the Authors' Society at the time) under which each broadcaster gave us a licence to include his (or her) broadcast in the proposed book in consideration of a share in the royalties proportionate with his (or her) contribution. But one unduly jealous publisher made a tremendous fuss about the contract we drew up with the BBC, and the arrangement was not continued after its expiry at the end of three years. In consequence, fewer such symposia are published in book form, which is perhaps no great loss because their sales are seldom, if

Publishers *v.* W. H. Smith & Son

Michael Hornby shaking hands with S. U.

Christmas tea at Lenzerheide

S. U. between the Geishas with the President of Maruzens and David

ever, as great as the sales of a book by any one of the better-known contributors, and the labour involved in the rendering of so many small royalty accounts is out of proportion to the amounts involved. Furthermore, the better a script is for broadcasting, the less satisfactory it tends to be for book publication.

In the course of my broadcast I had referred to Northern Europe as 'a bright spot in the book world' but at that time had never been there. For some reason which I don't remember, I was deprived of my usual winter sports holiday in Switzerland in January 1932, and as I particularly wanted to visit Norway and Sweden, I decided to have a week's ski-ing in March at Geilo (Norway) where the season is later. It was a quite different type of ski-ing from what I had been used to in Switzerland (Lang-lauf not Berg-lauf) but it suited me admirably. Instead of steep climbs and quick descents one covered vast stretches of hilly country in which one could easily lose oneself if one did not take the precaution that I did of going with a Norwegian who knew the terrain.

On my arrival at Oslo I found a telegram from Mr Karl Otto Bonnier, inviting me to a book trade dinner at his home during my stay in Stockholm. I accepted with alacrity. Little did I know what a magnificent reception was ahead of me. Old Mr Bonnier possessed a wonderful house in the Skansen Park at Stockholm, which he maintained in regal state. No more wonderful banquet could have been prepared in any king's palace. Everything was superb. All the leading Stockholm publishers and booksellers, besides many members of the Bonnier dynasty, were present. How many in all I could not count—my eyes were hypnotized by the number of wine glasses allotted to every guest. How was I, a teetotaller, to cope with the situation? The Swedes are very formal in their manners, and it is *de rigueur* when anyone drinks your health ('*Skol!*') to respond with the same wine. Fortunately, one of the young Mrs Bonniers came to my rescue. 'Have *all* your glasses filled with water,' she said (and there were, I think, eight of them), 'and make sure you use the right one'—incidentally no easy task. During the dinner Mr Bonnier made a most charming speech (in English) expressing appreciation of my international activities, to which of course I had to reply. At the conclusion of the banquet, we all walked round the table to shake hands with Mrs Bonnier and to say 'Tack för mat', which literally interpreted is, I suppose, 'Thank you for the meal'. It was a most impressive evening and one I am never likely to forget.

I took the opportunity during my stay at Oslo and Stockholm to make a thorough study of the book trade organization in Norway and Sweden. It seemed to me so desirable that the British book trade should know about it that I published a detailed description in a shilling booklet. It aroused no interest in the British book trade, but many copies were sold in Norway and Sweden, where booksellers and their assistants pride themselves on the completeness of their personal collections of books on their trade. Five years later I visited Denmark and published a similar booklet on the Danish book trade organization with the same result. In Scandinavia and several other European countries this determination to possess a complete library of books on one's own trade or industry is not confined to booksellers. It is universal. But how rare in England!

One incident soon after my return from Sweden I look back upon with great satisfaction. That most excellent old bookseller, the late W. J. Bryce, had got into financial difficulties. I felt that it would be a tragedy if his services, and those of his quite outstanding colleague, Mr I. P. M. Chambers, were lost to the book trade. The amount involved was small, so I bought the assets from the receiver, formed a new company with the two of them as directors, leased them a corner of my building in Museum Street on favourable terms, and gave them a fresh start. I felt confident that with a little financial supervision and greater caution in buying, they would not fail to make good. My confidence was fully justified, and today W. J. Bryce Ltd. must be among the most efficient and prosperous of the smaller bookshops in the country. A few years later they in turn were able to help a German refugee bookseller (the late Dr Hans Preiss), owner of one of the finest bookshops in Unter den Linden, Berlin, by letting him have a corner of their shop until he had built up a sufficient connection to justify taking larger premises. As a refugee from the Nazis, Dr Preiss was unable to take any of his money out with him, but he hit upon an ingenious method of outwitting them. At the time (a) about 12 marks = £1, (b) the Nazis were advocating the despatch of copies of their official paper, the *Voelkische Beobachter*, to people abroad. Dr Preiss accordingly arranged for friends to post him regularly copies of the paper with a few twenty-mark notes tucked inside, thus augmenting his meagre resources.

But Dr Preiss was not the only Berlin bookseller to find refuge in England. Some years later Dr Homeyer, of Collignon & Co., a firm with exceptionally good export connections, managed to secure permission to make a brief visit to London. Although there was every likelihood of his being sent to a concentration camp on his return, and J. & E. Bumpus were ready and anxious to put him in charge of their foreign department, all my attempts to help him to prolong his stay had failed. The Home Office was obdurate and I was in despair. By a lucky—some would say providential—chance, twenty-four hours before his time was up I found myself seated at the same table for lunch at the Reform Club as the late Sir Percy Harris and Mr Graham White, both then Members of Parliament. They were talking about the treatment of refugees, and I at once cited the case of Dr Homeyer. They agreed that it was criminal folly to send back to Germany a bookseller who could bring us valuable export connections, and took immediate and successful action. Instead of ending his days in a concentration camp, therefore, Dr Homeyer worked for more than a dozen years for J. & E. Bumpus, to their great satisfaction, until his retirement in August 1951.

Just before I paid the visit to Denmark to which I have referred, tenders were invited for the purchase of the assets of John Lane the Bodley Head Ltd. The business was insolvent at the time of John Lane's death, but so great was the prestige attached to the firm that there was competition to acquire it. There were five directors, and a further one was brought in with capital to bolster up the business, but as they all expected to be paid, and the profits were not there out of which to pay them, there could, of course, be only one end. It is astonishing for how many years a book-publishing business can continue its insolvent way before the showdown comes. The receiver said that the sealed bids would be opened on such and such a date, and that the highest bidder would be expected to take delivery forthwith. Now on that day I was due as President of the International Publishers Association (as it is now called) in Copenhagen to participate in the centenary celebrations of the Danish book trade organization, and there were at that time no other directors of George Allen & Unwin. When thinking the matter over, it suddenly occurred to me that it would be amusing to run the John Lane business co-operatively with two of my competitors. I accordingly approached my two fellow officers of the Publishers Association, W. G. Taylor (Dents) and G. Wren Howard (Capes) with whom I was constantly in touch. Would they care to join me to the extent of, say, one-sixth each? They, too, thought it an amusing idea and agreed. Would they like to check my valuation and agree my bid? 'No' was the answer. 'What is good enough for you is good enough for us.' And so it was that, on my return from Copenhagen, I learnt that my bid had been accepted and that I was chairman of something new in publishing—a business owned by three competitors. The war hit it badly. Over half a million books, for which there would have been a ready sale, were 'blitzed', and we had no paper with which to replace them. Our ration was inadequate to cope with any growth of the business. The Excess Profits Tax would have hopelessly crippled us had we not been able, as an outcome of a letter to *The Times* and the intervention of Somerset House, to call to our aid the heavy reductions in their capital structure made by our predecessors. The profits were all ploughed back to finance the growth of the business except for one year, when we paid a quite modest dividend. The results of that dividend as far as I personally was concerned are set forth in the following letter which appeared in *The Times*:

'The anomalies under the "special contribution" are manifold, but the following case is startling. A company was formed in 1937 to acquire the assets of a bankrupt concern and is now doing a substantial export business. The chief proprietor drew no remuneration, and, to finance the development of the business, no dividend was paid on the ordinary share capital until 1947, when a small one was declared, yielding the proprietor £100 gross. But the income tax, sur-tax and special contribution on this modest remuneration for ten years' daily attendance at the business amount to £127 10s 0d. The encouragement for building up an export business is thus in this case a fine of £27 10s 0d plus, it may be added, 2 per cent interest, because the proprietor was in New Zealand on business when the assessment was made.'

We thereafter refrained from paying dividends.

When we first took over the business we appointed Percy Howe (the authority on Hazlitt) to manage it. He had been a director of Martin Secker Ltd., and with the failure of that business, and the sale of its assets to Mr F. J. Warburg, was immediately available. He was succeeded in May 1939 by C. J. Greenwood, the assets of whose firm, Boriswood & Co. Ltd., had just been bought by The Bodley Head. At that time there was little competition to acquire businesses which had failed, and in addition to the assets of Boriswood, we acquired those of R. Cobden Sanderson Ltd., Martin Hopkinson & Co. Ltd. and Gerald Howe Ltd. John Lane thereby became the publishers of the work of that delightful author Adrian Bell, besides establishing many other useful connections.

One of the most interesting incidents during my chairmanship was the publication of Alan Wood's *The Ground Nut Affair*, an exposure of the disastrous post-war Government scheme for the production of ground nuts on a vast scale in East Africa. At least one publisher had been deterred from issuing the book because of the threat of Governmental intervention or a libel action. My colleagues have reminded me that when a distinguished Allen & Unwin author wrote congratulating me on my courage, I replied: 'I cannot claim to be a particularly

245

courageous person, but I am not easily intimidated when I am on my own ground and know what I am about.'

The experiment of joint ownership worked out most pleasantly, but, with added responsibilities in other directions, I found after twenty years of daily attendance and supervision that it was becoming a burden. We had succeeded in doing what we set out to do; the company was prosperous—much more so than it had ever been—in fact, 1956 was an all-time record, and we accordingly decided to sell it. The wisdom of this decision was accentuated by the fact that if anything happened to me the business would have immediately to be sold to help pay my death duties, and quick sales of publishing businesses are nearly always disadvantageous to the seller. After leisurely negotiations with various people, some of them exasperating, the entire shares of the company were eventually sold on January 7, 1957, to Henry Ansbacher & Co., who entrusted the further management of the company to Max Reinhardt Ltd., under whose auspices it is now being run.

* * * *

In the summary in these last two chapters of my personal work as a publisher in the nineteen-thirties, I have said little of my other activities which were more time-absorbing, particularly in 1933, than in any other period of my career. From 1931–1937 I was an officer of the Publishers Association (President for the middle two years), and President or Vice-President of the International Publishers Association throughout the whole period.[1] Within twenty-four hours of my return from the International Publishers Congress at Brussels, when I was President of both Associations, my brother-in-law died. As one of my New Zealand brothers and my father had died just before, and the latter's death involved the winding up of my mother's estate, I found myself simultaneously confronted with four executorships, in addition to a most unwelcome job as arbitrator between two publisher

[1] See Chapters 21 and 22.

colleagues, and service as a juryman in the King's Bench Division lasting many days.

My own business and my own affairs perforce received quite inadequate attention. The effect upon my publishing profit and loss account was devastating, and I should not want to face the post of President of the Publishers Association again. But it was an interesting experience, and the tributes paid to me at the end of my term of office by Sir Frederick Macmillan, Mr H. S. Scheumeier (of Nelsons) and others were most consoling. It was pleasant to be able to pass on the task to one in whom I had such unlimited confidence, W. G. Taylor, of J. M. Dent & Sons, and together to start thinking about the preparations for that great event, the London meeting of the International Publishers Congress in 1936.

It had not made my task as President any easier that for six months I was needlessly racked with the most painful neuritis— needless because my dentist had refused, until my doctor insisted upon it, to 'waste' a plate upon an X-ray photo of a wisdom tooth which appeared to be in perfect condition, but was in fact defective at the root and the source of my trouble. Before its removal I had gone to Bath for treatment—a treatment prematurely ended by an intimation that my elder son had fallen from a pony on to frozen ground and smashed up his elbow.

For one reason and another I had been so much criticized and abused by booksellers that I was not a little surprised, and much comforted, to receive at this opportune moment a quite unexpected letter of appreciation and thanks from a distinguished Scottish firm. It is a letter to which I still turn when in a doubting mood.

In looking through the correspondence of the period, I was glad to observe that my lifelong battle for books was not interrupted. I noticed, for example, three letters to Ramsay MacDonald, one in 1932 expressing the hope that if a tariff was held to be necessary there would be no question of the taxation of knowledge, i.e. that books would be exempted, and that no barrier would be erected to prevent the free exchange of thought; a later one urging that the Incitement to Disaffection Bill should be dropped, adding that even the Council of the Publishers Association (a very conservative body) had instructed me as President to make a formal protest concerning the way the Act was likely to jeopardize the position of bona-fide book publishers; and another asking whether anything could be done to ensure that the book trade was less of a Cinderella where national functions were concerned, and pointing out that we always seemed to fall between two stools. If the professions—architects, lawyers, doctors, etc., were being represented, publishers were excluded on the ground that they were connected with trade, but that they were equally excluded if representatives of industry were being selected.

When the late secretary of the Royal Academy said something pleasant about our issue of English editions of the Phaidon Art Books, I took the opportunity to draw his attention to the fact that, although presidents of many organizations and associations were from time to time invited to their yearly banquet, no President of the Publishers Association ever had been, though if there was one group of people who above all helped young artists at the start of their careers it was book publishers. I added that as my period of office as president was at an end it was my successors, not myself, I had in mind. He most kindly invited me personally on one or two occasions, and most delightful it was, but I don't think any president of the Publishers Association has to this day been invited as such.

The question of 'status' is one I have always felt keenly, because if once books receive the recognition to which they are entitled most of our difficulties will solve themselves, or never arise. Even the BBC might then comply more fully with its 'duty of carrying on the service as a means of disseminating information, education and entertainment', and be less scared of giving vital information about books of an educational character for fear that they should be accused of doing something for books which they could not do for any other commodity.

If, as I concluded a long address to the Association of Assistant

Librarians[1] about that time, I have shown in such matters undue and possibly un-English enthusiasm for my job, I hope that I may be forgiven, and that there will at any rate be some who will be inclined to say with Ecclesiastes 'I perceive that there is nothing better than that a man should rejoice in his own works; for that is his portion'.

[1] *The Library Assistant*, December 1933, Vol. 26, No. 11.

CHAPTER 15

THE SECOND WORLD WAR

Unlike 1914, the Second World War took few people by surprise. My elder son, David, was working during the middle of 1939 as a volunteer in Lauffer's Bookshop in Budapest and suggested that the family should spend their summer holiday with him at some ideal spot in Hungary. It sounded delightful, but I had no wish to be caught in such a place if war broke out. I said that we would come as near to him as we could in safety. A glance at the map showed that place to be Liechtenstein, and to Gaflei—high above Vaduz—my wife, our two other children and I repaired towards the end of August 1939. The outlook was so threatening that we cabled our son to join us at once, and he caught the last plane out of Budapest to touch down in Germany.

We had had just one happy day together when I heard the raucous voice of Hitler on a loud-speaker announcing the invasion of Poland. This meant war, and we left at once. We should have had difficulty but for a loan from a fellow-visitor at the hotel, a Swiss, to whom I explained that although I had a letter of credit for £250 the bank at Vaduz refused to honour it for even £20 on the ground that they did not know on what basis to calculate the rate of exchange.

When we eventually got to Zürich in a train packed with Swiss soldiers who had immediately been mobilized, we found that we could proceed no farther because, in view of the French mobilization, all services through France had been suspended. It was thus at Zürich we learnt that Great Britain was at war. The British Consul recommended us to proceed at leisure to Geneva, where all stranded visitors like ourselves would be collected and repatriated. This we accordingly did, after visiting the International Exhibition at Zürich and spending a few days in Luzern. When the time came for departure from Geneva, every seat in the train was numbered and occupied. We were warned to have provisions with us for forty-eight hours, and were taken via Lyons round much of France, finally arriving late at night at Dieppe. The crossing was fearsome because it was thought that we might be torpedoed at any moment. The vessel was so crowded that it was almost impossible to cross the saloon without treading upon recumbent bodies. We arrived, three weeks after we left Liechtenstein, in a panicky London anticipating bombs which did not come. It was the period of the phoney war to which so many people settled down as if it were going to last.

Experience of the First World War had shown me the importance of rapid adaptation to changed conditions, and I switched over to the production of Air Cadet, Junior Officer, Observers' and Spotters' handbooks which enjoyed a ready sale. Alan Michie and Walter Graebner's *Their Finest Hour* was one of the first books to record factual accounts of individual heroism in wartime; it was an immediate best-seller and the demand continued throughout the war. But the book which gave me the greatest personal satisfaction was Frau Litten's *A Mother Fights Hitler*, showing what miracles a fearless aristocratic woman could achieve in defence of her son.

A problem which deeply concerned me and was uppermost in the minds of thoughtful people at that time, was the future of Germany, and we published a number of books on the subject. Only second in importance was the question of self-government in India, a subject likewise reflected in our list.

The kind of difficulty with which we were confronted at this period is exemplified by the following incident. We had published many books by C. Delisle Burns, with whom our relations were of the happiest, and he sent us about this time his *magnum opus, The First Europe*. We told him at once that we should be proud to publish it, but had not at the moment sufficient paper on which to print such a big book. His reply was that the printing and publication could wait for paper, but what was urgent was that he should be able to correct the proofs in person. As he was a very sick man we expedited the typesetting, and he had the satisfaction of passing the proofs for press just before he died.

The basement of our new building, 28 Little Russell Street, was requisitioned as an air-raid shelter in September 1939, and we were instructed to place it immediately at the authorities' disposal who simultaneously demanded that the floors should be strengthened. As all our stock was stored in the basement this was tantamount to putting us out of business, and as the floors had been constructed to carry more than double the normal weight that part of the order was palpably absurd. We were allowed to retain part use of the basement for our stock, but on the strengthening of the floors the official concerned was adamant. Characteristic of many war-time bureaucrats he would pay no attention to any remonstrance, however justified. He knew better. I told the Kleine flooring people that this was a reflection upon their work, and their engineer so overwhelmed the official with facts and figures that he had no alternative but to give way, and the order for the strengthening of the floors, which would in fact have weakened them, was quietly dropped.

But the use by the public of what was our stock room was an expensive one for us. Whenever there was an air-raid warning, people of all descriptions flocked in, and, despite all our precautions, helped themselves to our books. One of the worst offenders proved to be a well-dressed lady, who walked into Bumpus's with four copies of an expensive book which she wanted to sell. Mr Wilson's suspicions were aroused and he telephoned to me. I quickly ascertained that the copies came from our basement, but by the time I had done so the 'lady' had taken her departure. Collectively our losses from theft were substantial though insignificant compared with what happened elsewhere, because when I arrived at the office on November 8, 1940, I learnt that during the previous night the warehouse at Edmonton, where our sheet stock was stored, had been completely gutted. In that one night we lost one million four hundred thousand books affecting two thousand one hundred titles on our list, and leaving us in many cases with only small stocks of bound copies.

I recalled those pregnant remarks of the Australian bookseller about the 'knock-out' blow I had had in August 1914; thought how much better equipped I was to cope with this appalling blow and smiled. Later in the day I ran across a fellow publisher who said, 'I hear you have had a gigantic loss'. I replied, 'Yes, over a million books'. 'You don't seem very perturbed', he said. 'Well, I can't do anything about it, can I?' I replied. When we heard later that we had lost twenty thousand books here and thirty thousand there, it seemed by comparison unimportant.

As I had foreseen, the compulsory War Risks Insurance, though intended to be fair, penalized the provident and endowed the improvident for the reasons shown in the chapter on the Publishers Association in the Appendices (page 391). Suffice it to say here that we received only a few thousand pounds for stock which over the years would have yielded more than twenty times the amount.

Nevertheless, I regarded myself as lucky, because at one time or another we had six bombs within a hundred yards of my home in Oak Hill Park, Hampstead, one within fourteen yards of where my wife and I were sleeping. That one was a time bomb which did not go off; had it done so, I should not be writing this. Under police instructions we had to vacate the house until, three weeks later, the bomb was removed. We took refuge with friends in Essex, and I went to my office daily from Bishop's Stortford. It was a wonderful respite for my wife and myself, and, apart from very occasional week-ends, the only one we had out of London during the whole war period. One bomb destroyed the Lodge at the entrance to Oak Hill Park near our house, and I have a vivid recollection of Mr (now Sir) Geoffrey Faber, who then lived opposite us, falling into the crater it formed—a crater which effectively blocked the road.

Like most Londoners I had other narrow escapes which it would be wearisome to recapitulate. When the raids were at their worst it was my practice at home to put on a record of Dvořák's

New World Symphony at full blast so that I could hear nothing else. At the office, my secretary and I saw no reason to allow Hitler to interfere with the even tenor of our way, and when the sirens sounded continued with dictation.

Naturally we had our share of casualties. One of our employees returned home to find his wife had had a direct hit from a bomb and that there was virtually no trace of her; another lost his home and everything he possessed, apart from the clothes in which he arrived at the office. These are incidents best forgotten, but I like to recall the story of one of the girl invoice clerks, who was an air-raid warden and voluntarily out on duty night after night. She arrived punctually as usual one morning and informed us that, whilst she was attending to some casualties the previous night, all the windows but one at the back of her house had been smashed by blast. A few days later she apologized for being a little late, but she said that all the windows on the other side of her house had been blasted, and it had made rather a mess. Then she added cheerfully, 'We've still got one window'. A week later she announced with a smile, 'Our last window has gone', as if there were now nothing to worry about.

In the course of a broadcast on Saturday, October 19, 1940, I said:

'Air raids can prevent our doing much that we enjoy, but fortunately they cannot deprive us of many of the things that matter most. On the contrary, for example, they bring to many of us increased opportunity to indulge in the pleasures of reading. . . .

'We hear much about "Liberty of Thought". True freedom consists not in the liberty to think, but in the freedom to express our thoughts, and in the liberty to hear and read the thoughts of others. It is of that liberty Hitler wants to deprive us. One of my favourite books is a little volume by Lowes Dickinson entitled *A Modern Symposium*. In it the full and free expression of thought is seen at its best. A group of distinguished people meet at a country house, and one by one express their attitude to life. Each speaker carries conviction by his obvious sincerity, and in listening to them one realizes as perhaps never before the many-sidedness of Truth and the value—nay more, the necessity—of the right of every individual to be free to express his views.

'It is said that a man can be known by the company he keeps. So, too, can he be known by the books he reads because in reading them he keeps company with their authors. If we have chosen our books wisely, we have enjoyed the companionship of the elect, and have done also that most satisfying thing, the cultivation of our intellectual and spiritual gardens.

'A distinguished bishop is said to have advised people during those nightly air raids:

> To commend themselves to God.
> To read a book.
> To go to sleep.

'That seems to me peculiarly sound advice.'

Worse in some ways than the loss of over a million books was the unpleasantness and bitter complaints it involved. Letter after letter arrived, 'Why don't you reprint this?' 'Why don't you reprint that?', 'When *will* you be in a position to supply this or that?' To all of them we could but reply that we might be stupid, but we knew of no way of producing books without paper; that our ration was a particularly small one, and that because we had been bombed at the wrong time we had not been granted (and were never at any time granted) a compassionate allowance to replace our losses like those who were bombed at the beginning or end of the war.

But that was not the only way in which we suffered. Author after author wrote to us to say that one or other of the mushroom firms (nearly all long since extinct) which sprang up overnight and took advantage of the idiosyncracies of paper control, had told them that they had plenty of paper, and that as we hadn't any they felt compelled to turn to them. One of these firms run by a Hungarian refugee, now deceased, built up in one year on so-called 'free paper', a turnover greatly in excess of what my paper ration would yield. While the going was good, and every book was over-subscribed, he lived in considerable splendour, but when the inevitable day came when his books became less readily saleable and a receiver was appointed his creditors did not get a penny in the pound. I am happy to add that the creditors included printers who had co-operated with him in securing illegitimate paper. The position was admirably summed up at the time by Alan Moorhead in some paragraphs in the *Daily Express* from which I give the following excerpts:

'Something strange is happening in the book-publishing business, and the more you look into it the stranger it is.

'If you look at the advertisements in the papers you will see new publishers are popping up everywhere. Inquiring into it today I find that some 200 new firms have entered the profitable business of supplying the book-starved public since the war began and, unlike the older firms, they have plenty of paper.

'When the paper shortage began at the beginning of the war the Government limited all existing publishers to a percentage of the paper they used in 1939, an erratic year for publishing. The quota at present is 40 per cent.

'That meant that all the old firms had to cut down drastically and the supply of books has never caught up with the demand. Any reasonably good or topical book sells out at once. "The last thing I want," one of the old publishers told me, "is a best-seller on my hands."

'However, there is nothing to stop a jobbing printer or anyone else setting up as a publisher any day he likes. And since he did not publish in 1939 he has no quota. He is limited only by the amount of paper he can get hold of—and there is still a great deal of paper lying round in the country.

'There is nothing to stop anyone buying paper. If you are an old 1939 publisher you have to declare the purchase of these extra stocks and deduct them from your quota. If you are a new publisher you go right ahead.

. . . .

'As you can imagine, the old publishers are in a bit of a ferment about all this. They complain that their authors are being taken away from them. . . . They say that the responsibility for keeping up the tradition of this country's publishing must rest on the old permanent houses who publish good stuff, not stuff that is merely popular.'

It did not make the situation any more pleasant that some of these many newcomers boasted of their acumen and openly described the old-established firms as sleepy and unenterprising because they abode by the regulations and respected the wish of the Paper Controller that they should not form subsidiary companies or seek dubious means to increase their meagre rations. In practice, the better publishers were consistently penalized, and the unscrupulous allowed to get away with all their illegalities.

As an illustration of the way in which old-established firms suffered, Chambers's *Twentieth Century Dictionary* was out of print from December 1943 to June 1944, when some further copies became available owing to an allocation from the Moberly Pool.[1] But these further copies did not enable Chambers to supply 25 per cent of the orders they held and they were unable to say when further copies would be available. At that same time their *Encyclopaedia* as well as their two-volume *Encyclopedia of English Literature* were out of print. Two-thirds of their total paper ration was allocated to purely educational books and they were only able to publish two new titles in 1943 and were compelled to cease altogether to publish children's books.

Certain literary agents added to the publishers' difficulties by serving them with notices that unless they reprinted this, that or the other work (which for the lack of paper they couldn't) the rights would revert under the terms of their agreements. When publishers united in self-defence, and entered into a gentleman's agreement not to acquire their competitors' authors as the outcome of such notices, the Society of Authors was most indignant. But in view of the way established publishers were treated over paper it is difficult to see what else they could do, although the distress of some authors deserved every sympathy.

A large proportion of my time during the war was occupied by a prolonged fight for paper for books, and evidence of some of my activities will be found in Chapter 19. How necessary the fight was will be seen from the following figures:

[1] About which see page 398.

PAPER RATIONING

		TONS
Newspapers		**250,000**
H.M. Stationery Office		**100,000**
Periodicals	*nearly*	**50,000**
War Office (*included in H.M.S.O. quota*)		**25,000**
Books (*including the extra* 2½%)	*less than*	**22,000**
American Book Publishers' quota for 1943 was		128,000

It is a tragedy that for lack of another 8,000 tons we were compelled to hand over many of our export markets to America, to deprive students of necessary text-books, and to be unable to supply the liberated countries with the books they so badly needed immediately the war was over.

I hope that one day a thesis may be written upon the treatment of books during the Second World War, with special reference to the limitation of paper for their production and the statistics collected by the Publishers Association of the number of books which went out of print.

One of the greatest consolations of this difficult period was the sympathetic understanding of people who mattered. Mrs Sidney Webb, for example, although she had no business to discuss, spent over an hour with me one Saturday morning just as a friendly gesture, and a fortnight later wrote: 'I so much enjoyed my talk with you and if you should ever be in this neighbourhood do let us know and come to lunch or tea'—an invitation which, owing to lack of transport (my car was compulsorily laid up), I was unable, to my everlasting regret, to accept. Later, though there was no reason why she should trouble about me, she wrote:

'We were so grieved to hear of your great loss. It reduces our own almost to a minus quantity. However, I see you are bringing out, like Longmans is, new books, and yours are always especially interesting and up to date. So I think you will live to see another accumulation

of millions; and for those of us who are over eighty, as we are, it
is not of much consequence if our books are out of print. With kind
regards from my husband.'

She was a fascinating person to talk to and it was a great deprivation that I did not see more of her.

Again, Margaret Storm Jameson, then President of the PEN
of which I am a member, who served with me on the Books and
Periodicals Committee of the British Council, went out of her
way to cheer me at this depressing time when, apart from losses
and scarcity of paper, we were short-staffed. In connection with
the last, the following paragraph from the *Bookseller* tells its own
story:

'Long Service'

'Some of Messrs George Allen & Unwin's employees seem to be
fairly certain of immunity from calling-up notices. On November
9th a third member of their staff, Mr J. James, who for so long has
presided at their trade counter, completes fifty years' service with the
firm. He started as a messenger with George Allen & Unwin's
predecessors, Swan Sonnenschein & Co., in White Hart Street,
Paternoster Square, on Lord Mayor's Day 1890 at the munificent
wage of six shillings a week.

'Life with the firm seems to have agreed with him, because, like
Mr Stallybrass, who has nearly completed fifty-nine years' service,
he has not even a grey, let alone a white hair! Two other members of
the staff with long service records are looking forward to scoring
their fifty not out before long.'

We were indeed fortunate in having these old employees and we
cherish happy memories of their loyalty, devotion and faithful
service.

Just as a spoilt child who cannot get his own way delights in
destroying things, so the Nazis in their anger over their failure to
invade England seemed to derive satisfaction from destroying
Wren churches and other beautiful buildings. Their success in
this peculiarly non-military activity rapidly became universally
known. News of their achievements in book destruction took

longer to reach the outside world. When it did, indications reached me from Sweden, Switzerland, and more distant parts of the world that publishers and booksellers abroad were under the most astonishing misapprehensions about the nature of its effects upon the British book trade. It seemed desirable to publicize a counter-blast to the Nazi suggestion that we had been completely put out of business. I pointed out, both in a broadcast and in print, that, unlike Wren churches, books could easily be replaced, and that, given paper, modern printing machinery could reproduce books faster than any Hitler or Goering could destroy them; that within a fortnight all the firms whose premises were destroyed in the City fire had established themselves elsewhere and were carrying on business. The rapidity with which they did so was startling, and I cited the following actual instance. A publisher learned at 9.30 one Saturday evening that his premises were on fire as the result of enemy action. He telephoned at once to inform his brother, who, by chance, was spending the week-end with a book trade colleague. Nothing could be done that night because the fire was not yet under control, but the brothers agreed to meet at daybreak. When their book trade colleague, who insisted upon accompanying them, saw the devastation the fire had caused, he said: 'Come along at once; we must clear a floor in my building for you.' All day Sunday the three of them, with some watchmen and others, worked steadily. On the Monday morning, when the publishers' staff arrived to find their usual premises gutted by fire, they were sent on at once to the alternative accommodation which had been prepared for them, and work continued without interruption.

I emphasized that although the book trade had had peculiarly hard knocks, there was no sign of any depression. On the contrary, at no period of the war had there been greater determination to carry on imperturbably or with more complete confidence in ultimate victory. By way of counter-offensive I pointed out that, unlike those in Totalitarian countries, we were still free to read just what we wanted and—apart from the printing of anything which would give information to the enemy—a thing no reputable publisher would want to do—there was no censorship. In the midst of war we remained even in that respect a free people. There was no Gestapo lurking round any corner or behind any door. There was no official telling us book publishers what we might or might not print. All kinds of opinions were as freely expressed in books—and for that matter by orators in Hyde Park—as in more peaceful times.

During all this period I, like others, was occupied with Fire Guard and similar duties, but what was more exacting were the responsibilities thrust upon me in connection with Oak Hill Park where I lived. It is an estate of about seven acres in a most peaceful corner of Hampstead. It won a first prize at the Great Exhibition of 1851 for a group of gentlemen's dwellings, but today the site has greater value without the wonderful Victorian houses. George Smith lived at Oak Hill Park Lodge in the early *Cornhill Magazine* days, and his weekly receptions held there were attended by such famous Smith Elder authors as Thackeray, Trollope, Mrs Gaskell, George Eliot, and Wilkie Collins, to name but a few. The Neave family who had long owned the estate, had for some time granted only short leases of the houses. When, therefore, I heard that the Park was to be sold, I realized that unless I took some action the site would be bought for development[1] and I should lose both my home and my tennis court. It so happened that the Sir Halley Stewart Trust were on the look-out for a large mortgage for which this estate offered excellent security. At their request I formed a small company to buy it with the money largely provided by them. I did so on the definite understanding that I should be absolved of any responsibility for the day-to-day management of the property, which was entrusted to a retired surveyor who was appointed a director for the purpose.

With the outbreak of war some tenants just left and repudiated all responsibility; one, to whom special consideration had been shown, 'flitted' overnight with arrears of rent—still unpaid. Only a minority—a small one—gave due notice and attended to their dilapidations. There came a moment when my wife and I were

[1] As 22 years later it now has been.

almost the only residents left in the Park. For adequate reasons the director in charge retired to the West of England, and I was left to 'hold the baby'. At this point the War Office stepped in, and, as an indication of the reckless behaviour of some of our war-time masters, here are two or three instances.

(1) They requisitioned two houses, which they never used except to turn on the water (which I had carefully turned off at the main), the day before we had one of the worst frosts for years, with the result that both houses were completely flooded. The compensation paid for the damage as assessed by the War Office (no appeal allowed in war-time) was £87. The condition in which the houses were eventually handed over was such that a surveyor I consulted said that they were only fit to be pulled down.

(2) We had just spent over a thousand pounds on converting one house into two maisonettes, for which we had tenants waiting. The War Office requisitioned the house and then left it empty for so long that it got into poor shape. All responsibility was repudiated.

(3) Cars identified as belonging to the Military drew up outside one house, and their occupants entered it by one of the windows. They eventually left carrying a basket which contained a toy railway that had been stored in the basement, apparently relying upon any criticism of their behaviour in war-time being regarded as 'unpatriotic'.

But to revert to publishing. It was already clear that there would be a pent-up demand for British books, and for translations of British books, throughout all the occupied countries the moment the war was over. We even published Czech editions of books by Masaryk and Čapek knowing that any stock not bought by Czech exiles in Britain and elsewhere would be readily sold in Czechoslovakia as soon as it was liberated. But we went further. In conjunction with that experienced publisher, Julius Firt, of the firms of Borovy and Melantrich, who had escaped to London, we acquired Czech translation rights in a number of books so that translations could be made in readiness for immediate production and publication the day an armistice was signed. The venture was most successful, but, alas! my share of the profits, which was to be used for another trip to the Tatra Mountains, remains in the form of blocked Czech currency in Prague.

In addition to my close connections with Czechoslovakia, for which I had received in 1938 at the hands of the late Jan Masaryk the Order of the White Lion of Czechoslovakia, I acted in an advisory capacity on publishing matters for the Netherlands Government in London. They wished to pay me a fee, but I declined, laughingly saying that I would much prefer a free holiday in Holland or Java when the war was over. One piece of advice I gave them they unwisely disregarded. I pointed out that their National Library, and probably one or two others, would unquestionably need copies of the more important British war-time publications, adding that they were easily obtainable through a good bookseller on publication, but as they were all being rapidly sold out many would be out of print and difficult to secure when the war was over. Their then legal adviser (a Boer) found reasons why they could, or should, not adopt this obvious course. The Norwegians, thanks to the intervention of the poet Grieg (brother of the publisher and grandson of the composer) to whom I had deplored the unwisdom of the Dutch, immediately implemented my proposal, with the result that the first ship that left for Norway after the war carried a consignment of books for the National Library at Oslo. The poet Grieg never learnt of the joy his action had brought to Norwegian librarians because unfortunately he was killed in a bombing raid over Germany. Some years later, when I mentioned the matter to some Dutch librarians, they were indignant, and when they asked whether I had ever been thanked for my honorary services, and I had to answer 'No' they were very upset. Whether as an outcome I do not know, but in 1950 I was made an Officer in the Order of Orange Nassau.

In March 1944 I received the unusual honour of being invited by the Royal Institution to deliver one of its celebrated Friday evening discourses. The subject was 'Publishing in Peace and War', and it was the first time in the long history of the Institution that one of the discourses had been devoted to publishing. It was also, I imagine, the first occasion on which the Government of the day had been openly attacked on such an occasion because I denounced in no measured fashion the mean and deplorable way in which paper for books had been handled. I reprinted the lecture, in slightly expanded form, together with some notes on 'The Future of British Books on the Continent after the War' and 'The Status of Books', as a pamphlet.[1] It was widely noticed in the Press, which had consistently advocated more paper for books, knowing what a small quantity was involved and how much it would achieve. I sent a copy to Lord Beaverbrook, then Lord Privy Seal, from whom I had a gracious acknowledgment, saying that it was of great value to him as a publisher and as a member of the Government because it was written with the unrivalled authority which I commanded. He expressed the hope that we were very near to the day when British publishing enterprises could go forward without the trials and difficulties to which the war had subjected them. His wish was not fulfilled in the ensuing ten years.

I was anxious that when my colleague (then Major) C. A. Furth was released from the Army he should have more material with which to build up our educational list. Accordingly when the firm of Ivor Nicholson & Watson went into liquidation, I bought from the receiver the assets of their subsidiary company, Elkin, Mathews & Marrot which they had changed from *belles lettres* into an educational business. A little later, owing to the death of its founder, an enthusiastic geologist, the much more important firm of Thos. Murby & Co. came into the market. At that juncture no publisher wanted to be burdened with additional complications, and there are plenty of problems facing anyone who takes over the assets of a business which has for some time been in the hands of a receiver. But it is at such times that

---

[1] *Publishing in Peace and War* (London: George Allen & Unwin Ltd., 1944).

an advantageous purchase can be made. We became overnight the leading geological publishers, but what was less attractive was to find ourselves purveyors of specimen minerals, geological hammers, and in fact anything of interest to a geologist, including many appliances of which I had not previously heard. Although we merged the business into our own, the goodwill of the name Murby in connection with geology was too valuable to lose. Accordingly we retained the Murby imprint for all geological books and used it for our own geological publications whenever we had cause to reprint them, adding, of course, in the books themselves, and on the Thos. Murby notepaper, the words 'Proprietors: George Allen & Unwin Ltd'. It was a most satisfactory purchase because it included so many 'bread and butter lines', that is books with a continuous and steady sale.

In the same year we had the privilege of introducing two most promising new authors to the public, Peter Abrahams, the South African, now a distinguished novelist, and the poet Alun Lewis, whose genius was quickly recognized. His untimely death as the result of an accident while serving in the forces in India in 1944 deprived Britain of a poet of outstanding promise, all of whose books we keep steadily in print.

At the request of the late Hermon Ould, then Secretary of the PEN, we embarked upon a series of 2s od booklets which it was hoped would augment their income. Unfortunately, despite the eminence of the authors, few of the volumes enjoyed any substantial sale and the continuous rise in production costs made it impracticable to continue the series after the twenty-first volume.

A book which strained our paper resources was Sir William (now Lord) Beveridge's *Full Employment in a Free Society*. It was a subject of the deepest interest at the time, for Sir William presented his work as a sequel and complement to the famous *Beveridge Report on Social Insurance and Allied Services* issued by the Government in 1942. Few people who lived through the First World War could have forgotten what an appalling problem unemployment had presented thereafter. The minds of the working classes were dominated by the fear of its recurrence.

Probably nothing contributed more largely to the failure of the Conservative Party at the ensuing election than their hypocritical attitude to the Beveridge Report. At first they denounced it on the ground that it went much too far; then when protests came from all over the country they promised a scheme that would go further. It was difficult for anyone to believe their protestations. Meanwhile the book sold merrily, and paper for it was the major claim on our meagre ration, much to the annoyance of some of our other authors. Nevertheless a subsequent more topical book by Lord Beveridge went to a mushroom publisher with unlimited paper, so impossible was it for us to compete in that respect though, granted paper, our resources and unique export connections were much superior.

Another book sadly affected by the paper situation, but in a quite different way, was the fourth volume of Lancelot Hogben's Primers, Hamilton's *History of the Homeland*. We had been so successful with our publicity for the first three volumes, *Mathematics for the Million*, *Science for the Citizen* and *The Loom of Language* that we knew that the advance orders for *History of the Homeland* would be formidable. They exceeded our most optimistic expectations. We had saved up paper from our ration for a very substantial first edition, but it looked as if it might prove inadequate. There was no paper in sight for a reprint. What were we to do? There had been bitter complaints from booksellers about publishers boosting books which they were unable to supply, forgetful of the fact that advertisement space had to be booked long in advance before the publisher could possibly know what the position would be. In the circumstances we soft-pedalled our publicity, with the result that, though the *History of the Homeland* continues to sell, it has never achieved the spectacular success of its three predecessors as it otherwise might well have done.

In publishing one has constantly to make quick decisions based on prophetic inspiration, helped, of course, by past experience. One cannot always be right. The successful publisher is the one who makes fewest mistakes.

As the war proceeded, more and more important groups of people became agitated about the acute shortage of books. The medical profession, for example, pointed out the absurdity of calling for more young doctors, and at the same time making it impossible for them to take their degrees for lack of text-books. Teachers drew attention to the foolishness of raising the school-leaving age without making any provision for the additional text-books that would be needed. The Ministry of Education alone were complacent. They never lifted a little finger to help the campaign for more paper for books. It was pointed out to them that we started the war with big reserves because it was the practice to print a five or six years' supply of most text-books, binding them as required; that, apart from losses by bombing, the shortage of paper had compelled publishers to reprint at most a years' supply at a time so that at any moment endless books would be simultaneously out of stock. Their reply was that no difficulty had thus far been experienced (a statement which any headmaster or mistress could have refuted) and it was not until it was too late to prevent the crisis that they bestirred themselves in the slightest and then it was to call for priority (out of the existing ration) for text-books, as if other books were not essential to education.

Although most publishers gave them priority in view of the value of their work overseas, the British Council became agitated about the number of important books completely unobtainable, and I had occasion to write on January 19, 1944, to the late Sir Malcolm Robertson, the then Chairman:

'I can only confirm that the book shortage is as acute as, if not more acute than, ever. The demand for *good* books, and I mean in particular those that have stood the test of time, is incredible, and the proportion of those unobtainable is both alarming and a disgrace to a cultured people. A visit to any good bookshop will confirm this statement.

'The treatment of established book publishers by the Government has been niggardly in the extreme. . . .

'The question is one of national importance and not of private profit because the realization of pre-war stock, coupled with poor standard years, has put most publishers on an Excess Profits basis. (Some are paying 95 per cent and will end the war with no stock and little cash.) . . .

'We are losing our overseas markets. Canada . . . has already gone. . . . Other markets which we could hold if we were in a position to deliver the goods we are now beginning to lose. . . . And the extraordinary thing is that the trouble could easily be remedied—so little would accomplish so much. Perhaps now that the War Office has once again made the startling discovery (it took three years in the last war as it has done in this) that a mental ration is essential for the maintenance of morale, something more may be done. Let us hope it will not be another case of "too late".'

Although letter after letter had appeared in *The Times* and other papers emphasizing that paper for books, unlike newsprint, was neither a dollar nor a shipping problem, Lord Woolton, CH, then at the head of the Ministry of Reconstruction, when addressing a group of publishers deplored that we could not have more paper for books *because* it was a dollar and a shipping problem. I naturally seized the opportunity to enlighten him, and followed up what I had said in a letter fully explaining the position. Alas! it apparently had no effect.

With the fourth year of war the British book trade entered a new and strange phase. Most people will remember the story of the old Scottish clergyman who prayed long and fervently for rain and who, when his prayer was interrupted by a cloudburst which penetrated the roof, looked up at the descending rain and remarked: 'Good Lord, this is ridiculous!' Well, for nearly forty years I had prayed for an increased demand for books, and it was indeed ridiculous that it should come at a moment when it was impossible to supply it.

But having smiled at the absurdity of it all, it is worth while to consider whether the demand was an entirely healthy one, or merely a feverish activity from which the patient arose sadly weakened when the fever abated.

The more closely one examines the situation, the more clear it seems that some of the 'prosperity' was illusory, and much of the demand ephemeral. The position of publishers and booksellers in relation to this feverish activity was by no means identical. Before examining the publishers' position there is a question of concern to booksellers which deserves most careful thought. It arose from an actual occurrence, and, indirectly, it throws light upon one of the publishers' war-time problems.

A bookseller had a copy of a certain standard work (in the field in which he specialized) which he always made a point of stocking. It had cost him 25s od. It went out of print owing to enemy action; its value rose, and a customer offered, and he accepted, £6 for it. Splendid! Unexampled good fortune for a deserving bookseller! Real cause of rejoicing! But wait. I have said a book essential for him to stock. He observed that a copy was up for auction, and as he could not attend himself, he gave instructions to someone to bid up to £6 for it. It went for £6 10s od; an accident, perhaps. A second copy turned up at another auction, which he was able to attend, and he secured it for £6 5s od.

Now let us analyse his position. As far as stock is concerned his position was unchanged, but with this great difference; the book stood in his stock valuation account at £6 5s od instead of 25s od. But what about his cash position? He had paid out 5s od more then he received, and incurred a liability of 10s od in the pound income tax on his £5 profit. (To simplify the issue I am treating gross profit as net profit, but ignoring the 100 per cent excess profits tax for which this particular bookseller was liable.) His turnover was £6 up and he was £2 15s od out of pocket. Now here is the question. Is it, or is it not, true that *in effect* he had paid £2 15s od for the privilege of writing up the value of his stock from 25s od to £6 5s od, and had not made any real profit at all?

The publisher's position was more complicated. There were so many contradictory factors. The destruction of stock by enemy action might mean extra sales, and it might mean loss of sales. Here are examples of both. We had an order from India for between 400 and 500 copies of a 12s od book of which our stock was short. We reprinted 1,000 copies and executed the order. The consignment was sunk; we bound up the balance of the edition, collected payment in full for the first lot from insurance and duplicated the order. The second consignment went to the bottom of the sea; we collected payment in full once again; reprinted a further 1,000 copies, and sent a third consignment, which arrived. Admittedly a quite unusual case, but our turnover was trebled; our profit on that peculiar transaction more than trebled. Here is the reverse side of the picture. On the day that I heard my firm had lost over a million books by enemy action, we received an order for 250 copies in sheets of an old book, if we could supply them at one dollar per copy as before. The day before we possessed 250 sheets, but as we had held them for many years and home sales were small, they had been written down to a nominal penny per copy. Had the order reached us a day or two sooner, we should have been over £60 in pocket because we should have been paid 250 dollars instead of the 250 pennies which we received from the War Insurance, and, as I need hardly emphasize, the profit in the case of a book of which a small edition is printed lies in the sale of the last 250.

That incident multiplied itself many times, and throws light upon the effects of War Risks Insurance. It endows improvident publishers by enabling them, in case of loss, to turn over-valued and possibly unsaleable stock into cash at inflated prices, and penalizes the provident publisher who has written down the value of his stock. There was no way out of the dilemma for the provident publisher, because, if he insured on the basis of replacement cost he was not able to get the paper with which to replace the books, and the difference between his balance sheet valuation and what he collected from insurance was treated as excess profits and taxed 100 per cent. Can anyone suggest that such profits are other than illusory?

The effects of enemy action were much more far-reaching than is indicated by the two examples I have given. Book destruction created a general shortage so that the losses of Publisher A might greatly benefit Publishers B and C, not merely because the general shortage sent up the values of all remaining stock and rendered hitherto unsaleable books easily marketable, but because the inability to obtain the standard work on any subject created a demand for substitutes. Normally, as we all know, supply readily catches up demand. When labour and materials are freely available the speed of book production is so incredibly rapid that no amount of bombing could keep up with it. But the acute paper shortage and the bottle-neck of binding made it impossible to replace stock as fast as it was sold. Associated with this partial breakdown of production there were many new and unusual demands for books. I have already referred to the duplication of lost shipments, which probably accounted to some extent for the maintenance of export turnover, despite the cutting off of market after market. But what may be termed Governmental buying was a very big factor. The demand for books from the three Services was almost overwhelming, and the educational work undertaken by them accentuated it. The Ministry of Information, the British Council and the Red Cross were all large war-time buyers, and there was the ever-increasing supply of books to prisoners of war. The replacement of blitzed public libraries was another unusual source of orders, but perhaps even more important than this was the demand arising out of changes of occupation, and the immigration to these shores of airmen, soldiers and civilians of varied nationalities.

If you take a young man from a city office and put him in the RAF, you almost compel him to buy books. He will want to brush up his maths., and to acquire all sorts of works of instruction, whether it be on astro-navigation or on meteorology. A large proportion of the continental emigrés were book-lovers, and, as far as their means permitted, book-buyers. It would be easy to go on citing these new causes of the war-time increased demand. But on top of these many factors there were (a) the freedom of books from purchase tax, which made them *relatively* cheap despite price increases, (b) the shortage of supply or complete absence of nearly all competing commodities or forms of entertainment, and (c) the black-out which kept people in their homes.

One could go on almost indefinitely citing reasons for the spurt in publishers' turnover, but perhaps more instructive is the reason for the temporary increase in profits *on new books*.

The most expensive item in the running of a book-publishing business, as I have already said, is publishing fallibility. That item, for the time being, almost entirely disappeared. The paper rationing reduced the number of new books any publisher could issue, and there was the curious situation of publishers weighing in the balance the return any particular book would yield for the paper expended. There was no need for a publisher to take risks if he did not want to.

Furthermore, the restriction in the selection of new books resulted in the demand for them being spread over a smaller number of titles—in other words an increase in the average sale of the new books, which in its turn minimized the possibility of loss. The larger the edition, the larger the margin of profit if it is all sold.

In this connection the experience of British bookbinders is of interest. In the first few years reduction in turnover resulted in losses, but during the next twelve months the size of the average binding order so increased that binders with the appropriate machinery were able to maintain their output with a much depleted staff. The binding bottle-neck would have been even more of a handicap but for that fact, and the costs of binding would have shown still more substantial increases than they did.

Even as it was, the constant price increases in printing and binding had serious repercussions very similar to the effects of inflation during the First World War. This was a matter of deep concern to publishers with pre-war stocks of books which they knew they would have to reprint at greatly enhanced prices. Many of us were busily engaged, though we were often unconscious of it, in selling stock at less than it was going to cost to replace. During the period of inflation in Germany, many a publisher whose profit and loss account showed huge profits from the realization of stock, woke up to discover that these fabulous profits would not replace even one-tenth of the stock he had so joyfully sold. We did not reach that stage, but the experience of the bookseller to which I referred is an object lesson worth study.

That there were silver linings to those most dark and threatening clouds I should be the last to deny. There was indeed one most reassuring fact about which all were agreed. Young people were buying books, and not merely books, but good books. They wanted the best. The war created a new reading public. Many acquired the reading habit who had never turned to books before, and there is much comfort in the realization that they did so for the acquisition of knowledge and the enjoyment of good literature, and not merely as an escape from the war. It is the pleasing responsibility of the book trade to see to it that this interest is maintained.

At the end of 1944 I received an inquiry from my good friend, the late W. W. Norton, the distinguished American publisher, for my views on a number of questions, including the absurd proposal of Morgenthau that Germany should be converted into a purely agricultural state. My reply, which follows, summarized the views I held, which were entirely contrary to those to which wide publicity was being given in the States.

'Your letter of November 13th arrived just before Christmas, whilst I was in University College Hospital celebrating, in room 60, my sixtieth birthday and thirtieth wedding day having an operation for the removal of a torn cartilage from my knee—a young man's complaint, as the surgeon remarked.

'It was a curious sensation to lie there with my leg effectively pinioned first in a splint and then between sandbags listening to rocket bombs and occasional alerts, knowing that if one came my way (which providentially it did not) I couldn't move a foot to help myself. It gave me plenty of opportunity of thinking about the problems you raise. I don't believe war can be made decent; consequently if the Germans foolishly believe that V1, V2 or Vx are weapons which will help them, I refuse to get emotional if they use them, but the mass cremation of Jews—a measure of no military significance—is another matter. How people who behave in this sadistic fashion are to be redeemed is an appalling problem. About one thing I am clear and that is, it will be solved neither by the vindictive people on the one hand, nor the sloppy sentimentalists on the other. It is certain that whatever the treatment it must be consistently and persistently applied. Vindictiveness soon exhausts itself and brings reaction; sentimentalism and pacifism are regarded by the Germans as a sign of weakness and therefore stimulate them to try again. (At the moment a V2 rattled the windows by way of encouragement to solve the problem.) I do not see how we can avoid a long period of complete and effective, though reasonably benevolent, international control. Benevolent, not because they deserve it, but because otherwise you and we may withdraw the control prematurely. The technologists must devise plans which still will effectively prevent Germany from secretly rearming.

'Personally, I think we are all inclined to under-estimate two factors:

'(1) Germany has for the first time really tasted her own medicine.
'(2) The Russians may occupy Germany first and set up a quasi-Communist regime, as they have done in Poland (thanks partly to the short-sightedness of Polish leaders in London).

'Despite what ignorant Left Wing people here and many in America have to say, it may prove to have been touch and go that we have not had a completely unrepresentative Communist Dictatorship in Greece established by sheer intimidation. It is not going to prove easy to ensure that the will of the majority prevails in some of these European countries.

'Turning to fundamentals, we have got to avoid like poison decisions based upon passing emotions. Every question must be examined in the light in which it will appear ten years hence. The mental state of Germany's youth may affect the European situation for twenty or thirty years; it is not a fleeting problem. If a really decent element gets on top in Germany we must within reason encourage it, and not, as on the last occasion, snub the democratic element and fawn upon the anti-democrats (another V2 at this point!). Above all we must steer clear of policies which our respective countries will not in fact be prepared to carry through. How far will your Senate go? World affairs are more dependent upon the veto of a minority of your Senate than it has any business to be. Don't you agree?'

March 1, 1945, remains the proudest day of my life. It brought me a letter from Sir William Hamilton Fyfe, Principal and Vice-Chancellor of Aberdeen University, reading as follows:

'You will have been formally notified by the Secretary of this University that it is our wish to confer on you the honorary degree of LL.D—a poor thing, but our own, and the best we have.

'Universities owe much to your profession, but seem slow to give public recognition of their debt, so it is a pleasure to us to do what honour we can to a Publisher who has always shown enterprise and a sympathy for brains, and to register our conviction that not all publishers are the second cousins of Barabbas.

'I hope you may be able to come to Aberdeen and take your medicine publicly in the summer.'

To which I replied:

'Few letters have come to me as such a surprise, or given me such pleasure, as yours which greeted me on my return home last night.

'That I should be one of the first publishers to be thus honoured is almost overwhelming. That a Scottish University on the other hand should be the first to give this most acceptable public recognition of the part played by book publishing in our national life is entirely appropriate. Whenever I have criticized lack of interest in things of the mind I have always made it clear that I was referring to England and not Scotland, and I have many times pointed out that no Scot is afraid to enter a bookshop whereas many adults are in England.

'I appreciate this recognition of publishing more than I can possibly say. You will not misunderstand me when I add that it means even more to me than any personal aspect of the matter.

'I will indeed come to Aberdeen and take my medicine publicly in the summer. I never realized before that any medicine could be so palatable.'

At the ceremony on June 28th I was one of those selected to respond to the toast and did so as follows:

'Sir William,

'Confession is good for the soul. I am an Englishman who cannot claim one single drop of Scottish blood in his veins. Moreover, like my father and grandfather before me, I am a cockney and rather proud of the fact.

'Nevertheless I can say with complete truth that the letter you, Sir, sent me about today's ceremony gave me a greater thrill than I should have received from any similar letter from any part of England, and the explanation is simple. For at least forty years I have observed and have frequently alluded to the fact that you in

Scotland take education much more seriously than we do in England. You really believe in it; and with that belief comes a recognition of the vital importance of books and the essential part they play, and rightly play, in any civilized community. It was, I think, my knowledge of your deep concern for education which caused me in my boyhood to be so deeply impressed that when that very great Scotsman, the late Alexander Whyte of Edinburgh, wanted a tutor for his children, he chose one of my elder brothers for the purpose. It certainly explains why I am so deeply moved at finding myself your honoured guest today.

'Most of those on whose behalf—in association with others—I am responding to this toast, have long and intimate associations with Aberdeen. They have the satisfaction of returning, as it were, to their home, and we all of us know what a deep and touching thing the approval of one's home circle can be. I have a different, but in its way equally moving thing for which to thank you. It is not merely for honouring a comparative stranger, but for setting a precedent in honouring a publisher of books. But then Aberdeen University has never hesitated to set precedents for others to follow. An Icelandic bookseller has just reminded me that forty years ago, almost to a day, Aberdeen University honoured Thomas Hardy before any English University thought of doing so, and there are many other examples which could be cited.'

My facetious younger son, when he read the speech, quoted Dr Johnson's remark that 'Scots learning is like bread in a besieged town. Everyone gets a little, but no one has a full meal', but it did not change my views.

Late on New Year's Eve, six months after the grant of this honorary degree, my wife learnt to her surprise, as the result of a trunk call from the printer of an Aberdeen newspaper, that the issue of the paper he was printing included my name in the Honours List. When I went to Buckingham Palace to receive the accolade, I was delighted to find myself in the company of the distinguished surgeon who, on my sixtieth birthday just over a year before, while the bombs were dropping, had so successfully operated on my knee.

Just before the end of the war a Conference of Ministers of

Education of the Allied Countries was held in London, and it was agreed that in future there should be no obstacles of any kind to impede the free flow of books from one country to another. But as I had occasion to remark in my pamphlet on *How Governments Treat Books*:

'Resolutions are not enough. They are too often merely "good intentions" with which the road to hell, according to the proverbs of many countries, is reported to be paved.'

Five years later there were more obstructions than ever, and at the Cultural Conference of the European Movement held at Lausanne I spoke about them and produced a most devastating chart listing them. At the close of the proceedings the following resolution was unanimously passed:

'That the Cultural Conference of the European Movement deplores the many kinds of obstruction and many forms of taxation set forth in the accompanying chart which hamper the free flow of books from one country to another and regards it as vital to the well-being of Europe that all such restrictions should be swept away.

'The Conference accordingly urges the European Movement to press the various European Governments to take immediate steps to remove all obstacles to the free flow of books.

'Furthermore, that the European Governments should be urged to ensure that in the event of shortage of currency, books, in view of their vital character and the relatively small amount of money involved, should be granted priority.'

A few of the obstacles have been removed, but an equal number of new ones have taken their place. The battle is still on.

CHAPTER 16

POST-WAR YEARS

Those of us—publishers and a vast public—who confidently expected that with the end of the war the supply of books would rapidly increase suffered bitter disappointment.

Everybody knows that if water is drawn from a reservoir more rapidly than the supply flows in, the largest reservoir must empty; but for some mysterious reason the same principle was not generally supposed to apply to books. Throughout the war far fewer books were produced than sold, and of the huge reserve of pre-war stock, no fewer than 20,000,000 volumes were destroyed by enemy action. The reservoir was practically empty, and nothing effective was done by the Government to enable publishers to augment the scanty supply, let alone to replace the 20,000,000 lost volumes.

On the other hand, we heard of Swedish wood pulp reaching the USA at the rate of 100,000 tons a month, and of so much paper already being available that the USA authorities could safely dispense with paper control altogether, whereas book production in Great Britain was left in a more precarious state than it was at any period during the war.

British publishers were still allowed collectively only about 2,000 tons of paper a month, out of which they were expected to replace 'blitzed' stock, and were urged in the national interest to build up their export trade. As the whole world was crying out for British books, and the hunger for them in liberated territories was intense, publishers were expected, in effect, to achieve something approaching the miracle of the loaves and fishes—but it just could not be done. And the sad thing was that, as the authorities left it so late, an increase in the paper ration could not *alone* solve the problem.

The book printing and book binding industries were hopelessly short of labour. Men of 79 and 80, who worked throughout the war (some of them came out of retirement to do so), dropped out, and at the other end of the scale boys of 18, who were just beginning to be moderately useful at their job, were called up, and there was no corresponding release from the army. On the contrary, even prisoners of war returning from long periods of incarceration in Germany, who were pining to restart regular work at book printing, were sent back to the army, where most of them had nothing useful to do. One such man, knowing how hard pressed his old firm was, offered to give up his leave to lend them a hand. But King's Regulations and Trade Union rules defeated him.

Printing was supposed to be on the priority list, but that seemed to have little effect. When in connection with Governmental requirements temporary release was sought for a key man, the War Office said that his work was much too important to warrant it. A day or two later he was given a new job—as a lorry driver.

Were books a luxury with which we could readily dispense there would be little to be said, but never were they a more vital necessity than at that moment.

It would be wearisome to recapitulate the many directions in which the shortage of books proved disastrous. Suffice it to emphasize that our whole educational system at home and our prestige abroad were at stake.

The Government rightly called for exports. Had it granted book printers and binders the labour, and book publishers the paper, publishers could soon have produced substantial exports, because, despite preferential treatment to export orders, we never got anywhere near to satisfying the demand.

Even in 1946 we were still confronted with paper difficulties, and they affected my firm cruelly in connection with Bertrand Russell's *History of Western Philosophy*. A really adequate supply would have absorbed more than our exiguous paper ration for a whole period. By setting aside all we could during the best part of a year, aided by an allowance from the Moberly pool, we were able to produce a first edition of 18,000 copies. Meanwhile the American edition was percolating into our export markets. We accordingly took the drastic course of allocating the whole 18,000 to export. The home market had to wait until, with the assistance of another grant from the Moberly pool, a larger number could be reprinted. Up to November 1959 we had sold over 95,894 copies—an agreeable figure for a not inexpensive work on philosophy. In the early stages we were seldom in a position to supply all the copies booksellers wanted, and in view of this fact and the outstanding success of the book, the booksellers' orders for Russell's next book, *Human Knowledge: Its Scope and Limits*, were fantastic. Now, unlike *History of Western Philosophy*, there were chapters in this later book quite beyond the understanding of the ordinary intelligent reader. I did what I imagine few publishers would have done. I went personally through the orders and reduced all those which seemed to me excessive, with the result that no one got 'landed' with the book, which remains a steady seller to those for whom it was intended.

This incident reminds me of a famous occasion when I rang up the late David Roy (then the chief buyer for W. H. Smith & Son) to tell him that he had ordered too many of one of our books, and he gasped, 'Well, you are the first publisher to suggest that'. It made him very attentive afterwards if I hinted that he had not bought enough, because, as he rightly said, the publisher *ought* to know. Unfortunately, too many publishers are prone to maintaining that all their geese are swans, a mistake I resolutely refuse to make. Works of genius or outstanding saleability are too few and far between.

So many of the younger generation of the book trade were beginning to ask me why I recommended this or that course in *The Truth About Publishing* (originally published in 1926) under the impression that the recommended course always had been normal and unaware that it followed the recommendation, that I felt I ought to make an effort to bring the book up to date. I had of course made a good many notes of the changes that had taken place during the twenty years that had elapsed since the book was first published, and when I examined them it became clear that much of it would have to be rewritten. It was too big a job to attempt in odd times. I did what I have done once or twice in the writing of this book—I took a week off and retired to St Deiniol's Residential Library, founded by Gladstone near his home at Hawarden, Chester. There for an additional shilling a day over and beyond most modest charges for board, one is provided with a private study where one can work completely undisturbed. It is a monastic existence, largely self-service, and with rigid punctuality at meals, upon which little time is wasted. If one writes for eight hours a day, as I did, with an hour's quick walk in the grounds of Hawarden Castle in the afternoons, it is astonishing how much one can accomplish in the way of first drafts which can be polished subsequently at leisure after they have been typed. It was in this way that the fourth edition was prepared. It was greeted with—if possible—even more enthusiasm than the first edition, and led to the appearance of several more translations, including one in Turkish, financed by the Turkish Authors' Society for the guidance of Turkish publishers. Fifth and sixth editions have been called for, each with minor additions or emendations.[1] What, of course, has pleased me most is the international prestige the book has achieved. I had dedicated the first three editions of my book to those of my fellow publishers who believed in co-operation—a very small minority. Perhaps the most striking feature of the fourth edition was the omission of that dedication because with one notable exception, all my fellow publishers had learnt the value of, and believed in, co-operation.

In looking through our list of publications of the years immediately following the war, I was agreeably impressed by their wide variety. Biographies predominated, and some of them were for one reason or another of special concern to me. An excellent biography of Ernest Bevin caused anxiety during his unsuccessful

[1] I printed an extra large number of the sixth edition, anticipating that it might be the last, but it sold out more rapidly than I expected. Owing to the many changes, e.g. in copyright, I have again had to rewrite large portions of the work for its seventh edition.

efforts to suppress it. Then some members of the Lloyd George family feared that a Life of Dame Margaret by her eldest son would be indiscreet, and ought not to be published, though it proved a delightful, humorous and quite inoffensive book. My connection with Bernard Shaw was renewed by the publication of his *Impressions of Sydney Olivier*, and my family pride enhanced by finding an uncle and two aunts included in a volume of *Victorian Portraits*, to refer to but one or two titles in a long list.

One book of a very different character, *Surveying for Agricultural Students and Planters*, calls for mention on purely technical grounds. It contained algebraical and other symbols which would have involved most complicated typesetting, but it was never set up. My school friend, Neville Brooke, of the Berkshire Printing Company, who brought the book to me, reproduced it lithographically from most carefully prepared typewritten copy with startlingly good results. It is a process now often used, but this was the first case of a complicated technical book being prepared in this fashion, and it has never been bettered.

An interesting feature of this period was the growing interest in Eastern Philosophy. We published *Vedanta for the Western World* by Aldous Huxley and others, as well as a new translation of the *Bhagavadgita* by Radhakrishnan, and thanks to the initiative of the late H. N. Spalding, who, with his wife, had founded at Oxford a Chair of Eastern Religions and Ethics, were able to embark upon a most interesting series, *Ethical and Religious Classics of East and West*, edited by Professor A. J. Arberry, Professor Radhakrishnan and others, which promises to be of permanent value. A big work on *The History and Culture of the Indian People*, of which we published the first volume, was transferred to India owing to the shortage of British compositors and the inability of British printers to give us in consequence any reliable date for its completion, one of the many unpleasant results of the refusal of the printing trade unions to recognize that the problem, unlike that following the First World War, was over-employment, not unemployment. This brings me back to Lord Beveridge, who, apart from more topical books, had been busily engaged upon the study of *Voluntary Action*. Of the book under that title which we issued for him more will be heard when the reaction comes from the expectation that everything should be done by a benevolent state. At the same time we published *Family Allowances* by that most remarkable woman, the late Eleanor Rathbone, whom to know was to respect for her complete independence, her fearlessness and integrity. If anyone demonstrated the value of the University Vote, and the desirability of having a few disinterested Members of Parliament free from Party obligations, she did. Any Parliament would be the richer for such a woman; would that there were more like her.

Long before she became famous, we were impressed by the work of Barbara Ward, who had contributed to *Hitler's Route to Baghdad* which we published before the war, and in 1942 we contracted with her to write a book for us under the title *People With a Vision*. Years went by and it was not forthcoming, so that when in 1948 she brought us *The West at Bay* we were highly gratified. It was an immediate success both here and in the States.

Almost immediately after the conclusion of the Second World War I went to Spain at the urgent wish of the Spanish publishers and the British Council to investigate the whole position of British books and Spanish translation rights. I have referred in the chapter on the British Council to my whirlwind campaign for the increase, or total abolition, of the quota on British books entering Spain. Here I wish merely to record the astonishing amount of help I received from my Spanish colleagues, and their amazing hospitality. Thirty or more of them took the whole day off to escort me *en masse* to Escorial, where I was royally fêted. The colleagues at Barcelona went—if that had been possible—even further. Still more of them accompanied me to Montserrat. When the time came for lunch, I was shown into a huge room magnificently laid out with beautiful floral decorations. I gasped, 'Surely this is not for me?' 'No', came the reply, 'this is for a wedding party; we are in the next room.' On entering the next room I felt as if I should like to sink through the floor, so much more elaborate and grand was it than the first. And as if that were not enough, half a dozen of the leading publishers took the next day off to escort me along the coast in the opposite direction to the Costa Brava, finishing up with supper at the home of one of them in Barcelona just before midnight. Could anyone imagine half a dozen leading London publishers taking two days off in that way for anybody? 'No', was the response of an irreligious publisher to that question, 'not even for God Almighty.'

In July 1947 I received an unexpected invitation from the British Military Government in Germany to open in Berlin the first book Exhibition on an all-German basis to be held since the war. It was a notable occasion, not only because it was a quadripartite function (the Russians wanted to exhibit the post-war productions of Leipzig) but because the keynote was the power of the printed word, rightly used, to facilitate the reconciliation and understanding of people. The Oak Gallery of the Charlottenburg Palace was crowded with allied representatives and members of the German book trade, and bore its own evidence of the persecution to which writers were subject under Hitler. Memorial panels commemorated the names of publishers, novelists, poets, essayists and journalists, and told of their end—murdered by the Nazis, died in exile, or cast into Auschwitz.

More than 5,000 books were displayed and represented a remarkable achievement at a time of severe scarcity. It was a curious experience for me to be confronted with a German book trade audience that knew much less about the pre-war German book trade organization than I did. They were mostly newcomers to publishing and bookselling because war casualties had taken a heavy toll; others were still prisoners in Soviet Russia, and those with a Nazi record were at that time excluded from the trade. Mr Robert Birley, then Education Adviser to the Military Governor, and later Headmaster at Eton, was one of the other speakers.

My visit to Vienna, Prague, Bratislava and Budapest in October 1946, just three weeks before the Communists seized power in Hungary, was made for the British Council at the instigation of the Hungarian book trade, who were determined if possible to maintain contact with the West. The enthusiasm of the reception they gave me was remarkable. If ever Hungary regains its freedom Budapest will be, as it always has been in the past in relation to its population, a wonderful market for British books. The trip was in one respect a costly one for me because, owing to the fact that it unexpectedly took me seventeen days to squeeze through the Iron Curtain, and I was consequently late in returning, I lost a most important book for the Muirhead Library of Philosophy. As I was not back on the promised date the not too philosophical author refused to wait. But I think that it was to his loss as well as ours that he took his book elsewhere; and later work of his came to us.

But publishing has its compensations as well as its trials, and a very substantial compensation came our way soon thereafter in the shape of *The Kon-Tiki Expedition*. It has always been my practice whenever any senior member of my firm takes his holiday abroad to suggest that he should take a few additional days in calling upon any publishers or booksellers within easy reach. Accordingly when my nephew, Philip Unwin, decided to exchange houses with a Norwegian teacher who, like himself, had a wife and two children, I suggested his visiting Oslo, where he naturally looked up my old friend, Harald Grieg, of Gyldendals, from whom he learnt about *Kon-Tiki*, and of course at once arranged for an early set of proofs of the original Norwegian edition to be sent to us. Both readers to whom we showed the proofs were enthusiastic, and I immediately cabled a substantial offer, which was accepted. The author, Thor Heyerdahl, himself came to London to fix the details of the contract with me. Our readers' reports had convinced us that we were confronted with a most remarkable book, and Heyerdahl's lecture to the Royal Geographical Society on the occasion of his London visit fully confirmed that view. But the moment we read F. H. Lyon's translation we knew that we had a 'best-seller'. Every member of the firm who read it became wildly enthusiastic. When we tried to convey our enthusiasm to our representatives and booksellers we were met with the response that the title was hopeless and that we should call it 'Across the Pacific on a Raft' (as if it were a story by Henty), and my reply that Kon-Tiki was a name easily pronounced which would, within a few months, be a household word, left them incredulous. (One of them reminded me of my prophecy when the Kon-Tiki was referred to in a jest on the BBC Light Programme.) This incident recalled to me once again the dictum of that outstandingly successful publisher, the late Sir Ernest Hodder-Williams: 'Listen carefully to all your travellers have to tell you—and then do the opposite.'

Our publicity in connection with the book was both diverse and interesting. First, I arranged with my good friend the late Ralph Deakin, then Foreign Editor of *The Times*, that he should have the first serial use of material for an article about the book six weeks ahead of publication. This proved to be a magnificent piece of advance publicity which at once 'started people talking'. Then we sold the serial rights to the *Sunday Chronicle*, and later to the *Liverpool Post* and other papers.

Almost double the normal number of review copies were sent out and I wrote personal letters to many leading critics and editors. The *Daily Mail* chose it as their Book of the Month, thus ensuring still more publicity for us.

During those final weeks before publication, we had been steadily feeding booksellers with facts about *Kon-Tiki*, including the story of its striking success in Scandinavia, where over 140,000 copies had already been sold. With the help of a young architectural student we had made models of the Kon-Tiki raft for bookshop window display, and these proved immensely popular.

We now heard that Thor Heyerdahl could be in London for the week prior to publication, and this at once opened up fresh possibilities. He had already arranged to lecture to the Royal Anthropological Institute and to show again the silent film of the voyage which had already been seen by the Royal Geographical Society on his earlier visit. This inspired us to hire a private cinema for a special showing to London booksellers. There is no doubt that this, coupled with the personal appearance of the author (who provided a running commentary in excellent English), really brought home to booksellers the thrill and achievement of the expedition and the tremendous possibilities of the book.

During that week Philip Unwin arranged for Mr Heyerdahl to appear in a television programme, and the largest of the raft models was also televised. We had already interested the BBC in a full-length feature programme on the book, and the author was able to provide them, at first hand, with additional material. He was in fact an ideal author from his publisher's point of view. He was completely reliable and efficient, and he was extremely co-operative over all that we wanted him to do for the publicity of the book. As the only cinema available for his film would not seat more than one-third of those we wanted to invite, he generously agreed to lecture with the film twice on one evening, speaking continuously for nearly four hours, a feat which he accomplished with no more than a plate of soup and a glass of beer for refreshment at half-time! He gave a third performance two days later.

Of medium height and powerful build, he has the traditional fair hair and blue eyes of the Norseman and a look of extreme physical fitness. His handsome face suggests great determination, but there is also an air of boyishness about him and he enjoys a joke.

Before the day of publication, March 31st, it was clear that our first large edition would be inadequate, and we felt still more confident that we were heading for a runaway success.

It was a foregone conclusion that it would be a Book Society Choice. The enthusiasm of Sir Compton Mackenzie, one of their judges, was so remarkable that we felt justified in doubling our already large first printing order. On March 8th we secured paper for another 10,000 copies, and searched for any other suitable paper we could find immediately available. Paper for a further 15,000 was found on March 10th, and for 2,000 three days later, with the result that a second impression of 27,000 copies was actually printed before publication. Seldom have I published a book which has had such instant recognition and about which all reviewers have been so enthusiastic. Every important paper seemed to review it during the week after publication, and the orders poured in. Our perpetual anxiety was to ensure a sufficient supply of paper. There is nothing which so effectively curbs the sale of a 'best-seller' as frequent periods of being unobtainable. The interest in it can evaporate so rapidly. I was determined that Kon-Tiki should never be out of stock for a day, and it never was, and that is more than can be said for any other recent 'best-seller'. But it was not achieved without colossal effort and much faith. There was one moment, for example, when we had about fifty thousand copies in course of production in excess of what would appear to be needed in the next five or six months. We had three printers and four binders simultaneously printing and binding it, in competition with one another over dates of supply, and some of them achieved miracles.

But what was most vital was the way our friends among the stationers rallied to our support. We pointed out that Kon-Tikis came, at most, once in a lifetime, and that we relied upon them to see us through, which they did most nobly. Everyone seemed to be pleased to be having a hand in Kon-Tiki's success, because all had read and appreciated the book.

The fun came with the Book Clubs, all of whom wanted it. Now they are accustomed to issue their editions twelve months after first publication, and to insist upon any book they select being exclusive to their particular club. Publishers are so anxious to secure a Book Club Choice that they will do almost anything to achieve it. It came as a surprise—I might even say a shock— when I said that there would be no Book Club edition in less than *two* years, and the statement that I wanted a second Christmas sale was regarded as pathetic imbecility on my part. But in fact we sold more copies the second Christmas than the first. The other important 'best-seller' was out of stock, and Kon-Tiki was not.

Furthermore, our provincial representatives had supplies in their cars with which they could supplement booksellers' stocks, and right from the start I had personally increased a large proportion of the ludicrously cautious orders booksellers sent us long after it was clear that whatever they ordered they would want more. The additional copies were marked 'see safe', but none ever came back; they were usually wanted before they arrived.

When the time came to arrange for the Book Club editions, and the claim for exclusivity arose, I dug my toes in. I admitted that they had always enjoyed exclusive rights, but said that *Kon-Tiki* was not available on that basis. They could go without it, but if they wanted it the conditions would be mine. My toughness caused much perturbation, but prevailed. I agreed the order in which each Club should have the book, leaving a month between each. Eventually it was taken by four Clubs, which resulted in a Book Club sale of nearly half a million. Such a thing had never happened before and has not happened since.

The appeal of *The Kon-Tiki Expedition* is universal. It is essentially an adult book, but children revel in it. Those who prophesied that women would not like it were confounded because the BBC serialized it in 'Woman's Hour'. Altogether it had over a dozen different 'treatments' on the radio.

A minister recommended it to all the Sunday School teachers of one denomination, and another preached a sermon about it.

It is no exaggeration to say that in its various translations the book swept Europe. It jumped straight to the top of the best-seller lists everywhere.

Many people were curious to know how these six men, restricted for over three months to a space the size of a large Persian carpet, managed to remain friends. I asked the author that very question when he was in London. He replied that he had realized that discord was one of the greatest dangers that confronted the expedition, and they had faced it at the outset. They agreed that if they felt like saying anything unpleasant they should keep silent; that if one of them failed, the others should remain silent. It worked, and they had no unpleasantness. On the contrary, they ended the expedition better friends than ever. Mr Heyerdahl thought it was a big advantage that none of them knew each other before the start, but then, he added with a smile, 'all the five' whom he had picked 'were very remarkable men'. And as they, I am sure, would agree with me, their leader was the most remarkable of all.

When we came to the issue of *Kon-Tiki and I*, the delightful sketch book of Hesselberg, the artist-navigator of the expedition, we encountered astonishing prejudice on the part of most booksellers. In Norway, one copy had been sold for every five copies of *Kon-Tiki*. I said that, although we might not equal that, we could not fail to sell one in ten. As few booksellers would at first stock the book, I gave instructions for a note to be printed at the foot of the last page of *Kon-Tiki* reading as follows:

Laugh with Kon-Tiki's Artist Navigator

'If you have enjoyed this book, ask your bookseller to show you *Kon-Tiki and I*, the entertaining sketch book of Erik Hesselberg, the artist-navigator.'

The effect was remarkable. The public insisted upon being supplied with it. More and more booksellers started carrying stock, but one I noticed consistently refused to do so, and ordered many more than a hundred copies from us *one at a time*. So satisfied was he that it wouldn't sell that offers of copies 'see safe' were scornfully rejected. The sales to date are over 65,000.

The good booksellers tend to assume that other booksellers are all like themselves (would that they were!), overlooking the fact that there are black sheep in every flock. But the black sheep are not the chief trouble. It is the bookseller who is dominated by prejudices who is the difficulty. It sounds unbelievable, but the chief buyer (since retired) of one large London bookshop was so determined that *Kon-Tiki* would not sell (because the hero was a Norwegian of all stupid reasons) that he refused to stock it, though his assistants told him that it was constantly asked for, until a quite small shop nearby had sold over 500 copies, mostly to people who had failed to get it from its bigger neighbour.

Probably we encounter this kind of thing more often than most publishers because we so frequently publish unusual books. The firm which is thinking all the time of tomorrow rather than yesterday, is bound to meet with prejudice, and we accept it as a compliment rather than the reverse.

We had done so well out of *Kon-Tiki* that we felt under an obligation to do whatever the author wanted in connection with his *magnum opus, American Indians in the Pacific*. It was more convenient to him that it should be produced in Sweden, and as we knew the standard of production would be excellent, we readily agreed. In view of its great size, and the extensive number of illustrations in colour, it was an impossible book to reprint in a hurry. Neither we nor the author wanted to run the slightest risk of being out of stock, and accordingly at his wish we printed a larger edition than seemed to us expedient. That would not have been serious but for one of those simple mistakes which occur from time to time in the best run businesses. Rates of exchange are something upon which I instinctively keep an eagle eye, but I was away at the time. Our Production Department is constantly converting Danish Kroner into sterling, and when confronted with the estimate in Swedish Kroner converted them at the rate for Danish Kroner, blissfully unaware of their great difference in value. It was a painful blow when it was eventually discovered how far out our estimates had been. Some increase in published price was unavoidable, but to put it up to the extent justified by the cost of production would make it impossible to sell the number printed. We compromised, waived all likelihood of profit, but consoled ourselves with the knowledge that *Kon-Tiki* would take care of us. Apropos of that last statement, a competitor remarked to me that anyone could show profits if he had a *Kon-Tiki*. Now I have always maintained that a publishing business ought to pay its way without dependence upon best-sellers and unexpected extraneous receipts from 'rights'. Accordingly I accepted my competitor's challenge and instructed our accountants to prepare a fresh set of accounts excluding *Kon-Tiki* completely from both sides. It was pleasant to find that the profits were within a few hundred pounds of what they had been the previous year. That is as it should be, because years may pass without a best-seller coming a publisher's way, and I do not believe that the best type of publishing can be maintained in dependence upon such an uncertainty.

Every now and again a typescript arrives written by someone who knows his subject inside out but who has not the dimmest notion how to select and present his material. Everything then depends upon finding someone with editorial experience and the infinite patience needed to sort out and rearrange a mass of good but chaotic MSS. One such book stands out in my memory, *The Arab of the Desert* by Colonel Dickson, than whom it would be impossible to find anyone with (in conjunction with his wife) a more intimate knowledge of his subject. In Mrs Lorimer, author of *Language Hunting in the Karakoram*, we found the ideal editor. Eight years elapsed between our acceptance of the book and its ultimate publication, and Mrs Lorimer was quite exhausted, but the result was an outstandingly good book which was a great success. A sequel, *Kuwait and her Neighbours*, that arrived after Mrs Lorimer's death was equally successfully tackled by that experienced author and editor of other people's work, Mr Clifford Witting.

Early in 1949 I was able to fulfil my wish to make a second world tour—this time with my wife (sister of my previous companion). The route to New Zealand was on this occasion via the USA and home via Colombo, Bombay and Suez. I had more than one objective. First, of course, was the wider distribution of British books, not excluding those of my own firm. Secondly, to visit Washington, the Grand Canyon and California. Thirdly, to see as much as I could of British Columbia, and lastly to see what I could do to break down the restrictions which were so sadly hampering the exports of British books to New Zealand.

At Washington I was able to see nearly everyone concerned with copyright and the tariff on books, to all of whom I pointed out that we had listened to many sermons from the USA on the wickedness of discrimination, and were beginning to wonder why, if they felt so strongly about it, they still continued to discriminate against us both in the matter of copyright and tariff, because it was only to books in English that the 'manufacturing clause' (that is the obligation to produce the book in the USA) and the tariff on books applied. I asked whether it would not be a fine thing for the United States to set us a good example and practise what it preached. There were many other equally embarrassing questions that I put to them which it is unnecessary to recapitulate, because in 1955 the USA signed a Universal Copyright Convention and abolished the manufacturing clause except for books of American authorship. The discriminating tariff still remains. As a revenue producer it is negligible but it is a formidable obstruction to the free flow of books, whether from individual to individual or from trader to trader. It gives irresponsible power to the United States Customs. It entitled them, for example, to prevent an English edition of a copyright work being passed into the States even with the approval and blessing of the copyright owner and American publisher. Even an author was not allowed to receive six complimentary copies of the English edition of his own work though his American publisher and a leading Senator urged the Customs to release them. High costs of production are compelling United States publishers to allow more and more copyright books to go out of print. In such cases, United States publishers are almost invariably willing to authorize the importation of the English edition, but if this permission is acted upon the copies are seized by the United States Customs. It was clear that economic factors would compel United States booksellers to look increasingly to Great Britain for the supply of books out of print in the United States, and that it was in the interests of both countries that they should do so. I preached this doctrine to all the booksellers in California. As an example I was able to point out that at that moment only one of Joseph Conrad's novels was available in a cloth bound edition in the USA, and that copies of the English edition in mint condition were readily available at less than half the cost of soiled second-hand copies of American editions. Throughout my stay in Washington I emphasized one fact familiar to publishers, but unfamiliar to others, including the

American printing trade unions, viz. any new book for which there is a big demand must in any case—protection or no protection—be separately printed on both sides of the Atlantic, because a supply thousands of miles from the demand is useless. It was a case of supplying at once or losing sales. In brief, the time factor protected the printers on both sides in all such cases. Furthermore, it was an indisputable fact that the production of small editions of slow-selling books was a class of business United States printers did not want and which the American printing unions were better without because their high wages were made possible by the use of costly machinery which was uneconomic for small editions. The idea that printing in the USA was still an 'infant industry' needing protection was laughable. The fact that America was better at BIG editions, and we were better at small ones, spoke for itself.

Apart from publishing problems, two things stood out at the end of my journey across the States and from one end of California to the other.

The ideas of most Americans about the British Commonwealth were about fifty years out of date. They had no relation to the present time. They were the greatest creditor nation the world has ever known, but still have a debtor mentality, and are blind to the obvious fact that their debtors can't pay them if they shut out their goods. That last point I found it necessary to emphasize in British Columbia, where many people were almost bitter about our failure to buy their products. In an address to the Committee of the Vancouver Board of Trade (March 1949) I pointed out:

'This does not mean that the people of Britain are not pining to buy more from Canada, because they are. I, for one, have an especial weakness for some of the products of British Columbia; in particular, your delicious fruit and excellent tinned salmon. But we are confronted with the unpleasant problem of how to pay for it.

'You people in Canada have been amazingly generous to us with your gifts, and have never begrudged us almost unlimited credit. But it is only a parasitic people who would be willing to rely indefinitely upon charity. Only a dishonest people would pile up liabilities which they saw no possibility of meeting, and we in Britain, as you would be the first to agree, are neither parasitic nor dishonest. What then can be done?

'May I first state the problem as I see it? During the hundred years or thereabouts when Britain was the world's biggest creditor nation we always took the precaution of importing rather more than we exported, thereby, be it noted, always enabling our debtors to pay their debts in goods and leaving them free to buy yet more from us with the certain knowledge that our imports would enable them to pay us. Two world wars have robbed us of most of our foreign investments, and of all the gold reserves we could spare. The year during which the Commonwealth was fighting alone landed us heavily in debt. There is now no way for us to get out of debt other than by exporting more than we import (and I, of course, include in our exports invisible exports, shipping and other services). In brief, we have to pay *in goods* for the excess amount of goods we imported during the war. There are two ways for us to get straight; one is to export more—a task upon which we are most diligently engaged. The other is to tighten our belts and make do with less—a most disagreeable and difficult thing to persuade people to do; nevertheless, the honest course.

'Now for years you and the United States were debtor nations and accustomed, as such, to export more than you imported. Overnight you, and still more the USA, have become creditor nations, but you have not, overnight, been able to change your commercial and economic traditions. But economic forces will compel you to recognize your changed position. If you want to export more, even if you want to export as much as you did, you will have to import more from your debtors.'

I then went on to speak specifically about the Canadian tax on books[1] and complete embargo on pocket diaries, greeting cards, and many forms of stationery, including 'blank books', a definition which gave their customs officials a wonderful opportunity to exercise their imagination and ingenuity. I concluded with the slogan 'Import more from us and your exports will take care of themselves'.

[1] Fortunately repealed in February 1953.

But I did not confine my attentions to the business world. I drew the attention of the University authorities to the changed position of the British book trade, and prepared the following statement for Dr Norman A. M. Mackenzie, President of the University of British Columbia, who raised the question at the National Conference of Canadian Universities.

'Since 1940, owing to the gigantic losses through bombing and our acute shortage of paper, British publishers were unable to maintain adequate supplies of University and other text-books. Through no fault of their own they were powerless to prevent the substitution of American books.

'It is much easier to lose a market than to regain it, but we are determined to get it back, and, indeed, it is in Canada's interests quite as much as in ours that we should do so.

'Without wishing in the very slightest degree to interfere with the freedom of choice, may I suggest the desirability of members of your faculty being officially informed that supplies from Britain can once more be relied upon.

'It might (may I hope?) be suggested that the possibility of reverting to British text-books should be considered; in fact, that in view of the importance of Canada buying more from Britain if we are to be put in a position to buy *and pay for* the many things we so badly want to buy from you, that the whole question of substituting British for American text-books should be studied.'

I suggested that an exhibition of University text-books might be organized, and this was subsequently carried out by the British Council.

Many newspapers have published interviews and reports about me, but none so entertaining as the *British Columbian* of New Westminster, BC (March 24, 1949), under the heading 'Sir Stanley Unwin dashes about Lumber Mill'.

When passing a shop window full of magnificent tennis shoes, I casually mentioned the temporary shortage of them in Britain, and the fact that I was not justified in using my restricted dollar travel allowance in making purchases of that kind.

Under a centre front page picture of me seated in a chair appeared the following, among other, paragraphs:

'Gaze long at this picture, for it is only once in a lifetime that you'll see a City Editor down on his knees. But after accompanying Sir Stanley Unwin, one of Britain's leading publishers, on a whirling tour of Fraser's Mills, City Editor, Bill Hamley, didn't have the strength to stand. He is helping Sir Stanley into new tennis shoes—a gift of the *British Columbian*. . . .

'The employees out at Fraser's Mills didn't know it, but the busy little man with the snow-white goatee who dashed around their plant has published as many books as they have handled boards. . . . This Englishman, whose age is "seventyish", dog-trotted around the plant behind salesman Gordon Saunders, former Adanac lacrosse star, asking questions and poking his cocky little beard into every corner he saw. At the end of an hour-long whirlwind inspection he stood unruffled and eager, while Saunders and the "Columbian" representative wilted. . . .'

When I reached New Zealand I found a very different position. Mr Walter Nash, their very able Finance Minister, who, when he decided to settle in New Zealand, went there as the representative of J. M. Dent & Sons Ltd. and my own firm, was under no illusions about the necessity of making imports and exports balance. On that issue I was naturally in complete accord with him. The question was what commodities should be regarded as luxuries, the import of which could properly be restricted, and which were necessities. It was a matter of priorities. I maintained that food for the body came first, food for the mind second, and that as New Zealand was self-supporting in food for the body, food for the mind (books) was priority No. 1, whereas their import had been so restricted that New Zealand was in danger of becoming 'a mentally starved nation'. That phrase caught on, and there were leading articles and interviews with me about it in all the New Zealand papers from Auckland to Invercargill. I found myself in the throes of a terrific campaign because the then Opposition found it a useful stick with which to belabour Mr Nash. The campaign culminated in a public debate between

Mr Nash and myself which was broadcast. Mr Nash suggested, and I conceded, that streptomycin and penicillin might be entitled to priority over books. (I did not know until a day or two later that the per capita consumption of drugs in New Zealand was higher than anywhere else in the world.) However, he promised that additional quotas would be granted in any case where they were clearly wanted for worthwhile books. The promise was implemented and the import of British books, which had dropped to £400,000 per annum, rose to £850,000 the following year. Whether my campaign had anything to do with the increase it is for others to say, but it occupied nearly all my time and reduced the three weeks' holiday I had planned to have with my family at the Hermitage (Mt Cook) to five days.

When I went to say farewell to Mr Nash, who had been exceedingly kind and had been responsible for a reception for me at Parliament House, I found him in great discomfort with a swollen face suffering from the ill effects of an overdose of penicillin, to which he was obviously allergic. I refrained from telling him how much I regretted conceding priority to penicillin over books.

In the course of my stay I called personally upon almost every bookseller in both islands, besides attending the conference of their association, to which I had been specially invited.

I returned to England to find that the successful publication of *Kon-Tiki*, of which, in addition to nearly half a million sold through Book Clubs, we had ourselves already sold well over half a million (and it is still selling merrily) had brought us many other books of adventure apart from those directly connected with *Kon-Tiki*, like *Happy Island* by Bengt Danielsson, the Swedish member of the expedition. Many titles spring to mind, but one stands out. I had given up a winter sports holiday to attend, on behalf of the British Council, the opening of a Book Exhibition at Oslo. I did not want to go, but as the Norwegian book trade associations had so flatteringly insisted to the British Council that they wanted me and that no substitute would do, I felt that I must accede to their wishes. I had heard much about the underground movement in Norway, and found that one excellent book about it had been so 'edited' and transformed by an American publisher as to be unsuitable for publication in England. When I deplored the fact to a Norwegian literary editor he said at once, 'I think Oluf Reed Olsen's work much better'. I found that Olsen had published two books, neither of which was suitable for translation into English because each contained so much about Britain that would be of little or no interest to British readers. But each contained thrilling Norwegian material. I sought out Mr Qvist, the bookseller-publisher, who had helped Olsen's underground activities, explained the position to him, and he quickly secured Olsen's permission to combine the Norwegian parts into one book. Neither of the titles of the two Norwegian books was attractive in an English translation, and of the many suggested I had no hesitation in selecting *Two Eggs on My Plate*. It was not a popular decision, but I felt sure it was right because the title would attract the attention of all airmen to whom the book would appeal, and, still more important, was one easily remembered. I had the greatest confidence in the book, a confidence not shared to the same degree by some of my colleagues, who felt that the size of a reprint I had ordered was excessive. Even I thought it would be sufficient to justify the distribution of the type. But the sales kept up to such an extent that seven further reprints have been called for. Each time we have said, 'Now we shall be able to distribute the type', but it never proved safe to do so. *Two Eggs on My Plate* is one of those rare, but most welcome, books which refuse to stop selling.

Our predecessor, George Allen, was the publisher of the works of Augustus Hare, and in particular (apart from the Guides) the six-volume *Story of My Life*, which had long since been out of print. Frequent reference to its merits prompted our editor, Malcolm Barnes, to prepare a two-volume abridged edition under the titles *The Years With Mother* and *In My Solitary Life*. They were accorded a most enthusiastic reception by the Press. Both editor and publishers were congratulated upon their enlightened enterprise, but the sales thus far have been disappointing. I say 'thus far' because I believe it to be a work of lasting value owing to the remarkable picture it gives of the country house life of the period described.

One of the really great men of my time and the period immediately before it, father of several distinguished sons, was Dr L. P. Jacks, for forty-five years editor of the *Hibbert Journal* which we had had the privilege of publishing since October 1938. His two volumes of autobiography, *Confessions of an Octogenarian* and its sequel, *Near the Brink*, written when he was ninety, make fascinating reading and reveal an unusually acute and balanced mind. He spent much of his eighties translating as a labour of love the work of Alfred Loisy, whom he held in great esteem and felt had never received the recognition he deserved.

Day by day I go personally through the pile of unsolicited MSS which descends upon us, still eagerly and optimistically hopeful that among the mass of rubbish there may be, if not a work of genius, something of outstanding interest. Usually I am disappointed, but one day the pile contained some love letters of Ruskin to Kathleen Prynne of which the world had known nothing. Sir E. T. Cook when editing the 39-volume edition of Ruskin's works had suppressed and succeeded in destroying three. My son Rayner, who has taken degrees in English Literature at both Oxford and Harvard, seized the typescript when I told him about it, and later said that he would like to edit the volume, which he did (I quote Evelyn Waugh's review in the *Spectator*) in an exemplary manner under the title *The Gulf of Years*, a piece of literary work which he followed up to my great satisfaction with a book on the peasant poets of England, entitled *The Rural Muse*.

There were many important books issued during this period to which I should like to refer, but I must confine myself to the most exciting, *The Lord of the Rings* by J. R. R. Tolkien, in connection with which my son Rayner played an important part. Like him, we were all of us at Museum Street *Hobbit* fans and were longing for a sequel, but when we learnt that it was a work of enormous length, primarily intended for adults, upon which Tolkien had been engaged for over twenty years, we were some of us rather aghast. But my son was not intimidated either by the appearance or length of this formidable manuscript. He pronounced it a work of genius which we simply must find a way of publishing, even if it meant issuing it in three volumes. I was away in Japan, and wrote at once agreeing to its acceptance even if it involved a loss of as much as £1,000. When on my return I was able to read a set of proofs I recognized at once that we were backing a certainty and that there would be no question of losing money. It was a book for all time, which will be selling long after my departure from this world. Its reception by booksellers to whom early proofs were submitted was both interesting and instructive. Real bookmen like J. G. Wilson of Bumpus's recognized it immediately as a great work; many were almost wildly enthusiastic, but a few said it left them completely cold. When we published the first two volumes, we confidently anticipated following them up immediately with Volume 3, of which we had the complete text of the story. But the author was not ready with all the supplementary material, and there was what seemed to all an interminable delay. Volume 2 had left readers in agonizing suspense, and never in over fifty years of publishing have I received so many letters from the public—some intensely humorous, more resentful, but all complaining that they could endure the suspense no longer, and complaining of our cruelty in delaying the publication of Volume 3. The burden of answering all these letters was such that we were as thankful as our correspondents when the production of Volume 3 was finally completed.

I mentioned that I was in Japan when my son reported upon the typescript. I was in the midst of one of the most strenuous of all my journeys abroad and round the world. With my elder son David, who came as my secretary, I covered about 26,000 miles, all by air, in just over three months between September and December 1952. The mere enumeration of the places visited shows the extent of the journey—Beirut, Karachi, Bombay, Madras, Colombo, Singapore, Djakarta, Bandung, Hong Kong, Tokyo, Bangkok, Rangoon, Chittagong, Dacca, Calcutta, Darjeeling,

Delhi, Srinagar, Lahore, Karachi, Basra, Kuwait, Beirut, Nicosia, Athens, Rome. At each place I called upon every bookseller, and, where there were any, the public libraries, besides interviewing many Governors, Prime Ministers and other officials. At almost every centre where the British Council had a Representative I found myself expected to give lectures and broadcasts. On my arrival at Karachi, for example, I received a telegram from the unfortunate man at Dacca, asking how many lectures I could give in the forty-eight hours I had planned to be there. I say 'unfortunate' because so few possible lecturers pass through Dacca, and he had no funds with which to pay their fares to come there. My son and I agreed each to give a lecture. When the time came, owing to my son's illness, I had to give them both, to attend two receptions, to give a broadcast, to address the booksellers collectively and subsequently to call upon all of them individually in the forty-eight hours I was there.

On arrival at Karachi I found that virtually no books were being imported because of regulations which called for a deposit of 75 per cent of the cost of any order at the time of placing it, i.e. months before the goods could be received. Furthermore, such books as were imported were subject to a postal (or customs) 'handling charge' of no less than 8 annas (then 1s od) on each package, however small, which made books needlessly expensive and penalized students, whom the Pakistan Government professed to want to encourage with their studies. I let fly with a whirlwind campaign, interviewing countless officials. On my return from Japan in two months' time, I had the satisfaction of being able to announce at the banquet given in my honour by the Karachi booksellers that both the 'deposit' and the postal handling charge had been abolished.

In India I interviewed Governors and Prime Ministers about the application of the Sales Tax to books. In Indonesia I devoted much energy to trying to secure the removal of the many obstacles to the free flow of British books to a country where English has been substituted for Dutch as the second language, and there is a huge demand for them. In Japan I was able to rebuild connections that had been lost during the war and the subsequent American Occupation, and to secure Japanese co-operation in refusing to handle pirated editions.

Late in 1955 I made a fourth journey round the world by boat via Bermuda and Havana to Jamaica, and thence by air to Grand Cayman, Antigua, Barbados, St Lucia, Trinidad, Tobago, British Guiana, Venezuela, Curaçao and so (by boat) to New Zealand, returning via Australia and South Africa. It was my first visit to the West Indies and reference is made to it in connection with my work for the British Council.[1] It was a great disappoint- to me that, although my plane touched down at Grenada, it was not practicable, owing to a devasting hurricane, for me to spend any time there.

I was determined that on this further visit to New Zealand I should not be deprived of a holiday. It had long been my ambition to visit Samuel Butler's *Erewhon* country, and my New Zealand doctor nephew kindly agreed to accompany me and to make the necessary arrangements. I don't think that we either of us realized upon what a strenuous undertaking we were embarking. Butler had a pack horse to carry his kit; we had to hump our own, and it included, besides heavy sleeping-bags and the usual impedimenta, food for four days. I have never carried such a weight. How heavy was soon revealed to me. My nephew is a great bird lover. When he drew my attention to one and I looked round, the weight of my kit deposited me on the ground. Without such a heavy pack, climbing over rough tracks and wading many streams would not have troubled me, despite the long distances between the disused shepherds' huts which were our nightly objectives. But constant falling was exhausting; nevertheless it was huge fun. We were warned that the huts were derelict, and that the only thing we could count upon finding was a billy in which to boil water. The billies were indeed there, but they all had holes in them. However, it was wonderful country and I wouldn't have missed those four days for anything. But I will admit that it was a joy

[1] See Chapter 23.

to get back to the old Homestead at Orari Gorge and to visit Mesopotamia—the site of Butler's home—by car.

Though these various journeys were strenuous, they were certainly successful, and greatly stimulated the sale of British books, including, I need hardly add, those published by George Allen & Unwin Ltd. In fact, on my return on both occasions I found our warehouse in difficulties. Our turnover had increased to about five times the pre-war amount, but our premises were the same size, and the fact that the proportion of export turnover had increased to about 56 per cent of the whole added to our troubles, because export orders require so much more space for looking out. Our forethought in buying all the adjoining free-holds availed us nothing because we were refused permission to do anything in the way of building or rebuilding. We were in the ludicrous position of being urged by one Government department to increase our exports, and simultaneously prevented from doing so by another, and the bitter thing is that we are stopped by a chimera—a grandiose scheme, involving millions of pounds, which will never be carried out and which nobody really appears to want. Premises which are partly, and ought to be wholly, condemned, must remain untouched because they are in a 'designated area'. The fact that the Holborn Borough Council objects most strongly to the prevention of any development in this large part of their borough is disregarded. The pipe dream of some mysterious bureaucrat is sacrosanct and any objections to it are over-ruled.

Between these two journeys—in January 1954—I completed my first fifty years in the book trade, and my three fellow directors felt that it was an event deserving celebration. They arranged a most delightful dinner at the Cutlers Hall, at which about 130 members of my family and friends of the firm were present. They were all handed a little volume of Tributes paid to me by some of our most distinguished authors (such as Professor Gilbert Murray, Bertrand Russell, Sir S. Radhakrishnan), and leading publishers and booksellers from all over the world, which they had secretly prepared.

Madrid Book Fair with José Zendrera

SPAIN, 1945

At Montserrat with Mr Gili, Mrs Janés and Mrs Simpson

INDIA, 1952

NIGERIA, 1957

The President of the Publishers Association, Mr Ralph Hodder-Williams, who was familiar with my early Nonconformist background, proposed my health in a delightful speech. In my reply I related some of the hardships and difficulties with which I had contended, and made it clear that the current impression that I had been born with a silver spoon in my mouth was far from true.

A few weeks later, the Publishers Circle gave me a luncheon at which my health was most eloquently proposed by Basil (now Sir Basil) Blackwell, and I was presented with an inscribed silver fountain-pen. A week later the Booksellers Association took the unprecedented step of interrupting their deliberations 'to do honour to one who has completed fifty years in the Book Trade whose name is, without doubt, the most widely known in that trade, not only in this country, but in the whole world'. Mr Cadness Page, at the conclusion of a charming speech, presented me with an enormous birthday cake in the form of a book and invited me to cut it, which I most happily did.

The completion of my first fifty years in the Book Trade seems an appropriate moment with which to conclude this section of the book. I would like, however, to add that I have much enjoyed the first five years of the next fifty.

Part II

CHAPTER 17

ON PUBLISHING

I have written about Publishing as a Profession in *The Truth About Publishing*, and have no wish to repeat here what is already available in print. Whether it be profession, trade or craft, publishing is certainly exacting. It is a most jealous taskmistress. It is more than what is known as 'a full-time occupation' because that is limited to office hours. The building up of a successful publishing business involves working non-stop and almost taking it to bed with one. For my own part, except for tennis on Saturday and Sunday afternoons, and during holidays when I shut myself off entirely from the business, I have for years on end worked non-stop and thrived on it. Even the reference to taking it to bed with me is not a complete exaggeration, because I have often employed the unconscious to solve problems for me while I slept.

Because the things handled are the product of man's imagination; because they may possess a quality which renders them imperishable, there is a fascination about publishing which all the prosaic details of estimating and production, printing and binding and distribution cannot destroy. There is a constant sense of adventure, of the probability of something momentous happening; every letter, every caller, offers the possibility of interest and surprise. And one day (who knows?) those daily piles of usually hopeless MSS may contain a work of genius which will make its publisher, as well as its author, famous.

'Of all the forms of merchandise', said the late Arthur Waugh, for many years Managing Director of Chapman & Hall Ltd., 'books are surely the most human and the most companionable, and the authors of books, taking them all in all, the veritable salt of the earth.' But publishing is more than friendship with authors, more than a wide and keen interest in literature. The late William Heinemann used to say that 'a publisher must be something of an accountant, and something of a lawyer. Above all, if the imprint of his firm is to be associated with great books, he must have a wide-ranging mind, keeping his finger on all new movements, knowing what the world has appreciated in the past, what it will need and appreciate today, and yet again what it will be asking for tomorrow'.

It is said that a man should enter upon marriage with his eyes wide open and keep them half-closed ever afterwards. My experience of book publishing is that people tend to embark upon it with their eyes half-closed and to open them very wide when they subsequently discover what it really involves. The knowledge that is needed for success in publishing cannot be acquired in a day nor yet in a year; it is often not till after a wide experience of ten or fifteen years that a publisher realizes most keenly how much there is still to learn.

Publishing is very different from what it was when I started more than fifty years ago. Paternoster Row is no longer the centre. There was a steady westward trend before the Row was bombed out of existence. At one time, strangely enough, Covent Garden seemed to be the magnet. More recently and more fittingly the neighbourhood of the British Museum looked like becoming the centre of the wide area over which publishing was spreading itself; but if the many acres in front of the Museum which have been 'designated' for a grandiose scheme are in fact put to that purpose, many publishers will regrettably be driven farther afield.

Publishing has moved westward in another respect; it has tended to become more American in outlook and method. That there should be greater interest in the best that America can pro- vide in the realm of literature is all to the good; that there should be increased concentration upon 'best-sellerdom' and stunt publishing is not a cause for equal congratulations.[1]

With most commodities it is true to say if there is a 'run' on them they tend to become scarce, and their price to rise. With

---

[1] See 'Books and Big Business' in *Books*, the Journal of the National Book League, No. 247 (April 1950).

books it is the reverse. The more they are bought, the more readily available and cheaper they can become. Nevertheless, as St John Ervine has pointed out, people who readily squander pounds on superfluities regard the expenditure of an equivalent number of shillings upon books as an almost criminal extravagance. What is often overlooked is that there are few things which books cannot help us to do better; that there are books, too, for every mood, and that nothing delights a good bookseller or public librarian more than to provide information about the best books available on any subject, or for any mood. I often hear people say of a famous writer, 'I should love to meet and hear *his* views on that question'. Well, we can meet these men in their books, and get something much better than a casual conversation; we can read their carefully considered opinions. Were these things more fully realized the publisher's problem would be much simplified.

Despite an increase in the number of public libraries that take their responsibilities seriously, scholarly publishing has become more difficult; but it has not become less vital to the intellectual well-being of the nation.

Here, merely changing the one word newspaper to book publishing, I should like to quote what the late C. P. Scott wrote about Newspaper Ideals, Character and Influence, because it applies so admirably to the better type of book publishing.

'A book-publishing house has two sides to it. It is a business, like any other, and has to pay in the material sense in order to live. But it is much more than a business; it is an institution; it reflects and it influences the life of a whole community; it may affect even wider destinies. It is, in its way, an instrument of government. It plays on the minds and consciences of men. It may educate, stimulate, assist, or it may do the opposite. It has, therefore, a moral as well as a material existence, and its character and influence are in the main determined by the balance of these two forces. It may make profit or power its first object, or it may conceive itself as fulfilling a higher and more exacting function.'[1]

[1] *Manchester Guardian*, July 2, 1955.

Most publishers, other than University Presses, when confronted with a scholarly work unlikely even to pay its way and which would certainly never yield a profit, immediately and naturally stand aside. To try to find a way of publishing such work is to embark upon a most perilous course. Publishers are not, as so often supposed, fairy godmothers. There are severe limits to what ordinary commercial publishers who are not endowed can do. It is one thing to give one's services and organization for nothing; quite another to be in addition out of pocket for the paper, printing and binding.

I have always been deeply interested in scholarly publishing; it was part of the Swan Sonnenschein tradition which I inherited. My firm has accordingly worked on the principle that we will gladly publish any scholarly work of importance from which there is no hope of deriving profit, provided we are not expected to do more than provide our services and organization gratuitously.

What many people find difficult to understand is our insistence upon complete knowledge of the financial and economic implications of every transaction, *coupled with* a readiness to act upon other than economic motives once the full implications of what is being done have been grasped by all concerned. Most people either ignore or act solely upon economic considerations. Our approach is disconcerting because it is unusual; in consequence some catch is suspected. Any publisher who follows this method of dealing with unprofitable but otherwise worthwhile books must not expect to be thanked for his services or his assistance to scholarship; he must expect abuse and a reputation for meanness. As an illustration here is an extract from a letter from a professor, who emphasized, when he first approached us about some philosophical essays, that he did not expect any cash reward from the book, but changed his mind as soon as we agreed to publish it.

'An economist friend described A. & U. as "the tightest-fisted publishing house in London". . . . It looks as if your caution about L.s.d. has frustrated other scholars than myself.'

312

Nevertheless I believe the principle is right, and, if it is, what people think or say about one is unimportant. Fortunately there are other professors and people of more importance than this correspondent who agree with me. In that connection a letter dated November 29, 1947, from James A. A. Porteous stands out. It reads:

'Now that the remaining stock of *The New Unionism* is to be sold off at a reduced price, I feel that this melancholy circumstance is also the occasion to recall to your mind four prophecies which you made at the start of its career.

'You foresaw that it might have good reviews, indifferent or poor sales, that it might be instrumental in getting me a job, and that years afterwards I would write to thank you and tell you just this tale. The first three prophecies were all fulfilled. It had good reviews; sales, as you know, were very disappointing (as things turned out, the international situation was against it); and it was directly instrumental in getting me an extremely interesting post—first as Assistant Secretary to the Scottish Economic Committee, where later I followed the late Sir William Goodchild as Secretary.

'Now, with a somewhat heavy heart but with very real gratitude I am fulfilling the fourth. I am afraid I have been a rather heavy liability, though I still hope one day to be able to recompense your firm with something more profitable. But that book meant a great deal to me personally. Frankly, if it had not been published, as far as I can see I should have been sunk. As it was, it enabled me, for example, to get married and in the course of time to build for myself a niche in Scotland.

'The book itself had, I think, an influence greater than might appear; and many of the reforms I advocated (which were then thought to be somewhat in advance of the times) have since been adopted or are now in the forefront of political thought. I foresee that some of its ideas will come much more to the fore during the next few years.

'So now I can only say, Thank you.'

Writing on this theme, with specific reference to works of research, Roger Burlinghame says:[1]

[1] *Of Making Many Books* (Scribner's 1946), p. 107.

'For most authors, satisfaction must come indirectly or in imponderable terms. . . . The immeasurable profit of "prestige" comes only from a book. A "great name" in literature comes wholly from a writer's books. No amount of magazine publishing, lecturing, radio broadcasting or movie production has a comparable effect. Yet all these profitable things are often made possible to an author because of the reputation he gains from one book which may be unlucrative or even costly in itself. For it is a curious fact that a book need not sell in great numbers to build a wide reputation.'

As an additional deterrent to any publisher embarking upon this perilous adventure of trying to assist the issue of scholarly work, he must expect that in the event of a reputation being built up through his services, the offer of the first commercially profitable book by the author may go to a competitor who would never be bothered with unprofitable books.

But there are compensations; above all the prestige of the firm; the respect of people who really matter, and the satisfaction of doing something pre-eminently worth while without becoming bankrupt in the process. It may even result, as it did in my case, in a letter addressed to:

Any Book Publisher,
London, England,

being marked 'try Unwin'.

As I have said, few people who have not made the venture realize how much easier it is to lose money than to make it at book publishing. Any man who has succeeded consistently (not merely through chancing on a 'best-seller') could have made more money in other directions, but he would have had a far less interesting life.

Making money, I can truthfully say, has never presented any difficulty to me. I could have been a millionaire had that been my objective in life; but that is nothing of which to be proud. I always agreed with my craftsman brother Bernard when he rubbed into me that 'the trick of making money out of almost anything was a special gift of very doubtful moral value'. Some men are born with this dubious 'gift' as clearly as others are with artistic genius. It enables them to see instinctively and immediately without conscious effort, the financial implications (where there are any) of every action.

Far be it from me to deny that it is a most convenient gift with the world as it is today, but whether it ought to be such an advantage is another question. Fortunately I have never been cursed with megalomania. There was a moment when I was in a position to acquire the controlling interest in Methuens and Chapman & Hall, which in association with my own firm of Allen & Unwin, Thos. Murby & Co., John Lane the Bodley Head Ltd., would have put me in the way of becoming the 'biggest' publisher, which the late Walter Hutchinson never was, though he claimed to be. But my object in arranging the purchase of these two old firms was to prevent their getting into wrong hands as there was grave risk of their doing, not to form a publishing combine. I was therefore content to acquire a minority interest, which I subsequently sold.

The absorption of small insolvent firms by financially stable publishers is an inevitable process, and I have myself thus acquired quite a number, but the amalgamation of big prosperous concerns would almost invariably be a disaster. In the first place, the character, personality and goodwill of the individual publishing houses would be largely dissipated. Unless they are merely manufacturers, most publishing businesses have a very definite character of their own, usually the reflection of the dominant personality who created them.

As has rightly been said, 'a publishing house is a long term business; it doesn't live from hand to mouth . . . it is deeply and inescapably personal; only the devotion and the individuality of its chiefs can make or preserve it; there is a part of their task which cannot be delegated, and it is that part which gives the firm its life'.

Mr Frank Swinnerton, the distinguished novelist, who has an intimate and practical knowledge of publishing equalled by no other author, has summed up the whole position admirably:

'That firm will stand highest, in ten, twenty, or fifty years, which has attracted to itself within this period the most valuable, the most amusing, the most typical books of its age. Therefore the great firms have all been founded upon the characters, the personalities, of those who established them; upon the foresight and courage of their ventures; and upon the degree in which those ventures added constructively to the culture of the period. . . .

'It is such an individual business that the death of a founder or the introduction to the firm of a new enthusiast may make an immeasurable difference to its calibre. And in the healthy rivalries of publishers lies assurance that no really good book, whatever its faults or eccentricities, is ever likely to remain unpublished. No British publisher *dare* miss the first class, even if, at first sight, he does not much care for it. . . .

'British publishers do more than any other class in the community to stimulate the production of masterpieces, and should enjoy our respect and thanks for historic service to culture.'[1]

It cannot be too strongly emphasized that publishers are not dealing with a mere commodity like soap or soda, where the advantages of mass production are overwhelming, but with the lively offspring of an author's mind. In a publisher, as I have said elsewhere, the recognition that he is *not* dealing with a mere commodity, but handling his sensitive and suspicious authors' children, each with an individuality of his own, is the beginning of wisdom. It is this factor which dictates the optimum size of a publisher's business, beyond which it is inexpedient to go.

The fact that under the influence of death duties, more and more family concerns are being turned into public companies is unfortunate. It means in the long run a loss of that personal author-publisher relationship which has meant, and means, so much.

I am often asked how I have managed to finance the development of a business which has grown as rapidly as mine. Has it not involved constant overdrafts at the bank? Many seem startled when I reply that my firm has never had an overdraft, and paid

[1] *Britain Today*, No. 94, February 1944.

off the last of its debentures more than thirty years ago. The explanation is simple. We have managed to avoid serious losses; we have put the requirements of the firm first and have always ploughed back more than half the profits; we have consistently valued our stock on a most stringent basis, which all publishers say they do but few succeed in doing because their profit and loss accounts would be too depressing if they did not deceive themselves about the value of their stock and rights. I had seen too many firms get into financial difficulties through this kind of optimism to want to follow their example. When there is a showdown it is astonishing how little stock realizes, as any liquidator or receiver with experience would readily confirm. Whether with taxation at its present level, firms will be able to finance their development out of revenue as in the past is to say the least doubtful.

In connection with this whole problem of finance I find Hilaire Belloc's views 'On Usury'[1] particularly interesting:

'The modern world is organized on the principle that money of its nature breeds money. A sum of money lent has, according to our present scheme, a natural right to interest. That principle is false in economics as well as in morals.'

With that statement I cannot but agree. The trouble is accentuated by the extent to which we are hypnotized by mere book-keeping entries, and our inability or reluctance to remember that money is only a symbol. If we made a practice of always asking ourselves what the symbols really represented we should avoid many pitfalls. A simple illustration will show what I mean. A thousand pounds lent at 5 per cent per annum to build a house or create a bomb may involve the same book-keeping entry. But in the first case the capital exists in the form of a house for the use of which it may be well worth while for somebody to pay £50 as long as it exists. After the bomb has exploded the capital has ceased to exist, but, much more serious, that bomb is supposed to create

[1] *Essays of a Catholic* (London: Sheed & Ward), 1931.

£50 per annum interest in perpetuity. Translated into facts, instead of book-keeping entries, the absurdity of that supposition is obvious to anyone. (It was doubtless this obsession with book-keeping entries that led a Somerset House official to maintain that, though the two hundred thousand unvalued copies of my firm's publications had admittedly been destroyed, we had lost *nothing* thereby because over the years this portion of our stock had been written off.)

This worship of book-entries and disregard of realities plays into the hands of the unscrupulous financier and distracts us from adequate study of this vital question of usury. Moreover, we are so preoccupied today with the filling in of forms, disentangling ourselves from regulations and fighting bureaucratic abuses of power that we are left with no energy (a thing which, thanks to my ancestry, I have never lacked) or time (which throughout my life I have found all too severely rationed) to cope with such vastly more important matters as this. I have given much thought to the problem, with Ruskin's theories all too clearly before me, but have no solution to propound. What is certain is that the fallacy of money breeding money must be squarely faced and not ignored, as it is apt to be.

Apart from the incursion of financiers into book publishing—a comparatively recent innovation—there have been marked changes in the book world, first and foremost, though of least direct importance to the public, in the organization of the book trade. It would be fair to say that fifty years ago there was no organization at all, certainly nothing comparable with what was, and is, to be found in many continental countries. Thanks to a very determined and on the whole successful, effort on the part of a comparatively small number of publishers and booksellers this is no longer the case. As will be seen in the chapter on its development and work, the Publishers Association has become an effective body with a wide sphere of influence. Among many other activities it takes its part in the work of the International Publishers Association.

To the public eye, the most obvious sign of change is in the quality of production. Here there has indeed been remarkable progress, particularly in typography. It was always possible with sufficient effort to secure the use of a good face of type, but the usual range in book printing offices fifty years ago was deplorable. Today it is the publisher's fault if his books are not set up in one of the many good founts now readily available. Greater care is taken today over the typographical arrangement of a cheap book than would have been bestowed upon an expensive one early this century. Even educational books have benefited, and no longer have the same dull and forbidding appearance to which an earlier generation was accustomed. Such a series as Understanding the Modern World or Secondary School Science which my firm issues are examples of modern school books which anyone can take pleasure in handling. Apart from an increasing use of fadeless cloths, there is not as much progress in binding, but dust jackets have an importance not even contemplated at the end of the Victorian, or even Edwardian, era. The time and care devoted to them, and the expenditure upon them, are prodigious.

It would take too long to enumerate all the other directions in which progress has been made, but two have given me special satisfaction. First the marked and consistent improvement in the standard of translations—a subject upon which I have had something to say elsewhere;[1] secondly, the development of photolithography—a process which enables books of which the type has been distributed and of which no stereoplates are available, to be reproduced photographically.

But that is only one direction in which photography is being applied to printing. Great advance has recently been made in the various mechanisms for photographic typesetting, which may at any moment supersede existing methods. This invention would at once sweep away lead, which has been the basis of printing from movable type since the days of Gutenberg. Instead, a series of master pictures of the alphabet would be photographed and the book be reproduced from these photographs.

[1] *On Translations* (London: George Allen & Unwin Ltd., 1946).

And whilst we are peering into the future, may we not one of these days buy our books in the form of long-playing gramophone records and be spared the trouble of reading them? Personally, I believe that even if such an alternative were available, most people would still prefer to read in peace and quiet. We already suffer from too much noise.

But that will not be the view of booksellers, many of whom when confronted with anything new, whether it be Penguins, Book Clubs, Television, or Book Sales, invariably feel that their end has come, though the innovation almost equally invariably turns out to their advantage. They are unaware of it, but owing to their shortsightedness they are their own worst enemies; not the publishers, whom they always suspect.

My personal secretary, who has worked for me with unparalleled devotion for over thirty-five years, has kept in touch with some of the early employees. I was interested to learn that one, who has been for a long time in South Africa, wrote to her on my completion of fifty years in the book trade, to say how much impressed she had been by the fact that I always thanked the staff when paying their wages. It was a quite unconscious act on my part, due doubtless to my strong feeling (a family tradition) that there ought to be something more than a cash nexus between an employer and his staff. When in London I go to all the employees at the place they are working to hand them their wages. This affords them a weekly opportunity to speak to me, or to make an appointment to do so more privately if they so wish. I try both to make it clear that I am readily accessible, and that I wish to preserve the feeling that we are a team, if not a big family. With a constantly growing staff, and the inconstancy of the younger female members of it, this becomes increasingly difficult. But it is well worth the effort. The dullest job becomes interesting when done with enthusiasm as one of a team.

It is a rule of the house that all complaints, whether from authors, booksellers, or others, are referred to me, and from time to time, for example, I am called to the trade counter to deal with someone dissatisfied with the information or decision that has

The Book Trade Delegation, 1926

been given. Fortunately I now have younger directors who relieve me of some of this responsibility. But I still see all the letters and orders that arrive (an ever-increasing task). This does not mean that I read them all before putting them in the tray of the person who is to deal with them. I know which letters to read and over which orders to pause. I expect my staff to deal with all correspondence without reference to me unless I pencil '? S.U.' upon it. That I do only when I am in possession of some facts that may be useful to them, or want them to consult me about the method of handling a particular situation. All the outward letters pass my desk; I know which it is expedient to read. This practice, thanks to my exceptional memory of what has gone before, often enables me to prevent tiresome mistakes or spot omissions. Very rarely I will completely re-dictate a letter, and ask the person concerned, if he thinks it an improvement, to sign and send it instead of his own version. One of the most common mistakes is the use of jargon or abbreviations which will convey nothing to their recipients; another is a failure to see the problem from the other man's point of view. A letter may be so worded as to invite the reply you want, or the reverse. Again, it has to be remembered that with some authors a mere expression of a hope that something might be practicable will be interpreted as a formal guarantee that it will be done. A man writing letters to authors has to be something of a psychologist. To ensure that letters of a type frequently needed (with or without modification) are correctly and happily worded, we make greater use of form letters than many firms. They are not necessarily printed, but the vital paragraphs are available. One letter in constant use, but never printed, was most carefully thought out and drafted in 1915 —more than forty years ago.

Apropos of mistakes, we all of us do silly things, most of which we manage to forget. One such incident I still remember. The chit which accompanied my pass book differed by £10 from what I expected, and assuming that as on a previous occasion there had been an error, I hastily scribbled across it that the substraction [sic] was wrong. One of Drummond's staff, the late L. P. Tremlett, with whom I was friendly and who was a bit of a wit, sent me the following delightful rebuke:

'Oh Publisher Great, I was quite devastated,
'Bewildered, bemused, and nearly prostrated,
'To think that once more I'd have to admit
'That Drummonds had made a mistake on their chit.
'But in spite of much study with slide rule and table
'To find our mistake I'm still quite unable.
'Dare I venture, I wonder, to ask you to look
'At Allen and Unwin's best spelling book,
'For I think you will find, 'tis merely a guess,
'That "subtraction" is spelt with only one "s" .'

CHAPTER 18

THE TRIALS OF A PUBLISHER

It has been said, by whom I don't remember, that 'Everyone knows about the trials of an author because, as writing is his profession, he takes care that his troubles shall not be hidden. But the publisher's trials have usually to be borne in secret.'

There are those who would maintain that the whole process of publishing is one prolonged trial from the arrival of the disorderly manuscript, bearing neither name nor address, to the vexatious libel action that may unexpectedly follow the publication of the most innocent work. But I am not one of them; I am too conscious of the many compensations publishing has to offer.

In the past, probably the chief trial of a publisher was that the day he became one he ceased to be an ordinary human being. He found himself regarded at one moment as an unscrupulous rogue with Machiavellian cunning, and the next as a philanthropist with unlimited endowments behind him. The rapidity of the change from one role to the other was sometimes startling. In my youth railway companies, until they took to prosecuting people and publishing lists of convictions, were regarded as 'fair game'. Publishers sometimes appeared to be in that unhappy position. I remember one author frankly admitting to me that he regarded it as quite all right to do a publisher down. Publishers in fact sometimes seemed to be regarded as being of a pariah class, in dealing with whom truthfulness and common honesty were superfluous. No doubt that was at the back of the mind of the author who, in my Fisher Unwin days, typed two copies of his manuscript and sold the copyright in his work for cash to two different publishers. Fortunately I was the prompter in producing the money, so that when the unfortunate publishers compared notes after both had printed the book, T. Fisher Unwin was

323

found to be the owner of the copyright and was spared the unpleasant job of prosecuting.

I sometimes used to think it was a pity that the late Herbert Jenkins, when he left his money to the RSPCA, did not add a proviso that, for the purposes of his legacy, a publisher was an animal. However, publishers *are* ordinary human beings, and fortunately today most authors recognize that fact and treat us accordingly. Nevertheless a publisher has to remember (and console himself with the knowledge) that almost everything he does will be considered wrong, and that the utmost publicity will be given to his every shortcoming; that as John Fox once wrote to Charles Scribner, a publisher is 'a man who is blamed if a book fails and ignored if it proves a success'. If he rejects a manuscript, he will be wrong in the author's eyes. If he accepts anything but those rare works of genius that may come his way but once in a blue moon, he will be wrong in the eyes of booksellers and critics. If he points out (correctly) that there is no probability of the sales of a particular book covering its printing bill—it is assumed not that there is anything wrong with the book or its subject, but that the publisher is mean and unenterprising. If, however, in a spirit of generosity, he publishes such books and finds his way to Carey Street, his creditors will be loud in their complaints. If he publishes a translation with the slightest blemish, he will be jumped on; but if he ventures on a mild protest when confronted with a translation too bad to be printable, he is apt to make an enemy for life. During the First World War I had just such a translation. It was so obviously, so palpably bad, that we had to have the work almost completely redone. It is our rule to give the translator's name, but in this instance we refused—I think quite rightly—to give the first translator the credit, or rather the unqualified credit, for the second translator's work. To do so would not only deceive the public, but might easily lead another publisher into the trouble we had experienced, because we ourselves had agreed to the author's choice of translator on the strength of a previous translation, which subsequent inquiry revealed was originally as bad as ours.

The translator was very angry, and found an ingenious way to vent her spleen. She persuaded a Scottish friend to sue us in Scotland for a debt of the predecessors of our predecessors, for which we were in no sense responsible, legally or morally. Some people doubtless understand Scottish law—I don't pretend to. Before our side of the matter was heard, the good lady had secured what is known as 'a writ of attachment', which prevented one of our biggest customers in Scotland from making any further payments to us till the matter was settled. We were advised that if we proposed to contest the claim it was essential to attend the court in person. With my colleagues and most of our staff away at the war, it simply couldn't be done. The amount involved was fortunately not considerable, so that it was simpler and cheaper to pay; but next time I shall go to Scotland.

Middlemen may be a great trial to a publisher for other reasons than is usually supposed. I am often accused of antipathy to literary agents, though I have some very good friends among them, because I have always maintained that they should be as open to criticism as publishers are, and have pointed out that just as there are good and bad publishers, there are good and bad agents.

My firm had gone to a great deal of trouble over a particular manuscript in which we were interested, and the author had recast it in accordance with our reader's detailed suggestions. At that stage a friend told the author that he ought to employ an agent, which he did. The book was shortly thereafter announced by another publisher. A year or two later the author returned to us, bemoaning the action of his agent—a well-known firm— because the publisher to whom the agent had transferred his work was now bankrupt. When we next had occasion to write to that particular agent, we mentioned, without giving reasons, that unfortunately we lacked confidence in his firm. It brought a strange letter from him the nature of which will be gathered from our reply:

'We have not accused you of the practice of "auctioning" books which you go out of your way to deny. But as you raise the question, it may interest you to know that I have at this moment on my desk a copy of a letter you wrote a few years back to one of your clients in which the following passage occurs:

> ' "On my report of the book, *supported of course by the fact that it is accepted by Allen & Unwin*, Messrs. —— are willing to publish it". . . .

'A subsequent letter reveals the fact that the publisher in question had not looked at the manuscript (over which we had gone to considerable trouble and expense) but had relied exclusively upon our judgment.

'The foregoing will perhaps explain our nervousness in negotiating with you.

'The result of the transfer to another firm of the book referred to in the correspondence proved most unfortunate for your client; but that aspect of the matter is not our business.'

A point which I think authors sometimes overlook is that almost inevitably and naturally agents have their special friends among publishers whom they tend, probably unconsciously, to think of first, whether or not they are necessarily the best suited for the particular book being offered. Moreover, some agents have no dealings at all with some publishers of repute and vice versa.

Whether as the author of *The Truth About Publishing*, or for some other reason I know not, but I am constantly asked for my advice about agents. Fortunately there are a few firms I have no hesitation in recommending.

Authors, even the most charming, are apt to suffer from illusions. One, harboured by most, is that it would be a disaster were their book not out in time for Christmas. Now unless it is a 'gift book' which no one would want to buy at any other time, this is often far from being the case. More books are issued in October and November than in any other months of the year, with the result that a smaller proportion are reviewed. Unless the books are published very early in the season they are too late for the Overseas Christmas season, which in some cases may be the more important. Furthermore, booksellers are confronted at that time with so many new books that they tend to be more discriminating and more cautious in their buying than at any other period except immediately before stocktaking. The publisher, whose sole aim is to sell his wares, is quite unprejudiced, and may be relied upon to give the best advice about the date of publication. The wise author defers to his publisher's judgment in such a question, but in this matter not all authors are wise. In a large proportion of cases, if a book cannot be published before the end of October it is best held over for publication in January or February—both excellent months, when people have Book Tokens to exchange.

Advertising can be a great trial. I wonder how many authors realize that probably nearly as much is spent to please or placate them as to sell their books. That peculiarly well-informed writer, Frank Swinnerton, has pointed out:[1]

'To authors it will come as incredible that advertising does not sell books. Yet that is the truth. *Advertising does not sell books.*' [His italics.]

The fact is that just as whipping will maintain, and even accelerate, the speed of a top that is already spinning, but will achieve nothing with one that is lying dormant on the ground, so advertising will maintain, and even accelerate, the sales of a book which is already being talked about, but will do little or nothing for one in which there is otherwise no interest. When we are told that a book has sold so well because it was advertised, it would almost certainly be true to say that it was extensively advertised because it was selling so well.

In the same way, many authors believe that their books would sell much better if they were on all the bookstalls, whereas the only books which justify that form of display are those that are very cheap, or for which there is already a demand, or certain to be a demand. A book will not sell merely because it is on a bookstall any more than it will sell merely because it is advertised. The secret is to get a book talked about. If that is achieved, sales, and probably bookstall display and advertising, will follow. But how is a publisher to convince an author of such unpalatable truths? We all admit that though you can take a horse to the water you

[1] *Best-Sellers: Are They Born or Made?* (London: George Allen & Unwin Ltd., 1939)

cannot make it drink, but how many authors really believe that though a publisher can take his (or her) book to the booksellers he cannot make them buy? Fortunately most George Allen & Unwin authors in all such matters seem to be endowed with quite exceptional wisdom and unusual understanding.

Another illusion, seldom entertained by competent authors, is that the publisher's readers and others are waiting to plagiarize their work. I think it may be said that the more worthless the manuscript, the greater the fear of plagiarism. The author who tells you that he 'has solved the riddle of the universe', whose manuscript won't stand five minutes' investigation, is of course confident that his ideas are going to be stolen. We had one amusing incident with a manuscript of so-called verse which had inadvertently been included in another package. The authoress was confident that the person to whom the MS had accidentally been sent would appropriate her priceless 'poems' and started discussing the amount of damages she would claim; yet the recipient in returning them to us said she had no idea that anyone would have the effrontery to send a publisher such worthless rubbish.

If a competing book is offered to a publisher on a subject in which he has specialized, his own author, if consulted, would in many cases want him to decline the competing book without a moment's hesitation. If the book is definitely not so good as the one already published, the advice is of course sound, but what if the book is as good, or perhaps rather better? Again, most authors would want it turned down. But in that case they would probably be wrong. There are advantages in a publisher having all the best books on a subject in which he has specialized. In the hands of another publisher the second book would indeed be a competitor. If both are handled by the same firm each can be made to advertise the other and both will benefit. The extent to which books in the same category or class can be made to advertise each other is seldom realized by authors, and not always by publishers.

I dare not dwell upon the multifarious troubles connected with book production, but I cannot pass over the difficulties that may attend the most insignificant printer's error.

In a biography of a worthy gentleman which we published, mention was made of the fact that when he was ill, Lady Blank brought him flowers—gay ones. In the course of printing, the last 's' disappeared. Any other 's' would probably not have mattered, but the sentence now read 'Lady Blank brought him flowers—gay one'. Lady B., a most virtuous and respectable old lady, objected vehemently to being pilloried as a 'gay one'. The sale of the book had to be suspended until the offending page was reprinted.

The dispatch of review copies would seem to be a simple process, particularly if the list has been mutually agreed. Unfortunately one or two editors are apt to be a little reckless in assuring authors that they have not had their books. (I admit the authors brought it on themselves by asking.) One distinguished literary editor (now deceased) seemed to take a fiendish delight in doing so. The trouble is that even if in such a case you show the author the formal receipt for the book, you do not necessarily satisfy him. In one case, to please a most important client, I sent a duplicate copy addressed personally to that particular editor, and got his initials on the receipt, but when next the author met him he still maintained he had not got it.

It used to puzzle me why important books failed to be reviewed in the one journal in which they would arouse most interest. The explanation proved to be simple. The editor had told the literary editor that he would review it personally, but found himself too pressed to do it until it was too late.

Apart from the destination of the review copies, the English publisher knows that the number he sends out is likely to be regarded as wrong. Either the author will think him stingy, or the Authors' Society will regard him as reckless. The German publisher suffers under no such disability. The law regarding publishing fixes the percentage, and for that matter saves him many of the English publisher's tribulations. It is recognized over there that both the publisher and the author need protection.

The answers given by some editors to importunate authors reminds me of many instances where over-zealous booksellers' assistants have assured authors that there has been such a run on their books that they have sold out, and have been unable to get further supplies. Imagine what such an author thinks of his publisher when the latter is called upon to disillusion him, and explain that there has been no run on the book, that it has never been out of stock, that the bookseller in question has never used a single copy, and refuses to put even one into stock.

Not only authors can regard publishers as philanthropists. A large body of people delude themselves with the notion that publishers live by giving their wares away; and consider it rather a privilege to encounter a recipient for them. The extent to which books are 'cadged' is unbelievable, and it is often the wealthiest who are the worst offenders. We receive book-begging letters of some kind almost every day, and often from institutions and people who would never think of 'begging' for any other commodity.

The misuse of the telephone is a very serious trial. The 'phone contributes far more to the inefficiency than to the efficiency of a publishing office—thoughtless people ring up for information needing hours of research; editors inquire about rights in illustrations of books long out of print, when a moment's reflection would tell them that an immediate answer over the telephone was out of the question. Some people—I fear a growing number—suffer from telephone mania. When they have nothing definite to do they ring up someone on the telephone. Publishers are interesting people with no particular occupation—let's ring up a publisher.

According to one distinguished novelist a publisher ought to spend most of his time entertaining authors. To do so at lunch can be one of the most pleasant aspects of publishing, but to devote one's entire home life to it would indeed be a trial. It is a trial which some publishers seem to survive with equanimity if not to enjoy, but one that I have successfully avoided. I find most authors agree with me that some part at any rate of a publisher's evenings could not be better spent than in reading their manuscripts in the quiet of his home.

Although many evening engagements can be a trial there are functions that are unquestionably worth while. An interesting feature, for example, in the literary life of the nineteen-thirties was the poet Sturge Moore's 'Bachelors' Evenings' at his home in Well Walk, Hampstead. Here one might meet, quite informally, most distinguished authors and artists. The discussions were often most animated, and in the background, though often taking part, was the benign figure of our host, Sturge Moore, a fine and lovable character. If memory serves me, these 'evenings' terminated with the outbreak of war in 1939.

I referred earlier to the question of libel actions. Providence having treated me hardly in my youth, has since been kind to me. I have had the excitement without the expense. Unfortunately penniless people who bring vexatious libel actions don't always show the consideration one man did to me. He died the day before the action was put down for hearing. Our joy was short-lived because his widow touched us for a donation instead.

The mention of widows reminds me of the experience of a publisher, who shall be nameless, which was related in response to the question posed by the PEN some years ago: 'Who suffers more, the publisher or the published?' He asked whether authors ever had to suffer from the persecution of publishers' widows as he had had to suffer from the persecution of authors' widows. He remarked that the Bible had something to say about importunate widows, but that the unjust judge had a charmer to deal with compared with some authors' widows. People are fond of saying that 'a little widow is a dangerous thing', but two of them, he remarked, using the publisher's body as a battlefield and regarding him as personally responsible for all the sins and shortcomings of the other widow, were indeed intimidating. The publisher had issued a number of books for the deceased, with whom his relations were of the pleasantest. In every case where there was a direct contract between them, the author had received more than the book had earned. But in many cases the author had sold his entire rights to an American publisher, who had in turn

331

sold the English rights to the British publisher. It will be clear at once that, with large unearned advances on all the direct contracts and the royalties payable to American publishers in all other cases, nothing was due by the British publisher, or ever likely to be. But trifles like that did not deter one of the widows. Here in his own words is an account of a day in that unfortunate publisher's life.

'The morning's post contained long letters from the author's agent (egged on by the widow), a solicitor acting for the widow, and a still longer one from the widow herself. Before I had time to read them, all three were on the telephone, and before the day was over all three had called on me. So had the widow's daughter, and a friend of the widow! A film company rang up to say that they understood that I owed the widow money and were they safe in advancing some cash on the strength of it, as also did a Government official. The agent admitted from the outset that all was in order and apologized for being troublesome. The solicitor, after examining agreements and correspondence, saw he was wasting time. Both resigned their jobs. But there are plenty of solicitors in London, and the game started afresh. The agreements became worn out with constant examination, because as each solicitor reported that everything was in order another was found. One had the temerity to suggest to me (at the instigation of the widow) that because the original contracts between the author and the American publishers, which naturally were in New York, could not be produced by me in London, I had no rights, and would it not be much better to pay the widow something to go away. I pointed out that if she found it profitable to make herself a nuisance she would never go away.' It was, in fact, a long time before she did.

The publisher's last words in answer to the question posed by the PEN were:

'In the struggle between the author and the publisher it is always the author who comes on top by the simple expedient so cleverly used by the ju-jitsu expert of feigning weakness. Unquestionably it is the publisher who suffers most.'

But this interlude has led me away from libel actions, which, until the Defamation Act of 1952, were a constant trial. I mentioned a couple in an earlier chapter. Here are two examples of the 'gold digging' variety to indicate the extreme forms these actions were taking.

An American novel mentioned an American boxer (who had never left the States) and who was 'down and out' years before a young English boxer of the same name (who had never left England) was even born. Nevertheless, when the book was published in England an action was brought on the ground that the name and occupation were the same. On Counsel's advice it was settled out of court for fear that there might be a boxing fan in the jury, though the plaintiff could not possibly have suffered any damage. Had the publisher fought and won the case it would have cost more because the plaintiff was impecunious.

In the other instance the complainant was less successful. He unwisely overlooked the fact that there had been other editions of the book on the market for seventeen years, which completely vitiated all his contentions. For the rash charges he made against the author he had the pleasure of apologizing instead of collecting damages.

Obscene libel, which may lead to a trial, is a perpetual trial to many publishers, and acutely so to those who publish fiction, when, to quote the pleasantly caustic phrase of the *Economist* 'a spasm of morality seizes the authorities' as in 1954. Under the ridiculous test of obscenity laid down a hundred years ago by Chief Justice Cockburn,[1] neither the Bible nor the works of Shakespeare could be defended. Even if all the leading literary critics were unanimous in regarding the offending work as a literary masterpiece it would not help the publisher, because he was debarred from calling expert evidence in his defence.

Fortunately the Obscene Publications Act (1959) redefines obscenity as an offence if its effect, *taken as a whole*, tends to deprave and corrupt persons who are likely, having regard to all the relevant circumstances, to read, see or hear the matter complained

[1] See Chapter 11, page 171.

of. Moreover, a person will not be convicted if he can prove that his publication is in the interests of 'Science, literature, art or learning, or other objects of general concern', and on this the courts will hear expert evidence.

This is a great relief to the reputable publisher whose position under the Cockburn test was an impossible one. I now hope to complete my career without finding myself quite unjustifiably in prison.

If publishing is such a tribulation why bother with it? When that question is put to me I answer with another. Does a mother cease to love the child who tries her? Does she not love him the more? Publishing is my child, and no trials or tribulations will make me cease to love it.

CHAPTER 19

HOW TO MAKE A NUISANCE OF ONESELF

I am probably more widely known in non-literary circles for my letters to *The Times* than for anything else I have done; they are thus part of my life, and a very amusing part.

Few people seem to realize either the power of a well-expressed letter or the vulnerability of Governmental Departments and large corporations, with the result that many ills are endured which could be cured, and many wrongs needlessly left unrighted. It is probably true to say that letters to *The Times* and questions in the House of Commons are the greatest defences of freedom and true democracy which we possess. But to be effective such letters need careful thought. The shorter, simpler and more cogent they are the more time has probably been devoted to their drafting. Hit hard but never in more than one direction is a sound principle; it is almost invariably unwise to try to make more than one point.

My first experience of letter writing was while still a boy. Everyone knows that if you prolong a railway journey you are entitled to pay the *difference* between the cost of the ticket you hold and the cost of a ticket for the distance travelled. This may be (and certainly often was) less than the cost of a separate single ticket for the additional journey. I wished on one occasion to excess my ticket at the beginning of the journey, but the booking clerk refused. He said that I must take a single ticket to the place from which my ticket started and that that was the usual procedure. I agreed that it was the customary practice and also the simplest because in most cases the amount was the same, but that on the basis on which the District Railway then arranged their fares there was in the present instance a difference of threepence-halfpenny, and that as railway companies were quite properly insistent upon their rights I saw no reason why I should not insist upon mine. The booking clerk remained adamant, but agreed that if I complied with his contention he would record the numbers of both tickets and I could take the matter up with the head office, which I accordingly did.

The first reply, as I anticipated, was an attempt to brush me aside with the bare statement that the action of the booking clerk was correct. I returned to the charge. There were continued attempts to bluff me, and finally a letter that they had nothing further to say, at which point they doubtless thought I would let the matter drop. But they were mistaken. I replied that I at any rate had more to say; that I was confident I was right, and did they wish to compel me to go to the trouble of suing them? The correspondence was then handed to their legal department, who likewise attempted to brush me aside. I asked them whether they were prepared to make a test case of it. They evaded the question. I repeated it. Were they, or were they not, prepared to make a test case of it? There was a pause while they took counsel's opinion. Counsel said that I was right. They wrote admitting as much and refunded the threepence-halfpenny. I thanked them, but said that in view of the unnecessary expense to which they had put me, the least they could do was to refund my out-of-pocket expenses for postage, which, as the correspondence had lasted for over three months, had become a substantial item. This they did. I had thoroughly enjoyed the battle, and as a mere boy, felt something of the satisfaction that David must have felt in overcoming Goliath, and the experience taught me much. From that moment I had no fear of Government Departments or wealthy corporations which, if tackled fearlessly when demonstrably wrong, usually prove astonishingly timid. Their status tends to leave them immune from open assault, and it is far too easily assumed that it is useless to speak out—perhaps I ought to say hit out—for what is right where such august people or bodies are concerned, whereas all are vulnerable and none likes to be made to look silly.

Perhaps the best test of letters to the Press and of the kind I have in mind, is whether they accomplish anything.

Unfortunately my first press-cutting book was destroyed. But from the excellent index to *The Times* I find that between 1923 and 1932 I wrote letters on such various subjects as the need for a Post Office COD system (introduced soon thereafter); the problem of tickets for children on the French railways (since solved); the property of Germans in England (a change was made); the taxation of commercial travellers in Scandinavia (since ameliorated); the need for third-class sleepers in Great Britain (introduced in 1928). One about *Alice in Wonderland* on March 27, 1928, had an interesting outcome. It read:

'It will be a national disgrace if the manuscript of *Alice's Adventures in Wonderland* leaves England. Is it too late to appeal to the owner to name a price at which it can be bought for the nation? If she will do so, I for one would be willing to make myself responsible for the raising of £1,000 towards the cost of securing it for the British Museum, and there must be many others who would gladly help.'

The owner (the original 'Alice' of the story) refused to name a price, and the manuscript was bought at the auction by an American dealer, and crossed the Atlantic. But my letter had not passed unobserved in the United States by Dr Luther Evans (subsequently Librarian of Congress). When the American owner died, and the manuscript once again came into the market, Dr Evans and a group of friends bought it, and I had the pleasure of attending the ceremony at which Dr Luther Evans generously handed over the manuscript to the British Museum, where it is now to be found.

There is, I suppose, no subject about which I have written so many letters as the burden imposed upon publishers to present five, and more usually six, copies of every book they publish to certain libraries, one of them in Dublin. The injustice of taxing British publishers for the benefit of a self-governing republic would seem to be obvious, and is not made less so by the fact that many of the books thus supplied are forthwith banned by that same Irish Republican Government. But though frequently exposed, the injustice has not yet been remedied. It is too easy to be generous with other people's property.

On May 11, 1934, I had an amusing encounter with H.M. Customs—a department of state whose activities need watching with special vigilance. The letter which follows appeared in both *The Times* and *Manchester Guardian*, and in the latter was appropriately headed 'By Hook or by Crook':

'On the ground that back numbers of American magazines were being dumped in England in large quantities, provision was taken under the Additional Import Duties (No. 6) Order 1934, to render them dutiable. That sounds innocuous; how does it work out in practice?'

'As the official agents for the sale of the publications of the International Institute for Intellectual Co-operation we import from time to time copies of an excellent bibliography of translations, compiled by the Institute at no little trouble and expense entitled *Index Translationum*. No sooner is this new "order" issued by the Treasury than a first consignment of 25 copies of an unissued number of the Index is detained by the Customs. A remonstrance is answered by a statement from the Customs that the package contains 25 books liable to duty at 20 per cent ad valorem. A further remonstrance pointing out that books are not dutiable brought a demand for the deposit of the duty on the ground that the Bibliographies, which they had previously described as "books", came under the heading of "catalogues, trade lists and advertising material".

'A suggestion that such a description was grotesque and if persisted in would result in a question being asked in the House of Commons, brought a reply from headquarters that this Bibliography was a periodical, and, although it had not been published by us, was a "back number" and properly chargeable with duty at 1/- per pound. And why was it a back number? Because, being a learned publication, it printed the date up to which its information went and not the date of issue. But even so the Customs were not satisfied. In a later communication they ruled that "since this periodical is equally a catalogue, it is also liable (irrespective of the month of issue) to an aggregate duty of 20 per cent which being the higher rate is the duty chargeable".

'As the subscription to the Index does not cover "duty", the copies have been returned to the Institute, and the Public Libraries and others wanting them must wait.

'Is this our idea of Intellectual co-operation?'

The copies of the Index were delivered forthwith. The head of the Customs telephoned to me protesting at my writing such a letter, making them look fools in the eyes of the whole Civil Service. I replied that I should do so whenever the actions of his staff called for it. 'Well, you might at any rate telephone me and give me a chance to put it right.' 'Very well,' I said, 'you shall have twenty-four hours next time.' 'There won't be a next time,' was the response, 'I've seen to that.' 'I'm afraid there will be', I said, and in less than a year the trouble recurred. The bumptious young man at the Customs would not listen to me when, in his own interests, I advised him to consult someone higher up, because otherwise he would be asking for trouble. I telephoned the head of the Customs. He was out, so I asked the lady who spoke whether she remembered the previous incident. She did indeed. 'Well, you have twenty-four hours', I said. There was no need for a letter to *The Times*; the goods were delivered by special messenger the same day.

On the 28th November of the same year, H.M. Customs gave me grounds for another letter in the *Manchester Guardian* about certain scholarly publications which it was not practicable to translate and issue in English unless colour-blocks produced for the original edition were used for the translation. In such cases British publishers were virtually compelled to print abroad because no provision existed for drawback of the duty on the return of the blocks. Moreover, the duty would be calculated upon their full value—a prohibitive amount—regardless of the fact that they had previously been used. It is interesting to note that there is now provision for drawbacks provided the blocks you have borrowed have *not* been used. Why it should be assumed that they are borrowed merely to be looked at H.M. Customs do not explain. We are then still compelled to have illustrations, and often books containing illustrations, printed in Germany and elsewhere on the Continent which could perfectly well be printed in the United Kingdom were our Customs regulations just a trifle more intelligent.

On September 28, 1935, as the agent of the League of Nations

Publications, I had yet again to tackle H.M. Customs. As the outcome of the fuss I had made of their ingenuity in finding a way of taxing the *Index Translationum*, catalogues (not being trade catalogues) and advertising material (not being trade advertising material) were placed on the free list. It was, I imagine, thought by those responsible for drafting the edict that they had solved the problem, at any rate so far as the League publications were concerned. But as I pointed out in a letter to *The Times*, they did not take sufficient account of the ingenuity of Customs officials:

'The Publications Department of the League of Nations sent to the London Office of the League a consignment of lists of League of Nations publications. These lists are in the possession of H.M. Customs, who, after over three weeks' deliberation, have refused to release them unless a substantial deposit is paid while a ruling is being obtained as to whether or not they are trade catalogues, i.e. as to whether the League of Nations is or is not a trading concern. Meanwhile, people who wish for lists of the documents published by the League of Nations must wait for them, though there probably was never a time when it was more important that information concerning the League should be readily available.'

Following that letter the lists of League publications were immediately delivered.

On February 19, 1937, I tackled the French Customs for a change, protesting against the examination at Calais of passengers' baggage in transit from Switzerland and Austria to Dover. On April 9th there was a letter in *The Times* from the Director-General of the French Customs that 'cette formalité est aujourd'hui supprimé'.

It is important when attacking abuses to choose the right medium so that when on two occasions some years later I felt called upon to pillory the Italian Customs, I did so in *The Observer*, which under the editorship of the late J. L. Garvin was regarded in Italy with special respect. One of the letters which had immediate effect is given below as it shows the technique that has so often proved successful.

'Almost exactly three years ago I drew your attention to the fact that the Italian authorities (the hosts of a UNESCO Conference) had celebrated the unanimous adoption of an agreement on the unrestricted importation of educational, scientific and cultural material, by raising the Customs duty on bound books, i.e. on practically all English books and particularly scientific books. That increase was subsequently withdrawn.

'But in the revised Italian Customs Tariff at present in force, there is a sub-heading which allows for a tax of 15 per cent on all leather *or artificial leather* bound books. Unfortunately there is no definition of what constitutes an artificial leather binding, and the Customs Inspector is able to interpret the regulation as he pleases.

'Now we all know that the ingenuity of Customs officials is unbounded. It is not surprising, therefore, to learn that books in imitation *cloth*, and even copies of the ordinary blue buckram "Oxford Companion to English Literature", are being classed as bound in "artificial leather".'

Cloth is no longer artificial leather in the eyes of Italian Customs officials.

Most Governments at some time and for some purpose seek excessive powers. As no Government, however genuinely democratic, can be trusted with such powers, special vigilance is needed when they try to obtain them. In 1934 there was talk of a Disaffection Bill, and as first drafted there were few intelligent people who could not have been prosecuted under its provisions. Fortunately the protests were immediate, vigorous and effective. I added my quota by pointing out that as the publisher of English editions of the works of Karl Marx and Friedrich Engels, issued by my predecessors more than fifty years previously, I was permanently in possession of 'seditious' literature, adding that as the publishers of much Quaker literature, considered highly objectionable by army authorities, I should at all times be liable to imprisonment under the new Act because this Quaker literature was always to be found on my premises. The Bill was wisely dropped.

But that did not prevent a further attempt being made soon after the outbreak of the Second World War, not merely to secure the same excessive powers, but to go even further. On October 31, 1939, *The Times* printed the following letter from me on Executive Powers in War-time:

'To one who had the privilege of publishing for many of the most distinguished members of the unpopular minority during the last war—one of whom subsequently became the first Prime Minister of the National Government—the wording of the new Defence Regulations is ominous.

'There can be few who would question the necessity for arming the executive with exceptional powers in war-time; but in a war for democracy against Hitlerism it is surely particularly important that we should not lose sight of fundamental democratic principles and that we should retain some regard for the liberty of the subject and honest freedom of speech.

'Even under DORA (The Defence of the Realm Act) one of our most brilliant intellectuals was sent to prison for a purely technical offence; the late Lowes Dickinson's masterly study of *The European Anarchy* was blacklisted, unknown to author or publisher (apparently under the illusion that it dealt with anarchism), and when copies of a certain review, approved and subsidized by the Foreign Office, were handed over to the Post Office for despatch they were secretly seized and destroyed by the War Office, though the review contained no reference to military affairs.

'These are just typical examples of what happened in the last war. Today, no one, I think, would have the temerity to suggest that the prosecution of the war was thereby assisted. But if they could and did occur under DORA despite the most categorical assurances of Ministers that the powers granted under the Act would not be misused, what must we expect under the new "Defence Regulations", one of which begins as follows:

' "The Secretary of State may make provision by order for preventing or restricting the publication in the United Kingdom of matters as to which he is satisfied that the publication, or, as the case may be, the unrestricted publication, thereof would or might be prejudicial to the defence of the realm or the efficient prosecution of war". . . .

'Space precludes a detailed examination of them all. It will perhaps suffice to point out that a regulation which begins by laying it down that no person shall "endeavour, whether orally or otherwise, to influence public opinion in a manner likely to be prejudicial to the defence of the realm or the efficient prosecution of war", and then goes on to define "public opinion" as "including the opinion of any section of the public" could be used to stifle almost any criticism of any Government action in war-time or even the discussion of war aims.'

I am happy to be able to add that the Defence Regulations were amended; that the war-time Government managed excellently without the excessive powers that had been demanded, and that, as will be seen in my chapter on the Publishers Association, the censorship worked as efficiently in the Second World War as it did badly in the First World War.

Not all letters have such immediate effect. One which appeared in *The Times* of August 7, 1940, accomplished nothing. It was in support of Sir Ellis Hume-Williams's plea 'for the issue once more of at least an outline of the Government's scheme for the ultimate reconstruction of Europe'. I pointed out that it was desirable not merely for the neutrals, but also for the German people.

'After the last war scores of Germans of all classes and of all shades of opinion assured me that had it been realized by the German people as it was by us that the only obstacle to peace in 1917 was Ludendorff's insistence upon the retention of Belgium, the collapse would have come a year sooner. We cannot state our aims too often or too clearly. Constant reiteration is one of Hitler's weapons which we should be well advised to use.'

The foolish cry 'for unconditional surrender' plays into the enemy's hands. It enables those in power to maintain the necessity of continued resistance and discourages the more intelligent and peacefully minded among our enemies from making an effort to overthrow the war-mongers. Finally, it leads, as it did in the Second World War, to the elimination of the better elements— such as the young Von Moltke—who might form an alternative government after the conclusion of the war.

The war might well have been shortened had we encouraged

343

instead of discouraged those in Germany who longed to overthrow Hitler.

More can of course be more readily accomplished in home affairs. The Post Office, for example, is vulnerable, as will be seen from the following extract from *The Times* of October 19, 1940:

'. . . Many letters complaining of long delays in the telephone, telegraph and postal services continue to arrive. Mr Stanley Unwin, the publisher, writes—

' "The complaints about the telephone, telegraph and postal delays are fully justified. I have had even worse experiences than some of your correspondents. For example, I asked my bank in Central London to post me a letter last Friday so that I might be sure of receiving it in Hampstead some time on Saturday. They did so, but the letter was not delivered until the second post on Tuesday. It thus took a day for each mile of its journey. This complete uncertainty when letters will arrive makes business unnecessarily difficult".' . . .

It had immediate beneficial effect.

Throughout the war I waged a ceaseless campaign for Paper for Books. The letters I wrote would fill a book. If they did not achieve all that was needed, it can be said that they were not without effect. I certainly made myself a nuisance and had I not done so the situation might have been even more disastrous than it was.

In face of the vast quantities of paper and cardboard used, and much of it wasted, for other and often inessential purposes, it was ludicrous for the officials concerned to pretend that the country's best interests were served by curtailing so drastically the amount of paper and strawboard allotted to the production of books. And it should be remembered that this was being done at the moment when the Government was showing a film emphasizing the place of books in the national war effort and opening with the following sentence: 'Books are the means whereby civilization is carried triumphantly forward.' The signature beneath those words was that of Winston Churchill himself. President Roosevelt went even further when he said: 'A war of ideas can no more be won without books than a naval war can be won without ships.' But an adequate supply of paper for books was never forthcoming. Even an additional six thousand tons would have made an immense difference and would have helped publishers to respond to the clamour for British books which arose the moment the armistice was signed from all those parts of Europe which Hitler had occupied.

During the correspondence about paper for books I had the unusual experience for a publisher of figuring in a *Times* crossword puzzle. The clue given was 'By no means a defeatist'.

A letter on the Excess Profits Tax in *The Times* of January 31, 1944, bore immediate fruit, as did a letter to the head of the Sabena Air Line in August 1947 regarding the treatment in Brussels of passengers in transit—a treatment so preposterous that a gallant captain who was one of the passengers had to be restrained from coming to blows with the official concerned who was merely carrying out orders from someone above. My technique in this case was to send copies of my letter to both Cooks and the Belgian Embassy. I received most categorical assurances from both the Sabena Air Line and the Embassy in London that such treatment would not recur. It was a more effective method than fisticuffs with an official who was merely doing what he was told.

In international matters a letter appearing merely in one country may be without effect whereas if reprinted in others may cause prompt action. An example is a letter on International Copyright which appeared in *The Times Literary Supplement* of August 28, 1948, and was reprinted in many continental book trade papers:

'Turkey, which has made such rapid progress in so many directions, has lagged behind in connection with copyright. A scheme proposing revision of the 1910 Turkish Copyright Agreement was prepared in the Istanbul University about nine years ago, but was never discussed in Parliament.

'Turkish authors, who deplore this neglect and suffer from the

THE TRUTH ABOUT A PUBLISHER

present unsatisfactory position, have just founded a Copyright Society to press for reform.

'Is it too much to hope that now that public attention is being drawn to the matter, Turkey will promptly bring herself into line with other civilized nations and sign the Berne Convention?'

Turkish adherence followed soon thereafter.

When I issued a pamphlet on *How Governments Treat Books* I was asked to authorize translations. My answer was 'With pleasure, provided you undertake to send copies of the translation to the Embassies and Consulates of the countries particularly pilloried'. The result was most beneficial. Governments don't like being made fun of any more than big corporations, and I had naughtily pointed out that one country classified booksellers with brothels for the purpose of taxation.

Letters to the United States press do not have an effect comparable with those to *The Times* or *Manchester Guardian*, but the following extract from one that appeared in the *New York Herald Tribune* of October 21, 1949, seems to me to deserve attention:

'Eire and Britain are now completely independent but both have agreed that the citizens of the other shall not be regarded as "aliens".

'Is it not time that the United States of America and the British Commonwealth followed that excellent example?

'Under present conditions it is not only desirable but vital that the Anglo-Saxon world should draw closer together. Is there any more effective way of doing so than by agreeing that our respective citizens shall not in future be regarded as aliens?'

The following letter of March 15, 1950, exhibits the Treasury at its soulless worst:

'It is obviously desirable, and in the interest of education, that children should be encouraged to love and to wish to possess books. An ingenious scheme was devised and successfully launched whereby they could obtain them by collecting and exchanging sets of sixpenny "book tallies"—sets in themselves of educational value. The immediate Governmental response was to decree (Notice No. 78, January 1950, by the Commissioners of Customs and Excise) that, although books were free of purchase tax, these book tallies were liable to 100 per cent tax. No question of revenue arises because if the edict is not rescinded, the scheme cannot be carried on. It is thus a question whether or not an excessively rigid interpretation of the purchase tax regulations should be used to stop a valuable educational experiment, and prevent children acquiring books by a novel means. Is this what Parliament intended or desires?'

Apparently it was, for the book tallies scheme was killed outright.

A brief letter to the *Manchester Guardian*, July 20, 1950, caused a lively correspondence with repercussions as far afield as New Zealand:

'Who is it that dictates that precisely two collars shall be provided with each new coloured shirt, and decides that at no time and in no circumstances shall an additional collar be readily obtainable? Is it a crime to want three collars?'

I am happy to say that it is no longer a crime.

As a method of exposing the ineptitude of the bureaucratic mind, the following letter is not without interest:

'We have become a protectionist country, but still conduct our affairs as if we were free traders. Protectionist countries grant facilities for the entry of goods intended for re-export after they have been increased in value. The British trader, on the contrary, encounters nothing but obstacles, and if he partially gets over or round them, is told not to do it again.

'We are invited to increase our exports to the USA, but when an American University Press asks us to produce for them on their immediately available paper a costly work, including Chinese characters, we are told by the Board of Trade that only a drawback on duty on all kinds of imported paper applied for on behalf of the whole trade, could be considered. We paid the heavy duty rather than disappoint our customer and lose the opportunity of earning dollars.

'Having done so, we received a solemn letter from the relevant Ministry admonishing us for using American paper (regardless of the fact that had we waited for British paper the order would not have been forthcoming) and instructing us not to misbehave ourselves in this fashion again.'

Apropos of the bureaucratic mind, it must be seldom I think that the officials who so readily draft regulations and 'designate' areas for our supposed well-being know the full implications of their activities. As the following letter in the *New Statesman* reveals, one can be sent to prison for being the landlord of a brothel, but prevented by another regulation from giving the brothel-keeper notice:

'The situation of the owner of war rent restricted property has become quite fantastic. Here is a case of a house in Bloomsbury at the absurdly low rental of £120 p.a.

'The landlord, who is liable to prosecution if his property is used for immoral purposes, suspected that the tenant to whom his house had been assigned was using it as a brothel. But the landlord had no power to prevent the tenancy being assigned and could not under the War Rents Restriction Act give the assignee notice. It is not easy to prove that a house is being used for immoral purposes, and it is expensive to make a mistake. Fortunately in this instance the police intervened and the tenant was convicted. Nevertheless that did not secure the landlord possession. He had to apply to the court. The tenant fought the case and lost. He then appealed, and again the verdict was against him. But he disregarded the order of the court, and a bailiff had to be called in. At that stage the tenant disappeared, leaving the landlord to meet all the costs, which exceeded a year's net rent. The premises were found to be indescribably filthy, and the landlord had to pay for the removal and destruction of the contents. But that is only half the story.

'It will cost about £700 to make the house habitable. Now with a rental of £120, half of which goes in tax, it would take over 10 years to recover that outlay, without allowing for interest or further expenditure. At the end of ten years, if not before, additional outlay is inevitable. There are tenants who would gladly put the house in repair in consideration of getting it at such an absurdly low rent, but if the landlord stipulated that they should do it *before* giving possession, or in consideration of getting possession, it would be regarded as the equivalent of key-money. If he gives possession first, the tenant can forthwith compel the landlord to do everything needed. The local authority cannot get permission to requisition the house.

The premises could be let for a substantial rental for business purposes, but under another Act that is forbidden.

'As the house is not available for sale, the landlord has apparently no alternative but to leave it empty to deteriorate yet further. He cannot even pull it down!'

The strange effects of taxation are illustrated in the following letter to *The Times* of September 17, 1952. It is included merely as entertainment:

'We are most of us conscious how complicated officialdom is making our lives. Here is an interesting, not to say startling, example. For business purposes, the chairman of a company had to embark upon a journey by air to Japan. His fellow directors felt it desirable that his company should insure him for £20,000 against accidental death. They assumed, as they could have done before the war, that if the premium was paid out of taxed profits and not charged as an expense, the firm would be entitled to the £20,000 as some compensation for his loss (in future years) should a fatal accident occur. It appears, however, that even when they are not asked to allow the payment of the premium as an expense, the taxation authorities would nevertheless regard themselves as entitled to income tax and excess profits levy amounting to about four-fifths of the amount, thus reducing the insurance to a nominal sum. To achieve what was desired, it would therefore be necessary to take out a policy for five times the amount, i.e. £100,000. The result to the company would be the same, but because in such circumstances the premium would very properly be charged as an expense, the Government would needlessly gamble on the life of the insured. It is most flattering to anyone to be valued so highly, even by the Government, but is it a desirable way of expending taxpayers' money?

'At that stage the Chairman intervened to point out to his colleagues that as his was a family business and not a public company, such an insurance might leave his family impoverished. Under a ruling of the court, cognizance could not be taken of the Company's liability to pay at a future date nearly £50,000 of the amount in income tax, and most of the £100,000 would be added to the value of his estate. In brief, the greater part of the £100,000 would be taxed twice, and its receipt would almost certainly cost his family more than the amount of the insurance. He besought his colleagues therefore to allow him to die uninsured by his firm against accidental death.'

Immediate action followed the next letter to *The Times*, January 2, 1953:

'In the course of a lengthy tour in the Middle and Far East, the worst advertisement of Britain which I encountered was the "British" post office at Kuwait. To effect a passage into this first floor stronghold is no mean feat in itself, for the near precipitous outdoor staircase is as narrow as a ladder and quite as awkward to negotiate. At the top is the dark, dingy and congested garret where, in the space of two small rooms and in an atmosphere of quite indescribable confusion the harassed postmaster and his staff are doing their utmost to deal with the heavy incoming and outgoing mails. The premises are a disgrace, which in spite of continued protests have apparently remained unchanged for years.'

Obscenity in books comes into the headlines at irregular intervals. It was very much to the fore in 1954 and as it doubtless will be again it may be appropriate to print two of the many letters I have written on the subject. The first appears in *The Times* on June 10th:

'The real question at issue is whether we ought to be satisfied with an *obiter dictum* of a Victorian Judge, delivered nearly a hundred years ago, under which much great literature could be prosecuted, or whether we should consider as more appropriate and intelligent the masterly judgment of the United States District Court, rendered December 1933, by the Hon. John M. Woolsey, lifting the ban on *Ulysses*. He emphasized that a book must be read (and judged) in its entirety, and that it must first be determined whether the intent with which it was written was pornographic—that is, written for the purpose of exploiting obscenity. He used the expression "dirt for dirt's sake", a definition of obscenity which would, I imagine, be accepted by, and secure the wholehearted co-operation of all responsible publishers.'

The other appeared in the *Manchester Guardian* on December 16, 1954:

'Now that the spate of prosecutions of reputable publishers has ceased for the time being with the acquittal of three of them, it seems appro-

priate, before there is any renewal of such activities, to examine the
contentions of the learned counsel briefed by the Director of Public
Prosecutions. Here are three quotations taken from the *Bookseller's*
report of the Heinemann case:

> 'The jury must bear in mind that the intention of the author
> and the publisher was a wholly irrelevant consideration. The
> fact that the book might contain fine prose, fine passages of
> descriptive writing, was equally irrelevant. "You can write
> obscene stuff well or badly." It made no difference whether the
> author was a Shakespeare or the author of cheap, paper-backed
> books. . . . It was sufficient, he said, if they found any one of the
> passages obscene, part being obscene making the whole obscene.
> . . . The purpose with which the book was written or published
> did not matter. . . .'

'In the case of *The Man in Control* counsel appeared to think that an
appropriate test of a literary work was whether it was suitable to give
to the office cleaner.

'In brief, it would appear that if a publisher who had the good
fortune to discover another Shakespeare had the temerity to publish
his work he would qualify for prison should the book contain a single
passage of the character of many to be found in the Bible. Apparently
to be on the safe side we publishers ought to be guided by the literary
advice of our charwoman.'

'Are we really expected to swallow such childish nonsense?'

It is always difficult to get prompt and adequate parliamentary
attention to International Copyright, hence the following letter
to *The Times* on October 15, 1954:

'The Brussels Convention was held over six years ago. The copyright
committee appointed to consider the legislation which ratification
involved published their recommendations two years ago. But nothing
more has been done.

'The United States has now signed the Universal Copyright Convention thus making it possible, at long last, to secure copyright in
British books in the United States, without formalities and without
the necessity of manufacturing them there. But the convention is
not operative until seven further countries have ratified it. Britain,

whom it will benefit, has not ratified it or taken the necessary legislative steps to do so. It is difficult to account for such Government inaction and what appears to be a surprising disregard of our export interests—not to mention our cultural prestige.'

The necessary legislation (which I had reason to know had long since been prepared) was promulgated soon thereafter.

Apropos of all these activities, which some may find obnoxious, I cannot help recalling the late H. W. Nevinson's delightful story of the days when fish were kept in tanks on the trawlers. The cod arrived in a flabby state until one day a catfish was put in a tank with them. Those cod were in superb condition; they had been so active avoiding the prickly catfish. It gave me a great respect for catfish and a readiness to make a nuisance of myself if I felt the cause justified it.

There are many ways of doing it besides writing letters to the Press. Here are a couple of examples. When I was in the West Indies I was appalled at the number of forms one had to fill in merely to travel from one island to another. On a day trip to the Cayman Islands, which administratively is under Jamaica, I had to fill in among other forms one certifying that I was taking no luggage with me—a form which I found great difficulty in persuading any official to take when I had carefully filled it in. On my return to Jamaica a few hours later a thermometer was solemnly placed in my mouth, presumably to ensure that I had not in those few hours acquired any infectious disease. I made fun of the West Indian passion for form filling to every official I met and had the satisfaction of hearing not very long thereafter that many of the forms had been abolished.

The fact is that we are all far too ready to put up with regulations and formalities which no longer serve any purpose, even if they once did. We are far too ready to acquiesce in unnecessary form filling. There are plenty of officials engaged in drafting forms; none in periodically examining whether they are still necessary. It is thus left for people willing to make a nuisance of themselves to ensure that some forms and formalities are occasionally dispensed with.

My West Indian trip afforded another occasion for action. I had planned to join a boat to New Zealand at Curaçao and had bought and paid for my ticket before leaving England. I learnt on arrival that there was a tax on tickets bought in Curaçao. On the ground that the New Zealand Company had not given me an actual ticket, subject to the confirmation of their local agent, but a voucher instructing their agent to issue me a ticket, I was held to be liable for the tax, and a tax, I may add, payable in Dutch West Indian currency (based on the dollar) of which I had merely a nominal amount. It was clear that the tax was never intended for people who had bought and paid for their tickets abroad, but the shipping agent was adamant. I found the hard currency with difficulty and paid under protest. I urged the New Zealand Shipping Company to take up the matter with the Dutch authorities and to make the slight change in their method of issuing such tickets to avoid a recurrence of such inconvenience to their passengers, but they refused to do either. Accordingly I took up the matter myself with the Dutch Government, and secured a refund. It is thus not thanks to the New Zealand Shipping Company that other passengers by their line will not be caught out as I was.

In Brazil my prolonged campaign to exempt books from Customs Clearance Charges, which worked out at eleven times the previous duty, resulted not merely in freeing books, but all goods which are exempted from Customs duty, including bulls, boars and donkeys for breeding, queen bees and manure.

I have cited these many instances to encourage others to realize how much any one of us can do, if he will but make the effort, to right wrong and check abuses, and to confirm how vulnerable are big corporations and public bodies, of whom there is a tendency to be afraid. As an illustration of the latter, I will conclude with an encounter I had with one (not the only one) of the five big banks.

It had always seemed to me regrettable that the facilities afforded to Post Office Savings Bank depositors were so restricted. Commercial banks, who themselves showed little apparent interest in that type of business, blocked the way. When one of them announced with a flourish of trumpets that they wanted to encourage small savings I decided to put them to the test. Instead, therefore, of opening a Post Office account for my daughter when she was born, I opened a 'savings' account with a branch of the big bank in question, and arranged for a governess in our employ to do so at another branch. The results were instructive. Before six months had elapsed the governess complained that she was made to feel so unwanted and was so humiliated that she did not wish to enter the bank again, and when my wife sought to pay in small amounts given to the child, she found herself frowned upon. This gave me the opening that I had anticipated. The upshot of the somewhat fierce letter I wrote to the Managing Director at the headquarters of the bank was a personal visit from him. At the end of an interesting talk, during which I had repeatedly to explain that I personally never encountered the treatment of which I complained, he asked what I recommended he should do. I replied, 'Instruct all your branches to give special attention to the small customers', and that, I know, was done. It was many years ago, and what permanent effect it had I cannot say, but my point is that one should not tolerate in big organizations, just because they seem all-powerful, treatment against which one would unhesitatingly protest were it a small concern. I still feel as strongly as ever that the facilities granted to Post Office Savings Bank depositors should not be so restricted. There would seem to be no reason (apart from vested interests) why they should not equal, for example, those obtaining in Germany. Unfortunately, however, our Post Office appeared, at any rate until recently, to be run as a method of taxation, not as a service.

CHAPTER 20

PURELY PERSONAL

It would be a most one-sided account of my life and activities if I refrained from mentioning the large part played in it by my home and family. It has been uniformly happy, and that is the last thing most people in these days seem interested to hear.

The Unwin family records demonstrate one trait—intense family love and devotion to the clan. It would thus indeed be an unrealistic picture which ignored it. It probably accounts for the strong feelings I have about home life and the upbringing of children, of which I shall have something to say. Perhaps it also explains why I still find the earlier practice of confining Christian names to the family circle and intimate friends commendable, and the present tendency to make even the most sacred things 'cheap' deplorable.

Much is said about the difficulty of living with one's 'in-laws', and it is often a very real problem, but it was never so with my wife and myself. After our marriage we had for a time no home of our own. Both our families pressed us to live with them and we both knew that we should be equally happy with either. In the end we compromised and spent half the time with each until we settled down in Maitland Park.

My wife and I have never been particularly interested in social activities outside our respective family circles. For one thing we followed my parents in having nothing alcoholic in the house, which limited our guests to those who would not find that too great a deprivation. Most of my business entertaining has always been done at my club, where my guests suffer no such limitations.

In our early married life we saw much of my wife's mother (her father, to whom I was devoted, died in 1917) and her elder step-brother, Wilfred R. Storr, who lived together at Hampstead.

As a young man he had worked at Williams & Norgate when the original owners were running it, and later he was for a time a partner in the small wholesale business of Castle, Lamb & Storr. This made him particularly interested in the founding and development of my firm, the progress of which we regularly discussed after lunch on Sundays.

Whether the anxieties of the time had anything to do with it I cannot say, but our first little girl, named after my mother Elizabeth Spicer Unwin, was born with a defective heart. It was not immediately apparent, but her lack of vitality soon proved disconcerting, and when Sir Thomas Barlow was called in he pronounced the sad verdict 'nothing can be done', which was true in 1916. Today an operation is sometimes successful in such cases. It was all over in twelve days and was a great shock for both my wife and myself. Those twelve days involved three nurses and three doctors, because we had to pay one nurse for not coming, another to go away, and a third whose devotion, skill and sympathy we can never forget, for looking after our daughter. The third doctor was needed for the cremation certificate.

With this experience behind us, it is not surprising that the arrival of our eldest boy in December 1918, just after the conclusion of the war, was a time of special anxiety. Nutrition during the First World War was not as carefully thought out as it was in the Second World War, and I think that most children carried during 1918 suffered to some extent from the diet deficiencies of the time. It certainly affected our eldest son's health. One thing I learnt in consequence, and that is how often if a small child is 'naughty' and completely unreasonable, there is a physical cause. The change in behaviour when the trouble passes is often startling in its suddenness.

Another important point insufficiently realized by many parents is that the decision who is going to be master has to be taken when the point *first* arises, usually when the child is three or four. If settled then there is no further trouble, but every time the decision is evaded the difficulty increases. It is sure to come at an awkward moment and the tendency is to postpone the issue and let the child get away with it. So important do I regard it that I feel that anything else should take second place. If that first battle is won, the child may put you to a test a second time, but seldom thereafter. It may mean taking the child to a part of the house where you can conveniently say with a smile, 'Now you may cry as much as you like'. Most children immediately realize that you are not to be mastered in that way, and will no longer want to cry. If this policy is going to be adopted it is essential never to tell a child to do something unless you are going to see that he does it. The occasions for a command are few and far between, but on those few occasions the command must be obeyed. It is very easy to 'suggest' what a child should do. One occasion when parental authority was disregarded by our elder boy can best be described in his own words because he remembers the incident vividly.

'I must have been very naughty because my mother took the drastic course of putting me to bed in the middle of the afternoon. Anyway, I was determined not to be kept there, because as soon as she left me I piled all the bedclothes in the centre of the floor, and proceeded to cover them up with every article in the room from tongs to hairbrushes, and from shoes to ornaments from the mantelpiece. There were three large cupboards along one of the walls, the first I remember containing household linen, and another innumerable bottles. The contents of all these were systematically added to the heap, the dimensions of which soon exceeded any castle I had ever built at the seaside.

'Just as I had finished, my mother opened the door. She saw with horror the gigantic pile, and, looking straight at me, said, "I must send for Daddy".

'For an hour I waited in suspense—wondering, fearing. I knew that he would be very angry, but could not think what he would do. I am never likely to forget. He just smiled and said: Well, you *have* given yourself a job; you've got to put all these things back exactly where they came from, and he watched over me while I did.

'It was a completely exhausted and contrite little boy who was glad to creep into bed two hours later to tell his Mummy and

Daddy that he was very sorry, and assure them (quite needlessly) that he would never do it again.'

One other incident my children never forgot. Each of them had a weekly ration of sweets of their own choice, and I had mine. But mine had a way of disappearing. I put a little note in the tin—

DO YOU NOT THINK *I* MIGHT BE ALLOWED A FEW
SWEETS?
I DON'T TAKE YOURS

Not a word was said and I had no further trouble. Later in life we had many a laugh about the shock that little note gave them.

I had had so much to do with my elder boy that the following incident on my voyage across the Atlantic in 1927 will perhaps not be surprising to anyone with experience of telepathy. It certainly made a deep impression upon me. I was suddenly awoken from deep sleep by David, then aged eight, calling out for me 'Daddy! Daddy!' Without stopping to think, I leapt from my bunk to go to him, but then realized that I was aboard the *Olympic* and that my son was many hundreds of miles away. I took a note of the hour and wrote to my wife to know whether our elder son had been ill. She replied 'yes', giving the date, and adding that he had called out for me in the night. Allowing for the difference in time, it was at the very moment that I had been woken up and jumped out of my bunk to go to him.

Throughout their childhood I always emphasized that Daddy and Mummy were one. There was no divided authority and in consequence, as with my parents and their much larger family, no occasion for physical chastisement ever arose.

All the foregoing observations on the upbringing of children are obvious and commonplace, but it is astonishing how frequently the obvious is, in practice, overlooked.

If, as I believe, it is the first seven years that are most important in the formation of character, no time spent by parents on their children during that period should be begrudged, however inconvenient it often is to put all else aside to attend to them.

Much has been said and written about the right of the child to express himself—a right which all too often is interpreted as a licence to do so at other people's expense or inconvenience. Later in life the child will have to learn—maybe through bitter experience—that he is a member of a community with equal rights. Can that lesson be learnt too soon? The most desirable and happiest way of expressing ourselves is in creation. We are born with a creative instinct, and one of the most important things we can do for children is to see that they have legitimate outlets for that instinct. Montessori and all the great educationists have emphasized it, but it is a truth much neglected. But for that neglect we should not have so many delinquent children. The child who has created things does not acquire a lust for destruction such as is all too evident today. In this matter my children were particularly blessed. Their enthusiastic governesses stimulated their interest in natural history and encouraged creative activities of all kinds.

It is usually possible to extract some good from misfortune, and my elder boy's frequent inability to go to school, and in particular one occasion when he was condemned to bed for three months, gave me an opportunity to teach him German. After I had done so for some months I remarked casually 'on one condition you could now accompany me on my next trip to Germany'. 'What condition?', he eagerly responded. 'Something that you will find most unpleasant. From the moment we cross the Rhine we must both speak nothing but German. Don't be in a hurry to decide; you had better sleep over it.' Later, armed with a little pocket dictionary, we set off for the Black Forest. 'Is this the Rhine?' he asked as we left Strasbourg behind. 'Ja! Jetzt fängst's an', I replied, and for three weeks we spoke not a word of English. Funnily enough I was the first to need the dictionary; I didn't know what a grasshopper was in German. It is astonishing how rapidly a child will learn a language if he doesn't hear his own, and at the end of three weeks in the Forest, accompanied part of the time by Hans Baedeker of Guide Book fame, my son found he could follow nearly everything that was said. The experiment proved such a success that we went the following year—that time to my beloved Türingen Forest. At the end of three weeks he had no fear of embarking upon conversation with anyone. This added greatly to his enjoyment of many subsequent family winter sports and other holidays at Lenzerheide, the Tyrol, and elsewhere.

I had benefited so much from foreign travel that I was determined that my children should see as much of the world as possible, and we often went abroad together. Unfortunately the Second World War brought such activities temporarily to a close.

But my children must be left to relate their own successful careers—David as a novelist and writer for children; Rayner as a naval officer, a graduate at Oxford and Harvard, and now a publisher; Ruth as the mother of a delightful and attractive family.

When he was Chairman of the British Council, I mentioned to Lord Eustace Percy (as he then was) that his grandfather, the Duke of Northumberland, was partly responsible for my having to earn my living at fifteen instead of having a University education. 'Well', he replied, 'have you any regrets?' to which I could but smile and answer 'No'. Nevertheless I am delighted that my younger son, who wished to go there, has not been denied the great privilege of happy years at Oxford and Harvard, and all they will mean to him in later life. I think he has benefited trebly because he spent six months in business before going to Trinity, and a period in the Navy before completing his course; I have long been convinced that the boy who goes direct from school to college, without having at any rate a few months of the rough and tumble of the business world in between, loses much, and I have been interested to learn from the President of more than one college that they are of the same opinion.

Most happy people have (or have had) a mission or purpose in life. The craftsman has the satisfaction of producing something beautiful or worth while, and so on. I have had an exceedingly happy life, have loved my work, and have throughout had two missions—some people would say ambitions . . . I prefer the Quaker expression 'Concern', or the German word 'Sendung'. Firstly, to create a book-publishing house of international repute;

secondly, to promote the distribution of British books throughout the world.

In my determination to achieve the first I have worked for my firm almost non-stop. I have tended it, and watched it grow from its disastrous start on the very day of declaration of the First World War until the present time. I felt that I had made some progress when I became President of the International Publishers Association for the second time, and when Basil Blackwell casually asked me whether I realized (which I had not) that my firm had become one of his firm's six most important accounts.

The second I hope that I have done something to achieve through over twenty-four years' service on the Executive of the British Council, and by calling personally on booksellers in every part of the world, as an outcome of which *Time and Tide* published a cartoon of me under the caption 'Stanley Unwin is putting British books on the map'. Mr Fred Melcher, editor of the *Publishers Weekly* of New York, evidently thinks I have accom-

Stanley Unwin is putting British books on the map

plished something because he described me as 'one who has kept the goal of better international flow of books before the literary countries of the world to a greater extent than any other individual'.

I am often asked why I continue to work so hard when it is quite unnecessary for me to do so. The answer is simple. I love my work. There is nothing more interesting or entertaining, and I am always learning something fresh about it. I am conscious of the truth of the motto that confronted me in the school chapel 'Labore est Orare', and believe with Carlyle[1] 'Blessed is he who has found his work; let him ask no other blessedness'. In consequence, when people inquire whether, if I had my life to live over again, I should wish it to be different, I can truthfully answer 'No'.

The least enjoyable period of my life was the three months spent at Leipzig. Had my step-uncle permitted me to spend them in a bookshop at Jena they would have been intensely happy, and I should have learnt just as much. That is the only change I would wish to make because I am so very conscious of how much I learnt from the less pleasing experiences in my life and from the necessity of 'doing without'. The last has given me an independence of material things which is inestimable. It is probably responsible for my instinctive reluctance to spend money on myself; my wants are so small. It may also account for my being so appalled by any waste of food in a world where millions are seriously undernourished.

My predecessor as President of the Publishers Association (the late Bertram Christian) and I frequently lunched together, and I have never forgotten the exasperation in his voice when he turned on me one day and said, 'During all the years we have lunched together I have never had as small a bill as yours'. It was quite unconscious on my part; I had not given it a thought. I can only plead that my instinctive economy on small things, which my elder son often bemoans when we travel together, has made it possible for me to do larger things which I felt much more important. My personal expenditure, other than on travel,

---

[1] *Past and Present* (London: Chapman & Hall, 1905), p. 169.

is probably less than some of my staff spend on cigarettes, but I have all I want, and there is no point in cumbering oneself with useless possessions, or as the Bible picturesquely puts it, to lade oneself 'with thick clay'.[1] In his will, my father-in-law, Rayner Storr, wrote:

'And lastly as to my worldly affairs I desire my children never to forget that the inheritance I bequeath to them is the result of much industry and frugality on the part of my revered and most unselfish parents who always set me an example of family and social responsibility and it is this sacred obligation which I wish to pass on to them along with the means necessary for discharging it begging them ever to bear in mind that capital is the fruit of human labour and should be made use of for social ends.'

With that attitude towards money I fully concur.

And this brings me to my own beliefs. The most popular broadcasts in the USA listened to by about thirty million, are the contributions to the series 'This I believe', in which men in all walks of life (Ministers of Religion alone excluded) are invited to state in 600 words what they believe. When I was invited to contribute, my first instinct was almost indignantly to refuse. On second thoughts I felt that I was being a coward because if at the age of close upon seventy I was not prepared to state my views, when should I be? I have seldom faced a more difficult task. After two whole week-ends of thought on the subject I wrote the following, with which I can appropriately bring this chapter to a close:

'I am not a philosopher, and make no claims to original ideas. I accept the Christian view of the nature and predicament of man. As a Nonconformist and an old-fashioned Liberal, I believe in such temporarily outmoded things as tolerance and reverence—reverence for beauty in all its forms, reverence for the things that have made England what it is, such as liberty, justice and law.

'Up to July 1914 I was so conscious of what appeared to be the ordered progress of things, that life seemed comparatively simple. I believed one had merely to endeavour to follow the Christian Ethic

[1] Habakkuk ii. 6.

and take one's part in furthering that progress in the many practical ways that presented themselves.

'In 1912, when, in the wide open veldt of South Africa, I had my first taste of real freedom (I had had my nose very firmly on the grindstone since the age of fifteen), I was able to experience "the wild joy of living", but in August 1914 the feeling that all was right with the world vanished overnight. But I could, and do, still believe—

> ' ". . . a sun will pierce
> The thickest cloud earth ever stretched;
> That, after Last, returns the First,
> Though a wide compass round be fetched;
> That what began best, can't end worst,
> Nor what God blessed once, prove accurst" '.[1]

'That I am able to believe this I owe to a consciousness of what Matthew Arnold described as "a Power-not-ourselves that makes for righteousness". A consciousness which nothing moves, a consciousness doubtless fortified by the many occasions in my mother's life when I observed at work, and thus experienced, the faith that moves mountains.

'I believe with the members of the Society of Friends that there is an "Inner Light" available for the help and guidance of those who seek it. I believe (in the words which Lowes Dickinson, in his masterpiece, *The Modern Symposium*, puts into the mouth of "John Woodman") that "Now, as of old, in the midst of science, of business, of invention, of the multifarious confusion and din and hurry of the world, God may be directly perceived and known", and, as he says a little later in the same moving address, "It is not by violence or compulsion, open or disguised, that the kingdom of heaven comes. It is by simple service on the part of those that know the law, by their following the right in their own lives, and preaching rather by their conduct than by their words".

'I believe that we are all of us born—though in varying degree—with a creative instinct, the exercise of which is essential to our well-being; and this belief accords with Karel Čapek's prescription for a happy life: "To do what we have to, out of love for the thing." '

[1] 'Apparent Failure', by Robert Browning.

Appendices

THE PUBLISHERS ASSOCIATION OF GREAT BRITAIN

THE INTERNATIONAL PUBLISHERS ASSOCIATION

THE BRITISH COUNCIL

THE PUBLISHERS ASSOCIATION

This chapter is an account of my personal connection with the Publishers Association, and particularly of my period as an officer: not a history of the P.A.

It seems, however, appropriate to add that since the Second World War, the Association has gone from strength to strength, and enlarged its services and activities in many directions.

I imagine that most firms now find it indispensable and wonder how publishers could have managed without it.

CHAPTER 21

THE PUBLISHERS ASSOCIATION OF GREAT BRITAIN

In my Fisher Unwin days I was a regular attender at the Annual General Meetings of the Publishers Association. They were strange and forbidding gatherings, and the attendance, apart from the members of the Council, was meagre. Again, except for the Council, to which the same people were almost invariably elected, few members knew one another. We were then such ardent individualists that it was rare to find two people in the body of the hall sitting next to one another. We avoided contamination by having two or three empty chairs between us. One observed members furtively taking each other in out of the corners of their eyes, and when the meeting was over, slipping away unobtrusively. It was unusual for any member not on the Council to open his mouth, and I still recollect the admiration I felt for the late Alfred Nutt when he had the temerity to stand up and ask a question.

Intercourse with the Associated Booksellers (as the Booksellers Association was then called) was largely confined to slightly acrimonious correspondence which led nowhere. The Council of those days—except so far as the Net Book Agreement was concerned—might appropriately be described as 'a gathering of important people who, singly, can do nothing, but together decide that nothing can be done'. The explanation is simple, the Association was formed primarily, if not exclusively, to watch over and protect the Net Book Agreement, and its founders not only had no wish to see its activities extended, but positively resented any attempt to use the Association for any other purpose. For years it was largely dominated by the three same individuals and it did not seem to matter which particular member of the triumvirate was President, Vice-President or Treasurer. Any form of co-operative activity (apart from supporting the Net Book Agreement) was abhorrent to them in principle, however beneficent it might be in practice. The prejudice was deep-rooted, and in one quarter still persists.

When in 1914 I took over the combined businesses of George Allen & Sons and Swan Sonnenschein & Co.—both firms long-standing members of the Publishers Association—almost my first act after taking possession was to apply for membership for the reconstituted firm of George Allen & Unwin Ltd. The application was turned down. Dear old William Poulten, then Secretary, who, even in old age and in the coldest weather, indulged in an early morning bathe in the Highgate Ponds, was terribly upset. In fact, as Beadle of the Stationers Company, of which my father was on the Court and my brother and cousin were Liverymen, he was so distressed that he came to see me in person about it. 'Wait and try again later', he urged. I am afraid that I merely laughed and said that it was the Publishers Association that would have to wait. It was, in fact, not until after the lapse of more than ten years that, under the joint pressure of a group of booksellers and influential publishers, I consented to re-apply for membership. I was then accepted, and almost immediately elected to the Council.

It was not, however, until still later that I discovered why I had been turned down in the first place. It was because Geoffrey Williams, a member of the Council, said that I had treated William Allen (the son of George Allen) badly. Now the sad or amusing thing is that I never had any opportunity of treating him well or ill. He had left the business six months before I bought it. I had neither cast eyes upon him nor had occasion to correspond with him. In fact, I only saw him once in my life, and that was much later when he asked for access to some of the old records of the firm, and I said 'with pleasure'.

We all know the effects of giving a dog a bad name. The bad name certainly 'dogged' all my early days. The fact that George Allen & Unwin published books for then much-hated people like Bertrand Russell and Ramsay MacDonald of course confirmed the diehards in their worst suspicions, and how suspicious they were is today inconceivable, and would be unbelievable were it not a fact. In the early days of the National Book Council it was desperately hard up, and it seemed to me absurd that any of its meagre income should be paid away in rent when I had vacant accommodation in a building which was to be pulled down when I could get vacant possession of the complete site. In my innocence I offered the use of the rooms, rent free—a not unnatural thing to do for one's own child, as the National Book Council was mine. The offer was accepted, but when it became known the fat was in the fire. It was assumed that in some mysterious way—no one could explain how—I was making vast profits on the roundabouts though I had demonstrably lost nothing on the swings, and there was no peace until the offices were moved to those of a publisher who charged rent.

I recently came across a letter I wrote about that time to the late E. W. Heffer, of Cambridge, who knew of my troubles, in which I explained that the National Book Council badly needed £150 to tide it over for the next three months; that I dared not myself offer to lend it free of interest, and would he be kind enough to cash the cheque I enclosed and send his own for the same amount, with a note that a friend of his was ready to advance the sum free of interest.

When I think of the sacrifices people readily make in these days for the good of the book trade, it seems laughable that even as recently as 1926 the offer temporarily to lend a paltry sum free of interest for a brief period could be regarded with suspicion. To one who, like myself, was conscious of having fallen so lamentably short of the example of public service set me by both my parents, it was all most bewildering and difficult to understand. But I learnt in due time the truth of the remark,[1] 'The world voluntarily opens a path to those who step determinedly'.

At this point I must go back to the formation of the Society of Bookmen, from which the National Book Council, and practi-

---

[1] George Meredith makes in *The Tragic Comedians* (London: Archibald Constable & Co. Ltd., 1904), page 49.

cally all the co-operative developments of recent years in the British book trade, sprang. Hugh Walpole—the founder of the Society—was inspired to start it by a speech made by Mr G. A. E. Marshall, of W. H. Smith & Son, at a meeting of the Whitefriars Club. Among those present at the first meeting held at 24 York Terrace on October 20, 1921, were J. D. Beresford, St John Ervine, John Galsworthy, Harold Macmillan, Maurice Marston, W. B. Maxwell, David Roy, Frank Swinnerton, Hugh Walpole (who presided) and J. G. Wilson. The meeting was 'called together to discuss further possible co-operation in the book trade', and Walpole suggested 'that a society should be formed on business lines with this aim in view'. I was a wholehearted believer in co-operation, and this was to me a heaven-sent opportunity, of which I readily availed myself.

The problems of book trade organization had interested me profoundly since 1904, when I left the German book trade with its excessive regulation and entered the British book trade, which seemed then by comparison to have no organization at all. In Germany people did what they were told; in England people pleased themselves. Now there is nothing more deadly than excessive regulation, but there are grave disadvantages in allowing everyone to be a law unto himself.

I had long realized how essential it was to attempt to regularize some, at any rate, of our trade practices, and to me the formation of the Society of Bookmen opened up immediate possibilities of discussing that, among other co-operative activities for the betterment of the book trade. Little did I at the time suspect the extent of the opposition and suspicion—I might almost say venom—with which any such movement would be confronted.

Some insight into the difficulty of bringing publishers together may be gathered from a long-forgotten volume by William Heinemann entitled *The Hardships of Publishing*.[1] Heinemann with his knowledge of book trade organization abroad knew how ill-equipped we were.

As it happened, book trade organization came later. Co-

[1] Privately printed in a limited edition, March 1, 1893.

operative publicity came first. Grant Richards had advocated it and aroused my interest, but it was a visit from a representative of Elders & Fyffes which fired the spark as far as I was concerned. He wanted information about a book we had published on the West Indies which I gladly provided. He then asked me if I could put him on to any others. He explained that he was preparing an advertisement folder about the West Indies and wished to include a list of the best books because if people read about the West Indies they would want to go there. 'How right you are', I said, 'I will willingly put myself out to help you', and I did so, thinking all the time, 'This is a job someone should be doing on behalf of the whole book trade. If one shipping company is prepared to publicize books in this way, why not others, and why only shipping companies? Are there not hundreds of societies and organizations interested in promoting the sale of books on their special subjects who would gladly compile such lists, pay for their printing and assist with their distribution? And what trouble it would save booksellers to have such lists to hand out to customers inquiring for books on those subjects.'

From this idea came the hundreds of bibliographies printed at other people's expense which the National Book Council produced and circulated in its early days. But there was a long and bitter fight ahead before the idea was accepted. The Council of the PA turned down flat any form of co-operative publicity; they would not at first even consent to appoint representatives to discuss it. The Society of Bookmen, which was wholeheartedly behind it, continued to work for it. But the rebuffs were so constant and formidable that Mr Maurice Marston (Secretary of the Society) urged me many times to drop it; I was knocking my head against a brick wall and it was a waste of time. But I persisted.

I still remember a talk I had with W. M. Meredith, one of the opponents. I asked him whether, if someone was prepared to advertise his books free of expense to him, he would have any objection. He would not. Would he object if, always free of expense to him, other publishers' books were included in the same lists? He would not. If, as I could demonstrate, there were many people who would be willing, given the slightest encouragement, to advertise books free of expense to publishers, would it not be worth while for publishers to provide the encouragement? It certainly would. In the end—and it was a long journey—I convinced him that it might be worth while to set up a modest— very modest—organization to secure free publicity for books.

Finally, in June 1924, the Council relented to the extent of being willing to examine the project. Six months later, in January 1925, the National Book Council was formed, and the Council of the Publishers Association voted £5 towards the preliminary expenses. But only a month later it had reverted to an ultracautious attitude, because at that time the voting of £5 for such a purpose was verging on the reckless. However, within three months the National Book Council was formally approved; and the Council meeting of May 1925 nominated the PA representatives to serve on the NBC executive. It was a long and sometimes bitter fight, but we had won.[1] There was, however, still a long way to go before the National Book League—the successor of the National Book Council—had the membership and prestige to which I felt it was and is entitled.

The early issues of the confidential Members Circular of the Publishers Association are revealing not only for what they say but for what they omit. The attitude of the Council of those days was almost consistently negative. Take as one example the question of restarting the International Publishers Congress, which before the First World War had been so ably and actively supported by William Heinemann. Two years after the war was over the Council expressed reluctance to restart it. A year later they agreed that it should be dissolved. A year later they pressed that it should be wound up. (Fortunately, thanks to the late Ove Tryde of Denmark, and the late Hans Lichtenhahn of Switzerland, into whose competent hands it was entrusted at the outbreak of war, it was kept in being.) Eight years after the war was over they

---

[1] For a survey of the first fourteen years' work of the NBC see 'Fourteen Years of Crusading' by Maurice Marston in *The Bookseller* of May 9, 1940, subsequently published separately. It begins, appropriately, with the sentence 'The birth of the NBC was a very undignified episode in the history of the book trade'.

informed Gustav Gili—the Spanish representative—that a meeting of the Committee of the Congress which he advocated would not be a success. A year later they were prepared to appoint a delegate, but still felt a restart inopportune. In January 1928 they were still discussing ways and means of stopping it. All this was unknown to me at the time, but as will be seen in the chapter on the International Publishers Congress, I learnt about it from my foreign colleagues and immediately took steps to back those who wanted these international meetings restarted.

But to return to earlier days, it was in connection with book trade organization that the Council was at its stickiest. I had delivered an address to the Society of Bookmen on German Book Trade Organization[1] which had aroused considerable interest, and as an outcome suggested that it would be a good thing for a delegation of British publishers and booksellers to inspect the organization on the spot. I said that it would be both desirable and more effective if official representatives of the Publishers and Booksellers Associations accompanied us. Accordingly in April 1926 an invitation was sent from the Society of Bookmen to the two Associations to nominate representatives to go to Holland and Leipzig with the delegation. This they did.

The Dutch and German book trade organizations put themselves out to be helpful, and what the members of the delegation saw was, as I anticipated it would be, a complete revelation to them. They came, they saw, they marvelled. Knowing how difficult it would be to get the delegation together when once we returned to London I stipulated that we should break our journey back and spend a couple of nights at Wernigerode in the Harz Mountains, both to rest from our labours and to discuss our report. After climbing to the top of the Brocken, consuming enormous Holsteiner Schnitzels washed down in most cases by much 'Helles', the delegation settled down to work.[2]

---

[1] It was reprinted in enlarged form in the first three editions of *The Truth About Publishing*. (London: George Allen & Unwin Ltd., 1926 and 1929), Chapter VII, p. 222.

[2] The report of which was widely circulated, and subsequently reprinted as an appendix in *British Book Trade Organizations*, edited by F. D. Sanders (London: George Allen & Unwin Ltd., 1939).

When the delegation returned from the Continent it met with scant courtesy, and the Council of the Publishers Association did not even want to give its conclusions a hearing. Not until they knew we should proceed with or without their co-operation would they consent to nominate two representatives to join us in forming a committee of survey to study the recommendations of the report. The meeting was in my office under my chairmanship, and I am never likely to forget the unique extent to which I was insulted by one of the Council's representatives, because I have never experienced anything like it before or since.[1] I fortunately kept my temper and made it clear that the Society of Bookmen was concerned merely with the initiation of reforms, not in their execution, and that there was not the slightest need for me to remain chairman if the proposed joint committee of the two associations was set up, but that I regarded it as essential that all those who had taken the trouble to study the book trade organization of Holland and Germany should be members of the committee. The Council's representatives then insisted upon a much larger committee (in the futile hope of swamping us) and to this we agreed.

When finally the Joint Committee was summoned, the Council's representatives did their utmost to make the terms of reference such as to prevent the Committee from making recommendations, and to limit it to an examination of the existing organization in Great Britain. A prolonged battle had to be fought to introduce the word 'critical' into the terms of reference, so that in the course of a critical examination the Committee could point out not only the defects and limitations of our then organization, but how they could be remedied. I tell this sorry story because it seems to me important that a younger generation should know that something more than apathy had to be overcome to attain whatever co-operation exists today in the book trade in Great Britain. But there was apathy as well, and we are still suffering from the results of it. However reluctant

[1] I suppose it is one of life's little ironies that years later I bought the assets of his business, and that he had to come to me for my signature to secure a job he wanted.

certain publishers were to serve on that first Joint Committee, not one who did so failed to realize at the conclusion of its deliberations what a useful purpose it had served. One of its chief opponents told me afterwards how much it had taught him. Certainly it marked a turning-point for the British book trade. Soon thereafter (November 1926) Dents and my own firm joined the Publishers Association.

Here I feel that I must take the opportunity of paying a tribute to one who helped so materially to change the spirit of the Publishers Association, though he is, I am sure, modestly unaware of the important role he played. I refer to William Longman, because it was with his election to the Presidency of the Publishers Association in 1929 that the change was accomplished. He had served as Chairman of the Trade Practices Sub-Committee of the Joint Committee with the late David Roy and myself. The would-be reformers knew how convinced William Longman was of the importance of the recommendations of the Joint Committee; the die-hards could not object to a Longman—there had always been a Longman—and he was accordingly elected with the approval of both sections. From that moment the Publishers Association has never looked back.

But the battles for the recommendations of the Joint Committee and certain essential changes in the constitution of the Publishers Association had still to be fought. They were sometimes not without their humorous side. I was by then (April 1929) a member of the Council and able to participate in its proceedings. Sir Frederick Macmillan had long since ceased to be President, but that had not prevented his acting as if he still were, should he feel that course desirable. On the first occasion when we came to one of these controversial items on the agenda he said at once 'Oh! We don't want that! Next item', and to the next item we should have turned had I not—to his surprise—intervened. I explained that it was a matter upon which some of us felt very strongly, and that if it was not to be discussed it should at any rate be put to the vote. It was, and Sir Frederick found himself, again I think to his surprise, in a minority, the votes being 8 to 3.

Now I had the greatest respect for Sir Frederick personally, for his knowledge of publishing, and for what he had done for the book trade. As each item came up I went out of my way to emphasize, as I could truthfully do, how much I regretted to find myself in opposition to one for whose judgment I had such great respect, but that I felt that the changes proposed were essential and recognized as such by the majority of the trade.

One of the most difficult things to put over proved to be the recommended appointment of a Joint Advisory Committee to examine applications for 'recognition' as booksellers (or 'Other Traders') entitled to trade terms. In the end I asked Sir Frederick whether, if the Council had the last word and made the final decision, it mattered that some booksellers had previously discussed the proposals with some of our members. On that note it went through. But the Council wisely prefaced its approval with the phrase (bitterly resented by booksellers), 'While in no way challenging or altering the publisher's admitted right to find his own channels of distribution. . .'. In practice the Council practically always accepted the recommendations of the Joint Advisory Committee. Occasionally it referred back a recommendation for further consideration, and when it did so the recommendation was usually reversed or altered by the Joint Advisory Committee in the light of the further information provided.

It must have been a most trying time for Sir Frederick, who before my arrival had never been thwarted on the Council, and I was intensely sorry for him. But the tide had turned, and in the end he recognized it. One of the proudest moments in my life was when, after my Presidency and shortly before his death, he wrote me in his own bold handwriting the following letter:

'Many thanks for your congratulations. As you know that I am 80, I hope you will forgive me if I seem rather old-fashioned in my views, but I am sure you will believe me when I say that if I do not always agree with my juniors I do not take it for granted that they are wrong.'

Not all even of the Joint Committee's recommendations were implemented. Two, to me, obvious desiderata about which I felt most keenly and for which I pressed hardest, an Orders Clearing Office and a Parcels Clearing House, were excluded by the Committee itself,[1] largely owing to the diligence behind the scenes of H. E. Alden, of Simpkins, a member of the delegation who undermined much of its work. Today it is realized to an ever-increasing extent that rationalization is inevitable if the book trade is to function efficiently. In 1928 I could only paraphrase a famous saying and put on record that 'Rationalization is lame but it comes'. Some of the Committee's recommendations were turned down by the Booksellers Association; some were adopted years later.

The uncertainty and confusion which existed in those days on such a simple matter as 'Allowances'[2] is exemplified by a letter I wrote to one bookseller in 1928, who expected us to exchange three copies of an early edition of St John Ervine's *Alice and a Family* for the new cheap edition which we had just published. I pointed out that he had not bought the books from us, that this edition had been published by Maunsel of Dublin ten years before, and that Maunsel had published a cheap edition *before* we took the book over!

About that time the Publishers Association was confronted with two difficult problems by the Library Association and the Australian Booksellers Association respectively. The Library Association had in March 1925 appealed to the Publishers Association for some discount upon their purchases; the booksellers, in spite of the fact that some regulation would protect the majority of booksellers against the pernicious price-cutting of a minority, had vigorously opposed the suggestion, and the Publishers Association had rejected the Librarians' appeal. But the librarians persisted. The Carnegie Foundation had allocated large sums to the building of public libraries and Colonel Mitchell, their

---

[1] See *British Book Trade Organisation*, page 42.
[2] A pamphlet setting out the regulations about 'Allowances' can be obtained from the Publishers Association.

secretary, felt very strongly that the librarians were being unfairly treated by the book trade[1] and gave the Library Association his influential support. As I had occasion to write later in the *Publishers Circular* of August 7, 1937:

'Public Libraries in the USA and Canada had been recognized; a Government report had urged that they should be recognized in Great Britain. The pressure was such that for those who had eyes to see it was clear that recognition would come, whether we liked it or not, unless some compromise was found. There were two alternatives: recognition or a compromise. The Library Agreement, signed on the 12th November, 1929 (amended in 1933), was the compromise. To suggest that it was unnecessary to do anything is to shut one's eyes to the facts, as well as to ignore what was at that time happening with an ever-increasing amount of library business up and down the country.

'What booksellers never seem to realize is that, based upon American and Canadian experience, recognition would have been the more profitable course to publishers (or, at any rate, to most publishers). It would not have meant putting public libraries on an equal footing with booksellers. They are supplied at a short discount both in the USA and Canada, and there is no reason to suppose that they would have been treated differently here. To the specialist publishers the advantages of direct contact would be considerable. Nevertheless certain publishers felt that, looked at from the point of view of the book trade as a whole, it was desirable that library business should be retained, if possible, by the local bookseller—or should we say "regained" because for the most part it had been lost to price-cutters. Some of these publishers made it very clear at the time that there would be no question of any modification of trade terms consequent upon the Library Agreement. Nevertheless a comparison of publishers' terms before the Library Agreement was signed and now would show that the concessions made by publishers during this period are vastly in excess of the amount conceded by booksellers to librarians. In case some bookseller is so innocent as to interpret that as a statement that publishers' terms are 10 per cent better than they were, may I point out that an average increase of 2 per cent on a bookseller's

[1] See Minto's *A History of The Public Library Movement*, p. 271 (London: George Allen & Unwin Ltd., 1932).

total purchases amounts to more than he concedes to libraries unless library business exceeds a fifth of his turnover.

'When one remembers the constant complaint of some booksellers about library business, and the anxiety of other booksellers to give commission to libraries which are not entitled to it, one is almost driven to wonder whether publishers were wise in supporting a move which was not to their own immediate interests.'

The Agreement allowing licensed libraries a discount of 10 per cent on their purchases of new books is confined to libraries in Great Britain and Ireland giving free public access and spending not less than £100 a year on new books. It came into force on November 12, 1929.

The Australian problem was a very different one and recurred later. It was a demand by the Australian book trade that British publishers should 'protect' their enhanced selling prices. Now irrespective of whether the increases were reasonable or excessive, about which much might be said, the demand involved many difficulties. It is one thing to maintain the Net Book Agreement at home; quite another to do so at the other side of the world, and if the principle is admitted as valid in Australia, why not elsewhere? In March 1925 the proposal was turned down, but the Australian booksellers persisted, and in February 1927 the Publishers Association wisely or, as I think, unwisely, persuaded most, though not quite all, of its members to sign what was in effect an Australian Net Book Agreement, thereby accepting responsibility for the enhanced Australian schedule of prices. The agreement soon broke down; almost as soon as it was signed the Publishers Association received a cable from Australia demanding that its members should cease to supply certain customers with whom they had been doing business for years. No convincing evidence was produced that those customers had been misbehaving themselves in any way, and in some cases it was merely that the Australian Booksellers Association did not want publishers to supply them. It was an impossible situation which was brought to a close by the devaluation of the Australian pound, which rendered the schedule invalid.[1]

The British Net Book Agreement originally applied only in Great Britain and Ireland, but in March 1929, largely on my initiative, it was extended to all sales effected in Britain wherever the customer happened to be.[2] This had the twofold object of protecting overseas booksellers from unreasonable competition and to stopping price-cutting and other abuses which were creeping in. It annoyed those who relied on price-cutting to secure the easy business, but assisted those who relied upon the quality of their services, which they could not give if they were left with merely the unprofitable orders.

Another trouble arose at this time owing to the action of a Co-op. next door to a bookseller, in putting notices in its windows, and inserting advertisements in the local papers, urging people to buy their Christmas Annuals at the Co-op. and collect their 'divi' on them. The bookseller not unnaturally asked whether he could allow discount, pointing out at the same time that the particular branch of the Co-op. carried no general stock of books. To grant one bookseller permission to break the Net Book Agreement was an impossibility. The Publishers Association had no wish to interfere with the Co-op. or to prevent them from using any profits on bookselling to enhance their general dividend, but the foolish action of that one branch compelled the Publishers Association to stipulate that no dividend should be allocated specifically to any net book. It caused a lot of trouble, but in the end nearly 200 branches of the Co-op. complied with the condition. As a matter of fact, few Co-op. branches have ever carried a representative stock of books or taken bookselling seriously. They are mostly content with quick-selling lines such as Annuals and cheap juveniles. They have never as a movement taken the

[1] In 1955, following a visit to Australia by Mr F. D. Sanders (Secretary of the Publishers Association), a compromise was achieved which, while absolving the Publishers Association from any responsibility for the schedule of the prices to be charged in Australian currency, gave the Australian booksellers the security against price-cutting which they regarded as essential.

[2] Colonial editions not being 'net books' were—unwisely as it proved—not at the time included.

advantage they might have done of the rise in the spending power of their customers to promote the wider distribution of books.[1]

One of the many things that impressed the delegates who visited Germany, and through them the Joint Committee, was the great financial benefit the Börsenverein derived from its ownership of the official Book Trade Paper and Directory. It was an example we were recommended, and ought undoubtedly to follow. Two attempts were made to have an official organ, and a book trade directory was produced. The obstacles were formidable, owing primarily to the existence of *two* privately owned trade papers, but partly to the unfortunate choice on April 25, 1928, of the late Geoffrey Williams as the first editor and to the reluctance of certain publishers to back the official paper, whichever it was. It is a long story with which I had much to do personally, and I don't like to think of the number of hours, days, weeks I spent on the negotiations and their implementation. There would certainly seem to be no point in spending more time in recapitulating the history of those sad and at times unpleasant experiments.

One of the first tasks that confronted me on my appointment as Treasurer of the Publishers Association, in March 1931, was the preparation of the 'copy' for the Association's monthly Members Circular. If the information in it was to be of value it had to be printed and circulated promptly. In those days the Council did not meet until after lunch, and there were cheques to sign, and other matters for the officers to discuss and attend to after the meeting, so that it was always well after 6 p.m. before I got back to my office. I knew that it would be fatal to wait until the next day, so my long-suffering secretary stayed while I dictated the complete 'copy', including the references to the previous entries on the same subject. Both the new President (the late Bertram Christian) and I realized that with all the additional work being undertaken by the Publishers Association, the part-time services of the Beadle of the Stationers Company no longer

---

[1] Since 1955 a more liberal attitude has been taken towards the Co-operative Societies. No objection is raised to a time-deferred dividend not specifically advertised in relation to books.

sufficed. In addition, the work of the various Groups (or sections), e.g. Educational, Fiction, Juvenile, etc., had vastly increased and was inconveniently carried on from another address. Clearly it was desirable for the whole of the Association's work to be carried on under the same roof by one responsible secretary. We received scores of applications and interviewed several candidates. Great pressure was brought to bear upon us to appoint an ex-publisher who would himself expect to have a secretary, but neither Mr Christian nor I had any doubts that the right man was the one we appointed, Mr F. D. Sanders, who occupied the post for twenty-five years. I think that both of us felt—I certainly do—that his appointment was the most useful and effective piece of work we ever did for the Publishers Association. Since then, anyway, no Treasurer has been burdened with the preparation of the Members Circular, though that does not say that he is not left with other and more onerous responsibilities, so greatly has the work of the Association grown. Today the Treasurer and Vice-President find themselves called upon to devote more than a third, and the President more than half, of their working hours, and sometimes the whole, to their official duties. It can truly be said that to be elected an officer of the Publishers Association is to be sentenced to six years' hard labour!

Soon after my appointment as Treasurer the question of the European market arose, and in July 1931 a recommendation was unanimously approved that in the case of books of British origin the British publisher's market was the world ex USA, with the possible exception of Canada, and that in the case of books of American origin Europe should be reserved to the British publisher. In October 1931 the decision that we must have the exclusive European market was reaffirmed and the members of the Publishers Association were urged to draft their agreements accordingly. It was pointed out that we had the backing of the Authors' Society in making the recommendation. In July 1932 the importance of the European market was emphasized again, and most members signed an undertaking to stipulate for the exclusive European market. Much trouble would have been saved years later had members implemented their undertaking. My firm always did, with the amusing result that after the Second World War when troubles arose over markets and an American publisher told me that he had invariably had an open market in Europe, I challenged him to find a single agreement during the forty years with which I had been doing business with him in which he had not granted me the exclusive right of sale in Europe. To his chagrin he could not find one. He admitted that I had an overwhelming case and we still have 'the exclusive sale in Europe' in our contracts with him as with many other American firms.

Another question which confronted the Publishers Association was the growing practice of British books being photographically reproduced in the USA and vice versa. It was clear that if a publisher, whether British or American, controlled the transatlantic rights, he might be ready to let his fellow publisher on the other side of the Atlantic reproduce his typesetting free of charge if thereby he could make a profitable sale of the rights from which he would benefit. It was equally clear that if the original publisher was by-passed and the sale was made direct by the author or his agent, it was inequitable that free use should be made of the original publisher's typesetting. It was obviously fair that in such cases the original publisher should share in the saving made by the photographic use of his typography. The following resolution was accordingly approved by the Publishers Association and the then American Association:

'This Association recognized the ethical principle to which their attention had been called, and agreed that when a publisher makes arrangements for the United States rights independently of the English house (or vice versa) he should pay something towards the cost of typesetting. The suggested basis of 25 per cent of the cost of composition might be equitable in many cases, but it was desirable that the amount of compensation should be arrived at by mutual arrangement owing to the difficulty of fixing any standard payment which would be fair in all cases. The attention of the members of the National Association of Book Publishers is being drawn to the fact that their Executive Committee have taken the position that some compensation should be made in every case where a book is reproduced photographically under an agreement to which the English publisher (or vice versa) is not a party. It is the intention of both Associations that the foregoing arrangement is reciprocal.'

But some publishers on both sides felt that a fee, however nominal, should be paid in every case. Furthermore, it proved a great mistake to mention any percentage because American publishers failed to realize that whereas a payment of 15 per cent on the British publishers' expenditure on composition might still make photographic reproduction highly advantageous to them, a payment of 15 per cent on the cost of American typesetting converted into sterling might show no saving at all to the British publisher. A uniform percentage ignores the fundamental principle, namely the sharing of whatever *saving* photographic reproduction effects. My firm has many times reset a book because the fee demanded by the American publisher exceeded the saving achieved by the use of photolithography. The test is, what does the use of the other publisher's typography save? In some cases it may be substantial, in others negligible. It cannot be calculated upon a uniform percentage of the cost of composition.

In April 1933 I presided at the meeting of the Council of the Publishers Association for the first time. I had always felt that the meetings dragged on far too long—too much time was wasted upon purely formal things and non-controversial decisions. Instead, therefore, of waiting for someone to propose the obvious, I put on the agenda what was proposed; I had then merely to ask whether we were all agreed. This not merely hastened the procedure, but left time for the adequate discussion of more important business. I was a little terrified when I found the meeting was over more than an hour sooner than usual and feared that members might feel they were being unduly hustled. It was therefore a relief when Sir Humphrey Milford and others took me aside afterwards to thank me for my expedition. It confirmed me in my view, which I found that most efficient chairman Lord Lloyd shared, that formal uncontroversial business should be taken at top speed—which it seldom is—so that there may be ample time for the things which matter. Despite this it is now found necessary to begin Council Meetings at noon, carrying on to 5 p.m. or thereabouts with but a short break for a sandwich lunch.

One of the troublesome things with which I had to contend during my presidency was due to the action of the bookbinders. They drew up a schedule of prices to be charged for binding; formed themselves into what they called the Book Manufacturers Association, and persuaded the Winterbottom Book Cloth Co. to undertake to withhold supplies of cloth from any binder who departed from the schedule. Now the danger to book publishers of any such move was obvious. No binder could at that time exist for long without supplies of cloth from Winterbottoms who were then not far short of being monopolists. To add yet further to their power was to place publishers as well as binders very much at their mercy. It was bad enough that the blockmakers had a ring which determined what we should pay for blocks. The position would become impossible if Winterbottoms and the binders could dictate what we should pay for binding. Who was going to police the binders' policeman, who already, in the judgment of some of us, possessed excessive power? The battle was long, arduous and occasionally acrimonious; but in the end we won and the Book Manufacturers Association was dissolved. It took a great deal of my time and called for no little determination because there was at any rate one publisher (if not two) in the binders' camp.

Another time-absorbing matter was the sudden and almost indiscriminate seizure of books as allegedly obscene in various provincial cities. It might well be that the seizure of a portion, possibly even of a large portion, of the books was justified. But among them were sometimes literary works issued by responsible London publishers. In many cases the small man who was prosecuted would plead guilty or at any rate take no adequate steps to defend the books that had been seized. Accordingly a distinguished author might find his work condemned as 'obscene' without either he or his publisher having the slightest opportunity of saying a word in its defence. The attitude taken in one locality was often quite different from that taken in another. The position of reputable authors and publishers was intolerable. I approached the Home Office and found to my surprise that the official responsible for such matters was a man who often sat at the same table as I did at the Reform Club. (This enabled us later to have many informal off the record discussions upon how best to deal with what is a more difficult matter than many people realize.) I started by asking whether, if an offence had been committed by selling one of the publications of a reputable London publisher, the right person to prosecute was the London publisher (the source of a supply) or a little newsagent in, let us say, Bootle or Bolton who happened to have a single copy in his stock. He agreed that it was obviously the publisher against whom proceedings should be brought, adding that I must remember that the local police were locally controlled and not under the jurisdiction of the Home Office. I suggested that nevertheless the Home Office was not without influence, and that it was unlikely that the various authorities would ignore a strongly worded recommendation that in cases where the offending books bore the imprint of a London publisher the case should be referred to them so that if action was called for it might be taken against the publisher. Eventually this was done and with most beneficial results. Some time later, when we happened to meet at lunch, I asked him whether he knew a certain distinguished French author. 'Oh yes!' he replied, 'very well. I was responsible for urging him to write *The Body's Rapture* which I regard as his best book.' 'Well', I laughingly replied, 'a copy of it has just been seized by a policeman in the West of England', naming, of course, the place. It was the last I heard of that particular incident.

But there were many other battles to be fought and won—too many to recapitulate. The problem of the supply of books to the Dominions through High Commissioners and Agents-General—bitterly resented by our overseas customers—was amongst the most time-absorbing.

Business had begun to be fraught with the many difficulties, tariff complications, customs and currency regulations, bureaucratic interferences, etc., with which we have since become so familiar. There was one minor triumph over our own customs. The taxation of books with headband or bookmarker containing an infinitesimal quantity of silk or artificial silk was dropped, and 'imperfections' and printed illustrations were put on the free list.

But to me the battle of paramount importance, and one which I have been waging all my book trade life, is for the improved status of the book trade. If books once achieve the status they deserve all doors will be open. Are books, as some of us are never tired of asking, an absolute necessity, or merely, as thoughtless people would have us believe, a luxury for those who have nothing better to occupy their minds? In brief, do books occupy a unique place in life, or do they not? Upon the answer to these questions much more depends than most people realize.[1]

I used my office as President to address myself to this problem. The following is a quotation from a speech made at Birmingham:

'In studying book trade organizations in all parts of the world, nothing has impressed us more than the important place that the book trade occupies in all civilized countries and its comparative obscurity in England.

'I must confine myself to one practical illustration. Whether you turn to Leipzig or Paris, Oslo or Amsterdam, you find the book trade in possession of their own freehold buildings—with headquarters and a meeting-place of their own. Is that not perhaps symbolic? It was in no case achieved overnight. It was the result of a consciousness that the book trade was a permanent as well as a living and vital thing. The young men of the book trades of those countries saw visions and the old men dreamt dreams.

'Ought we not to have a little more faith in the future? Is there any reason why we should not resolve here and now to start preparing for the day when the book trade shall occupy the place it deserves in the life of the country we all of us love?'

[1] See *The Status of Books* by Stanley Unwin (London: George Allen & Unwin Ltd., 1942).

My references to the subject provoked others, as witness the accompanying extract from a letter from A. C. Hannay to *The Church Times*:

'Has it ever occurred to your readers that book publishers enjoy less status and less recognition in England than in any other civilized country in Europe? Status and recognition are in themselves unimportant; it is the work that counts. But the publication of scholarly work is becoming increasingly difficult, and the publisher is more and more tempted to pursue the best-seller.

'You, Sir, have always shown appreciation of scholarly work in the large amount of space you have devoted to it in your columns; but in the absence of other forms of encouragement and recognition there is a danger that publishing in Great Britain may drift into the position of publishing in the USA where books with a mass appeal are now, apparently, the only kind which the general publisher welcomes.

'Recognition takes different forms in different continental countries, but in all the status of book publishers accords much more closely with the kind of work accomplished than with success at ballyhoo. Is there not a tendency here for the position to be reversed?'

Well, we have made much progress since then, but the battle is not yet won.

But there were other things to attend to besides battles. Years before, when Basil (now Sir Basil) Blackwell and I were not even members of our respective councils, we were dining together alone at the close of a Booksellers Conference in Edinburgh. We were dissatisfied with many things in the book trade. We decided that the only hope of remedying some of the defects lay in closer co-operation between our two Associations, which in turn depended upon a sympathetic understanding between the two Presidents. Having reached that weighty conclusion we looked at one another and said with a laugh: 'Very well. We must arrange to be presidents of our respective Associations simultaneously.' We did so arrange, but that we achieved all we set out to do neither of us would claim. We certainly at once cut out acrimonious correspondence between the two Associations by the simple process of meeting each other every week. In fact, the words of Isaiah were fulfilled—the wolf and the lamb fed together.

In pursuance of our plans we issued a letter to publishers and booksellers in June 1934 from which the following extracts are taken:

'We are convinced that if publishers and booksellers could meet more often on neutral ground, and in good fellowship and free debate, we should all benefit by it. . . . We believe that it would be worth while to try the experiment on a small unofficial conference of publishers and booksellers in the early autumn; and to that end we have engaged Ripon Hall on Boars Hill, near Oxford, from September 7th-10th. The Conference will begin on Friday evening and dissolve on Monday morning after breakfast. The transactions will not be recorded, and nothing said will be "used in evidence".'

The Conference was an outstanding success. My own part was an address entitled 'The Problem of Organization: Is a Holiday from Legislation Needed?'[1] in which I emphasized that the time had arrived to pause and take stock; to consider what we had set out to do about seven years before; what we had accomplished; where we had failed, and why.

I pleaded for a respite from resolutions whose *complete* implications had not been thought out and faced, and from restrictions which merely penalized the booksellers' best friends among publishers and benefited no one.

In view of the many new regulations which we had not assimilated, I might aptly have quoted the reply Louis XVI gave to a petition on December 4, 1775: 'There are already a large number of laws on the book trade, and we do not believe that the best way to ensure their execution is to increase their number.' Finally, I pointed out that the position of the book trade would not be bettered by any haggling over the business we were already doing, but by concentrating all our energies upon the vastly more important question of increasing the total sale of books.

With the termination of my Presidency, I still had two years as Vice-President ahead of me. During that period two new

[1] See *The Publishers Circular*, September 22, 1934.

schemes were promulgated and much discussed—Book Tokens, the invention of a publisher (Harold Raymond of Chatto & Windus), and the Book Agents scheme, advocated by another publisher (R. F. West of Baillière, Tindall & Cox). The Society of Bookmen helped at the initiation of Book Tokens, which at first were run by the National Book Council. It was intended to be a joint affair, but at a certain point the Booksellers Association took entire charge of it under circumstances which left some of us with an unpleasant taste in our mouths which we try, but find it hard to forget. The scheme has been of the greatest benefit to the book trade, though for a long time many shortsighted booksellers opposed it, as they are inclined to do with anything new which taking a broader view will be to their advantage. It strengthened the position of the Booksellers Association in more ways than one.

The Book Agents scheme had a stormy reception. Parts of it have by degrees been adopted, and to the limited extent that they have been used have been useful.

There were discussions with the BBC on what was 'reasonable use' in relation to the broadcast of extracts from copyright works. I was able to bring home to them that what would appear to them a derisory sum might be of importance to a poet, and suggested that something, however small, should always be paid for the use of extracts from a living poet's work, despite the shortness of the quotation. An amicable arrangement was duly thrashed out.

During my last term of office that perennial problem, the marking of review copies, came up for discussion, as well as the question of subsidiary rights, which was later to loom so much more largely in publishers' relations with authors and authors' agents. Still more important, at my instigation work was started on a Guide to Royalty Agreements, which had always been a pet project of mine. I had always hoped that such a guide might be a joint affair with the Society of Authors, in which, in the case of controversial clauses, each party would print their draft with a brief statement of their reasons for it. But this was not to be. The Guide is the sole work of the Publishers Association, though where they are definitely known, the views of the Society of Authors are mentioned. The Guide is in my judgment one of the most valuable pieces of work the Publishers Association has ever achieved. It would take too long to deal with the many other subjects which were engaging the attention of the Publishers Association while I was still an officer; the preparation of a new constitution; questions such as terminable licences, partial remaindering; reviews of books before publication, etc.

We were already being reminded that war might come by the receipt of a schedule of Reserved Occupations, an indication of the probable basis of conscription; and a recommendation for those who could do so without interfering with efficiency to move out of London in the event of war. Many useful activities ceased when war finally came and gave us so many more urgent problems to cope with. For example, a most useful Report on Coupon Advertising, which particularly interested me because it confirmed my contention that the bookseller profits rather than loses by the coupon type of advertising.

The first war-time problem to confront publishers was the War Risks Insurance Act, over which I took a very active part. Should publishers, or should they not, contract out? Personally I favoured contracting out and the setting up of a scheme to reduce risks by the interchanges of stock between publishers. It was clear to me at the outset that no insurance would cover the real requirements of a publisher of slow-selling scholarly books which had over the years been written down to nominal figures in his balance sheet. The problem was fully discussed at a special meeting of the Publishers Association. A bare majority was obtained for contracting out of compulsory insurance, but the Board of Trade had rightly stipulated for a three-fourths majority if they were to consider authorizing a trade to do so. Unfortunately my judgment proved right. The effect of compulsory insurance was to penalize the provident publisher and endow the improvident ones.[1]

[1] I dealt fully with this question of the valuation and insurance of slow-selling books in *The Accountant* of June 22, 1946.

Other war measures confronted us almost daily. The one that was handled most successfully was censorship, which, as I pointed out in *The Times*,[1] had been dealt with so idiotically in the First World War. It was decreed that the only ground for censorship was giving information to the enemy. On that basis the Publishers Association at once promised 100 per cent co-operation.

' "It is good news", wrote *John o' London's Weekly*, "that Mr Stanley Unwin and Mr W. G. Taylor have been appointed by the Publishers Association to advise the Press and Censorship Bureau about the censorship of books. Mr Unwin may be trusted to resist any attempt to curtail legitimate freedom of expression".'

As a matter of fact our services were never required. In doubtful cases publishers voluntarily and gladly submitted typescripts or proofs, and the censors dealt with them expeditiously. The expression of opinion remained free.

It was not my only advisory appointment. With Mr Walter Harrap I was consulted by the Import Licence Department of the Board of Trade, which had to restrict the import of books, like that of other commodities from abroad, so that overseas credits were not unduly depleted. The Department had no wish to interfere with the import of works of literary or technical value; Mr Harrap and I helped by classifying foreign books into categories and by advising on the doubtful cases. This restriction, of course, was not at all a matter of censorship.

Paper control was soon upon us. The Publishers Association tried to secure the postponement of rationing, and, failing that, preference for books. We were granted neither, but were threatened with dictation as to the way in which the paper allowed for books was to be used. In order to avoid the imposition of ill-advised governmental regulations, a committee, under the chairmanship of Mr W. G. Taylor, was set up by the Publishers Association to suggest the maximum economies in the use of paper which were practicable. It was a formidable undertaking. The committee held thirteen meetings in a fortnight—working

[1] See Chapter 19, page 343.

at the most intense pressure—and, despite the complexity and the highly technical nature of its task, achieved a 'Book Production War Economy Agreement' that prescribed the size of type, width of margins, weight of paper and the weight of boards, which was voluntarily accepted by the Publishers Association. It was a remarkable *tour de force* and owed a great deal of its success to the astonishing efforts of the late Guy Bickers of G. Bell & Sons. It resulted, as the Government wanted, in the creation of the maximum number of books out of the minimum raw material, but it compelled British publishers to produce an inferior article, which did us inestimable harm in Canadian and other markets where we had to face American competition.

Some of us moved heaven and earth to try to secure official encouragement of books at Cabinet level, but without success. When paper rationing came[1] it was based upon the usage of publishers in the year ended August 31, 1939, which in the opinion of most firms was a most undesirable choice. We appealed for an alternative period, or for an average of more than one year, without avail. The year selected suited certain manufacturers who were considered more important, so that was that. Right from the start the book trade just didn't count with those who had the last say in the handling of paper.

It was clear that if we publishers were to make any headway against this army of officials we must form an Export Group, because it was exports that counted, and this we were officially encouraged to do and immediately did. Furthermore, it was essential that we should have statistics. Now during my presidency I had appealed in vain for statistics. Later Mr Harold Raymond, of Chatto & Windus, had done so without success. Nothing would persuade many of the most important publishers to disclose their turnover figures, even to the most distinguished accountants under every guarantee of secrecy. But the moment it became clear that additional paper would not be obtained without statistics no publisher hesitated to provide them, and they have been forth-

---

[1] Incidentally books were completely left out of the first schemes, such was the official cognizance of their value.

coming ever since. Fortunately, when the forms were being prepared, I pressed for the inclusion of the figures for 1937 and 1938 as well as 1939, in order to give us the turnover for two complete pre-war years. The statistics have been invaluable and most instructive. Would that we had had them earlier. We should know much more about the book trade if we had.

Since the war much further progress has been made with the provision of statistical information. The export figures now show the relative importance of our many foreign markets, and there is a careful analysis of the scope and character of the home turnover.

In May 1940 my memorandum urging a reduction in Imperial and Foreign Printed Paper postage rates (Book Post) and my Book Export Scheme were both approved by the Council, but as the latter is fully dealt with in the more recent editions of *The Truth About Publishing* there is no need for me to refer to it here.

In June 1940 the Paper Control announced that book publishers would receive 60 per cent of the paper they had used during the prescribed reference period—the year ending August 31, 1939, and from that moment the struggle for more paper for books began.

'There is no such thing as culture in war time', proclaimed the *Daily Express* solemnly, and the Treasury duly seconded the motion. Immediately the Chancellor of the Exchequer announced the Purchase Tax, from which only food was to be exempt, I drafted the following letter to *The Times*, which I signed as Vice-President of the International Publishers Congress:

'Emphasis has properly been placed on the fact that the tax on purchases will not be levied on food for the body, but in characteristically English fashion there has been no reference to food for the mind. I hope no one will have the temerity to suggest that it is not needed, or that it is merely a luxury. The book trade is staggering under a series of blows, of which war risks insurance and acute paper shortage are but two. It would indeed be ironical if it were completely knocked out by a levy on the purchase of books—in effect by a tax on knowledge.

'The International Publishers Congress has consistently stood for the free exchange of books everywhere, and its efforts have met with almost uniform success. It would be humiliating if in a war for freedom of thought the sale of books in which man's highest thoughts are enshrined should be hampered by taxation.'

When I showed it to two Past Presidents of the Publishers Association, one handed it back to me with the comment 'waste of time'; the other said 'no harm in trying'. The immediate response was so great that it encouraged Geoffrey (now Sir Geoffrey) Faber, who was then President, to devote all his energies to securing the exclusion of books from the Purchase Tax. As the outcome of a long conference with the Board of Customs and Excise a masterly memorandum was drawn up on 'The Economic Case for the Exclusion of Books from the Scope of the Purchase Tax' which was submitted on behalf of the Publishers Association to the Chancellor of the Exchequer. Neither the Chancellor of the Exchequer nor the Treasury ever attempted to make any answer at all to any of the arguments placed before them. But the economic argument was only part of the whole case. A deputation headed by the Archbishop of Canterbury, consisting of Professor Sir Arthur Eddington, OM, Lord Hambleden, Mr A. P. Herbert, MP, Dr Albert Mansbridge, CH, Mr J. B. Priestley, Sir Charles Grant Robertson, Professor R. H. Tawney, with Mr Geoffrey Faber and Mr Wren Howard representing the Publishers Association and myself as Chairman of the Books and Periodicals Committee of the British Council, waited on the Chancellor of the Exchequer at the Treasury on June 21, 1940, and the Archbishop and others put the many arguments which as representing religion, science, education, scholarship and pure literature they could more worthily present.

The Chancellor's chief contribution by way of reply was that there were enough books in the country and that 'if I exempt books why not boots?' He seemed incapable of seeing any difference. I doubt whether any group of people left the Treasury building more infuriated. The members of the deputation determined then and there that the Chancellor should be compelled to learn the difference between books and boots, because there was no doubt that all the better elements in the nation were completely on our side. The following morning there was a magnificent leader in *The Times*; the *Manchester Guardian* and all the more serious papers and journals backed us equally wholeheartedly. The leader in *The Times* was followed up by an excellent letter signed by members of the delegation and leaders in the educational world. To help keep the pot boiling, a few days later I wrote a long letter to *The Times Literary Supplement*, which was duly published. Meanwhile Mr Geoffrey Faber, with the able assistance of Mr Gilbert McAllister, who had been appointed for the purpose, was organizing and carrying through an intensive campaign. A fighting fund was speedily raised and the National Committee for the Defence of Books was formed. The enthusiasm was intense, as was demonstrated at a public meeting held at Stationers Hall with Sir Hugh Walpole in the chair. The proceedings and the eloquent speeches by J. B. Priestley and others will be found in a booklet hastily printed for propaganda purposes.[1]

Mr Kenneth Lindsay, MP, and Mr Henry Strauss, MP, were most active in the House of Commons, and it was soon clear that there were so many on both sides of the House opposed to the taxation of books that the Government would have a stormy passage if they attempted it. A debate was expected, and I went to the House with Kenneth Lindsay, who had prepared a cogent speech in readiness. It was never delivered because the Chancellor bowed to the storm, and I had the huge satisfaction of hearing him explain to the House that you could not treat books just like any other commodity and that they were to be exempted from purchase tax.

The Associated Booksellers were enthusiastic and sent a gift towards the heavy expenses of the campaign, with a letter of appreciation of the work of Mr Geoffrey Faber and others, including myself. They described the achievement as 'an authoritative recognition of the unique national importance which our trade possesses. The trade as a whole had taken a great forward stride in the national estimation.'

[1] *The Book Crisis* (London: Faber & Faber).

This successful battle was one of many war-time occurrences which proved a stimulus to co-operation between publishers. As an example, the famous firm of wholesale booksellers, Simpkin Marshall, was 'blitzed' and its entire business, including a stock of about six million books, was completely destroyed one Sunday night. By 9 a.m. on the Monday, its chief competitor was already busily helping to deal with its orders. Before eleven its Managing Director was discussing future plans with me on the telephone, and within a matter of hours thereafter the Economic Relations Committee of the Publishers Association had got busy and three of us had undertaken to buy the goodwill of the wholesale and export side of the business with a view to its becoming a co-operative organization. Thanks to the assistance of the brothers Pitman and their Book Centre, and the determination of publishers generally (with two notable exceptions) that this important link in the chain of book distribution should not be broken, Simpkin Marshall was re-established with representative publishers and booksellers on its board. For reasons which it is unnecessary to go into, the final outcome was unfortunate.

The shortage of paper, the need for which was so greatly accentuated by the destruction of so many millions of books through bombing, was a very great trial—a trial not lessened by the knowledge that it could so easily be alleviated. I kept up a ceaseless campaign in the Press; the governmental replies were invariably disingenuous. They repeated with parrot-like insistence that it was a dollar and shipping problem, which, to put it bluntly, was a lie. Even in normal times, paper for books, a quite different commodity from newsprint, is not a dollar problem; in war-time it was not even a shipping problem, because paper for books was being made from home-produced straw, of which there was a surplus.

At first we innocently thought that the Paper Controller at Reading was responsible for our troubles; then we learnt that he took his instructions from the Ministry of Supply; later that that Ministry in turn worked under the Ministry of Production, who acted upon the advice of an Economic Committee of the Cabinet.

Although we did not know it at the time, though a few of us suspected it, the fact that the world was temporarily starved of British books and the British book publishers' foreign markets were presented to the USA was due mainly to the peculiar and unfortunate views of one member of that Cabinet advisory committee which had the last word in paper allocations.

In the end, one sensible thing was done. A special allocation of paper was made for the reprinting of essential books which their publishers could demonstrate they could not produce from their quota. It was known as the Moberly pool, because Sir Walter Moberly was the first officially appointed chairman of the committee which advised the Board of Trade about its allocation. The committee consisted of four publishers nominated by the Publishers Association, whose names should be recorded in letters of gold, because it was such a thankless and time-absorbing task wading through the applications. There were, in fact, 10,000 of them, and each of them was separately considered. The applications followed these four unfortunate publishers about for seven years, wherever they went, at home at week-ends and even on holidays. The four who made this major contribution to the interests of the trade were: B. W. Fagan[1] (later awarded a CBE), R. H. Code-Holland, R. J. L. Kingsford and W. G. Taylor. They carried through their task with exemplary patience and objectivity, and the reading public, as well as publishers, are greatly in their debt.

Early in the war (December 1940), the bombing of Stationers Hall left the Publishers Association homeless. I had fortunately left the fourth floor of New Ruskin House, 28 Little Russell Street, vacant for just such an eventuality, though I thought it was my own offices in Museum Street which might disappear. I was thus able to invite them to occupy it, not free—I had learnt my lesson about that—but at less than the economic rent until they moved into their present quarters at 19 Bedford Square.

[1] Mr Fagan acted as chairman before the appointment of Sir Walter Moberly.

CHAPTER 22

THE INTERNATIONAL PUBLISHERS ASSOCIATION

Most professions and trades have found some form of international organization desirable, if not essential. It is clear, for example, that doctors, architects and printers, to name but three at random, have found that whatever country they come from, they have much in common with and much to learn from doctors, architects and printers in other countries. Publishers realized this more than sixty years ago, and the first meeting of the International Publishers Congress, as it was then called, was held in Paris as far back as 1896.

Having started my book trade career in Leipzig, I was always deeply interested in the international aspect of publishing. My step-uncle had told me about the meeting of the International Publishers Congress in Budapest in 1913, and what a huge success it had been, so that as the years went by following the end of the First World War, I began to make enquiries about what had happened to the organization. I found that it still existed, although the secretary, Alfred Melly, had died in June 1920; that the countries which had been neutral had formed a provisional committee[1] to keep it in being, and were most anxious to arrange for another Congress, but that unofficial soundings had shown that one or two of the more important countries (including Britain) had shown no enthusiasm—in fact, had suggested in August 1920 that the whole organization should be wound up. This did not seem to me good enough, and I wrote to various foreign publishers to say how keen I was that the possibility of holding another Congress should at any rate be discussed. This,

---

[1] For an account of the work of the provisional committee who, unknown to me, were most active in keeping the flag flying, see the opening article by M. Ove Tryde in the volume of *Rapports* (Paris: June 1931).

thanks to the good work of the provisional committee, helped to start the ball rolling again and a meeting of the International Commission of the Congress (i.e. a committee of not more than two representatives of each book publisher's organization adhering to the International Association) was summoned to meet at Berne in October 1929.

I volunteered to go as the representative of the Publishers Association of Great Britain, and as no one else showed the slightest interest I was duly appointed with Mr W. G. Taylor, an ideal associate, as my companion.

Much of the time of this committee meeting in Berne was naturally occupied by the report of those who had taken charge of the affairs of the Congress during the war, notably the late Ove Tryde from Denmark, who was in the chair, and making necessary revisions in the Constitution, in which the late Louis Hachette took a most effective part. But two important decisions were taken:

1. That in view of the past controversies about the place where Congresses should be held, we should follow chronologically the list of pre-war Congresses, with the proviso that any centre which had never previously had a Congress might, by consent, be interpolated, leaving the order otherwise unchanged.

2. That following this recommendation, the first post-war Congress should be held in Paris, and if possible in 1931.

The Paris meeting was a huge success, in fact, it set a standard which some of us felt at the time it would be hard to emulate. Apart from a very full programme of work, recorded in the printed *Compte Rendu*, there was a Municipal Reception, a Foreign Office Reception at the Quai d'Orsay, a luncheon at the French Colonial Exhibition, and finally to cap it all the members of the International Commission were invited to lunch—on gold plate—with the President of the French Republic at the Palais d'Elysée. Later two or three of us were made Officiers de L'Académie Français.

When we got home I wondered what we should do when our turn came to have the Congress again in London. I looked to see what entertainment had been provided on the previous occasion, and found that it was limited to a visit to Windsor Castle preceded by a luncheon at a local pub. We must obviously do better than that. However, it was the turn of the Belgians next, so that we had time. On the other hand, as our invitation had to be given at the Brussels Congress it was desirable that we should know what we could do before we committed ourselves. By a stroke of good fortune, owing to the fact that his father had been a director of Swan Sonnenschein & Co., I was in touch with Lord Wigram, the King's Private Secretary, and I turned to him for advice. I explained how embarrassing it would be if, following the French President's action, we could do nothing better than we had managed last time. Was there a possibility of the King receiving a few of the more distinguished foreign publishers? Lord Wigram proved most sympathetic and thought that it might well be practicable provided he knew the date of the Congress the best part of a year ahead and that, when the time came, a letter was forthcoming from the Prime Minister or Foreign Secretary expressing approval of the suggestion. With both conditions it proved easy to comply. On one of my morning walks with Ramsay MacDonald I broached the question of the Reception, and he at once agreed to give me any help I needed. In such circumstances the Council of the Publishers Association had no hesitation in authorizing Mr Taylor and myself to announce at Brussels an invitation to hold the next Congress in London.

In Paris (as on each subsequent occasion) I urged that there should be an interval of three years between Congresses, but was overruled. The German delegation in particular insisted upon the desirability and importance of having another Congress in two years. It was thus an interesting indication of the mounting indignation at the Nazi treatment of the Jews when, in April 1933, I received a discreetly worded letter from my good friend Dr Gustav Kilpper, the representative of Germany on the Executive, that, although it might easily be misconstrued if the suggestion came from Germany, they felt that, in view of the tension in the atmosphere, it would be wise to postpone the Brussels

Congress to 1934 in accordance with my original proposal. It proved, however, too late to do so.

At the Brussels Congress Dr Kilpper went much further than such an enlightened man had any justification in doing in defending the Nazis, who showed their appreciation by turning him out of office. Following the Congress he urged my son and myself to join him on a holiday on the Eibsee, which under other circumstances we would gladly have done. My reply read as follows:

'I very much appreciate your letter of the 11th July with its kind invitation. But the news that reaches me this morning of the glorification of the murderers of my friend Rathenau—one of the most enlightened and noble-minded men I have ever met—makes it more than ever clear that Germany under the present regime is no place for me. That an assassin could be regarded in 1933 as a hero is incredible. What are we coming to!'

No one expected the Belgian Congress to live up to the French one. Actually, more than we expected was done for us, but the organization left much to be desired. In fact, it continually broke down. My colleague, Taylor, who was destined to be chairman of the organizing committee in London, took careful notes of all the circumstances in which the breakdowns happened. He was rightly determined that no such hitches should occur in London. Nor did they. Every detail was thought out in advance; the organization, aided by Mr Sanders, was first-rate. But lest anyone think such an achievement easy, I can assure him that it involves an incredible amount of forethought and hard work, and the fact that one is dealing with people of many nationalities with different habits, not to mention languages, complicates the task.

The preliminary work connected with a Congress is in itself an arduous undertaking. The choice of subjects to be discussed, the selection of the speakers, the collection and printing of the papers for circulation before the Congress meets all take time. Eighteen months, at least, is needed for the preparatory work if it is to be efficiently done. Therefore immediately after the Brussels Congress was over in 1934, Taylor and I started to work. In

addition to Lord Wigram, I had consulted the late C. H. St John
Hornby of W. H. Smith & Son. He mentioned the possibility of
the Goldsmiths Company entertaining us, and to our great joy an
invitation was forthcoming. It proved to be the most memorable
event of all, except for the few who went to Buckingham Palace.
Even today when I travel abroad, foreign publishers remind me of
it. The whole setting, the gold plate, the beautiful singing of the
grace before and after dinner, the loving cup, the quaint ceremonial, not to mention the exquisite food and wine, contributed
to making it a unique event. As an illustration of unexpected
difficulties that arise with international gatherings, a few of the
delegates ignored the Goldsmiths Company's invitation under the
illusion that it was a business concern and an advertising stunt.
Bitter was their grief when they learnt what they had missed.

A special committee was set up to entertain the ladies and
much was done to make their visit to London memorable.
Gordon Selfridge personally presided at the lunch he gave them.

One of the many problems that confronted us was where the
members of the Congress were to have lunch between the sessions
on the first day (Monday). It seemed cruel to turn them out of
Stationers Hall into Ludgate Hill and leave them to fend for
themselves in the rush hour. Stationers Hall itself was out of the
question because we were fully occupying it, but fortunately
Cutlers Hall is just at the other end of Warwick Lane, and with a
little prompting the Cutlers Company came to our rescue as far
as the loan of their hall was concerned. I was most anxious that
the British Council should take its part in welcoming these many
foreign publishers, and suggested that they might appropriately
provide the luncheon, but their income in those days was so
trifling that they felt it was beyond their means. However, when
I pointed out what a simple meal was needed, and how small the
cost, they acceded and Lord Eustace Percy (later Lord Percy of
Newcastle), then Chairman of the Council, made excellent
speeches both in English and French, which gave the Congress a
good start. On the previous Saturday I had entertained the
International Commission to lunch at the Reform Club. Knowing

that it would interest them, I afterwards took them round the Club. When we passed in silence through the Library we found, as might be expected, a few old gentlemen indulging in an afternoon nap. To my amusement I discovered afterwards that my guests thought that I had arranged for 'sleepers' to be there to recreate the atmosphere of Thackeray.

H.M. Government gave us a Reception at Lancaster House, at which Mr Duff Cooper (later Viscount Norwich) and Mr (now Sir) Anthony Eden received the guests. Tea on the Terrace of the House of Commons was arranged by the late Sir Godfrey Collins; a visit to Oxford, with tea in the grounds of Magdalen College; and a magnificent Dinner at the Dorchester, given by *The Times*, were among the other events. At the last I found myself seated next to Lord Hewart, and I was able to tell him why a jury (of which I was a member) gave such contradictory answers to the questions he put to them in a case in which Thomas Cook & Son were the defendants.

As might be expected, the visit to Buckingham Palace was most impressive. I had received a summons a few days before to discuss the arrangements, and the first point Brig.-Gen. Sir Hill Child emphasized was that there must be no slip-up over the order of precedence. Fortunately I was ready for that question and he at once agreed the list I had carefully thought out and brought with me. He told me that we should assemble in one of the rooms in the Palace and the King would be in an adjoining room. As President I was to go through and speak to the King privately—which I did—and should then come through with him and introduce the others one by one.

On an earlier occasion when members of the British Executive were presented one after another to King Edward VIII (then Prince of Wales) I had thought how appallingly difficult it was for him to find something appropriate to say to so many different people of whom he knew little or nothing. I determined that he should have no such difficulty with the members of the International Publishers Congress. Accordingly I memorized one fact about each delegate which I could mention to the King while they were approaching to be presented, e.g. when the Finnish representative was on his way I said, 'They have one of the finest bookshops in Europe at Helsinki'. It made the affair far less effort for the King, and the effect on the delegates was startling. They thought it nothing short of miraculous that King Edward VIII should be so well informed. When the proceedings were over and we were leaving the Palace, the King sent a member of his staff to thank me for having made it so easy for him.

The official end of the Congress was marked by a Dinner at Stationers Hall on the Friday night, given by the Publishers Association, over which I presided. By way of light entertainment we had a conjurer, and how he succeeded in removing the braces of a tall Norwegian publisher without any one of the rest of us observing him do it, and to the intense surprise and embarrassment of the unfortunate publisher himself, is a mystery over which I found him still puzzling when years later I met him in Oslo.

Officially the Congress was now over, but seven or eight delegates had, I knew, set their hearts upon meeting Lloyd George, and he most kindly invited me to take them to tea with him at Churt on Saturday afternoon. He was in great form and gave us a wonderful time.

To those of us responsible for the Congress, satisfaction over its success was heightened by the first official recognition of the importance of book publishing.

The venue for the next Congress put me very much 'on the spot'. Few of us wanted to go to a Nazi Germany, and an alternative invitation from Switzerland had been secured. Unfortunately my predecessor in office, M. Zech-Levie of Belgium, whose responsibility it was, had not even dropped a hint to the Germans of the possibility of another country being interposed, and without such an intimation they were fully entitled to expect us to honour our agreement to follow chronologically the order of the pre-1914 Congresses. Accordingly the German delegation came fully empowered (no doubt by Goebbels) to invite us to Leipzig in 1938, and were both surprised and horrified when the proposal was put forward that we should defer going to Germany and accept an invitation to Switzerland. Nazi pressure was, I believe, brought to bear on the Swiss Government; anyway, the Swiss invitation was withdrawn and the chief Swiss delegate made an impassioned speech in favour of acceptance of the German invitation, and pointed out, correctly, that we should, as a professional organization, put ourselves completely in the wrong if on political grounds (there were no others) we broke the agreement unanimously made when the Congress was restarted. Albeit reluctantly, I could not but agree, though as the result of the acceptance the United States withdrew from the Congress. Needless to say I took every precaution to prevent the Nazis from making any use of the Congress for political purposes. I made it clear, beyond a peradventure, that were there the slightest sign of their doing so I should immediately withdraw and urge all the other delegations to do likewise.

Some busybodies, learning that the Americans were refusing to go to Leipzig, which they were entitled to do but which, holding the ivory gavel of office which it was my duty to hand to my successor I could not do, started an agitation. Without troubling to see me or ascertain the facts, they got petitions signed by leading authors and others condemning my action, and then, having blackened my name, asked me to receive a deputation, which of course I did. When they came I explained the position and ended by asking them what they would do in my shoes? Would they break the agreement and put the Nazis in the right? No, was the reply, but they would take steps to see that no use was made of the Congress for propaganda purposes. When I showed them the categorical nature of the assurances I had demanded and obtained, they admitted I could not have done more. I suggested that they might have ascertained the facts before condemning one who had fought for freedom of thought as I had done all my life, and they withdrew. I still possess that wonderful collection of autographs. The incident has made me very chary of adding my signature to any protests of that kind unless I know the facts.

In 1937 (the year before the Leipzig Congress) I was due to

attend an Executive meeting at Geneva, and thereafter to go to Copenhagen for the Danish Book Trade Centenary celebrations. One event during the memorable festivities at Copenhagen was a special banquet given by that distinguished Danish publisher the late Ejnar Munksgaard, at which he presented me with a handsome collector's item of which he had only a few copies printed:

'Hans Christian Andersen's visits to Charles Dickens as described in his letters—dedicated to Stanley Unwin on the occasion of his visit to Copenhagen 20th January 1937.'

It was a characteristically charming Danish gesture which I could never forget.

For reasons which will become clear, I wrote to the head of the Nazi Publishers Association to inquire whether it was safe for me to travel to Copenhagen from Geneva via Germany—the most direct route. It brought the expected reply that it was absurd to ask such a question. That enabled me to tell him that only a week or two before a cousin of mine, a Quaker who had participated in the feeding of German children after the First World War, had been arrested and clapped into prison by the Nazis because he had looked up some Germans with whom he had collaborated in connection with his Quaker relief work. It is true that he was soon released, but I said that I had no wish to go to prison for even one day just because I called upon someone whom I had known in earlier times. The attention paid to me as the outcome of this exchange of letters was embarrassing.

About this time the Nazis' campaign against the Czechs over the Sudetenland was in full blast, and the Czech publishers, whose guest I was to be after the German Congress, consulted me about going to Leipzig and virtually left the decision with me. I pointed out that a refusal would play into the Nazis' hands because they would be able to say that the Czechs were boycotting a professional gathering on purely political grounds. With misgiving they accepted my advice, and subsequently thanked me for having given it because nothing untoward happened and they had an enjoyable time. Needless to say, I impressed upon Dr Karl Baur, my Nazi successor as President, that he must not let me down, and, as will be seen later, he implemented his undertaking nobly.

The Congress, with the preparations for which the German organizing committee had the inestimable benefit of Mr Taylor's experience, opened in Leipzig in the magnificent Buchhändlerhaus, and later adjourned to Berlin. Here we had to listen to an oration, theoretically of welcome, by Goebbels. When it was over the members of the International Commission were presented to Goebbels and had the dubious privilege of shaking hands with him. I stood by my successor in office while he introduced the delegates country by country in alphabetical order. When the turn for the Czechs came, two Sudeten publishers who had gate-crashed tried to get received instead of the official Czech delegates, but Dr Karl Baur was too quick. He stepped in front of them and presented my two Czech friends and the Sudeten gate-crashers were turned out. The incident was happily over in a second, but might well have created trouble had it been handled less firmly or with less promptitude.

The reception over, Dr Goebbels intimated that he would like to have a little confidential talk 'unter uns'. He then proceeded to tell more lies per minute with greater composure and glibness than I had conceived possible. As one German publisher muttered to me, if only what he said were *true* how happy we should all be.

Two other functions stand out in my memory. At a Dinner I was seated next to a high Nazi official whom I had ascertained came from German South Tyrol. I bemoaned the hard lot of the South Tyroleans—their inability to have their own schools and to use their own language—and how favoured the Sudetens were by comparison. I said that if only Hitler agitated for the freeing of German South Tyrol instead of Sudetenland, he would have the English wholeheartedly behind him. It was amusing to observe the good Nazi's feelings being more and more worked up as I expatiated upon the woes of German South Tyrol. He dared not say that he agreed with me, but at the end of the dinner grasped my hand with both of his, and with tears in his eyes said, 'Sie haben mich tief berührt' (You have moved me deeply).

There was a special performance of the *Fledermaus* for our benefit, and as guest of honour I was given the use of Hitler's box at the Opera. My opening conversation with the 'Staats-Sekretär', who was my companion, was unfortunate. He had asked me whether I knew Germany, and I replied that I had in fact visited every town of any size with the exception of Breslau— adding unwisely that I gathered that I had not thereby missed very much. 'I come from Breslau' was his glum reply!

At the conclusion of the Congress I think that all were agreed that it had gone off better than any of us had expected, so that when the Germans brought great pressure to bear upon us to accept a Polish invitation to go to Warsaw in 1940 we were in no mood to resist. I think that they anticipated being in possession of Poland by that time, but when 1940 came they were busily laying Warsaw in ruins.

At the conclusion of the London Congress, the Czech publishers had invited me to visit Prague as their guest. It was, I believe, the first occasion that a Publishers Association had done such a thing, though it has happened to me several times since. I replied that I would gladly come at the conclusion of the Leipzig Congress. Accordingly, when it was over I flew to Prague and found to my surprise six of my Czech publisher friends at the airport to greet me and to convey me to the suite they had reserved for me at the Ambassadors Hotel. They knew that it was my ambition to see something of the Tatra Mountains and therefore kindly arranged for me to go to Strbske Pleso during my stay. Altogether I was given a wonderful time, and as my visit coincided with the PEN Congress I had a double dose of interesting functions to attend. Three things stand out in my memory. First the 'Sokol', a spectacle of voluntary and spontaneous discipline never to be forgotten; then a luncheon party with Karel Čapek at his home; and finally a meeting with Czech journalists and others at the Spolecensky Club. They all wanted to know what Britain would do if Hitler invaded Czechoslovakia. I asked them whether they wanted to know what Britain ought to do, or what we should in fact do. They replied 'both'. I said we ought to remember Czechoslovakia's strategic position in Europe, and tell Hitler what we subsequently, and much more rashly, did about Poland. But that, in fact, our large-circulation newspapers would emphasize that Czechoslovakia was a small country a long way away, and not our concern, and that our Government would do nothing. It was a great consolation to me that when subsequent events confirmed my diagnosis, no Czech could say that I had misled him.

All this had nothing to do with the International Publishers Association, but it was the Leipzig Congress that led to my being in Prague at that critical time. Oddly enough other events—as related in the British Council chapter—led to my being in Prague just before the Communist coup.

During the war the Nazis tried to capture the International Publishers Association and to remove it and its archives to Germany. But thanks to the vigorous resistance of two of our Swiss colleagues this was prevented. When the war was over, Dr Karl Baur, as a Nazi, was not allowed to continue publishing and had perforce to resign office. The two other Vice-Presidents and one of the other members of the Executive had in the meantime died, so that as First Vice-President I found myself automatically President once again until a further Congress could be arranged. I secured the agreement of the Polish representative on the Executive to interposing a neutral country such as Switzerland as the place for the next Congress, and as soon as practicable arranged for a meeting of the International Commission. I had hoped that on this occasion we might restart more promptly. The Commission met at Geneva on July 31, 1947, but it was soon all too clear that in the then state of the world, with iron curtains, hard and soft currencies, and other obstacles, it was a case of *festina lente*.

In April 1950 I was invited as President to participate at Milan in the eightieth anniversary celebrations of the Italian Publishers Association, and in September 1953 to address the opening meeting of the Frankfurt Buch-Messe, which has since grown into such an important yearly event. I was able on the latter occasion to recall my early happy relations with the German book trade, and to congratulate them that a Frankfurt Phoenix had arisen from the Leipzig ashes. Functions such as these kept me in contact with my continental colleagues.

By the time the International Commission met at Zürich on February 23, 1953, the whole position was fortunately much clearer. The Polish member of the Executive had died and the Polish Publishers Association (if it still existed) ignored both our invitation to attend the meeting as well as more than one application for their subscription. We were thus more than ever free to accept the invitation of our Swiss colleagues to hold the next Congress at Zürich in 1954.

In accordance with instructions given them at the meeting in Geneva, the Executive had drafted a statement of the aims and objects of the International Publishers Congress:

'Freedom of thought, both in speech and in print, is the nerve-centre of the spiritual life of man and of his mental activity. Without that freedom the whole of literature—the recorded fruits of that activity— would suffer to the detriment of human growth in character and in knowledge. All, therefore, who understand the value of freedom in thought, speech and writing, and not least the publishers and distributors of books, should unite in securing that freedom, and should stand firmly together in opposing its restriction, wherever attempted.

'The International Publishers Congress has the essential task of upholding and defending the right to publish and distribute the works of the mind in complete freedom, both within the frontiers of each country and between the nations. Furthermore, its duty is to oppose steadfastly every restriction of that freedom wherever attempted or threatened.'

The draft was unanimously approved at the Zürich meeting, as well as the change of name to the International Publishers Association.

At the request of the Executive a Swiss publisher, Dr Conzett, had taken over the secretaryship in an honorary capacity and he set about the transfer of the archives and collecting the arrears of subscriptions with admirable diligence.

Until Dr Conzett's appointment practically all the post-war secretarial work fell upon my shoulders. For this reason my report to the International Committee was largely the work of one man, viz. myself, which no one could regret more than I did. I was able to assure the members of the committee that, although there had been few meetings, the work of the Association had been carried on with no little vigour. I could report that in their name I had waged an incessant war against the innumerable obstacles which impede the free flow of books. My campaign had included a two-column article in *The Times*, contributions and letters to innumerable periodicals and journals in England and abroad, and a pamphlet on *How Governments Treat Books* which had been reprinted in several languages. Other efforts included:

(*a*) Two months' intensive and successful agitation in New Zealand against the restrictions on book imports.

(*b*) A vigorous and partly successful campaign in Pakistan to remove obstructions to the free flow of books and a handling charge on book packages. The latter was subsequently abolished.

(*c*) A campaign to exempt books from sales tax in Bombay, Madras and Calcutta. (They are exempt in Delhi.)

(*d*) Largely unavailing efforts to free the Indonesian book market from incredible complications.

(*e*) A successful campaign to secure the exemption of books from sales tax in Canada.

The price of freedom from obstacles to the flow of books is eternal vigilance and the International Publishers Congress can claim to have done its part with no little success in many parts of the world.

In the matter of copyright, Dr Mentha, late head of the Berne Copyright Bureau, would confirm that the adherence of Iceland and Turkey to the Berne Convention was due in part to my activities as President. Although the secretariat had been largely in suspense, the International Publishers Congress had been far from inactive.

We had also been of assistance to some of our colleagues through the supply of food parcels, etc.

The fact that the Czech and Polish Publishers Associations were dissolved relieved us from the necessity of deciding whether we must envisage membership of a State Publishing House where no other form of publishing exists, a course which would introduce a political and incongruous element which might well be detrimental.

When I parted with the gavel of office in 1938 I never thought I should be destined to hold it again, and it was certainly not my wish to do so. The responsibility during the long period when we were virtually without a secretary was formidable, and it was a relief to me once again to hand on the gavel to my successor.

The choice of Switzerland as the meeting-place in 1954 for the first Congress after the Second World War was indeed fortunate. It provided the right atmosphere and practically every country west of the 'Iron Curtain' was represented. As was to be expected, the Swiss organization left nothing to be desired. The work of the Congress was conducted efficiently and we had a delightful day's holiday on the Burgenstock. After the closing session the members of the International Commission left for Berne, where they were received by the Swiss President and the Presidents of the Canton and City of Berne.

When we restarted the International Publishers Congress after the First World War, we thought the world position so difficult that we were uncertain whether we should succeed. It was even more difficult after the Second World War, but on both occasions our doubts about the desirability of holding a Congress were soon resolved.

Much more important than the papers that are read, or even than the many resolutions that are passed, is the opportunity these Congresses afford us to get to know and to understand our publisher colleagues in other countries. There is much more that unites than divides us. Had we accomplished nothing at our business sessions, these Congresses would still have to their credit the promotion of goodwill at a time when it is sorely and urgently needed.

Following the agreed chronological order, the next (the fourteenth) Congress was held in Italy in June 1956. The invitation from our Italian colleagues to hold it in Florence was received with pleasure and enthusiasm. It was an outstanding success. Over five hundred book and music publishers from eighteen countries were present at the opening ceremony in the Great Hall of the Palazzo Vecchio, a setting of Renaissance splendour. Modern technology provided a contrasting note—headphones attached to each chair enabled the user to listen to a simultaneous translation of all speeches into English, French, German and Italian.

Before handing over the Presidential gavel to his Italian successor at the opening meeting, Dr Keckeis presented me with a specially designed medal 'in recognition of my eminent service to the International Publishers Association', and announced my election as an Honorary Member of the Executive. Moreover, the Italian Publishers Association most generously insisted upon my wife and myself being their personal guests throughout the Congress.

Dr Luther Evans, Director-General of UNESCO, was the opening speaker and he was followed by the Mayor of Florence and a representative of the Government of Italy. The emphasis of the speakers was on the increased part that books must play, especially in international contacts, and this emphasis became the dominant theme in the subsequent discussions. The sectional meetings were held in the Pitti Palace, which was also the Congress headquarters.

The festivities included a fascinating day in Siena, Tebaldi in *La Traviata*, an exciting game of Florentine football in the Boboli Gardens, Receptions and a Grand Ball at the Pitti Palace. The climax followed the adjournment of the Congress to Rome, where Pope Pius XII granted us an audience at the Vatican and gave an address (in French) on the need of maintaining ethical standards in books, especially those intended for young people. Later on the same day, Signor Gronchi, President of the Italian Republic, received the International Commission at the Quirinal.

The fifteenth Congress held, after this book was written, in the charming surroundings of Vienna, was attended by an even greater number of publishers, and once again my wife and I had the privilege of being guests. What began over sixty years ago as little more than a small group with a predominantly European membership, has now developed into a world-wide organization representing countries as far distant as Korea and Venezuela.

I cannot close this chapter without referring to one achievement of the International Publishers Association, of which I feel rather proud. Rescuing our members from prison is not included in the list of 'Objects' of the Association, but we succeeded on one occasion in doing no less. During the Spanish Civil War, that most distinguished medical publisher, the late Gustavo Gili of Barcelona, had his dwelling destroyed. He did what any of us might have done in such circumstances—took refuge in the flat of a colleague and friend. Unfortunately, on the very night he did so the flat was raided by the police, who whisked the unfortunate Gili into prison. Now during a civil war it is much easier to get into prison than to get out. All the evidence of his family and friends that he was a medical publisher who had taken no part in politics availed him nothing against the fact that he was sleeping at that particular flat. When all attempts to secure his release had failed, I was asked whether the International Publishers Congress could help him. I at once telegraphed and wrote at length to the Minister of Justice at Barcelona, who paid not the slightest attention to my remonstrance. Accordingly I wrote to all the other members of the International Commission of the International Publishers Congress to get their associations to telegraph to the Minister of Justice at Barcelona, protesting at the continued incarceration of their innocent colleague, Gustavo Gili. The effect of those messages, coming as they did with equal insistence from countries which were pro- and anti-Franco, as well as from neutral Switzerland, was electric. Our colleague was forthwith released. As he himself was good enough to say, but for the International Publishers Congress he might have died in prison, because he was in poor health at the time.

CHAPTER 23

THE BRITISH COUNCIL

I have devoted so much time and voluntary effort to the work of the British Council since its inception nearly a quarter of a century ago, that no account of my life would be complete without some reference to it. Moreover, I welcome the opportunity this chapter affords to relate some facts about it which are little known to the general public, and to express views which no official could even if he so desired.

The most serious trouble about the Council was the delay in starting it, which resulted in its not having got properly going when the Second World War broke out. I have no quarrel with the fact that it began in 1935 with a nominal budget of £5,000 with which to tell the world something about the British way of life, because experience shows that the most enduring and well-run organizations have small beginnings, whereas attempts to *start* organizations in a big way with huge funds invariably prove disastrous. You cannot build a cathedral overnight even though it may be possible to run up a showy Exhibition.

It was clear at the outset that books would play a vital role in the kind of work the British Council contemplated, and that it was essential that the Council should be entitled to buy them on trade terms. Mr W. G. Taylor and I, as President and Vice-President at that time of the Publishers Association, were accordingly consulted at a very early stage, and it was agreed that the British Council should be recognized as entitled to buy books on trade terms provided they procured them direct from the publishers. Mr Taylor suggested that, if they wanted to make a success of the distribution of British books abroad, I should be invited to become, as nominee of the Publishers Association, a Governor of the British Council and their consultant on book trade matters. After some hesitation the invitation was forthcoming on April 30,

1935, and I have thus been connected with the British Council from its inception, as well as the only member of the Executive nominated by an outside organization.

It was suggested that the £5,000 should be supplemented by contributions of £45,000 from wealthy firms and corporations, but the vital question whether or not such contributions could be charged as a legitimate expense in the firm's profit and loss account was not faced. The point was brushed aside at the first meeting I attended as unimportant, if not irrelevant. But it was far from being either. As I pointed out in a letter I drafted to *The Times*, which Lord Tyrrell, then Chairman of the British Council, begged me not to send, every firm contributing to that £45,000 would have to pay income tax at the then rate of 4s 6d in the pound upon its contribution, because the amount would be added to the firm's profits for the purpose of income tax assessment. In brief, if the £45,000 were forthcoming, the Government's contribution would be a minus quantity—£5,000 less over £10,000. As I pressed the point, Counsel's opinion was sought and I was assured that legally nothing could be done. But it was quite clear to me—though apparently not to learned Counsel—that no surcharge of the amount of the subscription would be made by income tax inspectors if some dignitary at Somerset House notified them that in the opinion of the Treasury it was a proper trading expense, as it would now be held to be.

The surprising thing is that we did in fact get some outside money for South America and certain other places. I remember that even the Publishers Association made a token payment out of its exiguous funds.

Our start was in many ways unfortunate. The choice of some of the leading personnel, with two or three brilliant exceptions, seemed to me to be accidental rather than ideal. Moreover, the war came before we were properly established. This necessitated rapid expansion, and as time went on we could only recruit our staff from those who were left after the Army, Navy and Air Force and other Government Departments had had their pick. It is not astonishing, therefore, that a few of those appointed proved unsatisfactory or undesirable. The trouble was that one blunder of one person in one place was fully publicized and used to tar the entire British Council organization, while not a word was heard about the painstaking, conscientious and successful work accomplished by the rest of the staff in scores of other places. But that was to be expected of pioneer work, the essential character and vital importance of which is only beginning to be adequately recognized.

At a very early stage I was invited to take over from the Poet Laureate, John Masefield, the Chairmanship of the Books and Periodicals Committee which at that time met regularly and now (1959) forms part of the British Books Overseas Committee. One of the first projects to which I set my hand was the creation of a set of pamphlets covering various aspects of British Life and Thought, which would be separately available for those interested in some special subject, and could also be bound together in one volume for libraries. As the pamphlets would be largely wanted for distribution it was decided that they should be produced by the Council under my supervision and that half a dozen leading publishers should be invited to tender for the work of distribution on a commission basis; that is to say, that the copies would be printed with the selected publisher's imprint; that they would sell all they could to booksellers and hand over the proceeds to the Council less a commission. It is seldom that such a commission adequately covers the publisher's overhead, let alone shows a profit, so that it was not surprising that one or two of those approached declined to tender. Messrs Longmans were appointed and they have been the Council's most efficient publishers ever since. *British Life and Thought* proved a most useful tool, and has been followed up by many other excellent series, including *The Arts and Sciences in Britain, Writers and Their Work,* etc. This aspect of the British Council's activities was later disastrously affected by the compulsory intervention of the Central Office of Information.

Meanwhile good work was being accomplished in building up British Council libraries in all the countries in which we were at work. To husband our resources we planned from the start to concentrate upon one main library in the principal centre in each country, from which any other branch libraries in smaller places could draw supplies. Just as in England any public library can draw from, or through, the National Central Library in Malet Place any specialist publication it does not happen to possess, so could the smaller British Council libraries secure books from the main library in each centre. It is difficult to exaggerate the value of these libraries in promoting a knowledge of British life and literature. Naturally all the more important periodicals, including many learned, scientific and medical journals, are made available in the same way. In all centres there has been the closest co-operation with Anglophil Societies where they exist, and, of course, foreign universities. These lending libraries are specially valuable in countries where lack of sterling makes it impossible to buy publications in English except those issued in America, Russia and China. Foreign libraries and institutions have been helped by occasional presentations of books and periodicals, and by the provision of authoritative lists of standard scientific and technical works as well as bibliographies on such subjects as 'British Civilization and Institutions'.

An excellent plan has been devised to secure reviews of British books in newspapers, journals and radio programmes in countries where they would not otherwise be noticed, the publishers supplying the copies free or at cost. The Council also arranges exhibitions of British books and periodicals in foreign centres and keeps continuously in touch with several hundred Anglophil societies throughout the world. It is the Council's policy to encourage and support such societies wherever they are founded by local initiative, but not to attempt to create them where no such initiative exists.

But the activities of the British Council are too manifold and too important to be summarized in a brief chapter, and if I have said most about books and less about science, medicine, drama, and the fine arts and music, and the invaluable work for students visiting England, it is because books happen to have been my special responsibility, though as a member of the Executive I have been deeply interested in all aspects of the Council's work.

Much might be said about the assistance the Council gives in promoting the efficient teaching of English, now the first foreign language to be learnt in most countries of the world. In Indonesia, for example, the Government decreed in December 1950 that English should become the first foreign language and a compulsory subject in all schools; and two years later, that all university lectures should be given in the Indonesian language or in English. It became clear that the most valuable work the Council could undertake was in the field of English language teaching, particularly since the shortage of trained teachers was acute. In view of the comparatively small resources available the Council's efforts were, and still are, concentrated on the universities and teacher training colleges. Two British Council officers are seconded to the State Universities and the Council has been able to provide teaching assistance for the various types of courses for teachers set up by the Indonesian Ministry, as well as to provide the heads of the English Departments at many new teacher training colleges. Among other activities the Council has co-operated in bringing Indonesian teachers to the United Kingdom for training in English language teaching methods and with the revision of school syllabuses.

In India, Pakistan and Ceylon, the British Council is the recognized authority on the teaching of English. It is therefore not surprising that the Council's resources have been stretched to the utmost in an effort to meet the requests made to it by the authorities in those countries. The Council's Education Officers have advised on state syllabuses, on text-books and on all kinds of problems relating to the language.

The Nuffield Foundation, acting in collaboration with the Council, have financed an English Language Institute at Allahabad for the training of teachers from state schools. The Council has seconded a member of its staff as Associate Professor; books, films, and other equipment have been supplied and arrangements made for the grant of scholarships to the United Kingdom.

The passion in some countries to learn English is incredible. In Brazil, the Anglophil societies (all independent, but in most cases receiving help from the Council) have over nine thousand members; in Argentina over seventeen thousand, quite apart from those being taught in schools and universities. On one occasion when people were invited to enrol for English classes in Athens the police had to be summoned to hold back the crowd.

When the war was over, there were no facilities for transporting books across Germany to countries like Czechoslovakia, Austria and Hungary. The need for British books in those areas was acute and it was vital that it should be met. For years all those countries had been cut off, not merely from British books but from any point of view of which the Nazis disapproved. It was highly desirable that without further delay British books should be made available, and the point was emphasized by our embassies and legations in those countries. Ernest Bevin made a characteristically wise decision. He said £5,000 worth of books must immediately be sent to each of these countries and as there was no alternative method they must go by air, despite the cost. The shortage of books at that time was extreme, but immediately the project was explained to the Publishers Association they urged their members to give the British Council's requirements first priority. The members responded with alacrity, and copies of books were produced from hoarded stores and everything possible done to help. On the arrival of the books, exhibitions were staged by the British Council representatives on the spot, and the public poured in. When the books had been exhibited at all the more important centres, it was agreed that they should be sold to the local booksellers on the ordinary trade terms. It was inevitable that with a collection so hastily gathered together there were a few unsuitable books, but with that insignificant exception the whole supply was sold forthwith. Now the interesting thing is that if, following the example of the Ministry of Information, the books had been given away there would not have been a word of criticism, but because the British Council sold them on the ordinary trade terms they were condemned in Parliament and in a section of the Press for trading at a loss in that they had not covered the cost of air freight, which would have made the price of the books prohibitive. It would have been easy to give the books away, but anyone with the most elementary knowledge of psychology is aware that a book for which money is paid is more effective in its influence than twenty given away and in consequence dismissed as propaganda. In brief, on this, as on other occasions, the British Council was thoughtlessly criticized for taking what was obviously the right course.

Later when the German railways were functioning again, it was possible to get books into these countries, but in some cases there was no possibility of the local booksellers securing the sterling to pay for them. This led to the development of an ingenious Book Export Scheme,[1] formulated in November 1939, under which the British Council paid for the books in sterling and used the resultant local currency to finance their own work in the countries concerned. Thousands of pounds worth of books were exported in this way to countries which otherwise would have obtained none. The scheme was eventually taken over by the Central Office of Information, but was naturally dropped as facilities for direct trade recurred. It was inevitable that some blunders were made and that there was at times inefficiency in the running of such a hastily improvised and novel scheme, but it served a most useful and necessary purpose.

When Lord Eustace Percy resigned the chairmanship of the Council in 1937 and it was announced that Lord Lloyd was to be his successor, my prejudices were such that I was aghast. Lord Eustace Percy told me (correctly) that I had no need for anxiety, that Lord Lloyd had a passion for education and for making known the virtues of the British way of life. After two Executive Meetings I was a complete convert. He was a Chairman after my own heart. He took non-controversial routine matter at top speed so that, as he rightly said, we might have ample time to stop and discuss any item on the agenda upon which anyone had anything to say. He recognized that it was a non-party, or perhaps

---

[1] See *The Truth About Publishing*, fourth, fifth and sixth editions, pp. 220-1.

it should be all-party, job upon which we were engaged, and no one could be more punctilious than he was to ensure that each decision was approved by representatives of all parties. His driving power was magnificent, and under his guidance the work of the Council forged ahead. His dynamic personality was particularly needed. The Council has never been without enemies. There are so many people to whom cultural activities are anathema, and at that moment (and there have been other efforts to suppress the Council) there were attempts to merge the work of the British Council in that of a political organization, the Ministry of Information, regardless of the fact that to introduce politics was to nullify the invaluable cultural work of the Council which we could carry on in countries where the Ministry of Information was excluded. As part of the campaign there was continuous talk of overlapping, though as the Council was specifically debarred from (and had no wish to enter) the political field, any overlapping was due to encroachments on the Ministry's part, who were doubtless actuated to some extent, if not largely, by the need and desire to use cultural work as jam to cover the powder of political propaganda. If they had succeeded, all British cultural work overseas would have become as suspect and unpalatable as was Nazi 'cultural' work. Lord Lloyd fought and won that battle. But it did not prevent the Ministry from hampering the Council's activities and sabotaging the granting of a promised charter. In the absence of a charter the members of the Executive were in the last resort responsible for the debts of the Council. In its early days that was not a great liability, but with the Council's war-time growth the situation became intolerable. With Lord Lloyd's concurrence, the Executive stated that they would not continue in office unless the Council was granted a charter and we were relieved of our personal liabilities. Then, and not till then, was it granted.

Those who would like to suppress the Council are unaware that were they themselves in office they would find themselves compelled to restart the Council the day after they suppressed it, so vital and essential are many of its activities. Furthermore, many of them arise out of treaty obligations, from which there is no escape.

The way the Council has been hamstrung in its activities is almost unbelievable. It has consistently been expected to plan long-term activities on a short-term financial basis. Consider how this worked out in practice. Take as an example Switzerland. For various excellent reasons it was considered desirable to open up there, provision was made for it in the budget, premises were leased, furniture bought, fittings installed, staff collected. A year or two later when real benefit from all this expenditure was about to be reaped, there was a drastic cut in the Council's budget and instructions had to be given to close down. Money had to be expended to break the leases, furniture had to be sold at a sacrifice, local staff compensated. The protests from Switzerland, and the importance of such a hard currency country in the eyes of the Board of Trade, resulted in the British Council being instructed to reopen its office, which it did just twelve months after it had been closed. Much the same thing has happened in other countries, with a corresponding loss of money, energy and national prestige.

Is any more wasteful method conceivable? But it is under such conditions the Council has had to function, and the members of the Executive are without redress and have usually been confronted with a *fait accompli* by the Treasury.

The most that the Executive can do is to send a deputation to the Prime Minister or Foreign Secretary to point out the disastrous effects of the policy being pursued. I have been a member of at least three such deputations to Mr (now Earl) Attlee, Mr Herbert Morrison, and Sir Anthony Eden, and led one of them. When my turn came I pointed out to all three that the Executive were like orchardists instructed to uproot some trees and drastically cut back others at the very moment that they were about to yield fruit, and it did not make the procedure more sensible that we were often simultaneously invited to plant fresh orchards. I cited not merely the case of Switzerland, but Ethiopia, to stay in which we had sacrificed the Sudan, but where, as the result of four cuts in five years, we were reduced merely to subsidizing six masters in the Wingate School. Not only was the method wasteful, but it left a bad impression behind. The fact that soon thereafter we were urgently pressed to return to the Sudan emphasized the short-sightedness of the action we were instructed to take. The interval of non-representation meant waste of energy and influence.

In many countries no immediate saving could be made by sudden withdrawal owing to commitments and the heavy compensation payable to local staff. Moreover, the Council could not hold its own best staff with these uncertainties. I also drew attention to the fact that there were certain activities *which would pay their way* (such as a theatrical overseas tour) upon which we hesitated to embark because the outlay would fall in one year and the receipts in the next, and under a then Treasury ruling we could not credit the receipts against the outlay.

On this whole question of continuity of finance I cannot do better than quote the first general conclusion of the Drogheda Committee's Report:

'British Council work . . . is a long-term investment, and the increases recommended should be embodied in a five-year programme of development with some guarantee that the necessary funds will be available to carry it out. . . .'

The miracle is that the Council has accomplished such wonderfully effective work despite the absurd conditions under which it has been expected to carry on. And in referring to its quality I speak (unlike most of the Council's critics) after studying the work overseas.

In 1945, for example, at the pressing invitation of the Spanish publishers, I spent two and a half weeks in Madrid and Barcelona, and took the opportunity to visit Lisbon, Oporto and Coimbra. Although I did not succeed in getting the Spanish import restrictions on books removed, I did get the quota raised, and in Portugal I helped to secure the abolition of the import tax inflicted by weight on books. I found time to visit the British Institutes in all five centres, and the notes made at the time record how impressed I was by British Council activities in all of them, and by the devotion of the staff to the work. The effects of the war, the trend of international affairs, the spirit of the age, have increased in Spain as in many other countries the interest in Britain and the desire to learn English, but it is the work of the British Council which has again and again given impetus and practical form to a movement of thought and feeling which might otherwise have remained vaguely inconclusive. Before the war, for example, Spanish doctors and other specialists made very little use of British books and periodicals. Today our publications stand second only to the French (which naturally head the list) not only in medicine and the sciences but many cultural fields, and I have no doubt whatever that this change is due largely to the Council's excellent libraries (which lend by post as well as to callers), and to the exhibitions of books and periodicals, the review scheme, the extensive circulation of *British Book News*, the Council's monthly guide to book selection, the answering of innumerable bibliographical inquiries, and perhaps most of all the informed skill of the staff working in Madrid and Barcelona. Here as elsewhere the Council covers a wide range of humanities, arts and sciences. I dwell on books simply because books are my business, and it has to be borne in mind that in their own cash value they now make a more important contribution than ever before to the export trade by which we must as a nation earn our living—if we are not to starve. But in the long run books and periodicals are the best of salesmen for all our exports, besides the most influential of ambassadors in making friends for us, and there is no better augury for our future relations, on all levels, with the people of any country, than an increase in their purchases of our publications.

On a visit to Switzerland in 1946 at the invitation of colleagues in the Swiss book trade, I was repeatedly told by Government officials and others how much the Swiss appreciated the Council's work.

It was the same story in Austria where, once again, I found a highly conscientious and enthusiastic Council Representative, fully alive to his opportunities and obviously doing valuable work. The Austrians' desire for greater knowledge of the British way of life and their appetite for British books was stronger than ever. The booksellers, like many other Austrians, were enthusiastic about the work of the Council and valued very much the information service about books provided by the Council Library.

When I went on to Prague I found that, as the publisher of books by both President Masaryk and President Beneš, as well as most of the work of Karel Čapek and other Czech writers, I occupied a unique position in the eyes of the Czechs, so that I was able to obtain quickly all the information which I needed. Once again I heard many favourable comments on the British Council. I found a similar appreciation at Bratislava, where the British Institute reading room was delightful, and at Kosice.

I arrived in Budapest on October 15, 1946, three weeks or so before the Communists secured control of the country. My experiences seem to me therefore sufficiently interesting for me to quote my report more fully:

'It took me seventeen days to squeeze through the iron curtain which the Russians had already drawn along the Hungarian frontier. When I did arrive in the capital, however, I found that, despite the uncertainty as to whether I should get through, a most careful programme had been prepared to ensure the best use of my limited time. In fact, the superb staff work of the Council Representative and his assistants enabled me to do far more in that week than I should have thought possible. Although I did not arrive until after the offices were closed on Tuesday, at ten o'clock the following morning I was addressing a gathering of the leading publishers and booksellers, and arranging for a further conference on the Friday, at which I answered questions for over two hours before dinner at the Fesak Club.

'By the end of my first day, I had not merely met and addressed all the publishers and booksellers collectively, but had met and addressed a large Press conference; lunched with two of the most important librarians, the President and Vice-President of the Hungarian Publishers Association and others; met and addressed a large group of authors, translators and officials over tea at the Teleki Institute, and had met the Prime Minister and others at a dinner party given by Mr Walsh, our Acting Minister.

'The first day was typical of what followed. I met and spoke to the Hungarian Librarians collectively; had a long talk with the leading officials of the Hungarian Ministry of Education, who subsequently entertained me at lunch; was entertained at dinner by the cultural section of the Ministry of Foreign Affairs; and later received by the Foreign Minister himself; given a dinner by the Hungarian Authors Society, and entertained privately by officials and friends.

'With so many important engagements it was not easy to squeeze in all the calls I wanted to make during my week's stay. Nevertheless I managed to visit every important bookshop and all the leading publishers, besides several librarians, and thus obtained a clear picture of the book trade situation.

'I found the Hungarians unbelievably enthusiastic about everything British, and that they were thirsting for British books there was no doubt. They wanted on the one hand scientific, technical, medical and what may perhaps be described as learned books, and on the other cheap editions of fiction and *belles-lettres* by well-known writers. Even during the war, eighty per cent of the translations published were from English while those from German varied between six and thirteen per cent.

'I had a most satisfactory interview with Mr Kemény, Under-Secretary of State for Finance, about the allocation of sterling for books, and he seemed to think that there was no doubt that the libraries would get the £5,000 they wanted. This was partially confirmed the following morning, because when I called upon the Librarian of the National Bank he said: "I am so grateful to you for coming to Budapest because this morning, as the direct outcome of your visit, my Director has told me that I can have sterling for British books, and hitherto he has declined."

'I found that the Hungarians were not masters in their own house, and even their Publishers Association, let alone more important organizations, already had Communist officials. I should add, however, that the Communist President of the Publishers Association proved to be efficient, charming, and most anxious to co-operate.

'The Council Representative was most energetic and capable, and was backed by a most efficient staff, all seriously overworked.

'I spent Sunday at Eger as the guest of the Municipality, and was shown some of their treasures, including a vast collection of incunabula. Their welcome to "their first English guest" since the war was astonishing. They were pining for English visitors, and hoped that, despite the proverb about the swallow, my arrival indicated the coming of Spring.

'More than three film shows a day were being given by the British Council in Budapest. During the week I was there 16,000 people visited our Exhibition of Photographs of Britain, viz. about twenty times as many as a Russian exhibition which was given vastly greater publicity.'

Three weeks later the Prime Minister with whom I had dined was a refugee in Switzerland.

In 1948 I visited Holland and Belgium, and took the opportunity to see something of the work of the Council in these countries, where it was proving most successful.

Three years later I made a tour of the Scandinavian countries, and of everything which I saw of the Council's work, including the excellent libraries, I formed the most favourable impression. What struck me most, and I am sure that any other visitor who moved amongst Norwegians would endorse this, was the unqualified enthusiasm which I encountered in all directions for the British Council and admiration for the excellent work which the Representative was doing. A rumour of a possible 'cut' in Council activities had reached Oslo, and it is no exaggeration to say that it created alarm and despondency throughout Norwegian cultural circles. Had I lifted a little finger there would have been a Press campaign of protest. The Norwegians have gone a long way beyond the normal expressions of goodwill, and the practical assistance offered elsewhere in demonstrating the high value they place on cultural relations with Great Britain, and the work of the British Council in particular. It would take too much space to enumerate all the material and other support they have so generously given, but reference must be made to the circumstances in which the Norwegian-British North Sea Foundation 'to strengthen British-Norwegian friendship . . .' was set up. At the time of the East Coast flood disaster in 1953 the Norwegian authorities supplied large numbers of sandbags to Great Britain. The Norwegian Red Cross most generously refused the reimbursement authorized by the Treasury and devoted the £14,000 and £11,000 from the funds collected in Norway for the benefit of the flood victims to creating this most valuable foundation. It is clear that it would be a disaster were we to fail in any way in maintaining this astonishing goodwill that has been built up.

The book exhibition reflected the greatest credit on all concerned. It was opened by our then new Ambassador in a most excellent speech in the presence of the Norwegian Minister of Education, and the attendance then and subsequently exceeded the most sanguine anticipations. It is difficult for me to report on the cordiality and enthusiasm of the reception accorded to me personally by the Norwegian publishers and booksellers. They could not have done more had I been royalty, and the Norwegian Press was apparently full of my visit.

In Copenhagen a few days later I noted:

'At the magnificent dinner party given me by Mr Halfdon Jespersen, the publisher, H.E. the Ambassador was present, and at the concluding banquet all the publishers turned out and there was a gathering of over fifty. Here, as in Oslo, I found the greatest enthusiasm for the work of the British Council.'

On the value of cultural work in Europe, which has suffered so largely from the frequent 'cuts' in the Council's budget, I cannot do better than quote from a recent chapter in one of the Council's annual reports:

'It is perhaps difficult for most people in this country to realize the particular importance attached to cultural interchange by European governments. It is characteristic that many British observers and visitors in Germany were astonished and even shocked when small German cities rebuilt opera houses and museums before rebuilding homes. This difference of outlook is partly due to temperament but partly also to the facts of recent history. We have not had our own cultural life sapped by a totalitarian regime or shattered by a foreign occupation. Again, the post-war multiplication of festivals all over the Continent is not merely a device for encouraging tourist traffic, although this is of course one of the motives behind it. It is one of the symptoms of a desire, partly conscious, partly instinctive, to restore the cultural circulation which *is* Europe. It is part of Europe's attempt to reclaim and assert its own identity in the face, as some Europeans express it, of two alien cultural forces, Russia and America, both of which threaten to overwhelm it, one from hostility, the other from sheer exuberance.' . . .

In the autumn of 1952, as I have mentioned in Chapter 16, I made an extensive Eastern tour on business. At all the many places I visited I went to the British Institutes, saw something of their work, and frequently lectured for them. No one who saw what was being done could remain unconvinced of the desirability and importance of the Council's work.

Late in 1955 I visited the British West Indies, British Guiana, and Venezuela to see something of the Council's activities in one of the few remaining parts of the world in which I had not done so. I came away more than ever impressed by the usefulness and effectiveness of what had been done to stimulate cultural work in these fascinating islands and to promote a knowledge of English and the British way of life in Venezuela. In the case of the West Indies, much has been achieved through initiating work such as library development by challenge grants. These libraries and such organizations as the junior branch of the Institute of Jamaica have now been taken over by the West Indians themselves. In view of the passion of the small black children for reading, the value to the West Indies of this and other developments is incalculable.

Early in 1957, on a business trip to West Africa, I was able to study the work of the British Council in Nigeria, Ghana, Sierra Leone and the Gambia. The fact that a resolution was proposed and unanimously passed in the Northern Nigerian House of Assembly, expressing appreciation of the work of the British Council, is the best evidence one could wish of its usefulness. At Ibadan the local authorities are so keen on the Council that they not only let them have premises in a most favoured site in the centre of the town for ten shillings a year, but are spending £5,000 on enlarging them. At Lagos I found equal enthusiasm. The site of which the Council has been granted a 99 years' lease at a peppercorn rent is superb. The Public Library at Accra which the Council helped to start, is now housed in a magnificent new building financed by the Ghana Government and is a model of its kind. At Freetown, Sierra Leone, I heard praise of the British Council from many people who had no idea that I had any connection with it. But perhaps the best tribute is the fact that it is regarded as a Sierra Leonean activity which would remain even if the British Government ever took its departure, and this is confirmed by a recent grant of £10,000 towards the establishment of a new Council centre at Bo.

I have since been to most parts of Brazil; here again it was the same story, and I cannot help wishing that the Council's detractors could see for themselves the enthusiasm the work of the Council evokes everywhere, whether in the colonies or in foreign countries.

Finding the right man to conduct the affairs of the British Council is a much more difficult problem than many people would suppose, and at times involves great patience. People like the first Lord Lloyd are scarce. Few fill the manifold requirements of the post. General Sir Ronald Adam had been granted an Honorary Degree by Aberdeen University at the same time as myself, and I had learnt what he had achieved in connection with Army education, and had the opportunity of talking to him of the work of the British Council, about which he was enthusiastic. When I mentioned his name at an Executive Meeting as a possible candidate for the post it met with immediate approval; the blessing of the Foreign Secretary was sought and obtained, and at the next meeting it was unanimously agreed to invite him to accept the post, which he did.

But when his period of office was up, a much longer time elapsed before the right man could be found. Those entirely suitable were not free to accept the post; many had some but not all of the essential qualifications, and it seemed wiser to wait for the right man. The Executive's patience was rewarded because when the Appointments Sub-Committee interviewed Sir Paul Sinker (at, I think, the suggestion of the Treasury) they had no hesitation in unanimously and enthusiastically recommending that with the Foreign Secretary's blessing, which was immediately forthcoming, he should be invited to become the new Director-General. The choice could not have been bettered and the appointment of Sir David Kelly as Chairman followed soon thereafter.

One of the Council's difficulties is that it has so often to hide its light under a bushel. Let me cite one instance relating to 1937. There was a demand for British books in Roumania, but the amount charged for them in lei was fantastic. The local booksellers pointed out that they could never be sure of sterling at the official rate and must therefore charge enough to cover the very high black-market price. They said that they would gladly reduce their prices to 'x' lei to the shilling if they were sure of a monthly allocation of sterling at the official rate. Now it was essential from the point of view of the British Council that British books should be available to students. Accordingly the appropriate authorities were approached; they proved sympathetic. In the end, *provided nothing was said about it*, the Bank of Roumania undertook unofficially to see that some sterling was made available to the local booksellers each month. The amount was not large, but it was certain. The booksellers reduced their prices as promised and the results were dramatic. So greatly enhanced was the demand that representatives of two of the leading booksellers paid a hurried visit to London to make better arrangements for supplies. Now if at the time a word had been said about this useful piece of work, Hitler and Mussolini would have brought pressure to bear, and the arrangement would have been stopped.

Commercial activities are not part of the British Council's functions, but it is astonishing how often 'trade follows the book', and how purely cultural work results in profitable business for Britain.

Before the British Council was formed, a committee under the chairmanship of Sir Eugene Ramsden (later Lord Ramsden) set up by the Board of Trade emphasized that if Great Britain was to hold its own in competition for foreign trade, it was vital to encourage foreign students to come here for commercial or technical education rather than go to our competitors.[1] The Council has been actively engaged in doing this very thing. Visitors in influential positions, or expected later to occupy influential positions, who visit the United Kingdom and obtain experience of our manufactures, or are given professional assistance while here, are among our best customers. It is probable in fact, though it would be unwise to publicize it even if it could be proved, that the British Council actually pays its way. Here are a few examples of the kind of thing which is apt to happen.

A South American scholar, immediately he secured a professorial post in Experimental Physics, ordered from a leading British firm a mass spectrograph value £14,000. Another ordered laboratory apparatus to the value of £5,767. After a visit, the Dean of the Medical Faculty at a Middle East University ordered a blood bank and anaesthesia equipment from Britain. Another ordered equipment worth £10,000 during his stay.

Turning to the East, a Council-sponsored postgraduate medical student placed orders for about £2,000 worth of medical apparatus after his return. Another visitor ordered scientific equipment worth over £600 for his school, a Burmese laundry-man who was given an opportunity to study British methods subsequently bought £50,000 worth of machinery. An order for trolley-buses from Portugal was directly due to an article in *Britain Today* in which they were discussed.

The construction of new buildings for Victoria College, Cairo, which has been largely the concern of the Council, resulted in the importation from the United Kingdom of building material and equipment to the value of over £26,000. The general activities of the British Council science officer in Italy have led to an enormous increase in the number of visits paid by Italian scientists to the United Kingdom, one of whom, a Rome dental surgeon, spent over £500 in a month.

I have in front of me a list of over sixty instances, which it would be wearisome to give in detail, of orders placed as the

[1] The FBI (Federation of British Industries) now realizes the importance of this and supplements on a considerable scale what the British Council does.

direct result of the Council's activities, and these are merely some of those of which the British Council happens unofficially and sometimes confidentially to have heard. In many cases they were the outcome of information and experience obtained by Council visitors during their stay in Britain; in others they followed lecture tours under Council auspices in the countries concerned. And in this connection I cannot refrain from quoting a sentence from the Report of the FBI Engineering Training Mission to Latin America in 1953:

'We feel strongly that more and not less financial support should be given to the British Council's very important activities in Latin America.'

British music was until a few years ago regarded as an unknown quantity abroad. Few people in this country realize how much the British Council has done—through the establishment of its libraries of British music and gramophone records, the sponsoring of recordings of many major British works, and tours of eminent musicians throughout the world—to stimulate and satisfy the demands for knowledge and information about this country's achievements and progress in music. On the purely economic side, it is interesting to observe that, arising from the Council's work, orders for musical instruments to the value of some £2,000 have been placed with British manufacturers from the Middle East countries, and an order for £3,000 from a single European country. The Council's recordings have brought in over a period of seven years a sum of approximately £11,000 in royalties on sales.

Even the Art Department, which is so apt and so mistakenly to be regarded as a luxury, has brought substantial financial benefits as well as prestige to Britain. Since the war British art has achieved wider international recognition than ever before. A dozen or more of the most coveted of international awards have been won by British artists, including the international prizes for sculpture at the biennial exhibitions at Venice and São Paulo, which have three times been won by British sculptors, and, most recent of all, the newly established Guggenheim Award, which has been won by a British painter. The British Council can justly claim that these unprecedented honours are the result of its work; indeed most of them have been awarded in recognition of work shown in the Council's own exhibitions overseas.

As a result British painting and sculpture is sought after by private collectors and the long list of living British artists represented in foreign Museums of art is proof of the position they now enjoy in the world. This in turn increases, to a degree far beyond its present financial resources, the demand for the Council's exhibitions abroad.

But it would be misleading to mention only contemporary art. English art of the past is almost unrepresented in collections overseas, except in the United States and some of the Dominions. It has been part of the Council's work to bring the very considerable achievements of our painters in the eighteenth and nineteenth centuries before the world by means of such outstanding exhibitions as those of English Landscape Painting at the Orangerie in Paris in 1953 or the exhibition 'Masters of British Painting 1800–1950' shown in New York, St Louis and San Francisco in 1956–57.

The work of the Film Department has created sales for British film projectors. One South American country has ordered a hundred at a cost of about £250 each, and orders for as many again are known to be forthcoming. Other orders for projectors as a result of British Council film shows have come in substantial numbers from many other countries.

A considerable proportion of the total receipts of the John Gielgud tour in the USA in 1947, which amounted to about £62,000, was brought back to the United Kingdom in dollars. The Old Vic in Australia made a large profit, of which £20,000 went to the British Treasury in 1948. The Sadlers Wells Ballet in the USA in 1949 proved itself to be a first-class dollar earner, and according to the New York correspondent of the *Daily Express*, 'Every town they visited has reported increased sales of British goods'.

The public is constantly told of British Council expenditure, but very rarely about the commercial benefits derived indirectly from it.

About 90 per cent of the criticism of the British Council comes from Lord Beaverbrook's papers. But it is difficult to take them seriously when they condemn the Council for confining its work to foreign countries and ignoring the Dominions, and then afterwards condemn it even more vigorously for opening up in the Dominions after being invited by the Dominions to do so. It is all very confusing since the British Council's mission is to make known the British way of life and spread information about the British Commonwealth, in which Lord Beaverbrook is such a whole-hearted believer. There have been fewer attacks on the Council since the Staff Association published a pamphlet quoting a large number of these attacks with the real facts of each case. This pamphlet had a large sale and aroused widespread comment and approval.

More serious troubles have I believe been due to the British Council appearing, until recently, to exercise the fascination of a Naboth's vineyard to first the Ministry of Information and then the Central Office of Information.

It will be remembered that when the Council started, the Publishers Association agreed to allow it to buy books on trade terms, and, during a time of acute shortage, saw that the Council had priority of supply. But in 1947 the Treasury decreed that in future the Council must buy all its requirements through the Stationery Office (by which it would inevitably lose privileges) and that all its own books and pamphlets must be produced by the Central Office of Information, who in turn would employ the Stationery Office (with additional cost and delay). All remonstrances were in vain, but the House of Commons Select Committee on Estimates investigated the matter and condemned the Treasury action in no uncertain manner. Nevertheless the Treasury refused to budge, and it was only some years later that the Council was quietly permitted to revert to the earlier and more efficient methods. But because delays in production by the

Central Office of Information had blighted the success of the Council's publications, further works of this kind were reduced to a minimum.

As the outcome of the continued sniping at the British Council, its organization and work have been the subject of no fewer than four inquiries, one of them by the Organization and Methods Division of the Treasury, which expressed itself satisfied with the way the Council funds are spent. The last investigation was made by the Drogheda Committee, members of which studied the work of the Council in Britain and in several countries overseas. Their report, like those of all the previous investigations, was most favourable, and in fact no one with first-hand knowledge has any doubts about it. With English now the recognized universal language, we have unique opportunities of carrying on our educational work, which it would be a tragedy to lose.

Our books are a multitude of unheralded ambassadors from Britain, and their vital message was never more essential than now. In them is enshrined all that Britain stands for, and continue to stand she must and will.

The publishers have done their part in supporting the British Council since its inception. They have presented very large numbers of books for exhibitions and for review purposes, and have backed publications like *British Book News* and *Britain Today* because of their recognition of the useful purpose they serve. 'What the book trade does' (said a memorandum to the Export Council) 'in general and apart from the particular purposes of particular books, is to publicize British habits, ideas and ideals over the entire world. The variety, vigour and freedom of British civilization are demonstrated through the whole range of its literary output, from the ordinary novel to the most serious critical and scientific works.' This accords with the aims and objects of the British Council, which are as follows:

'To make the life and thought of the British peoples more widely known abroad; and to promote a mutual interchange of knowledge and ideas with other peoples.

'To encourage the study and use of the English language, both in foreign countries and in the Crown Colonies and Dependencies; to assist overseas schools in equipping themselves for this purpose; and to enable students from overseas to undertake courses of education or industrial training in the United Kingdom.

'To bring other peoples into closer touch with British ideals and practice in education, industry and government; to make available to them the benefits of current British contributions to the sciences and technology; and to afford them opportunities of appreciating British literature, fine arts, drama, and music.

'To co-operate with the self-governing Dominions in strengthening the common cultural traditions of the British Commonwealth.'

Could there be anything more worth while? As I said to the Drogheda Committee, I should not have devoted a third of most normal people's working hours for nearly a quarter of a century to honorary work for the British Council had I not regarded it as a task of paramount importance in the world as it is today.

*　　　*　　　*　　　*

Fortunately since this chapter was written there has been a marked change in the atmosphere. There is now a member of the Government (Dr Hill) responsible for the Overseas Information Services, who is able to fight our battles at Cabinet level—something to which no Foreign Secretary, however well disposed, could possibly give his undivided attention. Moreover, following Sir David Kelly's death, Lord Bridges accepted the post of Chairman. At the moment (1959) the barometer is set fair, and the importance of developing the work of the Council is realized to a greater extent than ever before. The best evidence of this is that the budget which started at £5,000 is now £5,000,000.

2F

TWO YOUNG MEN SEE
THE WORLD

by STANLEY UNWIN and
SEVERN STORR

Sm. Royal 8vo.   *Profusely Illustrated*   *21s net*

As a very young man, Stanley Unwin made a trip round the
world to study bookselling conditions in such countries as South
Africa, New Zealand, Australia, Japan, etc. He was accompanied by
his brother-in-law, Severn Storr, and during the trip each young man
wrote an account of their doings.

This book consists of a selection of the two journals edited,
annotated, and united into one whole. It makes most amusing and
lively reading as the two young men were both very observant, and
they were by no means conventional travellers.

But although their adventures were varied and at times exciting, as
when 'Johnnie', guiding a party over a mountain through a mist,
led them all to the brink of a 4,000-ft. precipice, the true charm of the
book lies in its human interest. Because the journals are real documents
the characters of the writers emerge clear and distinct, as characters
always emerge in the best, but only in the best, travel books. When
the reader, having finished the World Tour, puts down the book with
a sigh, he feels that he has made two new friends.

'But wherever they went these young travellers found subjects to describe with
insight and enthusiasm. An Odyssey as delightful to read about as it was to
experience.'   *John o'London's Weekly*

'. . .packed with vivid description, set down without any thought of publication,
and consequently lacking the naive self-consciousness that mars so much of our
literature of travel.'   *New Statesman*

'They have no affections of style, but are content, happily, to write intimately
and breezily of everything that happened to them. The result is a pleasant
feeling that one is sharing, the adventures, not merely reading about them.'
                                                                The Listener